French Military Arms and Armor in America

1503 to 1783

by René Chartrand

René Chartrand
French Military Arms and Armor in America 1503–1783
Woonsocket, R.I.: ANDREW MOWBRAY INCORPORATED — PUBLISHERS
216 pages

ISBN: 1-931464-73-1

©2016 by René Chartrand

All rights reserved. No part of this book may be reproduced in any form or
by any means without permission in writing from the author.

To order more copies of this book,
call Mowbray Publishers at 800-999-4697 or contact www.manatarmsbooks.com

Printed in China.

This book was designed and set in type by Jo-Ann Langlois.
The typeface chosen was Garamond.

Copyright ©2016 by René Chartrand

All rights reserved. No part of this work may be reproduced, stored in a retrieval
system, or transmitted in any form or by any means, electronic, mechanical,
photocopying, recording or otherwise, without the expressed permission from the author.

ON THE COVER: French troops in early Louisiana, circa 1699–1717.
Left: a soldier of the Louisiana troops, 1716–1717. He is shown carrying the unusual arms and equipment of these troops at that time. The exact appearance of the musket is uncertain, but it must have looked much like the contract 1716 Tulle. Instead of a cartridge box, the men were issued with a powder horn and a bullet bag held by a narrow shoulder belt and a leather frog for a bayonet and a small hatchet (or tomahawk) hanging from another narrow shoulder belt. Amazingly, tomahawks replaced swords, but only for a short time, since swords were symbolic of men-at-arms in that era.

Right: a soldier of the shipboard *Compagnies franches de la Marine* on temporary garrison duty in Louisiana, 1699–1702. His flintlock musket could be fitted with the newly invented socket bayonet, which was slowly introduced for the shipboard marines from the later 1690s. The other weapon was the standard infantrymen's sword featuring a brass Musketeer-style hilt.
Watercolor by Eugène Lelièpvre. Private collection. Photo: Stuart Mowbray

1 2 3 4 5 6 7 8 9 10

DEDICATION

To the late E. Andrew Mowbray,
friend, mentor, admirer of arms and armor of superlative beauty;
his wisdom and spirit live on.

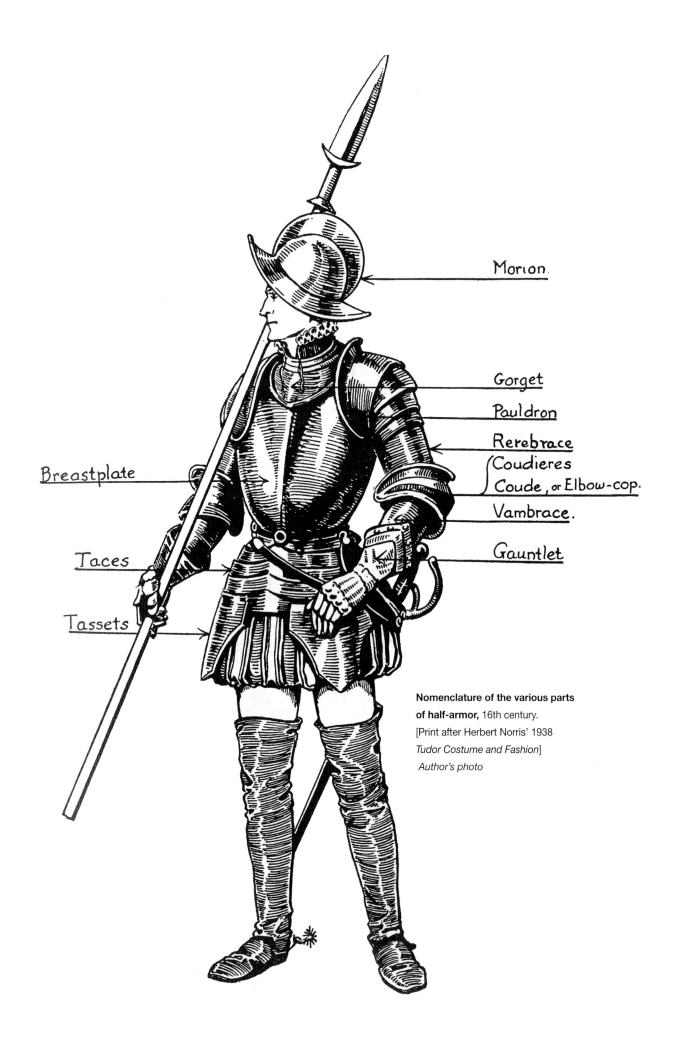

Nomenclature of the various parts of half-armor, 16th century. [Print after Herbert Norris' 1938 *Tudor Costume and Fashion*] *Author's photo*

TABLE OF CONTENTS

Acknowledgements ... vi
Preface ... vi
Introduction ... vii
Measurements ... xvii

Chapter 1
Explorers and Corsairs 1500 ... 19

Chapter 2
Early Settlements 1604–1663 ... 45

Chapter 3
Royal Government 1664–1674 ... 64

Chapter 4
Troupes de la Marine 1674–1713 ... 74

Chapter 5
Troupes de la Marine 1714–1769 ... 98

Chapter 6
Artillerymen 1500s–1763 ... 120

Chapter 7
Volunteers, Militiamen and Sailors 1660s–1763 ... 128

Chapter 8
Metropolitan Infantry 1746, 1755–1763 ... 158

Chapter 9
The Era of the American War of Independence 1760s–1780s ... 170

Chapter 10
Weapons Furnished to Allied Powers ... 194

Chronology ... 200

Appendices ... 201

Glossary ... 203

Select Bibliography ... 205

Endnotes ... 206

Index ... 210

ACKNOWLEDGMENTS

Over the last half century, many individuals have contributed data to the author that, as time passed, has made possible the writing of this study: Christian Ariès of Nantes (France), Francis Back of Montreal (Canada), Russel Bouchard of Saguenay (Québec, Canada), Jean Boudriot of Paris (France), Mrs. Anne S.K. Brown of Providence (Rhode Island), Simon Gilbert of Quebec (Canada), S. James Gooding of Bloomfield (Ontario, Canada), Erik Goldstein of Williamsburg (Virginia), Peter Harrington of the Brown University Library, Providence (Rhode Island), Kevin Gélinas (formerly Gladysz) of St-Sévère (Québec, Canada), Stuart Mowbray of Woonsocket (Rhode Island), Craig Nannos of Philadelphia (Pennsylvania), David Ledoyen of Montreal (Canada), Michel Pétard of Nantes (France), Harold Peterson (Virginia), David M. Stewart of Montreal (Canada), Don Troiani of Southbury (Connecticut), Luce Vermette of Gatineau (Quebec, Canada), and Stephen Wood of London (England).

We also wish to thank the staff in the many institutions in America and Europe that are named in the photo credits and have been of such superb assistance over the years. To one and all, may we humbly express our immense gratitude.

PREFACE

Deciding on how to organize the enormous amount of extremely varied data that makes up this study was a true challenge for this author. Ultimately, it was decided to split each chapter into two parts: The first section detailing data regarding weapons sent or carried in each French territory in America and a second "weapons" section discussing the types of arms (and armor, when appropriate) in the context of the era covered in the chapter.

This is not perfect, and there still could be confusion regarding weapons produced for and used by, say, the *Troupes de la Marine* as opposed to those used by the metropolitan *Troupes de Terre* that also served in America, but it seems a fair approach, especially from the mid-18th century when both types of troops served together.

All of this data, and indeed even more not presented here, has been gathered since the 1960s, not only because I have spent part of my professional life as a curator with the National Historic Sites of Parks Canada, but also because of a deep interest in finding out more about the early overseas French military establishments. Extensive research has found that, from the last decades of the 17th century, some French military weapons sent overseas were not quite the same types as those used by the French army in Europe. French arms historians Jean Boudriot, Christian Ariès and Michel Pétard (also an outstanding military artist) confirmed that they had come across the same differences during their archival research, while Harold Peterson and Jim Gooding, far from being taken aback by this new data on New France not found in their then-recent publications, encouraged me to go further and also provided much assistance.

This led to my meeting Russel Bouchard, who was equally passionate and did considerable research that eventually resulted in the publication of several excellent studies, notably on firearms made at Tulle. Historian and historical illustrator Francis Back scoured the probate and legal archives in Quebec, and much of that type of data for this book is thanks to his generosity as well as, more recently, Kevin Gélinas' great kindness in all aspects of research. As seen in the illustration captioning, a vast number of collections and museums were viewed over many years in America and in Europe. To the many friends and colleagues who always greeted me with much kindness and shared their wisdom regarding the topics in this study, I express my gratitude. And, finally, I cannot omit the input of Dr. Luce Vermette, one of the best and most thorough historians that I have ever met, concerning all aspects of material culture history, be it from sharing documents to visiting museums. And, yes, she is also the love of my life.

René Chartrand
Gatineau (Quebec)

INTRODUCTION

This work is an attempt to show the military weapons and armor in America used by French soldiers, settlers and sailors from the first explorers of the early 1500s to the achievement of independence by the United States of America in 1783. It is not intended as a study giving detailed mechanical descriptions, but rather to present a broad and comprehensive survey of the French military weapons used. The emphasis is on military weapons, which is to say, arms designed for a combat purpose.

In the modern history of armament, France has held a predominant place by its creation of sophisticated military weapons systems and its manufacturing capacity. This is true to this day, but it was not always so. When France (like Britain and Holland) became interested in overseas ventures, the weapons that armed its armies and the armor that protected its warriors often were imported from Italy, Germany and the Low Countries. As will be seen in our first chapter, some of the weapons and armor of the 16th century were remarkably fine. From what bits of evidence that have been found, such finery was also seen in America. Decades passed with more and more weapons being made in France; its gunsmiths and craftsmen of edged weapons became renowned for the quality and design of their products. By the 18th century, French-inspired military weapons systems were prevalent in most European countries.

French arms were, of course, used in French America, but adaptation of French military systems was also seen in the extensive Spanish empire. The British "13 Colonies" initially had English arms. However, during the American Revolution that spawned the birth of the United States, shiploads of French military weapons soon armed American soldiers, and they liked these weapons. American military weapons, up to the Civil War, were largely patterned after those used by the French armies.

One important aspect is that, in America, firearms were of patterns designed for the French navy from the 1670s until the 1740s. This was because, in the French royal government, it was the *Ministère de la Marine* (Navy Department) that administered the colonies in America, and this included providing troops and weapons for their defense. Therefore, it was the overseas military establishments of *Troupes de la Marine* that stood guard in America, and they carried firearms purchased by the navy that had specific features not found, or were somewhat different from those used, in the metropolitan army *Troupes de Terre* (land army).

Below:
Weapons of a soldier of the Compagnies franches de la Marine, c.1730. Contract 1729 and 1734 marine musket with its long-branched bayonet, brass-hilted soldier's sword and powder horn with brass measuring spout. [Drawing by Michel Pétard Collection and photo: National Historic Sites, Parks Canada]

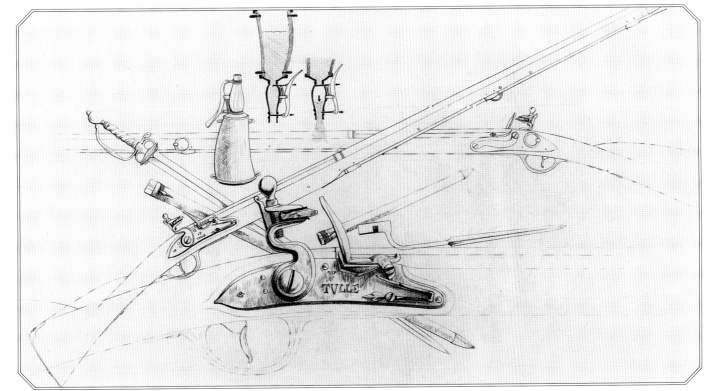

Such arms were carried not only by soldiers, but also by volunteers, militiamen and sailors, including freebooters and buccaneers. Certain arms that were not initially meant for military purposes nevertheless also became favorite weapons of war. For instance, hunting muskets in New France armed many a militiaman who might be a *courreur des bois*, as the roaming woodsmen were called. Excellent studies have already been made of this weapon that need not be repeated here, apart from an evocation of its main features. The "buccaneer" musket is another

Below:

Nomenclature of armor, early 17th century. Note the pistols shown at the top. [From *The Tactiks of Aelian*, London, 1616]

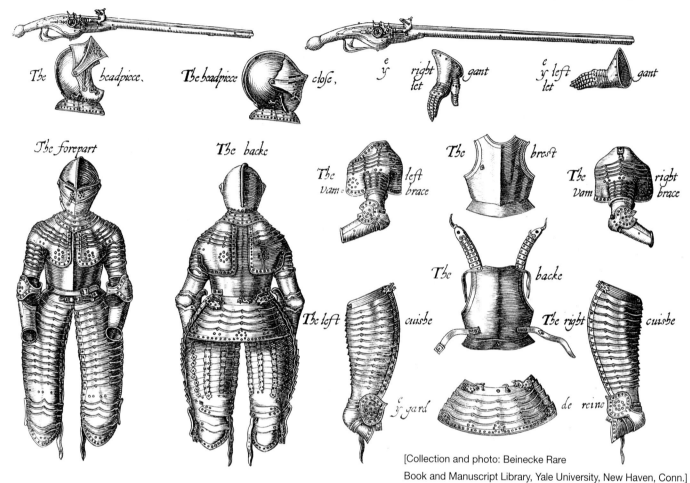

[Collection and photo: Beinecke Rare Book and Manuscript Library, Yale University, New Haven, Conn.]

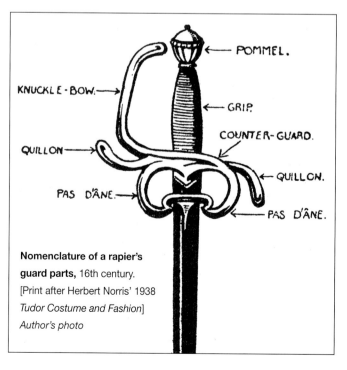

Nomenclature of a rapier's guard parts, 16th century. [Print after Herbert Norris' 1938 *Tudor Costume and Fashion*] Author's photo

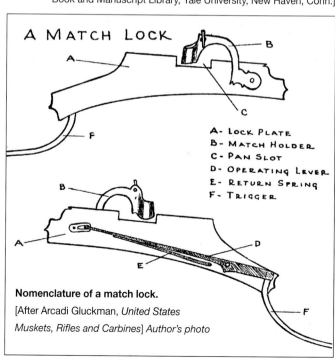

Nomenclature of a match lock. [After Arcadi Gluckman, *United States Muskets, Rifles and Carbines*] Author's photo

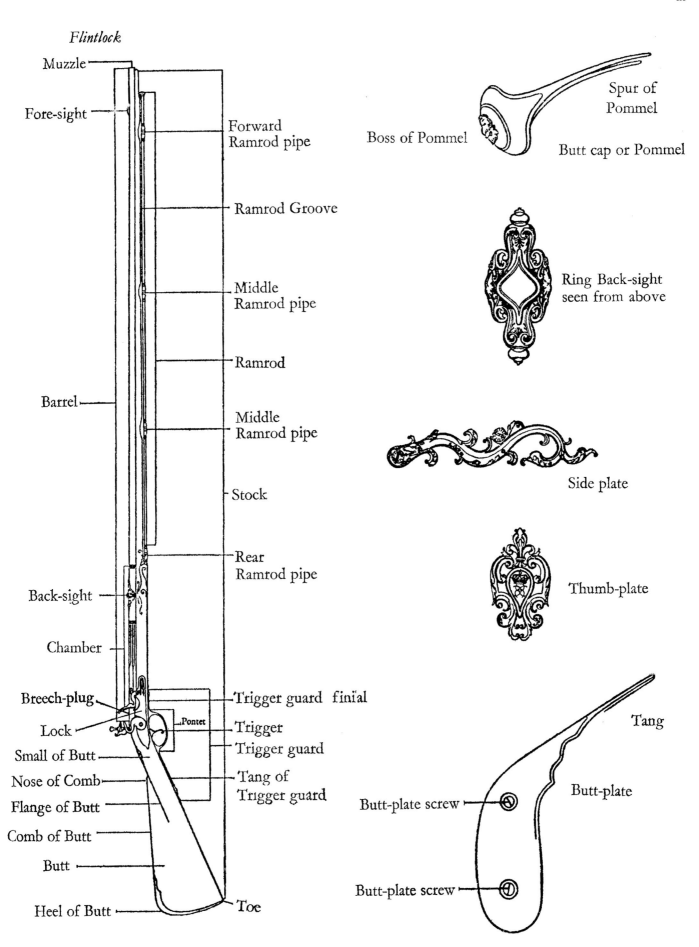

Flintlock musket parts. [After T. Lenck's *The Flintlock*] Author's photo

most peculiar firearm that evolved during the 17th century in the wild jungles of Haiti, as well as in the shops of shrewd gunsmiths in France. It was the firearm of choice for the "sea rovers," buccaneers and freebooters who sometimes turned to pirating. The French navy appreciated buccaneer muskets, too, and until the 1750s, they were the usual *fusils de bord* (ship's muskets) used to arm sailors on their warships. While this is not an exhaustive study of this still relatively unfamiliar type of musket, Chapter 7 offers some basic data on the buccaneer musket's varied specifications, as found in the archives.

Below:
Parts of the flintlock's lock.
[After T. Lenck's *The Flintlock*] *Author's photo*

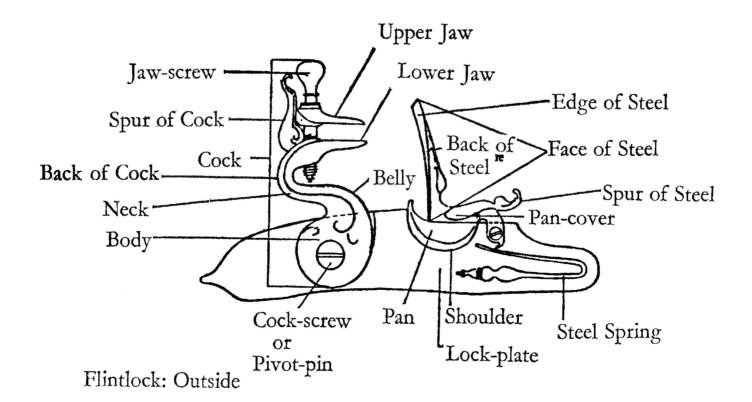

Flintlock: Outside

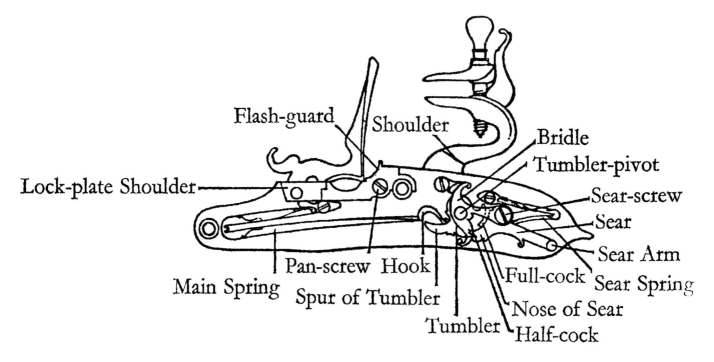

Flintlock: inside

Parts of a snaphance lock.
[After Arcadi Gluckman, *United States Muskets, Rifles and Carbines*] *Author's photo*

A SNAPHANCE LOCK
LATE FORM

A — Lock plate
B — Cock or hammer
C — Battery or frizzen
D — Frizzen spring
E — Pan
F — Pan cover (sliding)
G — Pan cover shaft

H — Pan cover friction spring
I — Pan cover opening bar
J — Main spring
K — Tumbler
L — Sear
M — Sear spring

This study gives much attention to military accouterments. Such items as cartridge boxes and powder flasks were part of any military weapons system, and firearms would be useless without them, as would swords and bayonets without their belts. They could have as many designs as dictated by individuals, but during the reign of Louis XIV, they became more standardized. Again, we note differences between those issued to the *Troupes de la Marine* compared to those carried by the metropolitan army.

Finally, this book has a wealth of illustrations taken from a vast number of sources. The onlooker will perceive that fine art paintings in leading museums and libraries often show men wearing weapons and armor in great detail. These offer an excellent visual context of what those items looked like when worn by the men at arms who used them. Some are often shown when they were quite new, as opposed to artifacts that reached us much damaged after several centuries. Sadly, there are practically no contemporary illustrations showing French soldiers, militiamen and sailors in America. Thus, to show the man, complete, bearing his arms, accouterments and uniform, we must rely on reconstructions based on archived documents, which have been made by some of the best and most specialized military artists of international stature. Observing all of these pictorial works, from old masters, as well as from the latest erudition, we may glance at soldiers as they were in the bygone eras.

Parts of a wheel-lock.
[After Arcadi Gluckman, *United States Muskets, Rifles and Carbines*]
Author's photo

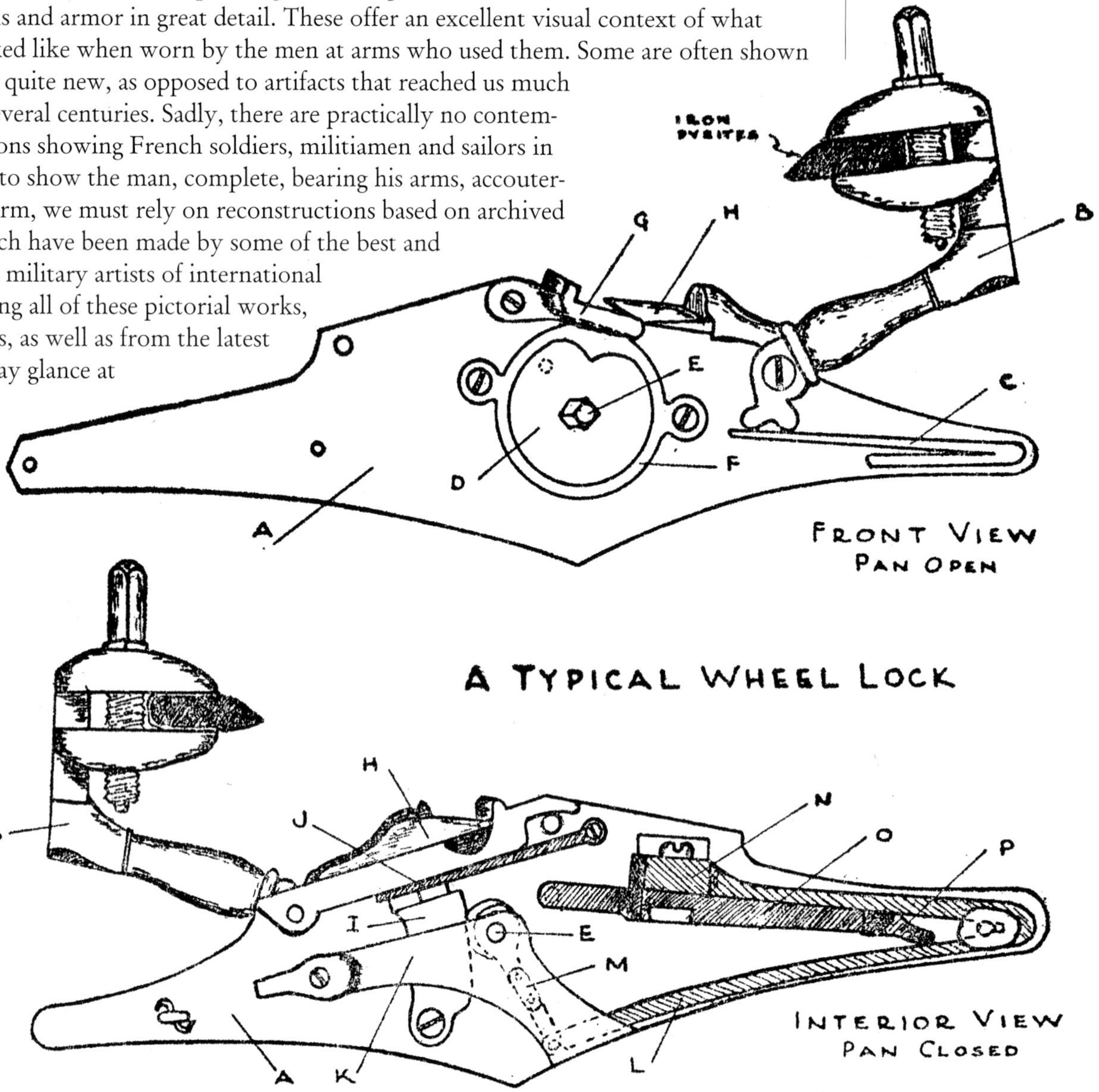

A — Lock plate
B — Doghead (hammer)
C — Doghead spring
D — Wheelock legend
E — Spindle or wheel arbor
F — Wheel housing ring
G — Flash pan
H — Pan cover
I — Pan cover shaft
J — Pan cover friction spring
K — Wheel arbor bridle
L — Mainspring
M — Chain
N — Sear bridle
O — Primary sear
P — Secondary sear

Administrative Territories of the French Domains in America

Only a few years after the 1492 discovery of America by the Spanish, French navigators were found lurking about its coastline. During the 16th century, French expeditions surveyed the American coast. They discovered and laid claim to part of what is now northeastern Canada and parts of Brazil, as well as the American states of Florida and Georgia. However, the French settlements failed or were destroyed by the Spanish and Portuguese. From the early 1600s, successful French explorations and settlements were made in much of North America, which now cover large areas of the U.S.A. and Canada, as well as in the West Indies and French Guyana on the South American mainland, north of Brazil. The relatively small colonies of Acadia (now Nova Scotia) and Placentia (southern Newfoundland) were ceded to Great Britain in 1713, but this was compensated by the settlements of Louisiana and of Ile Royale (Cape Breton Island) at that time.

From the 1660s and 1670s, France's domains in America were under the direct responsibility of the royal government and were administered through the Ministry of the Navy. There were originally two administrative government jurisdictions, and from 1714, there were three. These were each led by a governor general who had several local governors under his orders, as well as full-fledged territorial governors who, because of distance, corresponded directly with officials in France. Governors general and territorial governors were responsible for diplomacy and were the commanders in chief of the regular troops and militias posted in their jurisdictions. A governor general was assisted by an intendant for civil and financial aspects and also a bishop for religious matters.

New France covered much of North America (in the present United States and Canada). Thanks to explorers, followed by fur traders, it formed an immense arc around the British seaboard colonies and was interconnected by a string of forts in the wilderness. But its population was very small compared to the seaboard colonies held by Great Britain. New France was divided into three entities: Canada, Acadia and Louisiana.

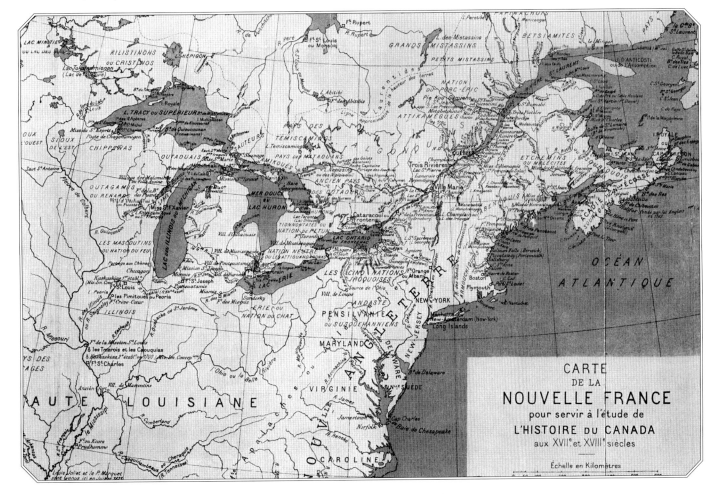

Map of New France.
[Print after Le Jeune's *Dictionnaire général...de la Nouvelle-France* — University of Ottawa, 1931]
Author's photo

Canada was ruled directly by the governor general at Quebec City with local governors at Montreal and Trois-Rivières. Canada had its own establishment of regular troops.

Acadia (now Nova Scotia and parts of New Brunswick and Maine) and Placentia (Newfoundland), until 1713, each had a governor and their own small establishment of regular troops.

Ile Royale (now Cape Breton Island) thereafter until 1758. The harbor and fortress of Louisbourg, where the governor resided, was built on Ile Royale from the 1720s. The jurisdiction of Ile Royale included Ile Saint-Jean (now Prince Edward Island). Ile Royale had its own establishment of regular troops.

Louisiana extended from the Gulf of Mexico northwards along the shores of the Mississippi River to Illinois. Its governor resided at New Orleans, and there also existed, due to distance, a "de facto" territorial administration at Fort de Chartres in Illinois ruled by a major or senior captain. Louisiana had its own establishment of regular troops.

Left:

The West Indian Leeward Islands. [From A.P. Newton, *European Nations in the West Indies*, London, 1933] Author's photo

Below: **Map of Acadia.** [Print after C.W. Jeffery's *Picture Gallery of Canadian History*]

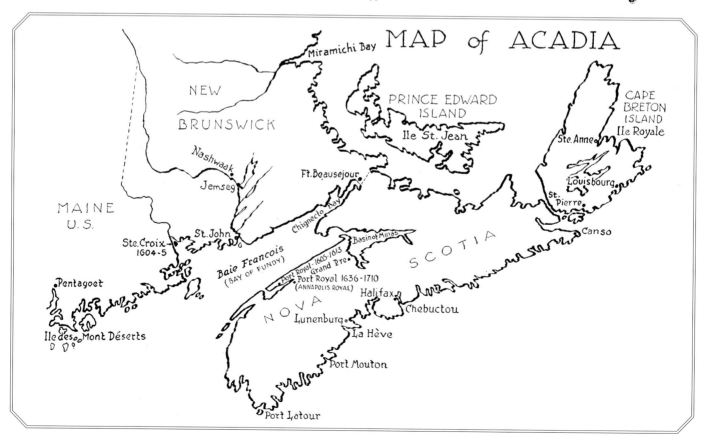

The West Indian Windward Islands.
[From Sir John Fortescue's *A History of the British Army*] Author's photo

The **French West Indies** were originally all under one governor general residing in Martinique. This included the smaller Leeward islands such as Guadeloupe, Grenada, the island of Cayenne that became French Guyana, and Haiti on the west coast of the large island of Hispaniola (today Haiti and the Dominican Republic). Originally the home of buccaneers that had turned planters, Haiti (then called Saint-Domingue) was the fastest growing and most prosperous of the French island domains From 1714, the French islands were split into two administrative jurisdictions:

Haiti, henceforth had its own governor general. It had three local districts: the northern, with its capital of Le Cap (now Cap-Haitien); the western, with Port au Prince as capital, and the southern, with Saint-Louis. Haiti had its own establishment of regular troops.

Map of Haiti (called Saint-Domingue before 1804). [From T.L. Stoddard, *The French Revolution in Santo Domingo*, Boston, 1914] Author's photo

The governor general of the Iles du Vent residing in Martinique was responsible for the French **Leeward** and **Windward Islands**, each of which had its local governor or commandant. The islands had their own establishment of regular troops. Cayenne (French Guyana) had its own territorial administration under a territorial governor and had its own establishment of troops.

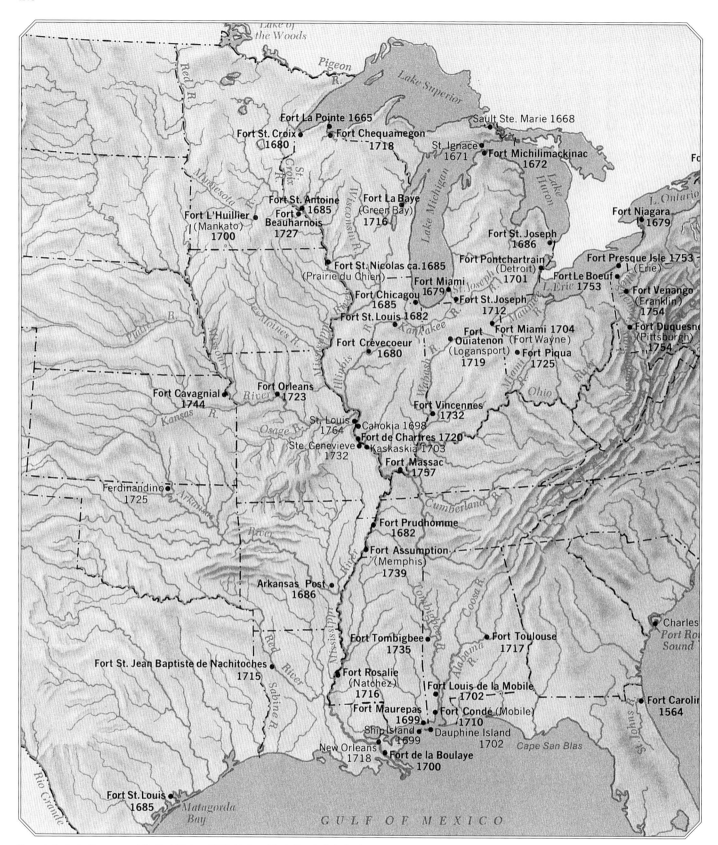

French forts in the present United States. [U.S. National Park Service] *Author's photo*

MEASUREMENTS

Measurements given in this book are of those in the old official French measurement system, used from 1668 until 1840, when the metric system became the only legal system in France and in its overseas territories. Before 1668, there could have been regional systems, although the Paris custom of legal measurements tended to be used.

A Frenchman taking caliber measurements hundreds of years ago did it differently than an American or an Englishman. Calibers were expressed in *lignes* (lines of an inch) or by the number of balls that was needed to equal one pound of weight. The ball was the measurement's rule, not the barrel's bore (as in Britain).

Calculation of caliber was achieved by the weight of the musket balls. Thus, the caliber 18 meant it took 18 musket balls to make a pound; the diameter of that one musket ball determined the musket's barrel caliber. This would make .65 of an English inch or 16.5mm for the ball, and the bore's measurement would have been .69 of an English inch.

The caliber 20 meant 20 smaller balls and thus a smaller caliber. This made .63 of an English inch and 16mm, the bore at about .67 of an English inch.

If the caliber was heavy, the weapon was also heavier due to its larger barrel. A lighter caliber, on the other hand, made for a lighter weapon such as the very popular .28 caliber for hunting and trade guns, but the impact of a hit was not as considerable.

Extreme precision in measurements was not technically possible at that time, and the size of a musket ball or the windage of a gun barrel could vary slightly. The tables below list the average calibers:

Source:
Lester A. Rose, *Archeological Metrology: English, French, American and Canadian Systems of Weights and Measures for North American Historical Archeology*, Parks Canada: Ottawa, 1983, p. 77.

French ball caliber	English bore	English ball	Ball mm
16	.73	.68	17.3
18	.69	.65	16.5
20	.66	.63	16
22	.65	.61	15.6
24	.61	.59.5	15
26	.59	.58	14.6
28	.58	.56	14.2

French lines	mm	Ball caliber (approx.)
8	18	16
7	15.7	20

GUN BARREL LENGTH MEASUREMENTS:

French measure	British	Metric (cm)
3 feet, 6 inches (42 inches)	44¾	113.69
3 feet, 7 inches (43 inches)	45⅞	116.40
3 feet, 8 inches (44 inches)	46⅞	119.11
3 feet, 9 inches (45 inches)	47⅞	121.81
3 feet, 10 inches (46 inches)	48¼	124.52
4 feet (48 inches)	51¼	129.93
4 feet, 6 inches (54 inches)	57½	146.18

Please remember that the length of the French foot was not the same length as the English foot. The French measurement is longer and equal to the English measurement of 12.787 inches.

Note:
The English-based measurement system is presently officially in use in the United States, Liberia and Myanmar (formerly Burma). All other countries use the metric system.

The official French measurements from 1668 to 1840 were:
2 Miles make 1 Lieue = 3.898 km
1,000 Toises make 1 Mile = 1.949 km (English mile = 1.61 km)
3 Toise make 1 Perche = 5.847 m
6 Pieds (feet) make 1 Toise = 1.949 m (English fathom = 1.83 m)
12 Pouces (inches) make 1 Pied (foot) = 32.484 cm (English foot = 30.48 cm)
12 Lignes (lines) make 1 Pouce (inch) = 2.707 cm (English inch = 2.54 cm)
12 Points make one Ligne (line) = 2.256 mm
1 Point = 0.188 mm

Above:

French musketeer with an early musket, late-15th/early-16th centuries. [Print after Viollet-Le-Duc from a contemporary illustration] *Author's photo*

Left:

French men-at-arms of the early 16th century. At left, the soldiers carry firearms, while those in the foreground have no armor. Those behind have cuirasses and helmets, as do the pikemen behind. A gunner attends the cannons at the middle ground, an officer in armor is behind, and trumpeters are at the lower right. [From a watercolor in the *Traité sur l'art de la guerre* of c.1500 by the Seigneur d'Aubigny (c.1452–1508), MS 659. Courtesy of Beinecke Rare Book and Manuscript Library, Yale University, New Haven, Conn.]

CHAPTER 1

Explorers, Settlers and Corsairs of the 1500s

The presence of Frenchmen carrying weapons in America goes back to the era of its discovery by Christopher Columbus as seen by the 1504 visit of Capt. Gonneville to Brazil. That same year, Norman and Breton ships were said to be fishing off Newfoundland, and in 1508, one Thomas Aubert had kidnapped some Indians there and brought them back to Dieppe. Indeed, there is evidence that Basque mariners were sailing in the general area of the Labrador coast as early as the mid-14th century and, in 1372, are said to have discovered what later became known as Newfoundland. The Basques, then as now, were based in northwestern Spain and southwestern France, so some of them certainly sailed under the flag of France. Like the Vikings who preceded them, they did not realize that the largely barren and frozen lands they sighted were part of a distinct continent that would become known as America.

Although recent studies describe the Basques as peaceful commercial fishermen operating on the very fringes of the known world, they were also involved in more warlike activities. The Vikings' Greenland sagas and traditional Inuit tales relate at least two raids on Greenland's Western Settlement that occurred in about the mid-or-late 14th century and were carried out by "strangers coming by sea" in three ships at first and then with a fleet. There seems little doubt that these obviously well-armed raiders were Basques, be they French or Spanish, or perhaps even both. In the latter part of the 16th century, French and Spanish Basques were known to fight each other during wars between their mother countries.[1]

The French, thus, had an early interest in the New World. Throughout the 16th century, they explored the eastern coast of North and South America and made many attempts to establish settlements, most of which were destroyed by the Portuguese and Spanish who were anxious to keep the newly found territories to themselves. The main French attempts are given below.

BRAZIL 1503–1504

The first clearly documented voyage by Frenchmen that mentions arms in some detail appears to be that of Capt. Gonneville's. In late 1503, he sailed from Honfleur on board the ship *Espoir* (of 80 tons bound for India) in the hopes of bringing back "spices and other rarities" to Europe with Portuguese assistance. Besides its cargo of European trade goods, the ship was armed with artillery, and the weapons on board for its crew of 60 men included: 40 muskets or harquebus or other types of *bâtons de feu* (fire sticks); 400 pounds of balls for the said fire sticks...; 2,000 (pounds?) of cannon powder, of which a fifth must be fine; 350 (sets of) slow match cord; 40 pikes, half pikes, partisans and *langues de boeuf* (beef's tongues, meaning daggers); and a dozen hand and war hatchets.

The ship ran into very bad weather after it crossed the equator and was totally off course. Land was sighted on January 5, 1504, and was reached the following day. Gonneville and his men had come upon the coast of Brazil at approximately 26 degrees latitude south. The ship stayed in that area of the Brazilian coast for about six months, frequenting the Indians, apparently Guarani, who were much impressed by the salvos of artillery and musketry fired by Gonneville's men. The men accompanied their captain with "fire sticks and artillery" on land, and on Easter Sunday (April 7th), they planted a cross 35 feet high "and well painted" in a ceremony accompanied by "drums and trumpets." The ship left the coast in July to go back to France, but ran into bad weather again and was blown further north on the Brazilian coast to the area of Porto Seguro. There they encountered fierce cannibal Indians that killed one man and took two others, one of which was "a soldier" that could not be rescued. After another landfall in the area of present-day Bahia, the ship sailed for Europe. As it neared France in March of 1505, it was taken by an English pirate. Gonneville and some of his crew, as well as Essomericq, a Guarani Indian who wished to come to France to learn, amongst other things, how to shoot artillery, finally made it back to Honfleur.

The account of this somewhat unlucky voyage appears to be the first that specifically mentions some of the weapons and ammunition carried to America by these Frenchmen. The mention of the unfortunate kidnapped "soldier," Jacques L'Homme, nicknamed La Fortune, confirms that a few soldiers were thought necessary to be part of such voyages besides a master gunner. These men, as well as officers and gentlemen adventurers who participated in such expeditions, surely also carried their own swords and daggers as well as helmets, shields and elements of armor, breastplates being the most common of several possibilities.[2]

Soldier playing dice, 1503. His halberd rests on the foreground. He wears a polished iron helmet with brass studs. The iron cuirass has breast and back plates, taces and tassets below, the arms protected by pauldrons, rerebraces, coudieres and vambraces. Much armor worn by French soldiers at that time came from northern Italy. [Detail from a painting of the Crucifixion by Milanese artist Adrea di Bartolo, nicknamed "Solario." Musée du Louvre, Paris] *Author's photo*

Musketeers, c.1530s. The muskets illustrated were likely the type used in the second and third quarters of the 16th century by French soldiers during the expeditions in Canada at that time. Belts with cylinder charges can faintly be seen on some of the background figures. Detail of a cartoon made between 1548 and 1554 in Brussels by Jan Cornelisz Vermeyen for a tapestry commemorating the 1535 attack on Tunis by a European mixed force led by Emperor Charles V. Vermeyen worked from notes he took during the expedition in which he participated as a war artist. [Kunsthistorisches Museum, Vienna] *Author's photo*

VERRAZANO 1524–1525

In 1524, King Francis I sponsored an expedition of discovery to sail along the North American coast seeking a passage to China. According to the account of Capt. Giovanni da Verrazano, a noted navigator from Florence, the ship *Dauphine* "armed for war" had a crew of 50 men equipped "with weapons and other engines of war and of the navy" with sufficient supplies for eight months. A few might have been soldiers, and there certainly would have been gunners. The ship reached the coast of the present-day Carolinas in early March and eventually sailed north along the American seaboard making occasional landings.

At about the area of Casco Bay, Maine, some 25 "armed men" landed and marched inland for some "two or three" leagues in spite "of the opposition from the inhabitants" who would shoot a few "arrows while making loud yells and then would run off in the woods." There seems to have been no casualties amongst the French, which might indicate that they had protective armor and would have undoubtedly occasionally shot firearms, and possibly crossbows, in defense. The expedition safely reached Dieppe on July 8th, where Verrazano reported that no passage had been seen.[3]

BRAZIL 1531

The first substantial attempt by the French to settle on the Brazilian coast occurred in 1531 when two ships and 120 men under the command of Jean Dupéret landed on the island of Santo Aleixo (near Recife) and built a fortified trading post. The Portuguese quickly intervened, captured the French ships on their way back to France and, in December of 1531, took and destroyed the French fort. It is safe to assume that Dupéret and his men were well provided with weapons.

CANADA 1534–1543

The next major expedition came out of Saint-Malo in 1534 led by Capt. Jacques Cartier who "discovered" Canada as his two ships went up the immense gulf and river that he named St. Lawrence. There is no precise record of gentlemen or men at arms being part of the 120 men of the expedition, said to have been sponsored by the king, but it is almost unthinkable that an ample supply of weapons was not available for such a voyage into the unknown. There certainly were gunners, because on July 6th, near present-day Port Daniel (Quebec), they landed to meet the natives and "fired two small cannons" and also shot off "two fire lances." This action both awed and frightened the Indians who ran off "in great haste."

On July 24th, at Gaspé, formal possession of "New France" was established by planting a cross of some 30 feet high fixed with a shield bearing the three gold lilies on blue with, and below, a board bearing the words *Vive le Roi de France* (Long Live the King of France), a scene that would certainly have involved many well-dressed and armed Frenchmen with Cartier as well as somewhat bemused native onlookers.

In 1535, Cartier was back in Canada during July with a more substantial expedition of three ships, this time including gentlemen volunteers, gunners and, undoubtedly, soldiers and armed sailors. When they got to Hochelaga (now Montreal), chief Donacona was surprised to see Cartier with so many of his companions armed with "war sticks" while the natives carried

Left:

Musketeer and an NCO, c.1530s. The musketeer at the far left is interestingly shown kneeling while reloading his musket. Also of much interest is the belt with charges he is wearing across his shoulder where some ten charges can be seen. The small bullet bag, usually seen on such belts in the 17th century, is not shown in this rendering. The central figure appears to be a non-commissioned officer or possibly an officer armed with a rapier and a polearm that could be a partisan or a half pike. Note the swordbelt. He is also dressed for a warm climate and wears no armor, as would be some officers and men in tropical climates such as found in Brazil. Detail of a cartoon made between 1548 and 1554 in Brussels by Jan Cornelisz Vermeyen for a tapestry commemorating the 1535 attack on Tunis by a European mixed force led by Emperor Charles V. Vermeyen worked from notes he took during the expedition in which he participated as a war artist. [Kunsthistorisches Museum, Vienna] *Author's photo*

Above:
Embarkation of an expedition during the first third of the 16th century. This detail of a south Flemish (modern Belgium and northern France) tapestry shows some sailors and men-at-arms armed with swords and polearms, indicating their probable everyday appearance on ships or at the first outposts in America. The muzzles of four iron cannon can also be seen toward the back of the ship. [Musée de Cluny, Paris] *Author's photo*

Right:
Soldier wearing an iron gorget, c.1530s. Note the chain mail under the gorget and over the cuirass. [Detail from a painting by Lucas Cranach the Elder. National Gallery of Canada, Ottawa] *Author's photo*

none. These "war sticks" were presumably pikes and halberds. The French were, in fact, on their guard, and Cartier was escorted by "the gentlemen and 25 well-armed soldiers." They eventually went back to France after passing a difficult winter in Canada housed in a wooden fort that was surrounded by "large moats, wide and deep, and a drawbridge gate."[4]

By 1541, founding a colony was now seriously considered and had royal support. Great preparations for establishing a settlement of "800 to 900 people" were underway. According to the April 1541 report of a Spanish agent spying on the preparations being made in Saint-Malo for Jacques Cartier and the Sieur de Roberval's expedition to Canada, the "soldiers and sailors would carry "harcquebouzes [harquebuses], arbalestes [crossbows] and rondelles [round target shields]..." Francis I, King of France, sponsored a substantial part of the expedition and supplied everyone with "white and black livery clothing," which were his royal colors. He also supplied three large ships with their artillery and some 300 soldiers for protection. Besides settlers, livestock and various supplies for an intended settlement, there was also "much good artillery" with: 400 harquebuses; 200 target shields ["rondelles"]; 200 crossbows "plus over a thousand pikes and halberds."

All these supplies came on top of the swords, daggers, pistols and other personal weapons and pieces of armor carried and worn by the soldiers as well as the gentlemen volunteers, numbered at 160 by the Spanish spy. For various reasons that remain somewhat hazy, the colony, which was established just west of present-day Quebec City, was dismantled and the settlers moved back to France during the

Above:

Soldier's Morion Helmet, second third of the 16th century. This type of helmet, associated with Spain in the popular media, was actually very popular with men at arms in all western European countries. This plain example was likely worn by a common soldier and has a French provenance. Note the plume socket at rear. [Musée Stewart, Montreal] *Author's photo*

Inset:

Captain holding a unit color with his soldiers, 1530s. [Detail from a print in Chasseneu's 1534 *Catalogas Gloriae*. Mundi published in Lyon. Anne S.K. Brown Military Collection, Brown University Library, Providence, R.I.] *Author's photo*

Left:

Jacques Cartier takes official possession of Canada at Gaspé on 1534 for King Francis I of France. Armed men are present. [Print after René Bombled in Guérin's 1904 La Nouvelle-France] *Author's photo*

Right:
Detail from a view of Hochelaga in Canada, c.1535. In the foreground, a number of small figures armed with polearms escort Jacques Cartier, who shakes hands with Chief Donacona, who was surprised to see Cartier's companions armed with "war sticks" while the natives carried none. Their attitude at the top of the wall shows they might defend themselves, at least according to this print published in Vol. 3 of Giovanni Battista Ramusio's *Navigation et viagi...* Venice, 1565. [Courtesy, Library and Archives Canada, C10489]

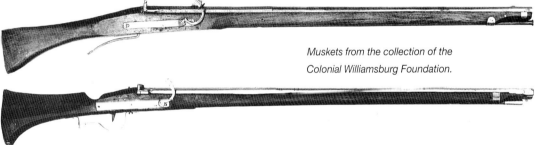

Right:
Matchlock muskets (top) probably Italian, (bottom) probably German; both 16th century. [Both courtesy of the late Harold Petersen]

Muskets from the collection of the Colonial Williamsburg Foundation.

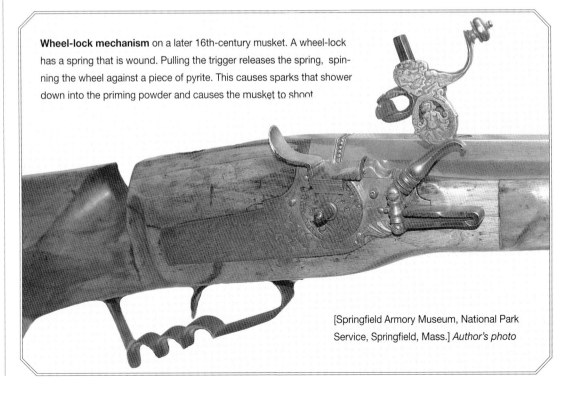

Left:
An early wheel-lock pistol, c.1530. Iron furnishings except for a few features in brass such as the butt stud and the flat rectangular lower left part of the lockplate. [Musée de l'Armée, Paris] *Author's photo*

Wheel-lock mechanism on a later 16th-century musket. A wheel-lock has a spring that is wound. Pulling the trigger releases the spring, spinning the wheel against a piece of pyrite. This causes sparks that shower down into the priming powder and causes the musket to shoot.

[Springfield Armory Museum, National Park Service, Springfield, Mass.] *Author's photo*

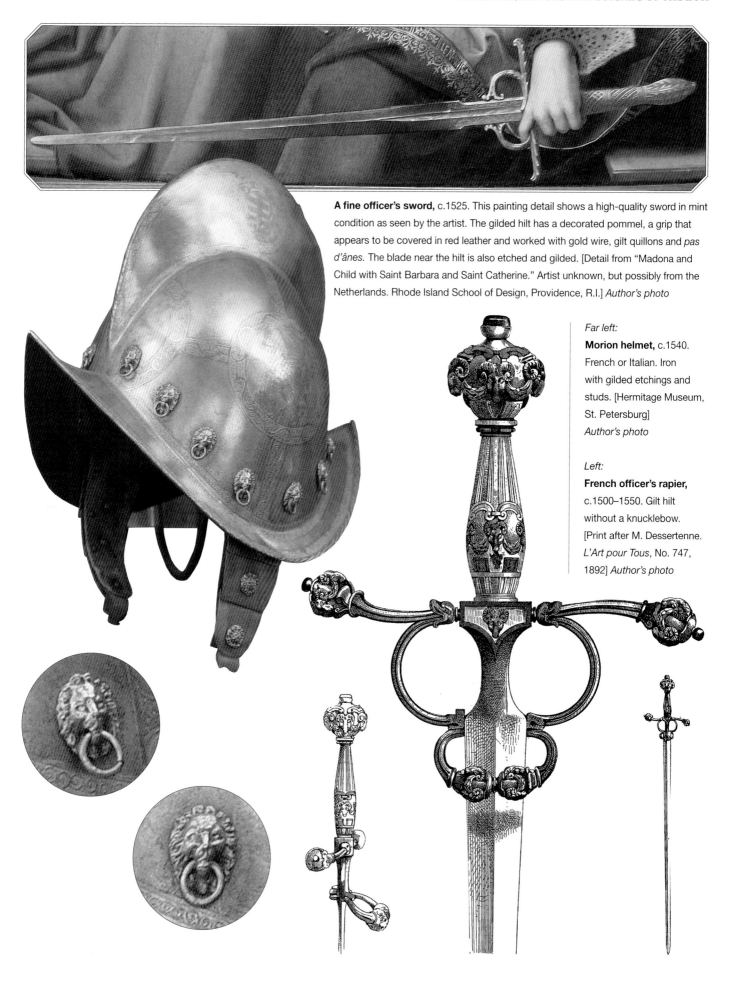

A fine officer's sword, c.1525. This painting detail shows a high-quality sword in mint condition as seen by the artist. The gilded hilt has a decorated pommel, a grip that appears to be covered in red leather and worked with gold wire, gilt quillons and *pas d'ânes*. The blade near the hilt is also etched and gilded. [Detail from "Madona and Child with Saint Barbara and Saint Catherine." Artist unknown, but possibly from the Netherlands. Rhode Island School of Design, Providence, R.I.] *Author's photo*

Far left:

Morion helmet, c.1540. French or Italian. Iron with gilded etchings and studs. [Hermitage Museum, St. Petersburg] *Author's photo*

Left:

French officer's rapier, c.1500–1550. Gilt hilt without a knucklebow. [Print after M. Dessertenne. *L'Art pour Tous*, No. 747, 1892] *Author's photo*

Right:
French troops receiving the submission of Italian soldiers, c.1530s–1540s. While a musketeer is seen at left, most soldiers of the time were still armed with swords, spears and shields. The painting appears to represent the surrender of Milan to King Francis I in 1515. [Anonymous French painting of the Fontainebleau school. National Gallery of Canada, Ottawa] *Author's photo*

Below:
French officer's cabasset, 1530s–1540s. A good example in iron, engraved with martial and scroll designs featuring gilt nails to hold the liner.

[Museo de Armas, San Carlos de la Cabaña Fortress, Havana] *Author's photo*

Below:
French soldier's cabasset, 1530s–1540s. Besides morions, this type of iron cabasset was fairly common in French armies.

[Château de Castelnaud, France] *Author's photo*

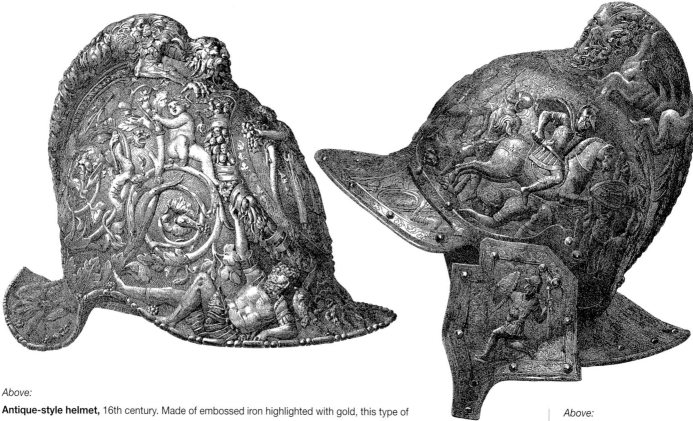

Above:
Antique-style helmet, 16th century. Made of embossed iron highlighted with gold, this type of French officer's helmet evoked Roman or Greek warriors by its shape and the scenes embossed, in this instance a battle between warriors armed in a Roman way. This helmet was made in Italy and exported to France. [Print after C. Kreutzberger. *L'Art pour Tous*, No. 287, May 31, 1872] *Author's photo*

Above:
Antique-style helmet, 16th century. French-made embossed iron helmet highlighted with gold depicting ancient mythological scenes. While men at arms in America are nearly always shown with morion helmets, French officers and gentlemen at arms could have other styles, such as this type. It is seen in numerous European battle paintings. [Print after C. Kreutzberger. *L'Art pour Tous*, No. 156, June 15, 1866] *Author's photo*

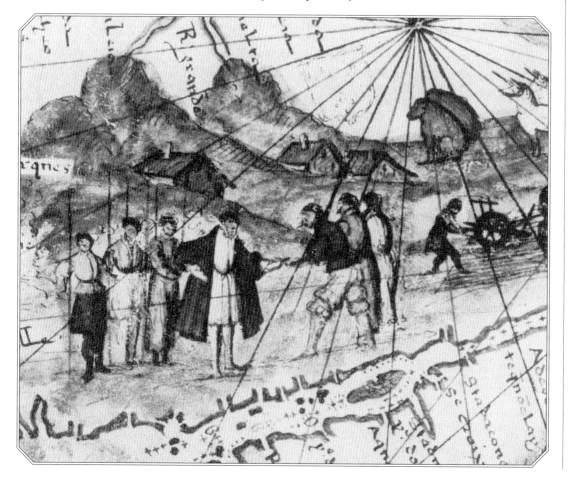

Left:
Jacques Cartier in Canada, 1542. He faces what appear to be musketeers. Behind is his escort of pikemen. [Detail from the Harlean map. Courtesy of Library and Archives, Canada, C21137]

EXPLORERS, SETTLERS AND CORSAIRS OF THE 1500s

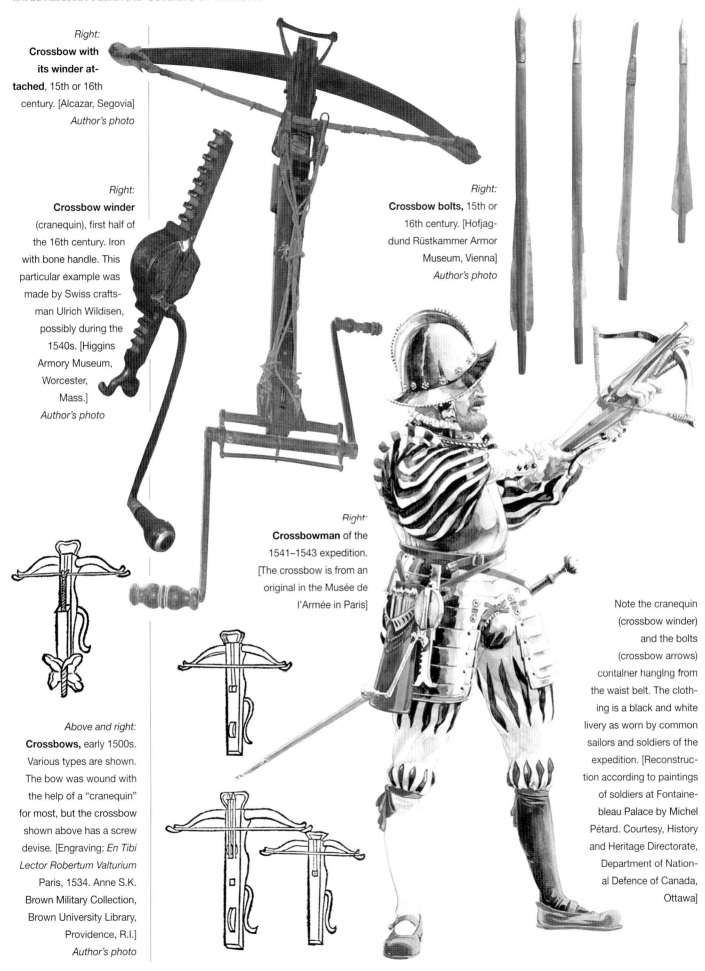

Right:
Crossbow with its winder attached, 15th or 16th century. [Alcazar, Segovia] *Author's photo*

Right:
Crossbow winder (cranequin), first half of the 16th century. Iron with bone handle. This particular example was made by Swiss craftsman Ulrich Wildisen, possibly during the 1540s. [Higgins Armory Museum, Worcester, Mass.] *Author's photo*

Right:
Crossbow bolts, 15th or 16th century. [Hofjagd- und Rüstkammer Armor Museum, Vienna] *Author's photo*

Above and right:
Crossbows, early 1500s. Various types are shown. The bow was wound with the help of a "cranequin" for most, but the crossbow shown above has a screw devise. [Engraving: *En Tibi Lector Robertum Valturium* Paris, 1534. Anne S.K. Brown Military Collection, Brown University Library, Providence, R.I.] *Author's photo*

Right:
Crossbowman of the 1541–1543 expedition. [The crossbow is from an original in the Musée de l'Armée in Paris] Note the cranequin (crossbow winder) and the bolts (crossbow arrows) container hanging from the waist belt. The clothing is a black and white livery as worn by common sailors and soldiers of the expedition. [Reconstruction according to paintings of soldiers at Fontainebleau Palace by Michel Pétard. Courtesy, History and Heritage Directorate, Department of National Defence of Canada, Ottawa]

summer of 1543. Declaration of hostilities between France and Spain is suspected as a prime factor of abandonment, as well as opposition from the native inhabitants.[5] The settlement's site has recently been ascertained at cap Rouge and archaeological surveys made. Amongst the fragments of objects found were pieces of chain mail, the iron tip of a crossbow's bolt (the crossbow's arrow, about 2.2 cm long), blade fragments, metallic scabbard tips, lead balls (about 15mm) and flints that would indicate that some of the expedition's firearms had wheel-lock mechanisms.

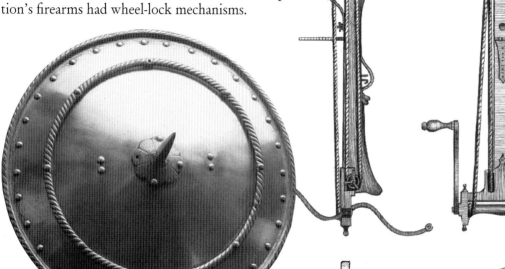

Left:
Side and top view of a crowsbow showing how its winder was fixed.

Turning the handle stretched the bow's cord. [Print after Delaunay's 1879 "Etudes sur les anciennes compagnies d'archers"] Author's photo

Far left:
A *rondache* round shield, first half of the 16th century. French or Italian, probably for an officer. Iron with gilt spike, nails and ribbed edges. [Hermitage Museum, St. Petersburg] Author's photo

VILLEGAGNON'S BRAZIL COLONY 1555–1560

In the early 1550s, Admiral Gaspard de Coligny, the leader of the Protestants as well as one of the most powerful persons in France, sought to establish colonies in America. The earlier French attempt at setting up a colony in Canada having failed, de Coligny's attention focused on "Antarctic America," which many Frenchmen then called South America. In 1555, the settlement of a Protestant colony in Brazil was decided upon. The Portuguese had settlements, notably at Salvador de Bahia, but they had not yet taken advantage of the superb bay of Rio de Janeiro, which had an excellent natural harbor. The French were also aware of this harbor and resolved to settle there. A fleet of three ships bearing some 600 men sailed from France under the command of the vice-admiral of Brittany, Nicolas Durand de Villegagnon, and landed at Rio de Janeiro on November 10, 1555. His group included "gentlemen and soldiers" and even featured a small personal guard of "Scottish soldiers" for de Villegagnon. The French Protestants settled on an island in the bay and built Fort Coligny and Henryville, named after the King of France, Henri II. They also set up a gun battery on a smaller island.

Two years later, Fort Coligny was partly rebuilt and, according to Jean de Léry who spent nearly a year in the colony, "a boulevard for the artillery was placed, reveted with masonry."

Above:
French *rondache* round shield, first half of the 16th century. This type of shield was still widely used by swordsmen at that time, and many are reportedly sent to Canada in 1541. [Print after Viollet-Le-Duc from a contemporary illustration]

Right:
Anonymous painting of St. Martin of Tours shows an officer in early to mid-16th-century dress and armor. Note the way the fingers hold the rapier's guard. St. Martin of Tours was a 4th-century Roman army officer who, upon seeing a scantily clad beggar near Amiens (France), cut his cloak in half and shared it. According to legends, he later dreamt that Christ told the angels that he had been clothed by Martin, and when Martin woke, he found his cloak intact. [Souillac Abbey, France] *Author's photo*

Below, right:
Nicolas Durand, Chevalier de Villegagnon, c.1550. The leader of the French Protestant's colony established on an island in the bay of Rio de Janeiro during the 1550s is shown wearing a quality half armor, possibly embossed. He was fond of costume. Jean de Léry states that "Villegagnon dressed in six suits that he changed daily: cassock and breeches always same, of red, yellow, tawny, white, blue and green…according to his humor…color of the suit he wore gave the humor he had that day…green and yellow…[was] not good." It was best when he wore "a long cloak of yellow edged black." [Contemporary French engraving. Museu Naval e Oceanografico, Rio de Janeiro] *Author's photo*

Above:
Quality iron gorget, mid-16th century. It holds a poudron, or shoulder guard. Made in Italy, possibly by Tommaso Fineguerra of Florence. [The Palace Armoury Valetta, Malta] *Author's photo*

Left:

"Ruse of Quoniambec" or Cunhambebe in Brazil, c.1555. Cunhambebe's ruse was to face away from his enemies with two muskets on his shoulders. As soon as he felt his enemies approach, he ordered one of his men to fire the guns. André Thevet's account emphasizes the chief's giant size and great strength. The muskets must have been obtained from the French, and this may be the earliest (or one of the earliest) images showing an Indian bearing firearms. Thevet, a Franciscan monk, traveled to Brazil with Nicolas Durand Chevalier de Villegagnon. He stayed only ten weeks, returning to France in 1556. [Print after Thevet's "La cosmographie universelle"…Paris, 1575] *Author's photo*

Left:

Portuguese attack the French Protestant's colony at Rio de Janeiro, Brazil, in 1560. The Portuguese ships are shown all around the French (who put up a spirited defense with guns and muskets) on Villegagnon's Island. [Contemporary French engraving. Museu Naval e Oceanografico, Rio de Janeiro] *Author's photo*

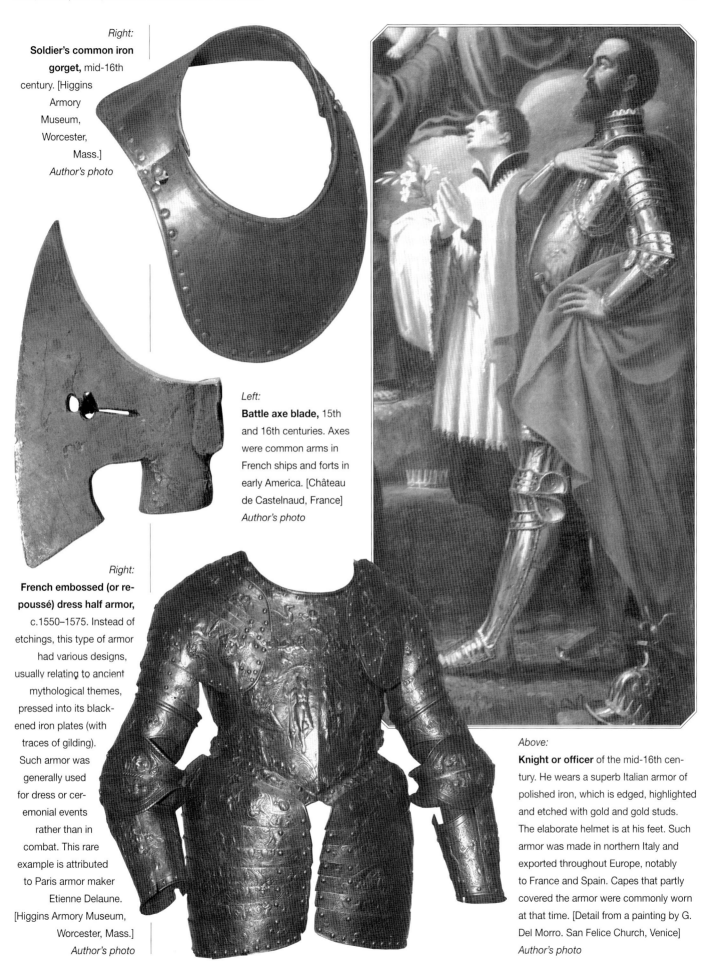

Right:
Soldier's common iron gorget, mid-16th century. [Higgins Armory Museum, Worcester, Mass.] *Author's photo*

Left:
Battle axe blade, 15th and 16th centuries. Axes were common arms in French ships and forts in early America. [Château de Castelnaud, France] *Author's photo*

Right:
French embossed (or repoussé) dress half armor, c.1550–1575. Instead of etchings, this type of armor had various designs, usually relating to ancient mythological themes, pressed into its blackened iron plates (with traces of gilding). Such armor was generally used for dress or ceremonial events rather than in combat. This rare example is attributed to Paris armor maker Etienne Delaune. [Higgins Armory Museum, Worcester, Mass.] *Author's photo*

Above:
Knight or officer of the mid-16th century. He wears a superb Italian armor of polished iron, which is edged, highlighted and etched with gold and gold studs. The elaborate helmet is at his feet. Such armor was made in northern Italy and exported throughout Europe, notably to France and Spain. Capes that partly covered the armor were commonly worn at that time. [Detail from a painting by G. Del Morro. San Felice Church, Venice] *Author's photo*

For all those efforts, the colony was soon torn by bitter theological disputes and supply problems. Relations with the nearby Indians were also strained when it was found that they practiced cannibalism. Some settlers plotted a mutiny to take over the settlement, but this was uncovered by the Scots soldiers and was repressed. Disputes and shortages continued, and in 1559, de Villegagnon went back to France leaving the command of the colony, now reduced to about a hundred souls, to his nephew Bois-le-Comte.

The Portuguese in Brazil, and eventually in Portugal, were most upset at the arrival of these new settlers. Not only were they French, but they were Protestants. Although initially slow to react to the arrival of the French, the Portuguese were determined to root them out of Rio de Janeiro. In early March of 1560, some 120 Portuguese soldiers, joined by about one thousand allied Indians, arrived within sight of Fort Coligny.

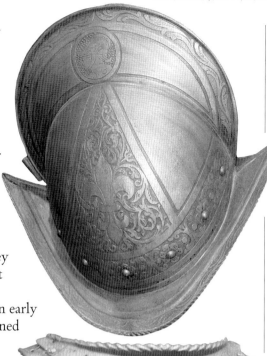

Left:
Morion, c.1550s. This iron morion is possibly French, as the fleur-de-lis decorative pattern was a popular one in France. At the rear is a plume holder. It may have been originally made in Italy and etched in France. [Museo de Armas, San Carlos de la Cabana Fortress, Havana] *Author's photo*

Left:
Officer's breastplate, mid-16th century. This European polished iron artifact is etched and highlighted with gold. [The Palace Armory, Valetta, Malta] *Author's photo*

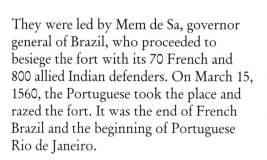

They were led by Mem de Sa, governor general of Brazil, who proceeded to besiege the fort with its 70 French and 800 allied Indian defenders. On March 15, 1560, the Portuguese took the place and razed the fort. It was the end of French Brazil and the beginning of Portuguese Rio de Janeiro.

Far left:
Charles de Magny in armor, 1550s. This remarkable statue shows typical, good-quality armor being worn and is an example of how it looked as worn by French officers and gentlemen-at-arms in the middle of the 16th century. De Magny was an officer of the royal guard, and he is shown taking a nap, indicating his eternal rest, because this was for his funeral monument. He died in 1556, and sculptor Pierre Bontemps of Paris made the statue the following year. [Musée du Louvre, Paris] *Author's photo*

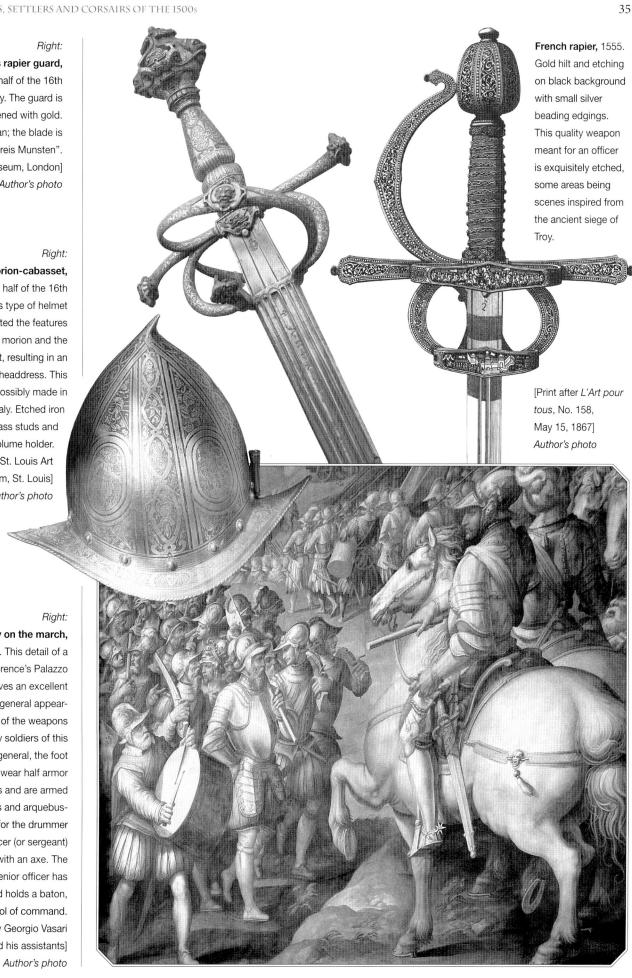

Right:
Officer's rapier guard, second half of the 16th century. The guard is damascened with gold. North Italian; the blade is signed "Andreis Munsten". [British Museum, London] *Author's photo*

Right:
Morion-cabasset, second half of the 16th century. This type of helmet incorporated the features of both the morion and the cabasset, resulting in an elegant headdress. This example possibly made in Milan, Italy. Etched iron with brass studs and plume holder. [St. Louis Art Museum, St. Louis] *Author's photo*

French rapier, 1555. Gold hilt and etching on black background with small silver beading edgings. This quality weapon meant for an officer is exquisitely etched, some areas being scenes inspired from the ancient siege of Troy. [Print after *L'Art pour tous*, No. 158, May 15, 1867] *Author's photo*

Right:
An army on the march, c.1560. This detail of a mural in Florence's Palazzo Vecchio gives an excellent view of the general appearance and of the weapons carried by soldiers of this period. In general, the foot soldiers wear half armor with helmets and are armed with swords and arquebuses except for the drummer and the officer (or sergeant) armed with an axe. The mounted senior officer has a rapier and holds a baton, the symbol of command. [Painting by Georgio Vasari and his assistants] *Author's photo*

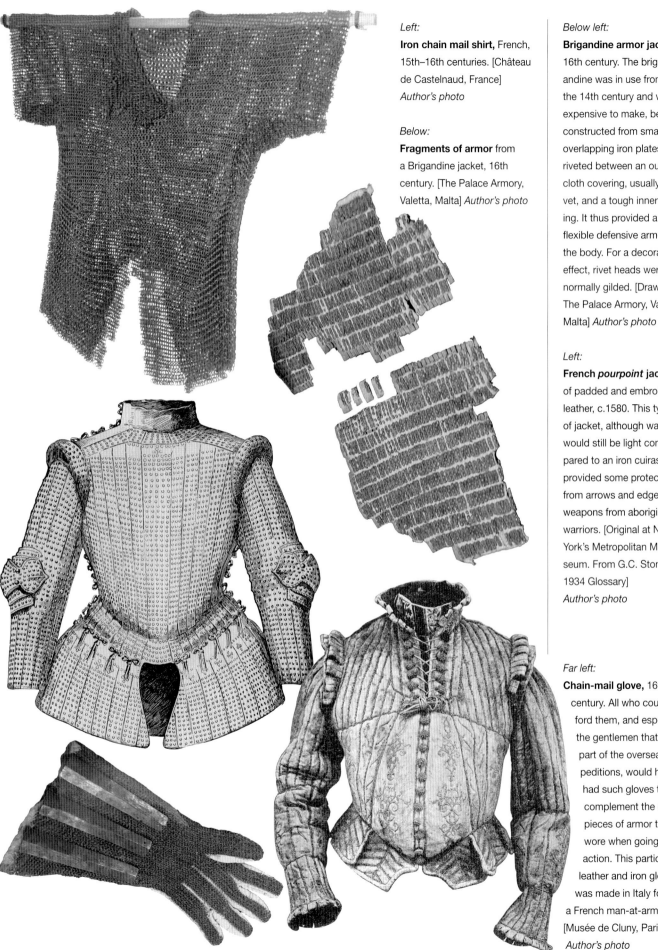

Left:
Iron chain mail shirt, French, 15th–16th centuries. [Château de Castelnaud, France] *Author's photo*

Below:
Fragments of armor from a Brigandine jacket, 16th century. [The Palace Armory, Valetta, Malta] *Author's photo*

Below left:
Brigandine armor jacket, 16th century. The brigandine was in use from the 14th century and was expensive to make, being constructed from small overlapping iron plates riveted between an outer cloth covering, usually velvet, and a tough inner lining. It thus provided a very flexible defensive armor for the body. For a decorative effect, rivet heads were normally gilded. [Drawing at The Palace Armory, Valetta, Malta] *Author's photo*

Left:
French *pourpoint* jacket of padded and embroidered leather, c.1580. This type of jacket, although warm, would still be light compared to an iron cuirass and provided some protection from arrows and edged weapons from aboriginal warriors. [Original at New York's Metropolitan Museum. From G.C. Stone's 1934 Glossary] *Author's photo*

Far left:
Chain-mail glove, 16th century. All who could afford them, and especially the gentlemen that were part of the overseas expeditions, would have had such gloves to complement the other pieces of armor they wore when going into action. This particular leather and iron glove was made in Italy for a French man-at-arms. [Musée de Cluny, Paris] *Author's photo*

Far right:
Men-at-arms wielding various types of swords, third quarter of the 16th century. A cutlass is held at lower left; at center, the soldier is armed with a *main gauche* dagger and a rapier; at right, an older gentleman draws his rapier. Facing them is a soldier who wields a great sword with both hands. His "rondachier" companion has a rapier and the round *rondache* shield. All hilts are of brass except for the great sword. [*Mores Italiae* 1575, MS 457. Courtesy, Beinecke Rare Book and Manuscript Library, Yale University, New Haven, Conn.]

Right:
Three rapiers once carried by French men-at-arms of the 16th and, probably, early 17th centuries. The first (top) is a fairly common iron-hilted weapon with a leather grip. The second (middle) is a quality weapon whose guard has small decorative engravings washed with gilt; note the open knucklebow. The third (bottom) rapier is a quality weapon with a blued and gilded hilt. Like many rapiers shown in artwork of the time, it has no knucklebow. Most, perhaps, all these types of weapons were made in Italy. [The Musée de l'Armée, Paris]
Author's photo

Far right:
An iron *main gauche* dagger, 16th century. Made in western Europe. [Museo de las Casas Reales, Santo Domingo, Dominican Republic]
Author's photo

FLORIDA 1562–1568

In 1562, Admiral de Coligny sent Navy Captain Jean Ribault to Florida with 150 colonists to found a settlement there. Charlesfort was built on present-day Parris Island, South Carolina, and Ribault came back to France leaving 27 men to guard the fort. The soldiers mutinied, Charlesfort was abandoned and most perished trying to get back to France. In 1564, de Coligny sent René Goulaine de Laudonnière with about 200 men and women to build a new settlement, which was done and named Fort Caroline (near Jacksonville, Florida).

Once the French flag was planted in Florida, Admiral de Coligny wanted to consolidate the French Protestant's colony. In the spring of 1565, he instructed Jean Ribault to return to Florida with the title of "Colonel and King's Lieutenant" and bring more soldiers, settlers and supplies — including weapons. The arms and armor intended for Fort Caroline that were loaded on board his ship in May of 1565 featured two calivers, two bastards, two petteraros, 12 arquebus, 300 pikes and 36 halberds. For armor, there were "corselets complete" with vambraces, "cuisses" and "bourguignottes" helmets.

The Spanish were not about to tolerate a French fort with Protestant settlers on the coast of Florida. They could use it as a base to attack the ships returning to Spain laden with silver. A powerful force under Don Pedro Menendez de Aviles made a successful surprise attack on Fort Caroline, which was captured. Jean Ribaut surrendered "about 60 harquebus, 20 pistols, a quantity of swords and bucklers, and some helmets and breast plates" as well as "the flags and arms." In the arms magazine there were 120 cuirasses, 300 pikes and many arquebuses on the racks: helmets and all new clothing, fine cloths in abundance. The Spanish account further related that "in the morning [of September 27, 1565], Juan Ribao [Jean Ribaud]...delivered to the Adelantado two royal standards, one of the King of France, the other of the Admiral, two field banners; a gilt sword and dagger, a very fine gilt helmet, a buckler, a pistol, a seal he had with him, which the Admiral of France had given him to stamp all the edicts."[7]

Above:

This halberd head had a thin point meant to penetrate between an opponent's armor plates. [Courtesy, National Historic Sites, Parks Canada]

Far left:

French soldier's cabasset with a halberd head, mid-16th century. The cabasset is of the same type shown in Le Moyne's plates of French troops in Florida. [Courtesy, National Historic Sites, Parks Canada]

The Spanish then put to the sword some 152 men, sparing only women and children. Fort Caroline was renamed Fort San Mateo. The French Protestants did not forget the Spaniards' cruel execution, and in August of 1567, one hundred French arquebusiers wearing

Left:

Pillar, erected in Florida in 1564, is adorned with France's coat of arms. This detail of a print by Jacques Le Moyne shows commander René Goulaine de Laudonnière escorted by a party of soldiers meeting with Indian Chief Timucua who shows them the pillar that was installed by Jean Ribault two years earlier. Laudonnière and his escort are elaborately dressed. Note the decorated breastplate and morions. [Print after Le Moyne. Private collection] *Author's photo*

EXPLORERS, SETTLERS AND CORSAIRS OF THE 1500s

Right:
French troops in battle, Florida, 1564. Note the cabassets mistakenly are shown with the point forward rather than backward; they pointed backwards so as to deflect a sword blow. [Detail from a print after Jacques Le Moyne. Private collection] *Author's photo*

Above:
French man-at-arms Italian-made morion helmet, 16th century. This sample is covered with etched engravings. [Print after C. Kreutzberger. *L'Art pour Tous*, No. 142, November 15, 1865] *Author's photo*

Right:
French soldiers in Florida, 1564. This is a party of musketeers with a sergeant carrying a halberd. Note the musketeers carry matchlock "petronel" muskets. [Detail from a print after Jacques Le Moyne. Private collection] *Author's photo*

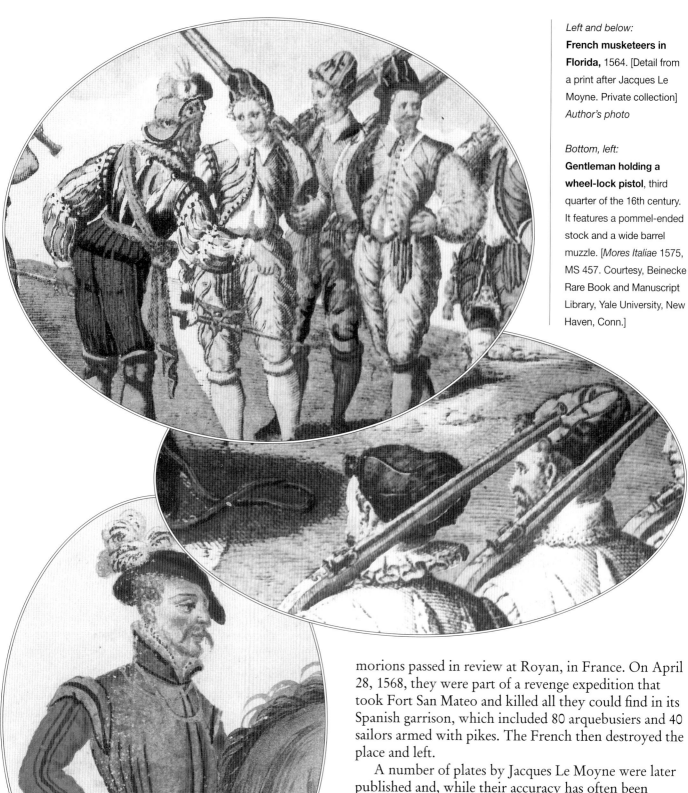

Left and below:
French musketeers in Florida, 1564. [Detail from a print after Jacques Le Moyne. Private collection] *Author's photo*

Bottom, left:
Gentleman holding a wheel-lock pistol, third quarter of the 16th century. It features a pommel-ended stock and a wide barrel muzzle. [*Mores Italiae* 1575, MS 457. Courtesy, Beinecke Rare Book and Manuscript Library, Yale University, New Haven, Conn.]

morions passed in review at Royan, in France. On April 28, 1568, they were part of a revenge expedition that took Fort San Mateo and killed all they could find in its Spanish garrison, which included 80 arquebusiers and 40 sailors armed with pikes. The French then destroyed the place and left.

A number of plates by Jacques Le Moyne were later published and, while their accuracy has often been debated, they remain the only fairly contemporary pictorial record of the Florida expeditions. As with all such plates, they are not modern "snapshots" of places or events, but they show French arms, armor and clothing convincingly. Some of the plates are reproduced in this book and they show a remarkable array of arms and armor typically carried and worn by mid-16th-century officers and men.

LABRADOR AND NEWFOUNDLAND 1580s–1590s

Spanish Basque fishermen were very active in whale hunting off the coast of Newfoundland and Labrador during the second half of the 16th century as attested by several recently found wrecks of galleons, vestiges of temporary work stations and burial grounds at Red Bay, Labrador. A large number of French Basques sailed from Bayonne and Saint-Jean-de-Luz in southwestern France, and while being whalers, they also were quite a warlike group that indulged in corsair activities bordering on piracy. The 1584 adventure of an English corsair, Capt. Hugh Jones of Falmouth, bears witness to the French Basque's willingness to seize anything afloat. After a year of pillaging the Spanish in the West Indies, and by the time Placentia, Newfoundland, was reached in mid-May, nearly all of the crew belonging to Jones' 90-ton ship *Jacquet* had perished of sickness except for the captain and the master. On May 19th, some 15 Basque ships from Saint-Jean-de-Luz arrived and seized the English ship with all its contents. Along with a "chest with all the Juelles and other things therein" as well as "300 Crownes" and many other items, the French Basques also took:[8] "One Copper Falconett; Thirtie Muskets with theire furniture; Fiftie Callivers with theire furniture; Tenne Cases of Pistolls [and] lock pieces; Tenne targettes and Tenne Armors of proofe; Twenty Corsleets; Twenty Jackes and cotes of plate; Swordes daggers and targattes of wood covered with lether; Long bowes shefes of arrowes & Pikes; Crosse bowes Slurre bowes with their arrowes & furniture."

How much of this armament was English or Spanish is impossible to say. And, probably with the exception of the long bows that were peculiar to the English, these weapons would now be used by French corsairs. It does, however, give an excellent idea of the arms found on board a ship intended for warlike activities at that time. Furthermore, in the 16th century, and a good part of the next century, weapons often made in Italy or in Germany found their way into France and other maritime powers such as Spain, Portugal and Great Britain, all of which also produced weapons.

Weapons and Armor of the 1500s

As can be seen from the descriptions above, a great many types of weapons and armor were carried to America by the French. As in other European nations, there were no regulation models, and even the calibers of firearms were not standard. Another factor was that many weapons and armor suits were imported into France from northern Italy or, to a lesser extent, from Germany. Those countries boasted the finest artisans of the time, as well

Pair of French wheel-lock pistols, 1570s. Decoration on the stocks copied in part from engravings by Étienne Delaune (Orléans 1518/19–1583 Strasbourg). Steel, chiseled, gilt, and inlaid with silver; brass; wood, inlaid with engraved staghorn and brass wire, with painted details. Both pistols have a caliber of 11.18 mm (.44 inch) and a length of 51.1 cm. [Courtesy, The Metropolitan Museum of Art, New York. Gift of William H. Riggs, 1913]

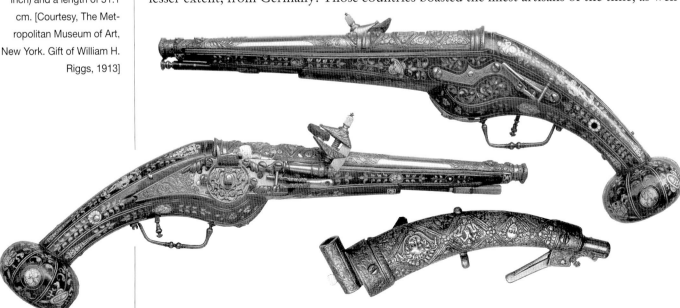

as numerous arms workshops that produced vast numbers of these items in a variety of qualities and prices. There also were some arms makers in France and Spain, but the bulk of the arms used in France appear to have come from Italy at that time.

The types of weapons used varied enormously. Those common in the Middle Ages were still widely used, notably pole-arms and crossbows. All carried swords because, in spite of the appearance of firearms, a great deal of the fighting was still done with edged weapons. Armies had large contingents of swordsmen who protected themselves with the round shields called "rondaches" or "rondelles." Indeed, 16th-century swordsmen in an army were often called "rondachiers" (those who carried round shields).

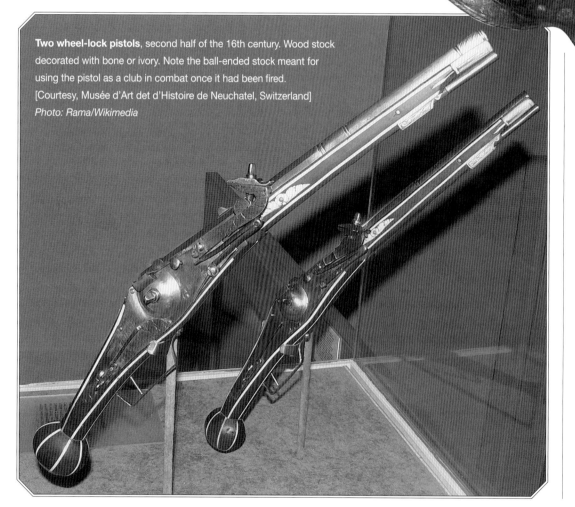

Two wheel-lock pistols, second half of the 16th century. Wood stock decorated with bone or ivory. Note the ball-ended stock meant for using the pistol as a club in combat once it had been fired. [Courtesy, Musée d'Art det d'Histoire de Neuchatel, Switzerland] *Photo: Rama/Wikimedia*

Above:

Morion-burgonet, 1585. This type of helmet, whose design was of Italian origin, became popular during the second half of the 16th century in France as well as Austria and Germany. This particular example is marked "1585" and may have been made in Augsburg, Germany. It is made of iron, etched with gilding, most likely worn by an officer or a guard unit. [Higgins Armory Museum, Worcester, Mass.] *Author's photo*

Below:

French match-lock petronel, 1570s. This curved stock design was common for inexpensive match-lock muskets for musketeers.

*E*xamples such as this one that feature inlaid decoration of bone were used by gentlemen. When aiming a gun of this type, the sharply curved end of the stock was pressed against the chest *(poitrine* in French), hence the name petronel. Caliber of 12.95 mm (.51 inch) and length of 114.9 cm. [Courtesy, The Metropolitan Museum of Art, New York. The Collection of Giovanni P. Morosini, presented by his daughter Giulia, 1932]

Below:
Musketeer's horn powder flasks, 16th century. European-made flasks made in a flat form were very widely used in all European armies. The cow horn's body could be left plain or, as with these examples, be engraved with mythological, floral or geometric designs. They had a metal spout and, usually, a cut-off at the top and bottom. A long metal hook was fitted to the back (invisible) and the flask was also provided with a hanging cord that ended with decorative tassels. [The Palace Armory, Valetta, Malta] *Author's photo*

Right:
Musketeer's powder flask, 16th century. Brass with gilding over black velvet. This item, carried by a French musketeer, appears to have been made in Germany. [*L'Art pour Tous*, No. 155, May 30, 1866] *Author's photo*

Portable firearms, the "hand-held cannons" or "fire sticks" of the 15th century, were ignited by a slow-burning match cord. They were certainly still common well into the next century as they evolved into "muskets," thus creating the "musketeer" soldiers. Despite its ease of operation, the matchlock musket was at a disadvantage when it was windy or rainy, because such conditions rendered the slow match inoperable. The solution to this problem came with the invention of the fairly complex wheel-lock mechanism in the early 1500s. This type of lock used a self-contained ignition system that featured a piece of iron pyrite or flint held in the jaws of a vice that was mounted with a spring-loaded serrated wheel wound like a watch. When a trigger released the coiled spring, its wheel would violently make the pyrite strike creating a shower of sparks. These sparks ignited the priming powder placed in the pan that connected through a small hole with the powder charge in the barrel. While this was not foul proof in bad weather, it was a great improvement. It was also relatively safe to use. Its main disadvantage was that it was a complex mechanism that was much more expensive than a matchlock, even in its plainer versions. From about 1550, the *platine à chenapan* (snaphance lock) appeared, which was an improvement of the earlier snaplock and the precursor of the future flintlock. This type of ignition system worked by a small spring-powered hammer with a flint attached at its end that, when released, caused a shower of sparks when it struck a small iron pan. It should be kept in mind that it does not seem to have been widespread in France, and we have not found conclusive evidence that in was used in its American domains.

There evolved three basic types of shoulder firearms. The most popular musket carried by troops was generally a matchlock, because it was much less expensive. Equipped with either a wheel-lock, snaphance or matchlock mechanism, the 16th-century infantry musket was a very heavy weapon with a caliber of 10 or 12 balls to the pound. Due to the weight of its barrel, it required a fork to hold it when aiming. It was a cumbersome weapon, but its efficiency against men wearing armor was useful on battlefields thanks to its heavy caliber. A much lighter shoulder weapon was the harquebus, because its caliber could be up to fours times as light. The disadvantage was that its hitting and penetrating power were far weaker.

The development of wheel-lock and snaphance mechanisms also opened the way to have smaller hand-held firearms — pistols — that could be used for combat at close quarters, notably at sea.

The arms and armor carried by 16th-century French soldiers appear to have been largely imported from northern Italy, although French smiths and artisans might alter or decorate some aspects of these items. Brantôme's *Discourse of the Infantry Colonels of France* mentions the early "Harquebuzes" as poor weapons that were badly assembled until some better examples came from Piedmont (northwest Italy) with barrels made in Milan, which led to increased importations by unit commanders. Eventually, French gunsmiths "imitated very well the foreign arms" and, to some extent, the imported armor. Be they muskets from Milan or made in France, the calibers could be "larger in one gun than in another," and this was apparently not a major problem at the time, although good-looking "harquebuzes of caliber" seem to have been especially appreciated. Brantôme also mentioned many weapons such as halberds, pikes (including some painted black), heavy matchlock muskets, pistols, corselets, gilded morions and even a rondelle shield covered with green velvet carried by one Captain Monein.

As can be seen in the illustrations, armor was commonly worn by 16th-century officers and men. In the early years of the century, the armor used was not very different from what had been used in the late Middle Ages. However, from about 1530, luxury armor made in Milan assumed new decorative patterns in tune with Renaissance art that was called the *Grande Maniera* (the Grand Manner), notably by the craftsmen of the Negroli family. These new patterns were inspired by the mannerism seen in Michelangelo's and Rafael's work based on ancient classical themes. The technique of polishing the iron and engraving it also evolved with decorative embossing, while gold wash or plate was increasingly used. The very best and most expensive armors could have jewels and enameled cameos added. Thus was the armor made by Francesco Negroni for the Dauphin of France who became King Henri II. The *Grande Maniera* soon came to France, and French artisans, often using Italian or German-made basic pieces,

Above:
Man at arms in armor, c.1590. The metal is blackened (a practice that became very popular in the second half of the 16th century) and decorated with gilt lines, edgings and studs. He may have been a French knight, while his armor is probably Italian. [Painting by Domenico Tintoretto. Museum of Fine Arts, Valetta, Malta] *Author's photo*

Left:
Pikeman's armor, c.1610. Iron painted black with brass or gilt rivets, fastening buckles, plume socket and top of helmet. Several heads of polearms are also visible. These items are shown as trophies at the lower left of a huge painting showing the queen being named regent on May 14, 1610, following the assassination of King Henri IV. The composition features Gods of Antiquity and the foot seen belongs to a nymph. [Musée du Louvre, Paris] *Author's photo*

produced their own versions of this style. Their works were generally more subtle with flatter embossing, but very few can be attributed outside of those made by the goldsmith Pierre Redon of Paris.

Nor was this decorative work only meant for the rich and powerful. Brantôme mentioned that, during the mid-16th century, morions and corselets imported from Milan were decorated far more cheaply and better in Paris than in Milan. Etching and gilding an officer's morion would cost eight "écus" at a Paris shop, while Negroli in Milan would charge 14 "écus." As a result, many French artisans took to etching and gilding armor pieces. Brantôme wrote that he had "seen a very great quantity [of armor] in France at low prices," so that this would also have been accessible to lower-ranking soldiers. All in all, Brantôme's account confirmed the other sources in that the variety in the weapons and equipment of the 16th-century French soldier was outstanding. And this was, of course, equally true in the New World.[9]

CHAPTER 2

Early Settlements 1604 to 1663

Below:
Pikeman, c.1596–1598. This drawing by Jacques de Gheyn II was prepared for a series of 116 engravings to demonstrate the use of firearms and the pike in *The Exercise of Arms* published in 1607–1608, in Dutch and in several other languages. This manual was also widely copied in France in the early 17th century for use with its own manuals. [Boston Museum of Fine Arts, Boston, Mass.] *Author's photo*

After nearly a century of unlucky attempts, the notion of establishing an overseas domain was still strong. The lure was, as previously, the possibility of amassing fortunes or at least some wealth in virgin territories. Most of South America, the larger islands of the Caribbean, Central America and Mexico were the domains of Spain and Portugal. There remained the Guyana area in South America, the smaller West Indian islands and North America. The latter first drew risk capital from businessmen eager to tap into the lucrative fur trade. These were to be trading stations, and the notion of settlements would come later. There would be adventurers of all sorts that came from France to America, not only fur traders but also seafaring and wilderness men that would become the *courreurs des bois* and the *boucaniers* — both fated to become larger-than-life figures — and all came bearing arms.

(NORTH AMERICA) ACADIA

In 1604, the expedition sailing for Acadia was provided with a "quantity of weapons and ammunition for warfare." The fort built on Sainte-Croix Island with "the banner of France" flying above had a gun platform, and its lodgings included quarters "for the Swiss" that seem to have been men-at-arms and, therefore, surely well armed. After a difficult winter during which many colonists perished due to epidemics, the settlement was moved to Port Royal in 1605, when a "company of some 40 men to relieve the sentinel of Sieur de Monts and his group" arrived. The French were armed with "muskets and swords." The following year, during a skirmish with Indians at the St. John River, and during another engagement, the son of the Sieur de Pont, one of the leaders, lost three fingers when his musket's barrel burst upon firing, because it had been loaded with too much powder.

Port Royal was abandoned in 1607, but in 1610, Poutrincourt came back with a party of men to reoccupy the place. In his account of his time spent in Port Royal that year, Marc Lescarbot mentioned that an Indian woman, thinking the French fort was being attacked, yelled "several times 'Ech'pada, Ech'pada' meaning 'to swords, to swords,'" and Sieur de Poutraincourt shot an "arquebusade" to bring down a deer while hunting — clear evidence of the weapons used by these colonists. In 1613, the Jesuit Order took over the settlement, but the missionaries had hardly arrived when the "English Captain Samuel Argal" and his men from Virginia successfully attacked Port Royal, killing a Jesuit and two other men. It was a pirate's raid, and after looting the place, the settlement was burned to the ground.[10]

In 1631, Charles de La Tour founded Fort Sainte-Marie on the shores of the St. John River (now St. John, New Brunswick). In the evening of September 18, 1632, an English corsair ship under one Forrester took Fort Sainte-Marie on the shores of the St. John River by surprise. Amongst the booty were four swivel guns, ten matchlock muskets and four harquebus.[11]

Isaac de Razilly (1587–1635) had been to Brazil in 1612 (see page 57) and later to North Africa. He was a knight of Malta and officer in the navy of the king of France. He was seriously wounded and lost an eye at the 1625 blockade of La Rochelle when his ship blew up in a fierce battle, but his valor was noticed by the powerful Cardinal Richelieu who sought his advice on naval and overseas affairs. In 1632, he was granted the prestigious title of "Lieutenant General of New France" and landed with 300 settlers at La Hève, on the southern shore of Acadia, to found a settlement there. He then soon sailed for Port Royal, took the place from the English and brought French colonists there as well. In 1635, his lieutenant, Charles de Menou d'Aulnay, took possession of Fort Pentagouet (Penobscot, Maine), thus restoring all of France's territories in Acadia as agreed by the 1632 Treaty.[12]

Razilly was content, but died at La Hève towards the end of 1635, and his probate inventory listed a number of weapons and accoutrements. There were "two firelock harquebus almost worn out," "two wheel-lock pistols," "two swords, one for thrusting, the other for use on horseback." Amongst the accoutrements were "two shabby baldrics embroidered in silver," "two other baldrics made of leather, one trimmed with silver and the other with silvered copper," "one sword-sling embroidered in gold and silver, new, with the belt." Other items included cloaks and cassocks bearing the cross of the Order of Malta.[13]

From 1640 to 1645, the area became embroiled in the "Acadian Civil War" fought between

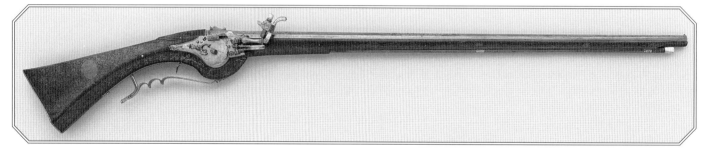

Below:
Wheel-lock short musket, c.1610. Engraved and gilt; wood, inlaid with silver and brass wire. Its caliber is 11.9 mm (.47 inch) and is 110.2 cm in length, the barrel having 79.4 cm. [Courtesy, The Metropolitan Museum, New York. Rogers Fund, 1904]

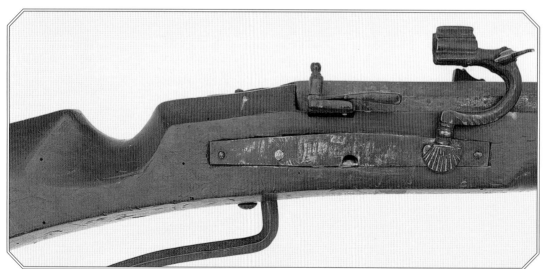

Left:
Matchlock musket lock, c.1600–1620. This example was made simply, yet was sturdy, and was meant for an ordinary infantry musketeer. [Courtesy Amoskeag Auction Company]

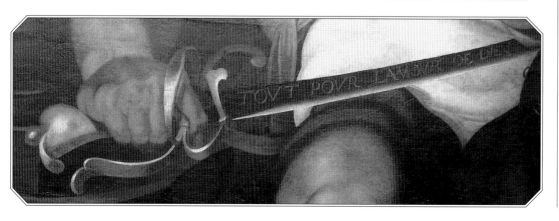

Left, bottom:
Cutlass c.1610–1619. This detail from a period painting shows the elaborate gilt guard of this weapon with the man's hand holding it with the forefinger, correctly grasping the lower part. The blade is engraved with the words: "TOVT POUR L'AMOUR DE DIEV" (Everything for the love of God) highlighted in gold. [From "La charité de Saint Martin" by Martin Fréminet. Musée du Louvre, Paris]
Author's photo

EARLY SETTLEMENTS 1604–1663

Right:
Claude de Razilly (right), Governor of Acadia, with one of his guardsmen, c.1635. The weapons and equipment shown are based on archaeological remains found in Maine. De Razilly was a kight of Malta and wears the black cape with the white cross of the Order of St. John. His guardsman has a red cassock with his coat of arms thereon, a red shield with silver lilies. [Drawing by Francis Back. Reproduced by courtesy of the artist]

Below:
Soldier, c.1628–1630. At his waist is an obscured but rarely seen *main gauche* dagger with a spike-like blade. The pommel of his sword shows above a cloak that covers the rest of this weapon. He is shown wearing the back plate of his cuirass. A white sash (the color that identified a French soldier) is slung over his right shoulder. [Detail of a painting by Valentin de Bourgogne. Musée du Louvre, Paris] *Author's photo*

the followers of competing governors Charles de Saint-Étienne de la Tour (a Protestant) and Charles de Menou d'Aulnay (a Catholic), so there were religious aspects as well as personal animosity. Several battles were fought, but information on weapons used is quite sparse. Cannons, muskets, swords and polearms were obviously present. Some soldiers probably wore iron helmets and cuirasses, since the manner of fighting in Acadia was typically European. Finally, in April of 1645, d'Aulnay and his men attacked La Tour's stronghold at Fort Sainte-Marie (now St. John, New Brunswick). La Tour's wife, Françoise-Marie, led the defense against a much superior force, but capitulated on April 18th, after d'Aulnay promised to spare the prisoners. He reneged and treacherously had La Tour's garrison hanged while Madame de la Tour was forced to watch the execution with a rope around her neck. She passed away three weeks later. The cruel d'Aulnay died in 1650, and ironically, La Tour then returned to govern Acadia and, three years later, married d'Aulnay's widow.

On August 16, 1654, Commandant de La Verdure at Port Royal capitulated to General Sedgwyck's New Englanders, his garrison being granted the honors of war. This meant the French garrison would come out with its colors deployed, each man-at-arms keeping his "matchlock musket or flintlock muskets on the shoulder, with match lighted cord at both ends" while marching to board a ship for France. Sedgwyck and his troops also captured La Tour at Fort Sainte-Marie, and Acadia became a ward of New England for the next decade and a half.[14]

Below:
Pair of wheel-lock pistols, c.1610. Made by Pierre Le Bourgeois at Lisieux. Blued and gilded, inlaid with silver wire and mother-of-pearl. Caliber: 12.4 mm. Overall length: 59.2 cm. [Courtesy, The Metropolitan Museum, New York. Gift of Charles M. Schott Jr., 1917]

Below:
Pair of wheel-lock pistols, c.1640. Made by François Du Clos with engraved decorations attributed to Thomas Picquot, both of Paris. Blued and gilded, inlaid with silver wire and mother-of-pearl. Caliber: 13.4 mm. Overall length: 58.7 cm.

[Courtesy, The Metropolitan Museum, New York. Rogers Fund, 1904]

Below:
Wheel-lock pistol, early 17th century. This .56 caliber weapon made in Italy is typical of the portable weapons carried by early traders and explorers.

[National Firearms Museum, Reston, Virginia]
Author's photo

Above:

Madame de La Tour begs d'Aulnay for the lives of her soldiers in captured Fort Sainte-Marie on April 18, 1645. This 20th-century reconstruction by Adam Sheriff Scott is a fine example of the problems encountered by modern illustrators who, apart from Champlain, have practically no period visual sources or vestiges to turn to regarding the early appearance of French soldiers and settlers in America during much of the 17th century. Since the fighting during the 1640–1645 Acadian Civil War was comparable to that in Europe, Sheriff Scott elected to show soldiers as in Europe, in this case armed with halberds and muskets and wearing pikemen's armor, which, under the circumstances, is possibly reasonably accurate. The image of D'Aulnay is based on a print said to be of his likeness. [Library and Archives, Canada] *Author's photo*

Left:

French soldier armed with a matchlock musket, 1630s. [Print from *Figures au naturel tant des vestements que des postures des Gardes-Françaises du Roy très chrétien*. Anne S.K. Brown Military Collection, Brown University Library, Providence, R.I.] *Author's photo*

CANADA

It was not until 1608 that the first permanent settlement was established at Quebec under the leadership of Samuel de Champlain. During these very first years, the little fort at Quebec was really a trading post. Its promoters were businessmen in France wishing to exploit the possibilities of trading European goods for the valuable furs in North America. This led Champlain and his companions to explore the interior in search of trading partners. Thus, the French became allies of the Huron and Algonquin Indian nations, but these alliances made them the enemies of the powerful and warlike Iroquois Confederacy of the Five Nations. As early as July of 1609, Champlain and two French companions were with a large band of allied Indians that encountered an equally large Iroquois force.

At this time, for main engagements, Indian nations fought each other in large groups while deployed in open fields. Warriors wore protective armor made of wood and leather, carried shields and were armed with clubs, spears, bows and arrows. On that fateful occasion, both Indian bands faced each other when Champlain stepped out in front of his allies, wearing a pikemen's armor and a plumed burgonet, then aimed and fired his arquebus. Two Iroquois chiefs were hit while, concealed in the nearby woods, two other Frenchmen also fired their guns. The startled Iroquois panicked and fled. The following years saw more engagements between the French, their allies and the Iroquois. Generally, although very few in numbers, the French prevailed because of their superior armament and iron armor.

Their offensive weapons were mainly matchlock muskets and swords.

However, from the outset, the French realized they faced combat conditions that were significantly different from what they had known in Europe. Indians also practiced furtive warfare with great skill. In order to survive and thrive in their new environment, the French quickly understood that they had to change their tactics

Left:
French Soldier in Canada, 1610s–1620s. A light arquebuss appears to have been the favored weapon. Shown here with a short barrel and a whell-lock, but it could also have been longer and with a matchlock. Helmets and pikemen's breastplates were worn for protection against arrows and spears. Reconstructon according to *Les Voyages… des Champlain* by Michel Pétard. [Courtesy, History and Heritage Directorate, Dept. of National Defense of Canada, Ottowa..] *Author's photo*

Left:
French burgonet, late 16th and early 17th century. Embossed iron highlighted with gold. This type of helmet became increasingly popular during the second half of the 16th century and was widely worn in French armies. The first governor of Canada, Samuel de Champlain, depicted himself wearing this type of helmet fighting the Iroquois in 1609. [Print after M. Dessertenne. *L'Art Pour Tous*, No. 759, January 31, 1892] *Author's photo*

from the type of fighting they knew in Europe and make substantial adjustments to the type of arms and accoutrements they carried as well as the clothing they wore.

During the first quarter century of their settlement, the small group of Frenchmen at Quebec included some soldiers that were hired by the monopoly companies that controlled the fur trade. These soldiers were very few, probably no more than a dozen, because of the cost to the companies who were mainly interested in turning out a profit. As soldiers, it would appear that their role was much

Left:
French "companions" of Champlain using an elevated wooden redoubt to shoot into an Onondaga town, 1615. [Detail of a print from *Les Voyages…de Champlain*. Courtesy, Library and Archives Canada, C5749]

Right:
Samuel de Champlain's defeat of the Iroquois in 1609. Details in this print show Champlain as wearing a burgonet and a pikeman's armor. His companions might have a breastplate. All three are armed with matchlock muskets and swords. From *Les Voyages…de Champlain*. The prints illustrating his works were made according to his sketches. They appear to have been fairly accurate in showing Champlain and his men, but the native warriors were simply engraved as naked men, whereas Champlain's texts described more clothing and armament such as shields. [Courtesy, Library and Archives Canada, C5750]

broader in a small settlement and included many other activities. Conversely, some of the traders also had military experience that could be called upon. Champlain himself, the colony's first governor for many years (1608–1635), was a veteran soldier

The French were not the only ones to adapt. Their Indian enemies also made dramatic changes in the way they were armed and the way they fought. The Indians instantly perceived the advantages of iron and firearms, and sought to obtain all they could. The French were forbidden to barter firearms for furs during the first decades of the 17th century, but certainly traded other types of military items. The Indians were not interested in heavy pieces of defensive armor such as breastplates and helmets. Instead they sought the efficiency that metal blades and arrow points had over those made of flints.

As early as 1623, Father Sagard, one of the early missionaries, mentions the increasing use of metal arrowheads amongst the Hurons allied to the French. The latter, to satisfy demand, bought thousands of old sword blades taken from stocks of discarded weapons in Europe and brought them to Canada to trade with the Indians. The natives, in turn, used the blades as spear points that were especially effective in hunting deer as well as in battle. These technical innovations brought about rapid changes in the way Indian nations in present-day eastern Canada waged warfare. Up to that time, they fought in two basic ways: the first was in large groups dressed in wooden armor fighting in an open field. The second was totally different, consisting of ambushes and surprise attacks carried out by small groups of warriors wearing no armor and hardly any clothing, since swiftness of movement was all-im-

Left:
Sword parts, early 17th century. These rusted iron remains are associated with Champlain and his companions' explorations and fights with his Huron allies against their Onondaga enemies. They were found at Cahiagué (Warminster Site) in Southern Georgian Bay of Lake Huron, Ontario. [University of Toronto, Department of Anthropology] *Author's photo*

Far left:
Officer's sword hilt, c.1650. Silvered hilt with iron blade. [Musée de l'Armée, Paris] *Author's photo*

Below left:
Soldier's Burgonet helmet, early 17th century. Side view. [Musée Stewart, Montreal] *Author's photo*

Left:
Soldier's Burgonet helmet, early 17th century. Front view. [Fort Ticonderoga Museum, Ticonderoga, New York] *Author's photo*

Above:
Infantry pike, 1620s. This was probably the type of pike sent to Québec in 1622. [Musée de l'Armée, Paris] *Author's photo*

French soldier armed with a wheel-lock musket, c.1630. [Print after Theodore Maas. Anne S.K. Brown Military Collection, Brown University Library, Providence] *Author's photo*

Above:
Young soldier with pikeman's armor, 1627. Capes were often worn by soldiers at the time, and this painting by Simon Vouet is probably very close to what an infantryman looked like on ordinary duty. [Musée du Louvre, Paris] *Author's photo*

Right:
Back view of French soldier aiming a musket, c.1630. Note the sword and the musket charge containers seemingly held in a bunch by a cord or narrow belt. [Print after Theodore Maas. Anne S.K. Brown Military Collection, Brown University Library, Providence] *Author's photo*

portant in this type of warfare. The wooden armor being increasingly ineffective against iron, the Indians gradually abandoned these and concentrated on camouflage and surprise attacks.[15]

The weapons and armor shipped to Quebec were identical to those used by troops in France. Champlain's account of his explorations and voyages in New France often mentions swords and harquebus as weapons used wearing pikemen's armor and helmets. This was a sufficiently lightweight outfit, and the harquebus was favored over the match (or wheel) lock musket because it was lighter. Wearing pikemen's armor was, nevertheless, very cumbersome in the Canadian wilderness. In 1610, Champlain complained of the immense number of bugs (probably black flies) that "cruelly persecuted" him and his companions — it seems some bugs would even get under the breastplates to bite the skin, and would, of course, be unreachable!

Left:

Ensign "marching on guard", c.1640s. Armed with a sword, he holds his unit's color. At that time, and until the end of the 17th century, the color's pike was short, only providing a handle to hold it — it did not rest on the ground. A gorget below his collar shows this young officer's status. [Both prints after Collombon's *Trophée d'armes*, Lyon 1650. Musée Stewart, Montreal] *Author's photo*

Below:

Lieutenant, c.1640s. Armed with a pike and a sword. His gorget is also seen below his collar. *Author's photo*

Officer's gorget, c.1630. This French gorget is of embossed copper and has its buff leather backing, the flaps of which are partly visible at the top of each end. The decorative embossing shows a battle scene.

[Private collection]
Author's photo

EARLY SETTLEMENTS 1604–1663

Right:
Front view of a French infantryman, 1640s. He holds his matchlock musket at the *Retirez vos armes* (withdraw your weapon) position. [Print from Lostelneau's *Le Maréchal des Batailles*; Paris, 1647. Private collection] Author's photo

Below:
French soldier in Canada, 1640s–1650s. Flintlock muskets are the predominant firearms used in Canada as early as the 1640s. Reconstruction according to probate records by Michel Pétard. The musket is taken mostly from early examples illustrated in Torsten Lenk's 1939/1965 *The Flintlock*.

[Courtesy, History and Heritage Directorate, Dept. of National Defence of Canada, Ottawa]

All the same, such armor offered good protection against spears and arrows, and they seem to have been used up to the 1630s.[16]

A shipment of arms and ammunition sent to Quebec in 1621 gives an idea of the type of weapons used by the garrison. This included two wheel-lock and two matchlock harquebus, 12 halberds, 50 pikes, two brass petards, two gens-d'armes armors (possibly three-quarter armor suitable for officers) and 40 sets of pikemen's armor (without the brassards). At first glance, this seems unsuitable for facing enemy Indians. However, besides the adaptations mentioned above, it must be recalled that Europeans in the New World also had to plan their defense against a sea-borne European enemy. That is indeed what happened at Quebec in 1629 when a strong force of English corsairs arrived. Resistance was pointless, and the French fort surrendered. What arms the English found in the fort included 14 matchlock muskets, two long wheel-lock harquebuses six to seven feet long, two others with match locks, 50 corselets without brassards, with burgonet helmets and the two gendarme's armors. Three years later, the treaty of Aix-la-Chapelle restored Canada to France and a new garrison arrived. It was probably armed and equipped in a similar way as before, since the soldiers entered Quebec carrying pikes and muskets. Champlain even suggested that the soldiers should wear protective chain mail shirts. In 1635, artillery was sent to Quebec as well as 23 matchlock muskets, 13 bandoleers, one wheel-lock harquebus, 20 pistols, four swords and, a sign of Canada's favorite future weapon, a "harquebus" with a flintlock — in effect, a flintlock musket.[17]

Meanwhile, a peace treaty between the French and the Iroquois had been agreed to in 1622. However, from the mid-1630s, tensions rose again, and there were increasing numbers of incidents. The Iroquois that the French would face were now much better armed than previously. Since the 1620s, the Dutch had established forts south of Canada at New Amsterdam (now New York) and Orange (now Albany, N.Y.) where they traded everything with the Iroquois, including guns. In 1641, war broke out between the French and the Iroquois. This time, many Iroquois warriors knew how to use the European firearms that they obtained from the Dutch.

This evolution in the armament of New France's Indian enemies led to changes in the equipment of the garrison's soldiers. The cumbersome protective items such as iron breast plates and helmets were no longer practical on service since mobility was now more important.

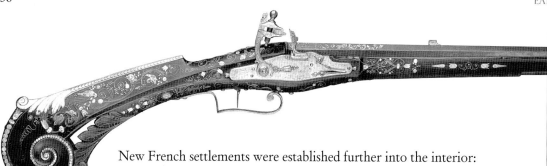

New French settlements were established further into the interior: Trois-Rivières in 1634, Montréal in 1642 and the religious missions with the allied Huron Indian nation on the eastern shore of Lake Huron. These new settlements and missions were closer to the enemy Iroquois nations, and all became targets for countless numbers of attacks during the 1640s. If the inhabitants of Quebec City lived in relative security, the same was not true for those who lived in Trois-Rivières or Montreal. There, all able-bodied men, be they soldiers or civilians, would never go out "without their muskets, swords and pistols." The number of soldiers available for defense was small, perhaps 40 in 1642 and about 60 two years later. Twenty-two of these soldiers were sent to the main mission at Sainte-Marie-amongst-the-Hurons, but the missions eventually fell to the Iroquois in 1649–1650. By the early 1650s, there were hardly 35 regular soldiers in the colony.[6] The situation remained very hazardous until 1665.[18]

In terms of weapons and equipment, soldiers and settlers in Canada quickly chose flintlock muskets as their favorite weapons. These appeared in the colony possibly as early as the 1640s and, according to various documents (notably probate records), were very common thereafter. Dollier de Canson mentions them from June 1651 in fights with the Iroquois, and it is obvious most men had already been armed with flintlocks for some time. Pistols, swords, knives and hatchets were also used as weapons. Various records, notably the probate inventories of deceased persons, give an idea of the types of weapons used in the early Canadian colony. A few examples are given below, and the reader should bear in mind that these items could have been used for many years previous by the deceased subject of the probate:

- A flintlock musket; 12 hatchets; a sealskin baldric (Louis Le Bicheur, Sieur de La Roche, soldier of the garrison, Trois-Rivières, November 26, 1654, ANTR, Ameau)
- Three very old locks for flintlock muskets; two bayonets; three flintlock muskets (Nicolas Godé, woodworker, Montreal, November 7, 1657, ANQM, Basset)
- A sword with its scabbard and waistbelt; a flintlock musket's lock (L. Biteaux, Montreal, February 19, 1658, ANQM, Basset)
- Eight flintlock muskets; two belt pistols; a sword with a guard; another sword with a baldric (Jean de Saint-Père, Montreal, January 12, 1659, ANQM, Basset)
- Two sword blades to fix a guard thereon; two axes (René Doussin, soldier, Montreal, May 26, 1660, ANQM, Basset)
- A flintlock musket's barrel of about three feet long with a lock (Jean Vallets, Montreal, May 26, 1660, ANQM, Basset)
- A sword with a "ollinde" [Holland?] blade and a silver guard, with its morocco leather baldric; another sword without a scabbard, with a black leather baldric (Louis Chartier, surgeon, Montreal, July 22, 1660, ANQM, Basset)
- A baldric of English cowhide with its iron buckle (Dollard Desormeaux, commandant of the garrison, Montreal, September 6, 1660, ANQM, Basset)

Left

French flintlock gun, c.1620s. This type of musket may have appeared in French America during the 1630s and certainly during the 1640s. Flintlocks proved especially popular in Canada. This particular fowling piece is one of the earliest firearms of French construction equipped with the flintlock. It was made for King Louis XIII (reigned 1610–43) in the workshop directed by Pierre Le Bourgeois' brother, Marin (about 1550–1634), to whom the invention of the flintlock mechanism is traditionally ascribed. The decoration of the gun includes the crowned monogram of the king. The scroll-shaped end of the gunstock is an unusual and especially graceful feature of this gun's design. The steel is chiseled, blued, and gilded; wood, inlaid with silver, brass, and engraved mother-of-pearl; gilt brass and bone. The caliber is 55 mm (.59 inch), length of 140.9 cm of which the barrel is 104.1 cm. [Courtesy, The Metropolitan Museum, New York. Rogers Fund, 1904. Rogers Fund and Harris Brisbane Dick Fund, 1972]

Left:

Sword hilt and blade remains, c.1625. These items were found during excavations in the foundations of the second Habitation fort built in Québec City during the early 1620s. [Courtesy, Ministère des Affaires culturelles, Québec]

- A pair of pistols; a small sword with the end of its blade broken and two baldrics of English cowhide; a flintlock musket with its grey serge bag; three trade flintlock muskets (Lambert Closse, sergeant major of the Montreal garrison, February 8, 1662, ANQM, Basset)
- A long flintlock musket; another such musket having been used with two or three burns on the barrel (Simon Le Roy, Montreal, March 17, 1662, ANQM, Basset)
- Two flintlock muskets, one made in Caen (Normandy) by Coupar with much decoration (Governor de Mésy, Montreal, May 6, 1665, ANQM, Faillon)

Items for personal protection such as armor and helmets seem to have been laid aside by the late 1630s or the early 1640s. All now wore ordinary French-style clothes, which increasingly included such Indian items as leather "moccasin" shoes. The "capot," a hooded sailor's coat, became one of the most popular items of clothing, both with the French settlers and with the Indians.[19]

A September 31, 1660, inventory of the Château St. Louis and its fort in Quebec City reveals that a number of items were now out of use. For instance, "seven or eight pikes" were stored in the roof's rafters, possibly some of those sent in the 1620s and since forgotten. In the arms magazine were found:

- 84 matchlock muskets of which 79 had locks with serpentine (the five others may have been wheel-locks), most old and nine unserviceable.
- 25 matchlock musket barrels of which seven or eight had burst.
- Five serviceable pistols and five old and unserviceable.
- 37 rifled carbines "such as they are."

There were also various parts for pistols, flintlock and matchlock muskets, 200 musket flints, nine pounds of match, 400 pounds of musket balls, musket and artillery powder and "in a secluded corner are a quantity of cuirasses and burgonets."

Of the above firearms, matchlock muskets appear to have been still viable and of some use to the soldiers in Quebec City. Indeed, in 1662, Colbert de Terron planned to issue some to arm with flintlock muskets obtained from one Girardeau for a hundred soldiers sent to reinforce Canada as well as send two or three hundred extra flintlock muskets.[20]

BRAZIL 1612–1613

In the early 17th century, the French looked again at Brazil, this time further north, in the Maranhao area. Daniel de la Touche de La Raverdière, a soldier and explorer, spent a few months there in 1604 and came back to "Maragnan" in July of 1612 leading an expedition for its colonization. Fort St. Louis was built, armed with 22 guns. In July of 1613, warfare erupted with the local Indians, and the 40 French soldiers fired some 1,200 musket shots in three hours, during which time the Indians shot back a "rain or hailstorm" of arrows that wounded a few Frenchmen but killed none. From this, it seems most likely that the French had half-armors on, presumably helmets and corselets with tassets.

Below:
Gentleman's flintlock pistol, c.1650. Possibly made in Liège or eastern France. Decoration includes military scenes with figures in 17th-century costume, trophies of arms, and Classical figures. This pistol, one of a pair, belonged to the Swedish general Carl Gustaf, Count Wrangel, who acquired it in Liège in 1651. It is a good example of a quality French-made weapon carried by officers. Its substantial pommel shows it could also be quite lethal in hand-to-hand fighting. Length, 62.7 cm; length of barrel, 43.3 cm. [Courtesy, The Metropolitan Museum, New York. Purchase, Arthur Ochs Sulzberger Gift, 2011]

Right:
Common flintlock pistol, 1650s. This type of plain but sturdy pistol, with no decoration, was undoubtedly the inexpensive sort of weapon widely used by all sorts of French men-at-arms on land and sea anywhere. Note the sturdy metal butt that could crack an opponent's skull in close combat once the shot had been fired. Steel, iron and wood, wooden ramrod with a bone tip. [Courtesy, National Historic Sites, Parks Canada]

Peace was soon concluded, and the local Indians were persuaded to abandon cannibalism. During a later ceremony at Fort St. Louis, some of the allied natives were described with swords, daggers, "rondaches" shields obviously given or traded by the French as well as carrying bows and arrows. The following year, the colony had up to 120 soldiers with sailors added. By then however, some 400 Portuguese troops arrived with hundreds of "Portuguezed Indian" allies to chase the French out. After some determined fighting in which "match cord" and harquebus are mentioned, the French were defeated and left the area.[21]

WEST INDIES

French adventurers had been roaming the West Indies for over a century in search of Spanish gold, either by smuggling or by more piratical practices, but they did not have a fairly permanent base until they took to roaming on the coast and the islands of the western end of Hispaniola (which is now Haiti) during the early 17th century. Its fields and jungles were increasingly populated by half-savage adventurers that were mostly French. They were, to quote Father Duterte's 1667 *Histoire générale des Antilles*, men that had "become skilled and valiant" by the nature of their occupation "which was to hunt [wild] beef to obtain their hides, and be hunted themselves by the Spaniards, who gave them no quarter." Although they had not settled the western part of Hispaniola, the Spanish would indeed hunt down any other Europeans found there since it was part of their realm. This made these mostly French adventurers resolute opponents of the Spanish who certainly had unluckily picked on some of the fiercest men anywhere. They "passed for un-disciplinable people" that could not "suffer any chiefs" and most of them had "taken refuge in these places" to escape being punished for "the crimes they had committed in Europe." They lived a wild existence that could be compared to trappers or mountain men in North America, and had no permanent homes. They cured meat and hides with smoke by making a "boucan," earning them their French name "boucaniers," which soon was translated into "buccaneer" by English adventurers who were also numerous in the area.

The Spanish considered buccaneers to be pirates, and once they went to sea, they did their very best to prove the Spaniards right. Hence the advent of the "flibustiers," translated as freebooters that roamed the Caribbean on board small vessels that looked for Spanish ships and small coastal settlements to loot. They needed a base, and the island of Tortuga, off Haiti's northern coast, proved to be ideal. In 1625, French and English adventurers arrived on the island. The Spanish drove them off in 1629, built a fort there, but then moved out most of their troops. A year later, the buccaneers were back, divided the island into French and English "colonies" in which they built a few plantations and, in 1633, imported slaves from Africa to work in them. There were many bloody disputes between French and English buccaneers, and some few Dutch ones too, but they would come together to fight the Spanish. In 1635, 1640, 1641 and, lastly, in 1654, the Spanish came back, but would ultimately retreat, and the *Frères de la côte* (Brethrens of the Coast) buccaneers would hold the place again. Indeed, the French had built Fort du Rocher that had repulsed the Spaniards in 1641.

A government of sorts had been organized by French Captain Le Vasseur in 1643, but he was killed by some of his discontented fellow freebooters ten years later. By then, the French royal government had developed a strong interest in the area and appointed one of Le Vasseur's lieutenants as "governor of Tortuga and the coast of Saint-Domingue" on November 28, 1656. It would, in time, become the French colony of Saint-Domingue, later known as Haiti, one of the most important and prosperous territories in the West Indies.

Below:
Armed and slovenly looking youngsters might be reminiscent of 1630s French adventurers in the West Indies. The musket has the lighter butt typical of that made in France. [Print from *Figures au naturel tant des vestements que des postures des Gardes-Françaises du Roy très chrétien*. Anne S.K. Brown Military Collection, Brown University Library, Providence, R.I.] *Author's photo*

Encouraged by their incursions in Tortuga, French adventurers went to St. Kitts (Saint-Christophe) in 1625, to Martinique and Guadeloupe in 1635, to St. Lucia in 1643, to Grenada in 1649 and to several smaller islands.

As can be imagined, all these adventurers from France and elsewhere in Europe came to the Caribbean islands fully armed with their swords and firearms. Since these were individually purchased and owned, records are scant other than passing references and occasional illustrations. The early French settlers of St. Kitts were described in the 1630s as never going out of their homes unless they had "five or six pistols suspended to a leather belt and a flintlock musket." Those of the Leeward Islands generally were said to go out barely dressed, wearing only a loincloth, and one might be armed "with a large knife, another with a cutlass, another with a lance that is like a half pike...another with a musketoon or a pistol." They hunted with dogs thus dressed and armed. As can be seen, they favored lightweight weapons, and flintlock muskets were, as in Canada, a favorite weapon.[22]

Some arms were, however, supplied by the monopoly companies that encouraged settlement. For instance, in 1637, the "Company of the Islands of America" sent six cannons for the fort in Martinique along with 400 matchlock muskets and 240 swords to be sold to the settlers. In January of 1658, the militia at Martinique paraded at the funeral of Governor Du Parquet "in good order, the matchlock muskets lowered and the pikes down" accompanied by the late governor's 12 guards wearing their "scarlet cassocks with the white cross, all with the musketoon and the bandolier." Since they had a bandolier, the *mousqueton* (musketoon) they carried was most likely a lightweight matchlock musket.[23]

Meanwhile, in 1649, a group of settlers took possession of the island of Grenada "bearing arms" while they built a fort and celebrated its completion by "10 or 12" artillery shots. Carib Indians soon attacked, were repulsed and were attacked in turn by the French the following year, who were armed with "flintlock muskets, matchlock muskets and other weapons" according to a contemporary account. Flintlocks are mentioned again in 1655 and 1658, which confirms they were widely used by the early settlers of the French West Indies.[24]

Below:
Attack on an Onondaga town by French and Hurons, 1615. Some of Champlain's French "companions" are shown firing with both a light type of musket and a heavy matchlock musket requiring a fork to support its weight when aiming. [Detail of a print from *Les Voyages...de Champlain.* Courtesy, Library and Archives Canada, C5749}

GUYANA

There were several settlement attempts by the French during the first half of the 17th century, but most failed due to Portuguese, English and Dutch opponents who wanted to control the area between Venezuela and Brazil. In 1635, merchants from Rouen built a fortified post on the island of Cayenne, but in 1654, the Dutch occupied the place until 1664. Nevertheless, by the mid-1660s, a small permanent colony with French settlers had been established when the French Guyana reverted to France. British and Dutch settlements were established further north.

Weapons

Shoulder firearms went through a certain evolution from about the 1620s. The harquebus was gradually abandoned as a weapon since its hitting power was too weak. The matchlock musket became the standard infantry weapon, but it was quite heavy and cumbersome since it required a fork to hold it steady due to the weight of its barrel. The army of King Gustav Adolf I of Sweden, considered the most innovative in the first third of the 17th century, was the first to adopt new, lighter weapons. A chronicler of 1632 reported having seen a company of Swedish soldiers, and "among them were musketeers armed with the new, very light muskets without forks." This was achieved by reducing the caliber and thus the weight of the barrel. By the second quarter of the century, the fork was vanishing and the lighter matchlock musket was predominant in European armies. Calibers were not yet standardized, but had decreased from about 12 to 20 balls per pound by the early 1660s.

The cause of this progress in France seems to have been due to Colonel Arnaud of the Champagne Regiment. According to a contemporary memoir, he "thought that the weapons [here meaning matchlock muskets] used by the infantry could be made to be more handy than those then used, and sent me patterns to be seen by the king and, if he [the king] concurred, to beg him to have some made in Holland from the funds of his regiment. I took these patterns to the king at his arms cabinet and His Majesty was so pleased that, not only did he agree to his [Mr. Arnauld's] wishes, but wanted the guards regiment [the Gardes Françaises] to have similar [muskets], and today the whole French infantry has no other type. Following the king's agreement,

Left:
Officer's partisan, mid-17th century. [Philadelphia Museum of Fine Art]
Author's photo

Below:
Officer's gorget, mid-17th century. Polished steel with etchings. French or German. [Philadelphia Museum of Fine Art]
Author's photo

Left:
Sergeant, 1630s, holds the halberd, his formal symbol of rank. [Print from *Figures au naturel tant des vestements que des postures des Gardes-Françaises du Roy très chrétien*. Anne S.K. Brown Military Collection, Brown University Library, Providence, R.I.]
Author's photo

Above:
Henri, Duc de Guise, a noble officer of some wealth, c.1635, wears a polished steel gorget, red edged with gold and lace backing. He has a gilt-hilted sword featuring a "Pappenheimer" shell guard supported by a buff gold embroidered shoulder belt. He also wears a buff coat decorated with gold thread embroidery. [Print after Van Dyck. Courtesy The National Gallery of Art, Washington, D.C.]

EARLY SETTLEMENTS 1604–1663

Right, top:
Iron-hilted rapier, later 16th and/or early 17th centuries. This weapon is made with a swept hilt, a rounded pommel and a wire grip. [Courtesy, Musée militaire vaudois, Château de Morges, Switzerland. Rama/Wikimedia]

Right, center:
Iron-hilted rapier, later 16th and/or early 17th centuries. This sword's swept hilt is somewhat elegant and features engravings. [Musée de l'Armée, Paris] *Author's photo*

Right, bottom:
A Pappenheim-style sword hilt, c.1630. This type of sword was popular in France during the reign of Louis XIII. Polished iron hilt. [Musée de l'Armée, Paris] *Author's photo*

Below:
Early example of the Musketeer-style sword hilt for an officer, c.1655–1660. This type of hilt quickly became universally popular. Made of iron, gold, wood, copper alloy and steel, this particular example was probably created in Paris. It has 104.1 cm overall length with 87.5 cm of blade. [Courtesy, The Metropolitan Museum, New York. Purchase, Arthur Ochs Sulzberger Gift, 2011]

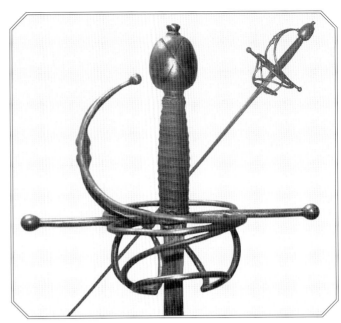

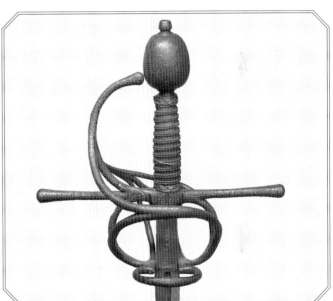

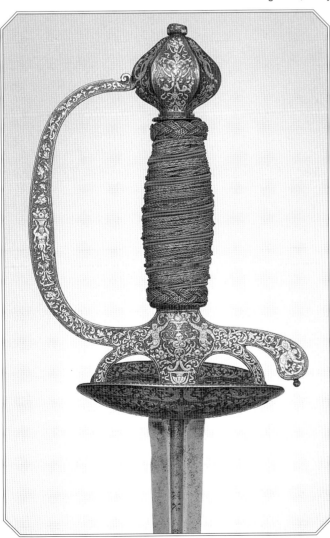

Mr. Arnaud sent Mr. Duplessis-Besançon to Holland to have these new arms made." The design of matchlock muskets also gradually changed from the rather heavy Germanic stocks to a lighter weight and more elegant shape, especially at the top of the butt, which became a hallmark of French gunsmiths.[25]

The flintlock ignition system was an improvement from the somewhat crude snaphance lock. The flintlock was a fairly efficient mechanism using a piece of flint fixed to a spring-activated hammer that, when released, would spark when hitting the lock's pan and ignite the black powder that set off the musket. This mechanism was lighter and cheaper than a wheel-lock. During the 1630s, French gunsmiths considerably improved the basic Miquelet flintlock into the *à la Française* (French-style) flintlock that spread to other countries. It provided a fairly dependable firing system that was suited to lightweight muskets and was ideal for pistols. As seen above, it quickly became popular in America. There are very few clues as to the features of the early flintlock muskets used in New France. One probate cited above mentions a barrel three feet long.

The flintlock also meant lighter calibers were possible for common soldier's muskets. French military authorities were reluctant to part with the matchlock musket due to its hitting power, and flintlocks were much frowned upon in the metropolitan army. This was for campaigns in Europe. In America, where fighting conditions were quite different, light weapons were more appropriate, hence the early arrival of flintlocks in North America and the West Indies.

Pistols passed from wheel-lock or snaphance to the flintlock ignition system during the first third of the 17th century, and their shape also changed, the grip taking a curved shape incorporating its ball pommel. Pistols became somewhat lighter as their barrel length decreased. Calibers were not standard, but seem to have stabilized at about 22 balls to the pound. Pistols used in America seem to have been of various types and were probably nearly always individual purchases.

Pikes, which usually were 14 feet high, armed many European soldiers, but in America they were not very useful against Indian or European raiders in the first half

Left:

Le Français en garde (the Frenchman on guard), c.1635. This well-appointed gentleman holds a rapier featuring a German-style Pappenheimer shell guard. Remnants of this type of shell guard have been found in the 1640s site of the mission of Ste. Marie-amongst-the-Hurons in present-day Ontario (Canada). [Print after Abraham Bosse. Courtesy, The Metropolitan Museum of Art, New York. Purchase, The Elisha Whittelsey Collection, The Elisha Whittelsey Fund, 1956]

Left:

Rapier made in western Europe with a German-style Pappenheimer shell at the lower part of the guard. This type of shell was found at the 1640s site of the mission of Ste. Marie-amongst-the-Hurons and may have generally had the appearance shown. [Higgins Armory Museum, Worcester, Mass.]
Author's photo

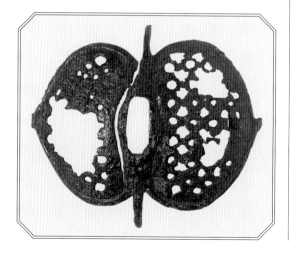

Left:

Part of a French soldier's sword guard, c.1645–1650. This appears to have been a German-style Pappenheimer shell from the guard of a rapier. Found at the site of the mission of Ste. Marie-amongst-the-Hurons. A small detachment of soldiers was posted there. [Courtesy, Sainte-Marie-amongst-the-Hurons Historic Site, Midland, Ontario]

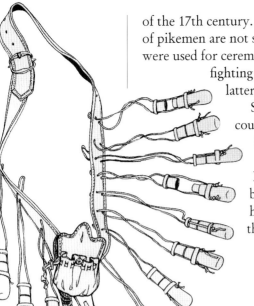

of the 17th century. Thus, while records occasionally mention shipments of pikes, distinct units of pikemen are not seen, and pikes are later found in recesses of storehouses. In America, some were used for ceremonial functions, notably in Martinique, but were abandoned as a weapon for fighting on land. The same was likely true for halberds and partisans, although the latter weapon is sometimes sent out later in the 17th century.

Swords (being personal possessions) were commonly carried, and the hilts could often be in the style of rapiers of various types. Vestiges of what may have been part of a "Popenheim"-style rapier have been found at the site of the 1640s mission fort of Sainte-Marie amongst the Hurons (Midland, Ontario). From about the mid-1650s, the new Musketeer type with its single knuckle-bow became increasingly popular. All main types of polearms, including pikes, halberds and partisans, were supplied to the various colonies. The extent of their use may have varied depending on local circumstances as seen above.

Equipment and Armor

During the first three quarters of the 17th century, the swords and accouterments were usually carried by shoulder belts or baldrics that could vary individually, but nevertheless had a certain similarity to one another. As previously, they were usually made of leather with metal buckles and would

Above:
Bandolier with charges in cylinders, 17th century. [Drawing by Michel Pétard. Private collection] *By kind courtesy of the artist*

Below:
Charge cylinder for a bandoliers, 17th century. [Philadelphia Museum of Fine Art, Philadelphia, Penn.] *Author's photo*

Right:
Early 17th-century powder horn. Made with deer bone, possibly antlers, and iron cap and spout. The carving shows a profile of King Henri IV of France. [Musée du Louvre, Paris] *Author's photo*

Right:
Musketeer, c.1640s. Armed with a matchlock musket and a sword. The bandoleer has the "Twelve Apostles" charges. [Print after Collombon's *Trophée d'armes*, Lyon 1650. Musée Stewart, Montreal] *Author's photo*

have the so-called "Twelve Apostles" that denoted, according to the humor of the time, the twelve powder charge containers suspended by cords from the shoulder belt. These bandoleers were generally carried by men armed with matchlock muskets, although those using flintlock muskets might have had them too, or else, a small bullet bag. There were powder horns and flasks, but some found that powder in a coat pocket was more handy even if more dangerous. But these men were used to dangers, and powder might even be used for pranks.[26]

Evidence that armor was sent out and sometimes used in action is found during the first third of the 17th century, but thereafter, it is obvious that it was progressively abandoned, not only in America, but also in France where the number of pikemen decreased.

By mid-century, pikemen of many regiments in France appear to have laid aside the iron helmets and simply wore hats.[27]

Left:

French infantryman, 1640s. This print gives a rare view of the soldier, revealing how his equipment was worn. At the lower part of the belt are three of the "twelve apostles" charges hanging by cords. A folded length of slow match cord is slung over the belt, a small bullet bag and a priming powder horn are in front of it. The soldier is shown holding his matchlock musket at the *Tournez vos armes derriere du coste gauche* (turn your weapon behind and to the left) position. [Print from Lostelneau's *Le Maréchal des Batailles* (Paris, 1647), private collection]
Author's photo

CHAPTER 3

Royal Government 1664 to 1674

Below:
Guard of the Governor General of New France and the French West Indies, 1664–1668. By royal permission, the Marquis de Tracy's guard company of 20 guardsmen had the same dress as the King's Musketeers, and they were armed with rifled carbines. The carbine held by the guardsman is from an original in a private collection. [Watercolor by Michel Pétard. Courtesy, History and Heritage Directorate, Department of National Defence, Ottawa]

During the early 1660s, young King Louis XIV heard that his colony of Canada was on the brink of destruction at the hands of its Iroquois enemies, while the islands seemed the domain of adventurers as well as the prey of Carib Indians and European opponents. Obviously, the monopoly companies did not have the resources and the resolve to efficiently defend and develop his realm in America, so the king installed a direct royal government. In October of 1663, he named the Marquis de Tracy as governor general of the French territories in America.

WEST INDIES AND GUYANA

The first phase of Louis XIV's policy of consolidating France's domain in America was to send warships to the West Indies in early 1664 bearing the Marquis de Tracy, escorted by his own 20-man guard company along with 200 soldiers detached from the Chambelle (or Chambellay), Orléans, Lallier (or Allier) and Poitou regiments of the metropolitan royal infantry. It was the first time French royal troops were sent to America.

The Marquis de Tracy's company of guards, consisting of a captain, a lieutenant, a cornet and 17 men, instituted the permanent practice of having such a unit as the escort of the governor general. High officials of equivalent status in France were permitted such companies, which added to their prestige and dignity. Tracy's guard company was even permitted by Louis XIV to wear the blue cassocks with a white cross of the king's own musketeers, although such companies normally wore the livery of their master. They were supposed to be mounted, but this proved impractical in America. All carried a sword and, most interestingly, a rifled carbine (see glossary), which were called *carabines*. The 200 royal infantrymen were armed with matchlock muskets with plug bayonets, and each would also have had a sword.[28]

On May 13, 1664, de Tracy arrived at Cayenne (French Guyana), which had been occupied by Dutch adventurers who had been chased out of Brazil by the Portuguese. They surrendered without a fight, and the fleet then sailed to Martinique where de Tracy arrived with all the pomp and circumstance seen in the age of the "Sun King," escorted by his guards and soldiers to the sound of artillery volleys.

Far left:

Private of the Carignan-Salières Regiment, Canada, 1665–1668. Armed with a matchlock musket with its plug bayonet (just the tip of its handle is visible), sword and equipped with a bandolier. The uniform issued in Canada was brown with grey coat cuffs and lining, black and buff hat and shoulder ribbons. All items are based on actual artifacts or archival documents. [Watercolor by Francis Back. National Historic Sites, Parks Canada] *Author's photo*

Left:

Infantry soldier, c.1660s. Armed with a matchlock musket, sword and equipped with a bandolier. A plug bayonet would also be part of his weapons. [Manesson Mallet, *Les Travaux de Mars*, 1672 edition] *Author's photo*

Left:

Soldiers marching near Grey in Franche-Comté, 1667. Several hold their matchlock muskets by the barrel with the butt up. [Detail from a print after Van der Meulen. Courtesy, Library and Archives Canada, NL15534]

In the Spring of 1665, after establishing royal authority and naming governors in the various island, Tracy and his royal contingent sailed for Canada.

In 1666, four companies from each regiment of Poitou, Navarre and Normandie were sent to Martinique, the last two of which fought off an English attack on St. Kitts in July 1667.

Right:
Infantrymen, 1667. The arms are fairly standard being matchlock muskets and swords, most having knuckle guards. The soldier holds what could be a pike or, more likely in the West Indies, a partisan or a halberd. [Print after Alfred de Marbot, who took his figures from works of the 1660s for the 1846 *Costumes Militaires Français*] Author's photo

Below:
Soldiers playing cards, c.1665. Note the matchlock muskets leaning against the barrel. [Detail from a print after Van der Meulen. Versailles Palace, France] Author's photo

French Guyana was also taken by English corsairs in September of 1667, who then found "400 small arms" in the place as well as "80 Back, Breast and head peeces" of armors that must have been old pikemen's armor that had been stored, obviously not used, by the soldiers. Four more companies of Poitou arrived in Martinique that year. Hostilities ended, and the companies of Navarre and Normandie went back to France, while it seems Poitou's contingent dissolved in the islands. The arms and equipment of these troops were matchlock muskets and swords.[29]

Following the Marquis de Tracy's departure for Canada in 1665 with his guards and troops, Jean-Charles de Baas was appointed governor general, and he also had a guard of carabins to attend him from 1667. Once peace had been signed and the regular troops had gone back to France, they remained the only regulars in the French West Indies.[30]

CANADA

In 1665, Louis XIV sent to Canada the whole Carignan-Salières infantry regiment, which amounted to 20 companies. Furthermore, the four companies detached from the Lallier, Chambelle, Orléans and Poitou regiments that had been sent to the West Indies the preceding year arrived in Quebec during the summer under the command of the Marquis de Tracy with his company of guards. The arrival of over 1,200 soldiers with about one hundred officers, as well as thousands of settlers who would also come from France over the next few years, transformed the colony. Villages and forts sprang up everywhere in the St. Lawrence and Richelieu river valleys. The French troops attacked the Iroquois in their own territory and destroyed some of their towns and crops. Grudgingly, the Iroquois signed a peace treaty with the French.

The soldiers who arrived in Canada during 1665 were royal troops and were armed and equipped like Louis XIV's army in France. Officers carried spontoons, sergeants carried halberds, corporals and privates had matchlock muskets with plug bayonets, and all had swords. The Carignan-Salières also had brown clothing and were one of the first units in the army to wear uniforms. No pikes were sent, instead, 200 soldiers of the Carignan-Salières regiment were issued flintlock muskets with plug bayonets, a remarkable innovation when one considers that the use of this type of musket was then forbidden in the metropolitan French army because its caliber was considered too light. This was not a problem in Canada, where increased mobility was required, and flintlock weapons were widely used by soldiers and settlers. They also received 200 belts for *gibicières* (seemingly ammunition pouches). Also issued were 800 *poires à poudre* (powder flasks).[31]

Several probate inventories mention arms owned by deceased officers. Ensign François Traversy of the Orléans Regiment, killed in action against Iroquois warriors in 1666, had a long-bladed sword with a silver hilt. The Sieur de Chazy of the Carignan-Salières Regiment, who perished under the same circumstances in 1666, owned a long-bladed sword with "a silver guard and grip" and a "small knife with silver guard and grip." When Captain François Pollet, Sieur de la Combe Pocatière of the Carignan-Salières Regiment passed away in 1672, he left a sword with a gilded brass guard, a sword with silver guard and grip, two bandoliers with grey fringe, a buff bandolier with black fringe and a pair of fine pistols. In 1678, Pierre du Pras, Sieur du Bray, who had been an officer in Carignan-Salières, left a bandolier with black fringe for his sword.[32]

The colony now being secure, most of the regular soldiers were either disbanded to settle in Canada or went back to France during 1667 and 1668. A few companies were maintained thereafter, but all were disbanded in 1671. The dissolution of these companies left a very small number of soldiers acting as town garrisons in place: 27 in Québec and only 10 each in Trois-Rivières

Above:

Soldiers in camp, c.1664–1667. The standing soldier at the center might be an officer. He holds a musket that seems to be short and thus would have been lighter, possibly a flintlock. He wears only a sword baldric, like the soldier sitting with whom he is talking, which reinforces the possibility that both are officers. He wears a hat trimmed with fur rather than the usual brimmed hat. [Detail from a print after Van der Meulen. Versailles Palace, France] *Author's photo*

and Montreal. With the 20 guards of the governors-general, the total amounted to 67 men.

The famous explorer La Salle agreed to have 10 soldiers with officers at his expense in Fort Frontenac from 1675. To provide a large body of men in emergencies, the Canadian militia was organized from 1669 as an obligatory duty for all men able to bear arms between the ages of 16 and 60 grouped in parish companies (see Chapter 7).

There are practically no documents describing weapons in Canada during this period, but Dominique de La Motte de Lucière's inventory reveals an amazing array of items, which mix European military and First Nation's items, which seem to date mostly from the late 1670s and early 1680s. While he was not a royal officer in the strictest sense, he was a nobleman, an early companion and officer under La Salle at Fort Frontenac in 1678, and became a Canadian seigneur in 1683. He had in his possession two swords, a gorget, a cane, two flintlock muskets of which one was without a buttplate, a bayonet, an ammunition pouch, a powder flask, a waist belt with a silver buckle and another with silver thread, a portage collar decorated with bead work and a very old *calumet* (Indian pipe) made of red stone. The First Nation's items could

Right:
Officers during the 1660s. This remarkably detailed painting by Belgian artist François Du Chatel shows what have been called officers, gentlemen, and erroneously, royal guard musketeers. It is a fairly rare view of officers from a contemporary source showing precise details. Both are armed with swords supported by elaborately embroidered baldrics. The mounted officer's sword is not visible, but his standing colleague has the new Musketeer-type sword as seen from its ornate gilded guard. Both have the fashionable summer dress trimmed with a multitude of ribbons and small buttons. The mounted officer is dressed in grey ornamented with light buff ribbons. The officer that is standing has a light brown jacket with dark reddish buff ribbons and brown breeches and stockings. Officers in the West Indies and during a Canadian summer could certainly have had a similar appearance. Horses were brought in numbers into Canada from the mid-1660s. [Musée du Louvre, Paris] *Author's photo*

have been from the Seneca Iroquois with whom La Motte negotiated to build Fort Conti on the Niagara River.[33]

Documents pertaining to Governor General Frontenac's company of guards during the 1670s have surfaced. The guards were still carabins and therefore continued to have rifled carbines, although their cassocks were now to the livery of governors general rather than the king's. Guard officers did not have cassocks or rifled carbines and found their own arms. Captain de Thomas de la Mouguère owned a buff baldric laced with silver with a morocco leather frog for his sword and a flintlock musket made by one Soullard. Lieutenant Philippe de Carrion, Sieur Dufresnoy, had a sliver-hilted sword, two baldrics with fringes, three pistols and three old "service" flintlock muskets.[34]

PLACENTIA

Placentia Bay in southern Newfoundland was well known by sailors during the 16th and 17th centuries. In 1660, a small group of French settlers attempted unsuccessfully to establish a colony there. But in 1662, another French party, led by Nicolas Gargot, who had been named its governor, arrived at Placentia with settlers and 30 soldiers. The garrison mutinied, the governor was killed and only eight soldiers survived. In 1663, Commandant Duperron Chalour arrived with 29 soldiers armed with flintlock muskets. Amongst their supplies were flints for muskets and 200 pounds of "powder for flintlock muskets" as well as "four iron moulds to make lead balls." He found the starving survivors of the previous settlement and set about building a fort. At length, the colony prospered, and by 1671, some 74 persons were making a living from fisheries at Placentia. There seems to have been no soldiers left, but the inhabitants were certainly able to bear arms. They are said to have repulsed five attacks by the Dutch and the English between 1672 and 1678.[35]

Weapons

By the middle of the 17th century, the types of weapons carried by military men holding the various ranks were fairly consistent. On the whole, apart from gorgets, armor had been laid aside for officers who were officially armed with spontoons (half-pikes) or occasionally partisans and swords. A sergeant should ideally always have had "a pretty sword, and an honest (meaning decent) bandolier, a good hat and take care of his halberd, as well as to avoid the reputation of drunkard, smoker and women chaser..." Soldiers were armed with muskets, plug bayonets and swords. There were also formations of pikemen in Europe, but they had vanished in America. Officer's spontoons and sergeant's halberds were carried for formal occasions until the 1750s and 1760s, but there were no further changes in the basic armament of enlisted men. Of course, especially in North American wilderness campaigns, officers and sergeants would carry firearms rather than pole arms.[36]

While standardization was not totally achieved, there were general rules of thumb as to musket proportions and calibers. These are summed up in Mallet's *Les Travaux de Mars*, which appeared in 1672 and again with a few updates in 1684:
- Matchlock musket, 1660s–1670: barrel 3 feet, 8 inches; caliber 8 lines; the lock is an iron plate; 3 ramrod pipes.
- Flintlock musket, 1660s–1670: barrel 3 feet, 8 inches; 4

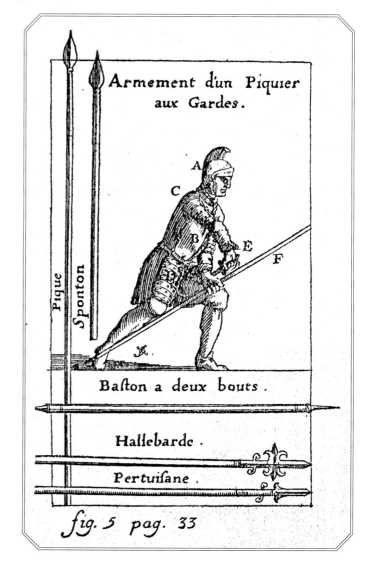

Below:
Armament of a pikeman of the (royal) guards in the 1670s. At left, the long pique, the shorter spontoon and, below the pikeman, the rod pointed at both ends, the halberd and the partisan. The halberd shown here was used in army units with the axe blade model, but apparently not by naval or colonial troops. [Print after Gaya's 1678 *Traité des Armes*]
Author's photo

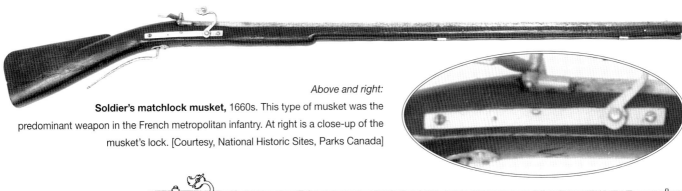

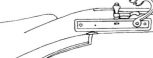

Above and right:
Soldier's matchlock musket, 1660s. This type of musket was the predominant weapon in the French metropolitan infantry. At right is a close-up of the musket's lock. [Courtesy, National Historic Sites, Parks Canada]

Above:
Profile of a standard French army matchlock musket, 1660s–1670s. [Drawing by Michel Pétard. Private collection. By kind courtesy of the artist]

Right:
A thin-bladed partisan and a halberd, c.1660–1680s. These types of weapons, as well as scythes and battle axes are more likely to have been used in the West Indies than in Canada. [Higgins Armory Museum, Worcester, Mass.] *Author's photo*

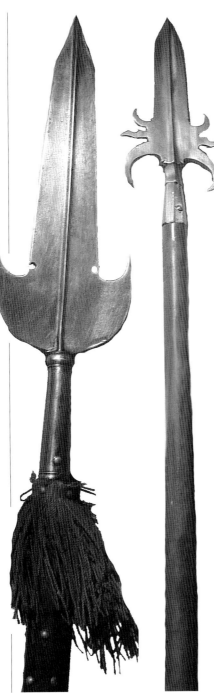

Far right:
French soldier about to hurl a grenade, 1660s–1670s. Elite soldiers performed this duty and became known as "grenadiers" at that time in European armies. Grenades were also used in French America. [Manesson Mallet, *Les Travaux de Mars*, 1672 and 1684 editions] *Author's photo*

Left:

Regimental infantry officers, c.1665–1672. At left, a color bearer; at center, a company or field officer; at right, an officer of pikemen. All three are armed with swords, and two have spontoons. The bottom of their gorgets are also seen below the cravats. The officer of pikemen wears a cuirass. Note that the color's pike was hand held and did not rest on the ground. All wear the new-fashion "justeau-corps" coat with long skirts that quickly became prevalent in all western countries. A company of pikemen wearing helmets and cuirasses is shown in the background. [Manesson Mallet, *Les Travaux de Mars*, 1672] *Author's photo*

Below, left:

Matchlock musket, 1660s–1670s. [Manesson Mallet, *Les Travaux de Mars*, 1672 edition] *Author's photo*

Below:

Flintlock muskets, 1660s–1680s. Mallet describes the flintlock musket as usually having an overall length of four feet, ten inches and a barrel of three feet, eight inches. [Manesson Mallet, *Les Travaux de Mars*, 1672 and 1684 editions] *Author's photo*

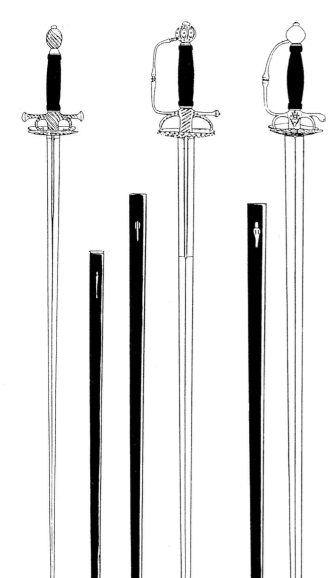

Below:
Sword types of the 1660s and 1670s. The "Mousquetaire" type with the knuckle bow became the prevalent model. The hilts could be iron or brass. [Drawing by Michel Pétard. Private collection] *By kind courtesy of the artist*

feet, 10 inches total length; lock 5 inches long; 4 ramrod pipes; iron furnishings.

- Bayonets: In the first half of the 17th century, bayonets became widespread within all European armies and became especially common in the French army during the 1640s. As seen above, they also appeared in America, carried for instance by the royal soldiers that served in the West Indies and North America from 1664. They could be quite varied in details, but the typical bayonet had a narrow grip that would fit snugly in the barrel's muzzle and a broad, flat and pointed blade. It thus transformed the musket into a short pike, but it could no longer be shot.
- Rifled carbine: the guardsmen accompanying Governor General the Marquis de Tracy were termed *carabins*, which in 17th-century French meant rifleman, and many years later, such weapons were listed in a New France governor general's probate inventory along with guard's cassocks. The type of rifled carbine is unknown, although such weapons were indeed used in certain guard units in France and also on ships.

The graceful "Musketeer"-type sword became the universal favorite and would remain so for over a century. As usual, officer's swords were more luxurious. According to Mallet's *Les Travaux de Mars*, during the 1660s and 1670s, soldiers' swords were to have a length of three feet, including the guard.

Equipment

As previously stated, soldiers had the buff bandolier slung over the left shoulder with the charges held by strings and a leather bag to hold bullets. It was described by Mallet as being three to four inches wide and two and a half feet long (presumably from the shoulder). The buff leather shoulder belt was four to five inches wide and was slung over the right shoulder.

CHAPTER 4

Troupes de la Marine 1674 to 1713

The last quarter of the 17th century saw the advent of truly regular garrisons being permanently posted to protect the various French establishments in America. As noted above, since France's American overseas territories came under the authority of the Minister of the Navy and his department, the troops posted in America belonged to the specially created overseas (or colonial) establishment of the "Troupes de la Marine," although they did not serve at sea. As seen in the appendices, upon their establishment, the overseas garrisons eventually exceeded substantially the number of naval troops based in France for sea duty. All naval troops, be they in America or Europe, were officially armed and equipped the same way from the same royal magazines. There were, of course, local variations, especially in America.

By the early 1670s, the troops that Louis XIV had sent to Canada and to the West Indies in 1664–1666 had returned to France, but those who wished to remain as settlers had been released from the army. Apart from the guards of the governors general of New France and of the French West Indies, with a few dozen soldiers attached to specific town garrisons at Quebec, Trois-Rivières and Montreal, there were no regular troops. The militias were therefore expected to provide the basic defense force. This was somewhat feasible in North America during the 1670s, since there was peace with the Iroquois, and the effects of the war with Holland were rather remote.

THE WEST INDIES

It was a different situation in the West Indies, which were much more subject to attacks by powerful enemy fleets with troops on board. This is what happened to Martinique in 1674 when Admiral Ruyter's Dutch fleet, bearing some 3,400 soldiers, attacked Fort Royal on July 20th, but was repulsed and suffered huge losses at the hands of about 160 determined defenders, 46 of whom were marines off ships or guardsmen, with the rest being militiamen. It was a lucky victory that sent shivers down the royal spine in Paris. It was realized that the defenseless islands might be lost, and the Navy was at once ordered to detach 400 troops to garrison them. The eight companies of what later became known as the overseas establishment of the *Compagnies franches de la Marine* were distributed throughout the various islands. This was the beginning of permanent colonial garrisons maintained by the government — in other words, the foundation of the French colonial army. In spite of their affiliation with the Ministry of the Navy, these *Troupes de la Marine* (Navy troops) that were stationed overseas were not shipboard marines, but were true colonial troops.

Left:
Private soldier of the Troupes de la Marine serving on board ships and in the West Indies, 1670s–1680s. He is armed with a matchlock musket and has the bandoleer. The uniform was grey with blue cuffs and breeches. [Sketch by Eugène Lelièpvre after Valmont's manuscript. Private collection] *Author's photo*

Right:
Infantrymen c.1670s–1680s. One wears the older style bandoliers replaced from December 1683 with waist belts and powder flasks, which are worn by the other soldiers. [Manesson Mallet, *Les Travaux de Mars*, 1684 edition] *Author's photo*

Below:
Drawing of a French infantry matchlock musket, c.1680s–1690s. Apart from its matchlock mechanism, this type of musket is, by the 1670s, generally similar to a flintlock. Note the shape of the lock, which resembles that of a flintlock. [Engineering atlas by Claude Masse. Service historique de la Défense, château de Vincennes] *Photo by Jean Boudriot*

Bottom:
French infantry matchlock musket, c.1680s–1690s.

In 1677, the establishment was raised to nine companies and then to ten companies in 1683. Postings varied, but in 1685, four were at Martinique and three were at St. Christophe (St. Kitts). There was also a company at each island of Guadeloupe and Grenada and one for both Marie-Galante and Sainte-Croix. Two at St. Kitts were transferred to Saint-Domingue (Haiti) in 1690. By 1693, the islands had 14 companies. Haiti's garrison was quickly augmented and had ten Compagnies franches by 1705 for a total of 30 companies posted in the French West Indies.

The soldiers sent to Martinique and the other West Indian islands from 1674 would have been armed and equipped much the same as their comrades of the 1660s: a matchlock musket with its plug bayonet, a sword and a bandoleer with a dozen charges. A 1680 shipment for the troops included 320 soldiers swords, 322 sword shoulder belts, 322 bandoliers with charges and strings (to hang the charge cylinders) and an extra "ten dozen charges and as many cords to refurbish the bandoleers that could be of further service," 18 halberds for sergeants and 10 drums with their belts and drumsticks for drummers. In 1689, 150 matchlock muskets were issued to the soldiers at St. Kitts and 50 with bandoleers at Marie-Galante, while 24 partisans and 24 spontoons went to Grenada. Some 400 more matchlocks with polearms went to Martinique in 1692.[37]

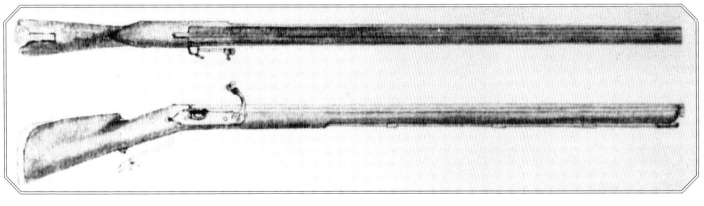

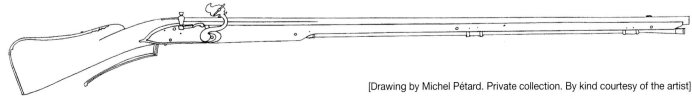

[Drawing by Michel Pétard. Private collection. By kind courtesy of the artist]

Many buccaneer muskets were also sent, and in July of 1695, the Minister of the Navy asked for "the matchlock muskets and flintlock muskets to [arm the six companies in St. Domingue] as well as swords, waist belts and cartridge boxes…" On September 5th, he added that, for the "six companies sent to St. Domingue…[there were] 200 buccaneer muskets, but you will see that they be light and such as soldiers may carry them…[ask] Mr. Ducasse [the governor] to sent back the ones they presently have which are too heavy. You will also send bayonets…" On September 27th, he wrote to the intendant of Rochefort that, "…the flintlock musket shipment that you propose to send to St. Domingue would be a double expense and of little use in the view that we have to send buccaneer (muskets) that are lighter than those that were issued to the new companies. So…it would be best to wait to send (them) by the ships that will depart in December and to have 300 light flintlock muskets made at the Tulle manufacture that you will mark the weight, caliber and the proportions to Sr. de la Combe; the soldiers will use them up (the ones they presently have), and they then will be stored…" From the above, it seemed that soldiers in Haiti were armed with both a matchlock musket and a flintlock buccaneer musket.[38]

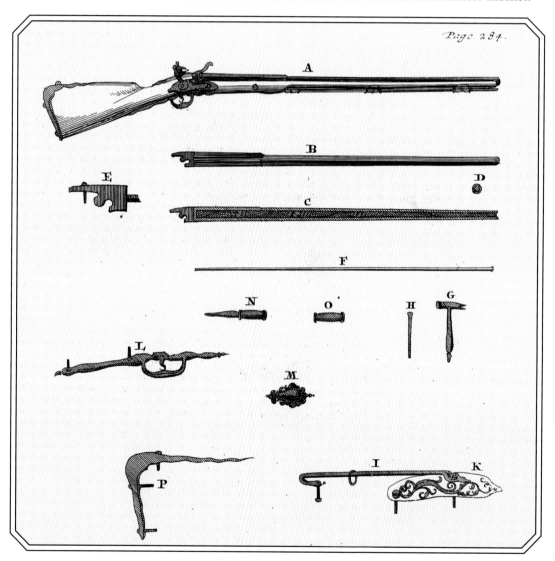

Left:
Carabine (rifled musket), which was carried by governor's guard units in Canada and the West Indies with some few that were also found in royal magazines. Rifles, however, were not widely used. [Print from Saint-Rémy's 1697 *Mémoires d'artillerie*] Author's photo

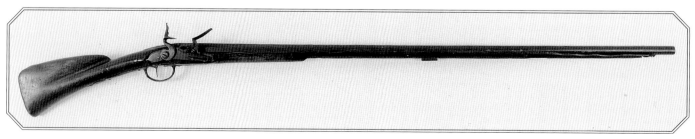

Below:
Tulle military musket made for the French Navy, c.1697. Found in Quebec, this extremely rare item has some of its parts missing or replaced (in the 18th century), but it is extremely helpful, in conjunction with the contracts, to have a fairly precise idea of these important muskets in North American and West Indian history. [Courtesy, National Historic Sites, Parks Canada]

A:
Triggerguard of the Tulle infantry musket, c.1697. [National Historic Sites, Parks Canada] *Author's photo*

B:
Butt of the Tulle infantry musket, c.1697. The metal buttplate has vanished, but its impression into the wood gives a fair idea of this design.

C:
Marking on the barrel of the Tulle infantry musket, c.1697. It reads: "PAVPHILE A TVLLE".

D:
Ramrod pipe of the Tulle infantry musket, c.1697. [All four photos from the National Historic Sites, Parks Canada]

E:
Design of the 1697 Tulle infantry musket. The grenadier model had a sling added. [Drawing by Michel Pétard. Private collection. By kind courtesy of the artist]

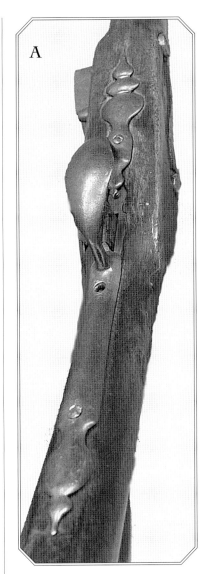
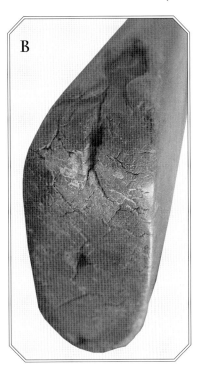

Indeed, the first article in royal order of October 12, 1695, regarding "the discipline and service of troops in the islands of America" contained a rather surprising statement: "the intendant will issue a matchlock musket, a buccaneer flintlock musket, and a powder horn to each soldier." Since this involves issuing two muskets to each soldier, an expensive undertaking, one can doubt that it was done for very long. Indeed, it may have been actually limited only to troops in Haiti, the place where the buccaneer muskets had originated. In 1697, an order to Tulle included 100 ordinary muskets "for the Islands" as well as 100 buccaneer muskets that may have been for regular troops.

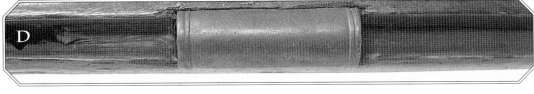
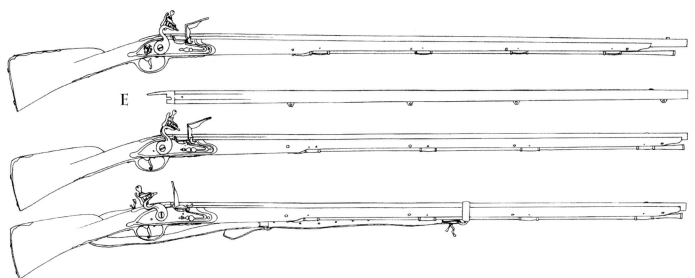

There is another shipment to "America" in 1700 that includes 650 buccaneer flintlock muskets, 100 ordinary flintlock muskets, 100 grenadier flintlock muskets and 200 matchlock muskets along with 200 pistols. This seems to have been for the militia, but some could have been for the regular troops, too. Nevertheless, the variety seems rather strange since there would not be enough matchlock muskets to arm 700 men. Thereafter, references to buccaneer muskets were consistently "for the inhabitants" and not for the soldiers.[39]

By the early 1700s, the soldiers were very likely armed with the standard flintlock muskets — most likely made in Tulle — that were used by the troops in North America and the marines in France. From the 1670s, the governors general of the "Islands of America" also had a company of guards consisting of a captain, a lieutenant, a cornet and 17 carabins indicating they were armed with rifled carbines like the guards of the governor general of New France.[40]

FRENCH GUYANA

In 1676, the Dutch took Cayenne, the only large settlement in this small defenseless colony. The following year, Admiral d'Estrées' French squadron retook the place, and from that time, three Compagnies franches de la Marine were posted at Cayenne, later raised to four companies in 1691. The first soldiers to arrive must have been armed with matchlock muskets, since the 1677 arms shipment mentioned "100 matchlock muskets to change," meaning in reserve. The 100 swords were probably also meant for both the soldiers as a reserve and for the militia. Two years later, the garrison was sent 81 sabers with silver hilts and 34 swords with silver hilts for its 120 men and NCOs. In 1687, the troops were sent 150 matchlock muskets, 150 bandoliers, 150 swords that were most likely of the standard brass-hilted musketeer style and 150 waist belts.[41]

(NORTH AMERICA) CANADA

In the early 1680s, the increasing tensions between the French and the Iroquois nations finally burst into hostilities, and French settlements were once again raided. The militia did what it could, but regular troops from France were urgently requested in 1683. In November, three companies of Compagnies franches de la Marine landed at Quebec City with many more following. By 1688, 35 companies of 50

Left and below:
Soldier of the French Compagnies franches de la Marine (front and back views) serving on ships and based in France's naval bases, c.1705. The musket was most likely made in Tulle from contracts passed with the French Navy in the early or mid-1690s. It has iron furnishings and no sling. The buff belt has frogs to accommodate a plug bayonet and the sword. The flap of the ventral cartridge box is fur covered. The uniform of these shipboard marines was a grey-white coat with blue cuffs, lining, waistcoat, breeches and stockings, brass buttons and false gold hat lace. [Copy by Lucien Rousselot after a period document. Private collection] *Photo: Jean Boudriot*

men each were in Canada, but this was reduced to 28 the following year. In 1699, the number of men per company was reduced to 30 for a total establishment of 840 sergeants and soldiers led by 84 officers.

The first companies to land would have been armed and equipped as marines in France. They carried matchlock muskets with plug bayonets and had bandoliers with the "12 Apostles" and a sword. In the Canadian context, matchlocks were not seen as an effective weapon. Since the 1640s, flintlocks had been used widely by soldiers and militiamen. Governor General La Barre sent back to Rochefort 740 matchlock muskets that had been sent in 1683. Some 500 flintlock muskets were sent in 1684, but quickly condemned as only "proper for children" by the irate

Right:
Compagnies franches de la Marine, Canada, c.1683–1692. Left to right: a drummer, a private soldier and a sergeant. These weapons and uniforms from France were generally identical to what was used in Europe with the exception that, in Canada, from 1685, all private soldiers were armed with flintlock muskets including plug bayonets and swords. Sergeants were armed with halberds and swords. Drummers were armed with a sword. Troops serving in cities and large forts used these weapons and clothes. Sergeants wore a grey-white coat with red cuffs, lining and stockings, gold buttons and hat lace. Drummers wore a blue coat with red cuffs and lining, while privates had a grey-white coat with blue cuffs and lining, both having grey-white breeches and stockings, brass buttons and false gold hat lace. Reconstruction of arms and clothing after documents in the French colonial archives by Francis Back. Early equipment included bandoliers with charges as shown by a soldier in the background, but these went out of use in Canada from the later 1680s. [By courtesy of the artist and of the Company of Military Historians]

La Barre who called for decent weapons. At this point, Viscount Denonville, who replaced La Barre in the post of governor general of New France, was advised in February of 1685, while still in France, that the 600 flintlock muskets asked for by his predecessor would be hard to come by since the gunsmith Maximilien Titon of St. Etienne asked an excessive price due to the unusual (and unknown) length specified for the barrel. Denonville felt that the specifications of the army's flintlock muskets "which are usually of 3 feet, 8 inches (barrel) and the butt is at most 14 inches" should do. Two months later, 600 flintlock muskets had been bought at 8 pounds, 13 sols (shillings) and 10 deniers (pence) each, which must have been the going price for such weapons. They were shipped to Canada along with 200 *fourniments* that were probably the new cartridge bags that replaced the bandoleers with charges. Two years later, 800 more flintlock muskets for additional troops were sent to Canada. They may have been made in Paris, although, in 1692, some 800 flintlock muskets made at St. Etienne were shipped to arm the troops in Canada.[42]

Left:

Officer of the Compagnies franches de la Marine in review order, c.1690, armed with a sword and a spontoon, the regulation weapons for infantry officers until the early 1760s. As military fashions changed, waist sashes disappeared in the early 18th century, but the weapons shown remained the same. [Reconstruction after officer's probate inventories of the era by Michel Pétard. Courtesy, History and Heritage Directorate, Department of National Defence of Canada, Ottawa]

Far left:

French officer's gorget, late 17th century. This richly worked silver-gilded example would have belonged to an officer of some means. [Musée de l'Armée, Paris] *Author's photo*

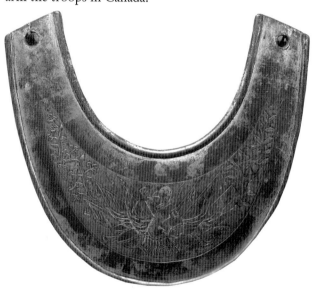

Thereafter, flintlock muskets made at Tulle armed the soldiers in Canada as witnessed by the remains of a remarkable soldier's musket found in Quebec City (made at Tulle), which could be dated to 1697. Archived documents pertaining to arms shipments confirm that the Tulle muskets soon became the only type used by soldiers in French America for many years after that.

Probate records listing the belongings of officers of the Compagnies franches in particular, but also of sergeants and soldiers, reveal that many had remarkable personal arsenals.

Ensign des Méloizes had in his possession at the time of his death in 1699 two old pistols, a powder flask, two new Tulle flintlock muskets, three swords

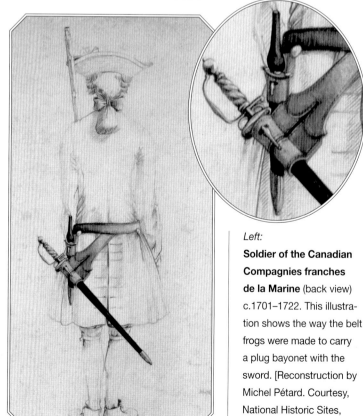

Left:

Soldier of the Canadian Compagnies franches de la Marine (back view) c.1701–1722. This illustration shows the way the belt frogs were made to carry a plug bayonet with the sword. [Reconstruction by Michel Pétard. Courtesy, National Historic Sites, Parks Canada]

Right and below:
Sergeant of a Canadian on-parade company holding his halberd, c.1710–1716. He has the new model that no longer features the axe blade, both sides now having a wavy point. [Watercolor by Michel Pétard. Courtesy, National Historic Sites, Parks Canada]

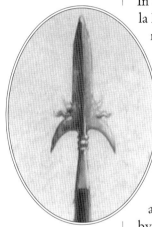

Right:
Capt. Hertel de Rouville, c.1710. This portrait, as was the convention for portraits of military men, shows de Rouville wearing what is supposed to be a breastplate, an item that the artist in Canada had probably never actually seen, except possibly in European prints. Armor appears to have been totally discarded by fighting men in Canada as early as the 1640s, and over half a century later, hardly anyone had ever seen it worn in the country, so that de Rouville wears a dark blue *plate* trimmed with red and edged with gold lace and a sort of frill on the upper breast. Several early Canadian officer's portraits have such strange-looking armor. [Print after portrait] Author's photo

with brass hilts, five regulation flintlock muskets "of a large caliber" with barrels and gun parts for five others. Captain de Lusignan had, in 1699, a pike (probably meaning a spontoon), two halberds and a blue (?) drum case with its sticks. He seems to have kept a few items for his company.[43]

Captain Jacques de Joibert, Seigneur de Soulanges, who died in 1703, had no less than eight gilt gorgets. Another officer had a gorget and a spontoon that year. Captain Daniel de Grelon, Sieur Duluth, who passed away in 1710, had a pair of pistols and a fine flintlock musket. In 1711, Captain Nicolas Rousselot, Sieur de la Prairie, left a spontoon, a gorget, a flintlock musket and an old pistol. Captain Jacques Lepicard Dumesny de Noré had, in 1714, three old flintlock muskets, a "sword of gilded iron, another sword" and his "enamel and gold" medal as a knight of the Order of St. Louis. Ensign Louis Mallerais, Sieur de la Moillerie, who died in 1714 after being wounded by a sword stroke "through the body" in a duel with Lieutenant D'Argenteuil, possessed a spontoon, a powder horn and a waistbelt. Perhaps he was attended to by surgeon-major of the Troupes de la Marine Pierre Goudot who had a sword when he signed his will a few years earlier.[44]

All of this shows that, from the 1680s and 1690s, many Compagnies franches officers in Canada quickly became wise to the ways of the wilderness, not only for hunting, but for warfare with muskets and pistols as well as swords. The spontoons were still required for formal parades as were the gorgets. This last item, however, was the insignia of officer rank and probably worn on campaign early on. Perhaps in a class of his own was Captain Duplessis Fabert, who passed away in 1712. He had a rather amazing five-shot flintlock musket, two bad pistols and two old cartridge pouches.[45]

Sergeants too laid aside their halberds for hunting and fighting in the wilderness, as did Sergeant Thomas Farabezolles who had a powder horn.[46] For wilderness expeditions, officers, NCOs and men were issued special clothing, equipment and armament. The first such expedition was the extraordinary 1686 winter overland trek from Montreal to

Hudson's Bay led by Chevalier Pierre De Troyes, captain in the Compagnies franches de la Marine with several Canadian officers, 31 soldiers and 70 Canadians volunteers. Soldiers each carried their issue flintlock musket with a plug bayonet, a brass-hilted sword, a buff leather waistbelt and a cartridge pouch on a buff shoulder belt. Other weapons were brought to arm the Canadian volunteers as well as the soldiers: 130 flintlock muskets with sheaths, 50 pistols, 100 plug bayonets, 50 grenades and 60 swords or sabers. Two rifled carbines were also issued to the group, a unusual occurrence in New France. Every man on any expedition certainly had a small hatchet or tomahawk and one or more good knives. To this day, these items are essential when spending any length of time in the wilderness. In the days of New France, besides their utilitarian use for camping, they could also be ideal weapons in close-quarter fights.[47]

ACADIA

This small colony had been returned to France by the 1667 Treaty of Breda, and like the other French colonies in North America, there were no troops there from the early 1670s. Unlike in Canada and the West Indies, the organization of a militia there never seemed to have been effectively made. In August of 1674, two Dutch ships took Pentagouet and Jemsec, destroying their forts. At best, during such emergencies, volunteers would gather to defend what they could while armed with whatever weapons they might have. However, some of the settlers were woodsmen, and with

Left:

Canadian militia volunteer and soldier of the Compagnies franches de la Marine, winter expedition to Hudson's Bay, 1686. As can be seen, much of the weapons, equipment and clothing for such a wilderness campaign in Canada were different than what was used in Europe or in settled areas of the colony. The men had flintlock muskets with bayonets, as well as swords or sabers and even hand grenades. Small hatchets were in any woodland expeditions. Clothing issued for this expedition was relatively uniform, the capot-style coats being blue with an edging of false gold lace put on those of the Compagnies franche soldiers. All had winter caps, mitts, musket bags, *mitasses* (Indian leggings), mocassins, snowshoes, etc. This type of equipment remained generally the same for wilderness expeditions until the end of the French Regime in Canada. [Reconstruction by Francis Back after 1686 documents. Courtesy, National Historic Sites, Parks Canada]

Left:

Canadian Compagnie franche soldier equipped for a winter raid campaign, 1690s. Note the cloth musket case, snowshoes, mocassins, mitasses (Indian leggings) and warm hooded *capot* coat. [Watercolor by Francis Back. Courtesy, National Historic Sites, Parks Canada]

allied Abenakis Indians, were redoubtable raiders on English settlements during the last part of the 17th and the early 18th centuries. In 1684, some 400 flintlock muskets were sent to Port Royal to provide the settlers with arms, and 222 are reported in a census two years later. Some must have had artillery skills since eight cannon were also sent at that time.[48]

A regular garrison was posted at Port Royal from 1685 when 30 soldiers of the Compagnies franches de la Marine arrived followed by 30 more two years later and another 30 in 1688 for a strength of three officers and 90 men. In May of 1690, a powerful American fleet from Massachusetts captured Port Royal and Fort St. Louis at Chedabucto, the dozen soldiers in the latter fort putting up a hopeless resistance. After destroying what they could, the Americans sailed away to Boston with booty and the garrison as prisoners. In 1691, five officers and 40 soldiers were detached from the Canadian companies by Governor General Frontenac in order to provide a garrison at the new Fort St. Joseph (or Nashwaak) at the mouth of the St. John River. These troops were reorganized into two companies in 1696. In 1700, the garrison went back to Port Royal, and in 1702, the establishment doubled to four companies. The Americans unsuccessfully attacked Port Royal in 1704 and 1707. The place finally surrendered to a large combined force of British and American troops and ships in 1710. Acadia was ceded to Great Britain by the 1713 Treaty of Utrecht.

Right:
Soldier of the Acadia and Placentia Compagnies franches de la Marine, c.1701–1708. The private holds the c.1697 Tulle musket. The plug bayonet and sword are shown in their scabbards; in Placentia, it was replaced by a socket bayonet. The soldier's uniform of the Acadia and Newfoundland companies was a grey-white coat with blue cuffs, lining, waistcoat, breeches and stockings, white metal buttons, unlaced hat, which was different than the troops in Canada. Sergeant's uniforms in Louis XIV's reign were often different than those of the enlisted men. Sergeants of the Acadia and Placentia companies were armed with halberds, wore blue coats with red cuffs, lining, waistcoat, breeches and stockings, silver buttons and hat lace. Drummers had a coat of blue with red cuffs and lining garnished with the red and white royal livery lace, blue waistcoat and stockings, unlaced hat. [Reconstruction of arms and clothing after documents in the French colonial archives by Francis Back. By courtesy of the artist and of the Company of Military Historians]

The troops posted in Acadia were armed from the outset with flintlock muskets, like in Canada, but some guns were missing in 1689 because 50 muskets were requested for the soldiers "of which half are unarmed." The Canadian Compagnie franches detachment sent out to Acadia by Governor General Frontenac in 1691 had muskets that needed replacement two years later. Required were 40 flintlock muskets with 40 extra locks and 40 "good bayonets to put into the muskets (barrels)" with their scabbards. Four years later, 50 "good muskets" and 24 spontoons (which must have meant naval boarding half pikes) with artillery and ammunition were needed. In 1701, 160 ordinary muskets for the troops and 160 more for the inhabitants, as well as 100 spontoons, were requested for Port Royal along with artillery. These supplies were shipped from Rochefort the following year. The soldiers also had swords, and in 1704, one hundred more swords with scabbards were requested along with leather and metal parts to make scabbards in the colony. A further request of 1708 mentioned "200 [soldier's] muskets with socket bayonets, 100 buccaneer muskets with brass furniture and 100 hunting muskets" that were surely intended for local sailors and militiamen, but it is unsure whether these weapons arrived before the Anglo-Americans captured Port Royal in 1710.[49]

PLACENTIA

To provide some protection for this Newfoundland port, a royal garrison of 25 soldiers with a captain of the Compagnies franches de la Marine, arrived at Placentia in 1687. It had a turbulent existence, with Placentia being taken by English "freebooters" in 1690. Some 40 more soldiers were sent the following year and fortifications built. English attacks were consequently repulsed in 1692 and 1693. The garrison was raised to two companies of 50 men each in 1694, augmented to three companies in 1696 that then participated in taking St. John's from the British. In 1704, they attacked Bonnavista and raided St. John's in 1705, which was taken again in 1709. In spite of these successful French military activities in Newfoundland, Placentia was ceded to Great Britain by the Treaty of Utrecht in 1713.

The 1687 detachment was almost certainly armed with matchlock muskets with plug bayonets, and they did have swords with waistbelts. In 1691, 40 matchlock muskets were sent with four flintlock muskets, possibly for the officers. Three years later, the matchlock muskets were found to be so unsuitable that they were "sent back to France," and flintlock muskets rearmed the garrison. From 1702, because the armament was "very bad," flintlock muskets with plug bayonets, waistbelts, *gargoussiers* were issued in 1704 with some 300 ordinary muskets sent "for the inhabitants." In August of 1708, socket bayonets were asked for, and the king approved, so they were probably on hand from 1709.[50]

LOUISIANA

This immense territory was explored during the 17th century, notably by Robert Cavelier de La Salle, who traveled down the Mississippi River reaching the Gulf of Mexico on April 9, 1682, and claimed the whole area that is now the American Midwest and part of its Gulf Coast for France and named it "Louisiana" in honor of King Louis XIV.

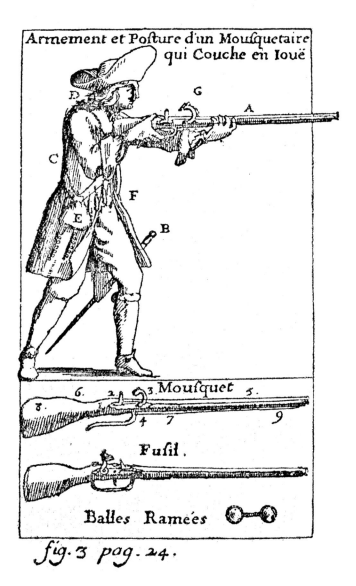

Below:
Armament and posture of a musketeer [infantryman] presenting during the 1670s. Besides his matchlock musket (A), he is armed with a sword (B) and is equipped with a bandolier (C) with charges hanging (F) and a ball bag (E) and a shoulder belt (D) for the sword. Below, crude renderings of a matchlock musket and of a flintlock musket. [Print after Gaya's 1678 *Traité des Armes*] *Author's photo*

Right:
Soldier armed with a matchlock having the German-style butt and a sword without a knuckleguard. The sword belt and the bandolier are worn over the shoulder, c.mid-1670s. [From Manesson Mallet's 1684 *Les Travaux de Mars*]
Author's photo

Below:
Infantry officers and men marching, c.1685–1690. The officers are shown carrying their spontoons and wearing Mousquetaire swords held by a shoulder bandolier. They have the sash around the waist. The enlisted men hold their matchlock muskets over the shoulder, and their Mousquetaire swords are in scabbards held by waist belts, a new arrangement introduced from 1684. The shoulder belt holds a bullet bag, and individual charges in cylinders have vanished. Compagnies franches de la Marine infantrymen serving in the West Indies, French Guyana, Placentia (Newfoundland) and as marines on board warships were armed with matchlock muskets and would have had the same general appearance. [From a large brass medallion by Jean Régnaud and Pierre Le Nègre. Musée du Louvre, Paris]
Author's photo

The king approved that a settlement should be made at the mouth of the Mississippi, and in 1684, La Salle led an expedition of four ships from France, sailing into the Gulf of Mexico with 70 sailors, 100 settlers and 200 soldiers on board (half at the government's expense and half at La Salle's cost). Unfortunately, it had several misfortunes including the fact that they could not find the mouth of the Mississippi and some ships being lost and running aground at Matagorda Bay on the coast of Texas. Fort St. Louis was built there, but La Salle was murdered in 1687 by mutineers, and the remnants of the colony vanished.

In 1684, arms were requested and supplied from the Navy's magazine at La Rochelle consisting of "50 flintlock muskets in port and 350 in the magazine," "150 swords and as many [150] sabers," 25 partisans and 25 halberd, 100 pairs of pistols with ammunition and tools. Recent underwater archaeology of the *La Belle*, one of the ships wrecked on the Texas coast, has revealed several remnants of muskets. It would appear that the flintlock muskets found there might be "ordinary" muskets as defined in the 1674 regulations that might have been carried by the troops. Overly long-barreled muskets would seem to be buccaneer muskets that might have been ship's guns (see below and Chapter 7).[51]

The territories that became the French colony of Louisiana saw their first permanent settlement at Biloxi in 1699. Other posts were built "on the Mississippi River," and eventually, the two main settled areas revolved around the towns of Mobile (now in Alabama) and New Orleans, the capital of the colony. Its early government was royal until 1712 when granted to financier Alexandre Crozat who obtained its trade monopoly in return of a colonizing effort.

The earliest settlement at Fort Biloxi in 1699 had a detachment of marines of the metropolitan Compagnies franches de la Marine until 1704 when two companies of Louisiana's own establishment troops arrived. These early companies were armed with flintlock muskets and bayonets (probably plug), since 6,000 flints were to be supplied in 1701, although there may also have been some matchlock muskets. A 1703 list of furnishings "for the fort" mentions 6,000 pounds of *poudre à mousquet* (matchlock musket powder) that could also have been used for flintlocks. The same list also requested 1,500 trade flintlock muskets with 5,000 pounds of musket powder. It suggests *poudre à mousquet* was used as a generic term. There was no shortage of flintlock muskets in the early French settlement and in the villages of neighboring Indian allies. The soldiers would also have had swords, cartridge boxes and powder flasks as did other Troupes de la Marine elsewhere.[52]

Weapons

In the metropolitan army, weapons systems used by the troops administered by the Ministry of War remained relatively diverse, and this had a great influence on the Ministry of the Navy's choices when it came to arm its soldiers, notably with regards to muskets. Before the 1670s, it can be said that there were no palpable differences in the basic armament of a French soldier in the *Troupes de Terre* (land army) with his comrade in the navy's Troupes de la Marine forces. Calibers were on the way to being standardized, which influenced the measurements and the weight of muskets. On the other hand, there was no standard pattern model that arms manufacturers could follow, or perhaps wished to follow, when it came to details. Rather, arms were produced by many gun makers with an understanding of general practices in the trade while following changes in style and fashion. There is not much that is technically different in a matchlock musket of the 1660s from one of the 1690s except that the appearance of the latter musket usually bears more refinements such as more stylish furnishings.

Flintlock muskets were still not accepted in the metropolitan army when a royal order of February 6, 1670, stipulated that flintlock muskets would have barrels three feet, eight inches long with a caliber of 20 balls to the pound. Each infantry company was to have no more than four fusiliers. The captains obviously took little note of it so that, on February 25, 1675, a displeased king confirmed the order again noting that "most soldiers carry flintlock muskets" and he "forbade most expressly" the captains to have more than four fusiliers. Soldiers thus armed would not be inscribed in the muster rolls, the captain's pay would be withheld and the money set aside by royal treasurers

Left:
Accoutrements for fusiliers, 1670s. Soldiers using flintlock muskets tended not to have the cylinders with charges stringed to their shoulder belts, but needed pouches for their flints and bullets. These pouches were initially of a modest size. [Drawing by Michel Pétard. Private collection] *By kind courtesy of the artist*

Below:
Infantry officers drilling enlisted men, c.1685–1690. The soldiers are aligned by an officer holding a cane. He is armed with a sword whose scabbard is barely visible behind the lower skirt of his coat. The soldiers hold their matchlock muskets. Their new waist belts and shoulder belts with bullet pouches are clearly seen. Compagnies franches de la Marine infantrymen serving in the West Indies, French Guyana, Placentia (Newfoundland) and as marines on board warships were armed with matchlock muskets and would have had the same general appearance. [Detail from a large brass medallion by Jean Régnaud and Pierre Le Nègre. Musée du Louvre, Paris] *Author's photo*

to purchase matchlock muskets for the soldiers. Nevertheless, the flintlock was not abandoned and continued its slow but irrepressible march to dominate the arms used in the metropolitan army. Later in the 1670s, the flintlock's caliber was lowered to 18 balls to the pound (or about .69 English inch). Louis XIV finally had a change of heart about it, and by his order of December 1, 1692, now announced that there would be as many fusiliers as musketeers in regiments and that grenadiers would henceforth be armed with flintlock muskets.[53]

The Ministry of the Navy had its own peculiar needs regarding weapons, and during the 1660s, defined what was needed on board the sailing navy's warships, the galley fleet based in Marseille and the overseas territories that came under its administrative arm. The navy was also responsible for France's coastal defense and was in charge of the large naval bases for the sailing warships at Brest, Rochefort and Toulon. This was not as powerful a ministry as the Ministry of War that administered the land army, but from the 1660s, it received a great deal of attention and support during most of Louis XIV's reign, a monarch who understood the importance of naval power in world affairs.

This included weapons systems that, from 1674, were defined insofar as to how sailors on board warships would be armed for action. Besides the soldiers' matchlock muskets, this included ship's flintlock mousqueton carbines for petty officers and flintlock pistols. Although not covered in the regulations, the flintlock buccaneer musket also made its appearance. These firearms for militiamen, buccaneers and sailors are described in greater detail in Chapter 7 of this book.

The 1674 and 1689 printed naval regulations defined the marine soldier's matchlock musket "to be used on all occasions on land or at sea" as having a barrel of 3 feet, 8 inches (9 inches in 1689), octagonal at the breech and tapering for a third of its length, a caliber of 8 lines (or 16 defined as "a one ounce ball"), serpentine, 6 inches long (7 inches in 1689), curved at 3.6 in.; barrel extends 2.6 in. beyond the walnut stock; forged iron ramrod pipes; wooden ramrod with iron tip; long trigger; weight: 6 to 7 lbs.[54]

Below:
Edged weapons used on board a galley, c.1700–1715. These weapons were similar to types on sailing navy ships. From top to bottom: bayonets, boarding axes, a sergeant's halberd (the newer model), an officer's sponton, a partisan, a boarding pike and a cutlass. [Undated document. Courtesy, Archives Nationales, Marine, G5, 203]

While the ban on flintlocks was kept up for naval personnel and marines, it is clear that it was not as stringent in the navy as in the army. The marines serving detached on board warships were armed with matchlock muskets, and initially, the soldiers of the Compagnies franches de la Marine posted in America were also armed with matchlock muskets.

We have seen in Chapters 3 and 4 that flintlock muskets were favored in Canada from the 1640s, and this ignition system was also adopted by West Indian buccaneers for their own peculiar muskets (see Chapter 7). Thus, the pressure to have flintlock muskets was obviously much stronger on the Ministry of the Navy than in the metropolitan army. Nevertheless, while it was becoming accepted in the 1670s that such weapons were suitable for sailors on board ships and for militiamen or adventurers in the colonies, it was a different matter when it came to regular soldiers of the Compagnies franches de la Marine that served as marines on board ships or garrisoned overseas territories. As seen above, the first huge change for regular soldiers from match to flintlock occurred in Canada during 1685 and spread to other colonies in subsequent years and decades. The early procurement of these flintlock muskets for Canada revealed uncertainties in the proportions of muskets to be used as well as from whom they could be supplied to the Ministry of the Navy at a fair price. Maximilien Titon at St. Etienne furnished mainly the army in France, but was also interested in business from the navy. However, the Ministry of the Navy was fearful that Titon would have a near monopoly in arms production.

From 1690, the procurement of firearms by the Ministry of the Navy became much more standardized thanks to foundation of the arms manufacture in Tulle by Michel Pauphile, a skilled gunsmith, and Martial Fénis de Lacombe, a royal attorney at the court in that city. The plant itself was on the shores of the Céronne River and was set up towards the end of 1690 and early 1691. This was the result of a previous agreement signed on September 4, 1690, by the intendant of Rochefort calling on Pauphile and Lacombe to furnish the navy's arsenal with flintlock muskets.

As will be seen below, the navy's need for firearms was substantial and was not restricted to muskets for shipboard marines, but also extended to colonial troops. Furthermore, hunting, trade, ships and buccaneer muskets and pistols were quickly added to the list so that, by 1692, the Tulle manufacture already had about 200 employees and was clearly a thriving business. Until it became a royal arms factory in 1777, the Tulle arms factory was a private business, but heavily committed to supplying the Ministry of the Navy with small arms. While this was the main core of its business, it also supplied some weapons to the merchant marine, notably bucca-

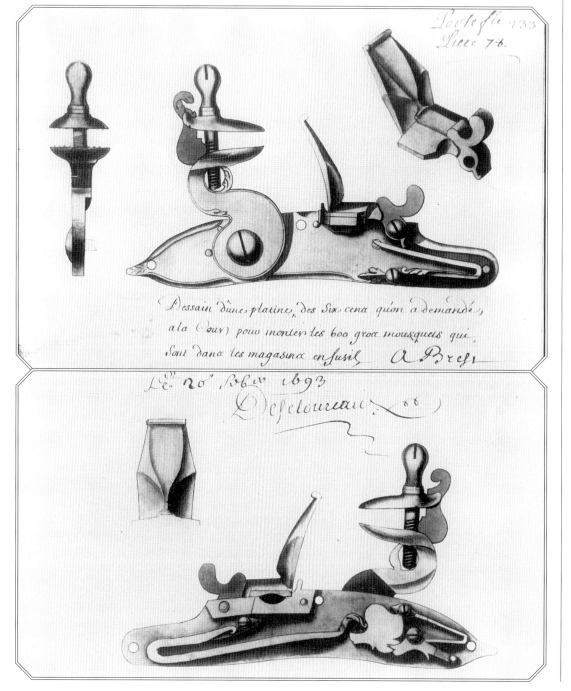

Left:
Flintlock plate for navy muskets, 1693. The drawing shows "one of the six hundred" locks requested to put on "600 large [matchlock] muskets that are in the stores" at the port of Brest to turn them into flintlock muskets. [Drawing dated at Brest, September 20, 1693. Courtesy, Archives Nationales, Marine, G5, 203]

Left:
Flintlock plate inside mechanism for navy muskets, 1693. [Drawing dated at Brest, September 20, 1693. Courtesy, Archives Nationales, Marine, G5, 203]

neer muskets and pistols as well as nails for shipbuilding. One of the reasons for Tulle's success was its proximity to Rochefort, one of the three most important naval bases in the nation and it specifically dealt with shipments of troops and supplies to territories in America. Also, Tulle could obtain the necessary iron ore, brass and wood relatively easily, being situated in south-central France, which produced these materials.[55]

Nevertheless, and especially in wartime, the navy also occasionally called upon gunsmiths at St. Etienne for some arms. From the early 1690s, it was agreed that Tulle would furnish weapons to Rochefort and Brest, the main naval bases on the Atlantic, while St. Etienne would supply Toulon and Marseille on the Mediterranean. As early as 1687, the navy obtained 400 flintlock muskets there and 450 pistols in 1690 and another 1,500 muskets three years later. In 1703, at the start of the War of Spanish Succession, the navy ordered again from St. Etienne 400 ordinary muskets, 400 carbines, 500 pistols, 300 grenadier muskets and 600 muskets with socket bayonets. A few hundred more muskets are delivered in the 1730s. All these weapons appear to have been intended for marines and sailors in French warships rather than for the American colonies. Substantial shipments of St. Etienne muskets occurred from the 1740s.[56]

Bayonets

All military muskets came with bayonets so that they could be transformed into short pikes of about 160 cm long for hand-to-hand combat. In the 17th century, the plug bayonet, whose handle went into the barrel's muzzle, was the standard model and the first type carried by the Compagnies franches de la Marine in France and America. This model had the disadvantage of preventing any shooting while it was fixed until Marshal Vauban invented the socket bayonet in 1688. The Marshal's invention was thereafter slowly adopted, especially in the overseas territories. The Compagnies franches in Placentia may have been the first to have socket bayonets starting in 1709. This type of bayonet may have also appeared in the West Indies at about that time, because in 1712, buccaneer muskets with socket bayonets were requested in Martinique for its militiamen. However, the old plug bayonets of the companies in other colonies were replaced later by socket bayonets.[57]

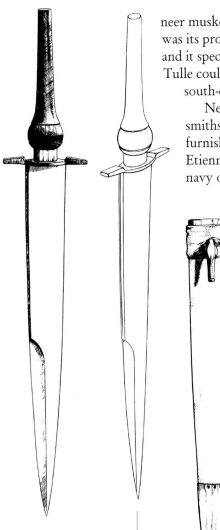

Above:
Plug bayonet with scabbard, c.1680s–1720s.
[Drawing by Michel Pétard. Courtesy, National Historic Sites, Parks Canada]

Right:
Bayonet models for naval and colonial troops, 1703. Model with the long branch was adopted in preference to the wide-bladed type.
[Document dated November 28, 1703. Courtesy, Archives Nationales, Marine, G5, 203]

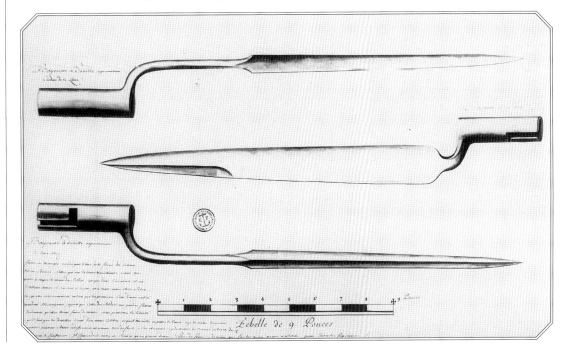

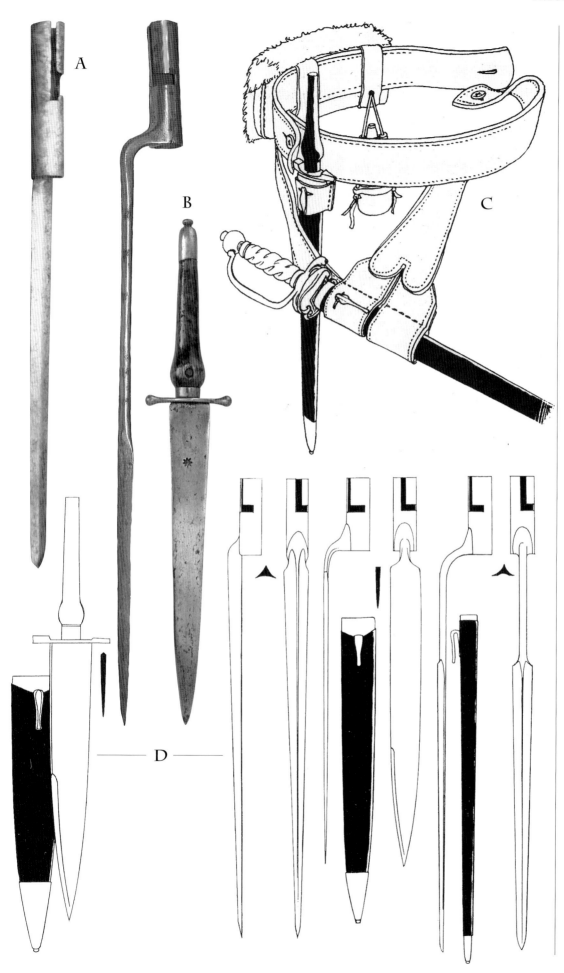

A:
Early socket bayonet, late 17th century. The first type proposed, in 1695, to be used by French marines and overseas troops. It has no branch and forms a complete blade. [The Palace Armory, Valetta, Malta] *Author's photo*

B:
An English plug bayonet and a long-branched socket bayonet, late 17th–early 18th century. [Private collection and George Neumann Collection. Valley Forge National Historic Park, Pennsylvania]

C:
Soldier's waist belt with bayonet and cartridge box, 1690s–1720s. [Drawing by Michel Pétard. Private collection] *By kind courtesy of the artist*

D:
Evolution of bayonets used by the naval troops, 1680s–1720s. [Drawing by Michel Pétard. Private collection] *By kind courtesy of the artist*

Right:
Flintlock infantry grenadier musket with a socket bayonet, c.1690s. The mountings, such as the buttplate and the triggerguard, seem elaborate, but are confirmed by actual examples. The early type of bayonet with a long branch is shown. The swivels are for the sling, which was then usually fixed only to grenadier's muskets. [After Saint-Rémy's 1697 *Mémoires d'artillerie*] Author's photo

Below:
Soldier's sword hilt, late 17th century to mid-18th century. Brass hilt. [Photo courtesy, National Historic Sites, Parks Canada]

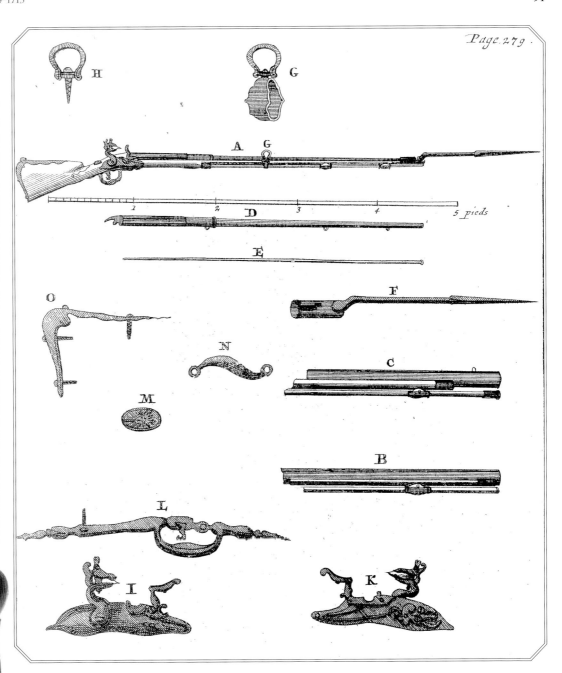

Swords

Soldiers' swords were important to the men who carried them in the 17th and 18th centuries. As a weapon, they were of minimal value and probably caused more casualties when used in tavern brawls and duels than on any battlefield. Only gentlemen, nobles, royal officials and military men were allowed to wear swords in France. Thus, a young peasant joining the armed forces was issued a sword not only as a weapon, but because it was the symbol of his status as a military man-at-arms. The infantry soldier's sword itself was not a quality weapon, but it did look good. From the mid-17th century, the *à la Mousquetaire* sword became prevalent, and by the 1670s, it was the only type seen. Only the garrison of Cayenne, French Guyana, seems to have obtained sabers and swords with silver hilts in 1679, but then received the standard sword in 1687. It usually had a brass guard featuring a narrow knuckle bow, a quillon, a pas d'âne, a cast brass grip or a wooden one covered with brass wire and a shell. The iron blade was narrow and sharp on both sides. Blade length varied. A few examples that were measured had blades that went from 69 to 78 cm long.

NCOs and officers had the same type of sword, but of higher quality. An interesting detail is that surgeons were also armed with swords. Although non-combatants, they were socially viewed as educated men and gentlemen as shown by the will of troupes de la Marine Surgeon Major, the "honorable" Pierre Goudot, who bequeathed his sword.[58]

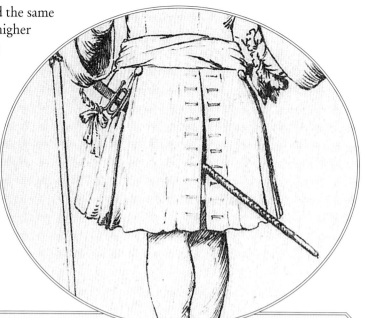

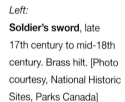

Left:
Soldier's sword, late 17th century to mid-18th century. Brass hilt. [Photo courtesy, National Historic Sites, Parks Canada]

Above left:
Compagnies franches de la Marine officer (rear view), c.1697. Note the way that the à la Mousquetaire sword was carried by officers and gentlemen. It was held invisibly under the waistcoat by a belt or a hook arrangement, the guard emerging at the top of the left skirt panel with the scabbard end extending beyond the lower part of the skirt. [Print after Lucien Rousselot. Private collection] *Author's photo*

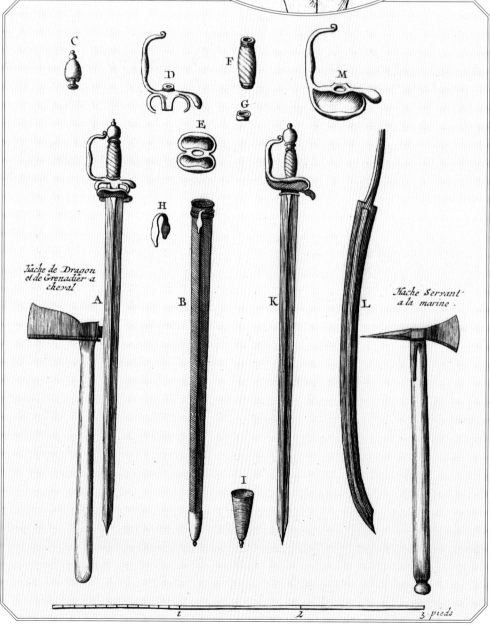

Far left:
Service cavalry swords and sabres with axes. [Print from Saint-Rémy's 1697 *Mémoires d'artillerie*] *Author's photo*

Polearms

Infantry officers from the rank of colonel to that of sub-lieutenant were to have spontoons seven and a half to eight feet long by royal order of May 10, 1690. It was further stipulated that officers would have their polearms at reviews and formal parades on pain of not being paid. The same order informed sergeants that their halberds would be six and a half feet high, including the ironwork. The above also applied to officers and sergeants of marines and the Compagnies franches de la Marine posted overseas.

By a royal order of February 25, 1670, partisans were forbidden to henceforth arm infantrymen. It was considered "much more useful" that they should be armed with muskets or with pikes. There were still pikemen in the metropolitan infantry, but they too were diminishing in numbers like the musketeers, while there were more fusiliers. Partisans continued to be used in the navy for certain duties, notably in the galley fleet by Pertuisanniers who guarded the prisoners that manned the oars. As late as 1686, a dozen partisans were sent to Haiti, obviously to arm a few militiamen who may have been assigned prison guard duties because there was not yet a regular garrison posted there.[59]

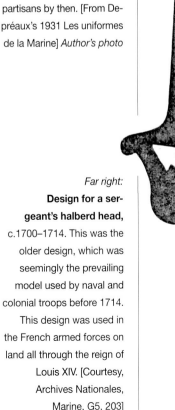

Right:
Partisan's head with an anchor design, 17th century. This item would have been associated with naval personnel, troops or constabulary corps such as Archers or *Pertuisianiers* of the navy. A corps of *Pertuisianiers* also existed in 18th-century Martinique, although not armed with partisans by then. [From Depréaux's 1931 Les uniformes de la Marine] *Author's photo*

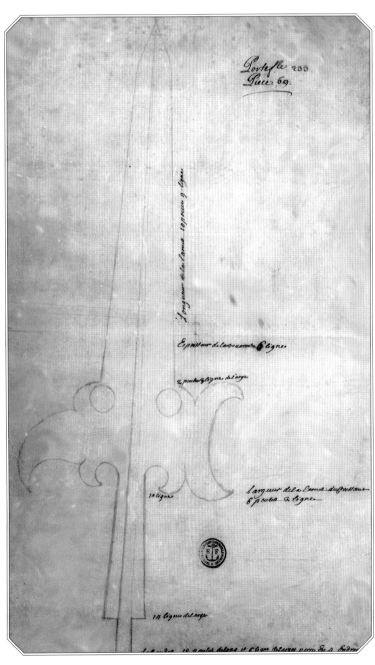

Far right:
Design for a sergeant's halberd head, c.1700–1714. This was the older design, which was seemingly the prevailing model used by naval and colonial troops before 1714. This design was used in the French armed forces on land all through the reign of Louis XIV. [Courtesy, Archives Nationales, Marine, G5, 203]

Left:

Polearms carried by sergeants, c.1670s–1680s. Type A: the most common model carried by infantry sergeants, the pointed top has a long pique blade 12 to 15 inches long (French measurement), one side having a form of crescent and the other, like a star (three wavy rays). Type B was a partisan. Type C was an *hache d'armes* (battle axe blade fixed to a pole). Type D was a scythe blade. Type E was a *fourche* (fork), which had two points and a downward-curved point that was "very good for attacks on outposts" for hand-to-hand combat "when there was no time to use firearms." The sergeants wear the post-1683 sword belt at the waist. [Manesson Mallet, *Les Travaux de Mars*, 1684 edition] *Author's photo*

Equipment

Before the 1680s, all infantry privates and corporals in most European armies were equipped with a wide buff leather belt worn over the right shoulder having frogs for the sword and bayonet on the left side. The frogs carried the sword and bayonet scabbards, which were of dark brown or black leather. For about a century, musketeers had been equipped with buff leather bandoleers with the "Twelve Apostles" charges worn over the left shoulder. These belts were thought to provide some protection against sword cuts, but were found to hamper movement. Bandoleers with charges had been found slower to load muskets than if the powder and ball were in bags or coat pockets.

By a royal order of December 14, 1683, the bandoleer was abolished for infantry musketeers and fusiliers who henceforth were each to carry enough powder to fire 30 shots, which came to about a pound. Obviously, this called for something different than a bandoleer so that, during the 1680s, soldiers carried a powder flask containing a pound of powder and a *fourniment*, which then meant a leather bullet bag, often covered by a stiff dark leather flap engraved with the king's coat of arms. This item could also be called a *gibecière*. The flask and the fourniment were carried by a buff belt slung over the left shoulder. A smaller flask called a *pulverin* was also seen, which contained fine powder used for priming the lock.[60]

The Compagnie franches' early powder flasks, usually made of wood, were covered with dark leather, and contained a pound of powder. They were often called *poire à poudre* (powder pear) due to their pear shape. These were replaced by powder "horns" made of real horn and garnished with brass. The powder horns, introduced in the Navy's troops from 1695, featured a brass mechanism, which measured the amount of powder necessary for each charge. This horn had enough powder for about 30 to 40 shots and was carried by its own narrow buff belt slung over the left shoulder.

From the 1690s, the cartridge was adopted in the French Navy's troops. It consisted of a paper cylinder containing the bullet and the powder charge. Instead of using the powder horn to load each charge, which took time, the soldier now would tear a bit of paper from the cartridge with his teeth, pour a bit of powder in the musket's pan, ram the rest of the cartridge down the musket's barrel with his ramrod and he was soon

Right:
Waist belt of the 1680s. A sword frog and a frog for plug bayonet is stitched to the belt, which also holds a priming powder flask and a bullet pouch. [Drawing by Michel Pétard. Private collection] *By kind courtesy of the artist*

Right:
Soldier of the Gardes-Françaises, 1684. This guard infantry unit was the first to wear the sword belt around the waist, and this is one of the earliest illustrations of this item. A frog was attached at its left to hold the sword's scabbard while the priming horn, bullet bag and slow match (for the matchlock musket) was attached to its right side. This being a guard regiment, the coat and belt have lace embellishments, but the basic aspect was the same for other soldiers. [Manesson Mallet, *Les Travaux de Mars*, 1684 edition] *Author's photo*

ready to fire. A reserve of cartridges thus increased the speed of fire as the charges were already prepared.

In 1696, the king ordered that "all soldiers of the Compagnies franches de la Marine should be given gargoussières instead of fourniments."[61] This newly invented *gargousssier* was a ventral cartridge box worn on the waist belt at the front or front right side. It consisted of a slightly curved elm wood block into which were bored nine holes for cartridges. The block went into a buff leather container with two loops to slip it on the waistbelt. It was covered by a flap of reddish brown *cuir de Roussy* or Russia leather. In front of the cartridge box, but invisible because hidden by the flap, were two small pouches of soft buff leather, one for flints, the other for extra bullets.

When the bandoleers were abandoned, the shoulder sword belts were also altered. They were now worn around the waist with the sword and bayonet frogs and scabbards on the left side and closed with a brass buckle in front. Since sergeants carried halberds, their buff sword belt only had the frog for a sword.

If officers used a buff sword belt, it was to

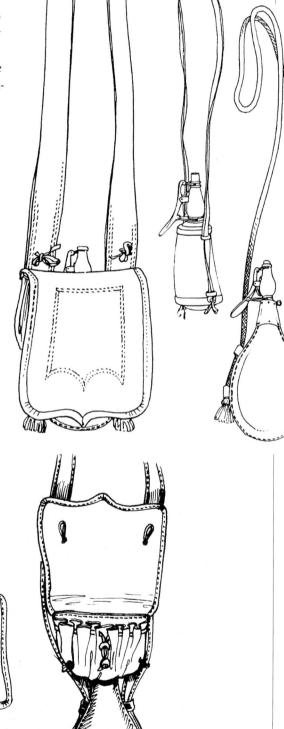

Left:
Ammunition pouch, powder horn and leather powder flask, c.1690. Reconstruction after period artwork and artifacts. [Drawing by Michel Pétard. Private collection] *By kind courtesy of the artist*

Below left:
Ammunition pouch with powder horn and socket bayonet attachment, 1690s. This rendering taken mainly from a 1697 St. Rémy print shows the pouch flap stamped with the royal arms. The powder flask is suspended behind and below the pouch, and the priming powder is attached on the shoulder belt. The very new and still scarce socket bayonet is shown here attached to the retaining belt, which was abandoned in favor of adding a bayonet frog above the sword frog on the waist belt. [Drawing by Robert Marrion. Private collection] *By kind courtesy of the artist*

Right:

Military powder horn, c.1700. The horn containing the powder had its top fitted with a thumb-operated brass measuring spout and a brass bottom. This particular horn is engraved to the *Cent-Suisses* guard unit, but it is typical of those used throughout the armed forces. The small round disk attached to the spout bears the museum's identification number and was not part of the original object. [Musée de l'Armée, Paris] *Author's photo*

be worn around the waist over the waistcoat, but under the coat. Officers could also use an unseen metal sword holder fixed to the waistband of the breeches under the waistcoat so that only the sword was visible.

On campaign, French soldiers used a large canvas or coarse linen bag that held their belongings and was carried on the back. This was not yet an item of regulation gear described in fine detail, but it was traditional equipment. These haversacks were usually made by the soldiers. There were two types — the most common was a rectangular bag with a large flap worn over the shoulder and slung by a leather belt, and the other type was made like a sack or bag, which opened at the top and was worn using two leather straps slung at each shoulder.

Each soldier also carried part of his squad's equipment, one having tent pickets, another the cooking pot, and so on. Nor was there a regulation model for water canteens, but a gourd (to which was added a wooden stopper and which was was carried by a cord), was the favorite. So much so that, even today, water canteens for camping are still commonly called "gourdes" in francophone Canada. However, some had canteens made of tin and perhaps also of leather.

Right:

Army on a march, c.1685–1690. This detail from a painting of the period shows infantrymen and horsemen. The infantryman at left carries pots and pans and might be a company cook while his companion has a fur-covered knapsack. At right, a fairly clear view of what appears to be a fusilier, since his shoulder belt supports a pouch and has no charge cylinders hanging from it. The waist belt is invisible, but worn under the coat to support his typical soldier's sword. He does not carry his knapsack. [Musée Condé, Chantilly] *Author's photo*

CHAPTER 5

Troupes de la Marine 1714 to 1769

Following the end of the Spanish Succession War (also known to Americans as "Queen Anne's War") in 1713–1714, the exhausted European powers entered into a relatively peaceful period for the next quarter century. The occasional flare-ups between nations did not degenerate into major, world-wide conflicts. In France's overseas domains, it was a period of consolidation and of expansion. Garrisons nearly doubled in the West Indies and were increased in Louisiana and Louisbourg. From the 1740s, the wars of the Austrian Succession (1744–1748) and the Seven Years War (1756–1763) put tremendous pressure on the French territories, and without a navy that could equal the British Royal Navy, France lost Canada, Louisbourg, Martinique and Guadeloupe during 1759–1762, while Louisiana was ceded to Spain in 1763. Martinique and Guadeloupe returned to France after the end of hostilities. Consequently, with Guyana, the French domain in America had not quite vanished.

CANADA

Although socket bayonets had been introduced starting at the end of the 17th century, their introduction was gradual, and in the overseas territories, the Compagnies franches in Canada may have been the last troops to receive them. The old plug bayonets of the companies in Canada were only replaced by socket bayonets from 1721 to 1725. This probably coincided with the issue of newer grenadier muskets that were likely of the 1716 contract type ordered from Tulle by the French navy. From 1745, St. Etienne muskets were sent to Canada that were certainly of the army's 1728 pattern, with the steel ramrod introduced in 1741.

Thereafter, the lists of weapons in Canadian stores reveal a mixture of weapons, some in bad repair. Of course, most of the best military weapons were not in stores, but were carried by the soldiers to whom they were issued with a reserve of these for replacements. The royal magazine at Quebec City had more variety than most, since some of its weapons included arms intended for ships' crews. On the whole, from the mid-1740s, soldiers of the Canadian Compagnies franches could be armed with either Tulle or St. Etienne infantry muskets that, from 1743 when barrel bands were added to Tulle muskets, were almost identical.

In 1743, a royal order signed on May 1st at Versailles arrived in Canada stating that, in the future, military muskets of the Compagnies franches in the colony were to be marked "AU ROY" (The King's) as well as bear the mark of the company captain on the butt. The markings were to be seared in by an official iron

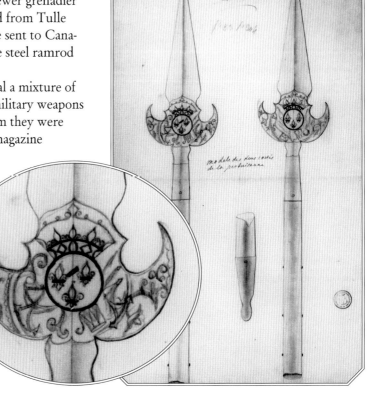

Below:

Design for a partisan, 1714. This model "sent in 1714" was intended for the Navy. Regular troops did not carry partisans, so they were probably intended for the Navy's Petruisaniers, whose duties consisted mainly as watchmen and prison guards. They were found in French seaports, and a small unit of Pertuisianiers was also on duty in Martinique. [Courtesy, Archives Nationales, Marine, G5, 203]

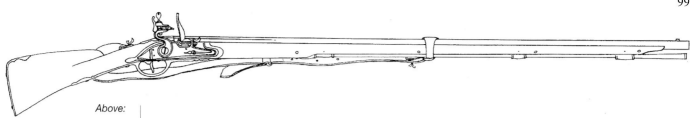

Above:
Tulle *grenadier* musket, contract of 1716 includes reference to sling swivels, indicating that slings were now a standard feature for muskets issued to the troops. [Drawing by Michel Pétard. Private collection] *By kind courtesy of the artist*

Above:
Butt of a military musket used in Canada. A royal order signed at Versailles stipulated that military muskets of the troops in Canada were to be stamped "AU ROY". As can be seen, the mark is stamped on the butt, but not the name of a captain. Instead, one sees the number "14", which may be the musket's rack number, carved or stamped above. Making a stamp to the name of each captain would likely have been impractical and expensive, so it seems that numbering was resorted to instead. This musket has had so many repairs and replacements so that it is impossible to say with certainty if it was a Tulle or a St. Etienne product. [Fort Chambly National Historic Site, Parks Canada] *Author's photo*

stamp to prevent counterfeiting. It appears that stamps with captain's names were not made, since this would have been impractical and expensive, but the "AU ROY" mark has been seen on a couple of musket butts to which were added other markings such as numbers that possibly denoted the weapon's rack number within a company. This order applied only to the Compagnies franches in Canada. Since very few surviving muskets have this marking, it would appear that this was done for a short time and then abandoned. There is no evidence that similar orders were sent to the troops of Ile Royale, Louisiana, the West Indies and Guyana.[62]

Officers in Canada, as in all French infantry formations, were to wear gilded gorgets and be armed with pikes and swords for European-style dres parades. But 18th-century Canadian officers, as their 17th-century predecessors, were also armed with an arsenal of firearms and edged weapons. Swords would normally have gilt guards, but there was variety as seen by Ensign Messein's "brass sword with a silver grip" noted in 1739. The commandant of far away Fort Ouiatenon had, for his part, "a silver [hilted] sword" with a yellow leather waist belt. Usually, the officer's sword belts were worn under the waistcoat and were thus invisible. In 1761, Captain and engineer Sieur de la Morandière left a "regulation saber."[63]

Extracts, by no means exhaustive, of Canadian officer's probate records reveal such items as pistols and tomahawks amongst personal belongings. These were far more useful during raiding expeditions in the wilderness (as well as for game hunting). They were nowhere in any regulation, but certainly essential in the North American context. When Lieutenant Joseph Dejourdy de Cabagnac died in 1737, he owned a long-barreled musket with a silver

Left:
Private of the New France Compagnies franches de la Marine, c.1750–1755. He is armed with a 1743 Tulle musket with its bayonet and a brass-hilted sword; note the rounded butt tang. The nine-hole cartridge box was still used by the overseas Compagnies franches, but the cover with the white anchor was replaced in the late 1740s by the stamped royal arms. The uniform was a grey-white coat with blue cuffs, lining, waistcoat, breeches and white gaiters, brass buttons and "false gold" hat lace. [Reconstruction by Eugène Lelièpvre. Courtesy, National Historic Sites, Parks Canada]

thumb piece, a pistol and a pocket pistol, a hunting horn full of powder, a powder flask and two bullet pouches. The 1752 probate inventory of Captain J.-B. Jarret de Verchères' belongings included his regulation weapon, which was "an old spontoon," and also non-regulation arms such as "an old Tulle musket, a pair of fine pistols" and "a small rifled carbine." In 1753, Ensign de Bouat had a brass gorget, a Tulle musket, a powder horn, a pistol, and an old hunting knife with its old waist belt. Lieutenant de Saint-Michel had, in 1758, a musket with its sheet (or bag) and some bark gargousses (meaning here cartridges) to fill with powder. François de Marillac, who died in

Below, left:

Sergeant, Canadian Compagnies franches de la Marine, c.1718–1730. He holds the new model halberd for French naval and colonial troops. The brass-hilted sword, which might be gilded, was officially a sergeant's only other weapon. The uniform was grey-white with blue cuffs, lining and stockings, gold buttons and cuff lace, gold hat lace. [Reconstruction by Michel Pétard. Courtesy, National Historic Sites, Parks Canada]

Left:

Halberd head, c.1730s–1750s. Found at the site of Fort Saint-Frédéric, now Crown Point Historic Site, [Crown Point, New York] *Author's photo*

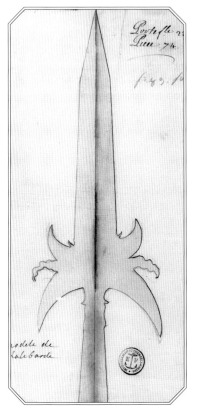

Left:

Sergeant's halberd head, 1714. This "model of the halberd" dated 1714 was "sent this year" for the use of the French Navy's marine and overseas troops. It was widely used in the land forces in the 17th century, but possibly much less so in the naval and colonial troops. From the beginning of the 18th century, it became the only type carried by sergeants in land and sea forces. [Courtesy, Archives Nationales, Marine, G5, 203]

Right:
French halberd heads, first half of the 18th century. The one at the center is the pre-1714 model. The two others would be later. Note one is a screwed-on type.

All of these halberd heads could have been used by sergeants at Fortress Louisbourg from the 1720s, when the city was founded, to 1758 when it fell to the British and was subsequently destroyed. [Found by archaeologists at Fortress Louisbourg. Courtesy, National Historic Sites, Parks Canada]

November of 1759 from wounds received during the siege of Quebec, had a double-barreled musket "mounted on wood with its lock" as well as two grenadier muskets and a pair of old pistols. The probate, drawn up in 1760, of Captain Joseph Langy, a Compagnie franches officer famous for his wilderness raids, revealed he had a saber with a brass guard, a sword with a silver hilt and its old red leather waist belt. In 1762, Captain de la Corne left two pistol bags, four musket bags and five tomahawks.[64]

Halberds and swords were the official weapons issued to sergeants. Indeed, Sergeant André Duplessis owned two swords with silver hilts when he passed away in 1753. Sergeant François de Sarrobert also had a spontoon (actually a halberd) head in 1756, but also two pocket pistols with their holsters. As for Sergeant Jean Megret, he owned a Tulle musket when he died in 1758. These few examples show that NCOs also could be armed with firearms in a Canadian warfare context.[65]

With regards to corporals and private men, their armament would also vary when posted in wilderness forts and engaged in raid warfare. In 1751, five Compagnie franches soldiers deserted from Fort Sandusky (in present-day Ohio). An officer-cadet, a soldier, nine Canadian militiamen and three Huron warriors soon caught up with the deserters who put up some resistance. The deserter Joseph Gorel (nicknamed *Prest à boire* — ready to drink) shot a pistol aimed at the officer-cadet, but missed, while a deserter corporal drew "his saber" before the deserters were overcome. Deserter Corporal François Boisrand was found "with his musket in its bag," which gives clues as to weapons available in a small and isolated frontier outpost. Clearly, non-regulation sabers were considered handy. They were probably naval boarding sabers. The remnants of such sabers, which had similar guards to those in the wreck of the frigate *Machault*, were found by archaeologists at Fort Saint-Frédéric (Crown Point, N.Y.) and as far as Fort de Chartres (Illinois). Pistols were a handy weapon, and they too were probably navy pistols that could be issued to the men — a useful weapon on a raid. Please see Chapter 7 for details on sabers and pistols.[66]

LOUISIANA

Since 1712, the small nascent Louisiana colony had been granted to Antoine Crozat's monopoly company, which passed in 1717 to the *Compagnie d'Occident* (Western Company) and in 1719 to the *Compagnie des Indes* (Company of the Indies) which, failing to make sufficient profits, handed Louisiana back to the royal government on January 22, 1731. Much further north was the *pays des Illinois* (Illinois Country) settled by Canadians in the early 18th century that was incorporated into the colony of Louisiana by a royal decree of September 27, 1717, and thereafter sometimes also called "Upper Louisiana." This made Louisiana an immense domain that went along the Mississippi River from south of Lake Michigan to the shores of the Gulf of Mexico. It remained a French territory until the 1763 Treaty of Paris, which ceded the east side of the Mississippi to Great Britain and the west bank with New Orleans and its area to Spain.

There were two companies in garrison starting in 1704, and Crozat's monopoly company added two more in 1715. The two companies sent in 1715 had "100 very good-looking sabers" and 200 Tulle muskets with bayonets, apparently ordinaire without slings, were sent for the four companies in Louisiana. Four more companies were raised in 1716, arriving in Louisiana during 1717. Although these Louisiana troops were supported by funds from a private monopoly company, they were also subject, to a certain extent, to the rules concerning the Navy's overseas troops. In 1716, the Navy specified that the Crozat's Louisiana troops would have the same arms, equipment and clothing as its overseas Compagnies franche, but to save money, Crozat stretched the rules to issuing uniform coats every three years instead of every two, and he changed the issuing of equipment to a powder horn and a bullet bag held by a narrow shoulder belt and a leather frog for a bayonet and a small hatchet (or tomahawk) hanging from another narrow shoulder belt instead of a cartridge box and a waist belt. The swords and sabers were withdrawn and went into storage. The muskets then issued were likely akin to those used by the Navy's troops and probably had socket bayonets. In 1717, the monopoly went to the Company of the Indies, and due to speculation followed by a horrendous financial crash, the Louisiana troop's establishment went to a high of 16 companies in 1721 as well as a short-lived Swiss company, their garrison then reduced to eight companies by 1728. The military muskets were wearing out by 1721, and some of the soldiers were using trade muskets instead. The swords and usual equipment were back in use since cartridge boxes and waist belts were shipped to the Louisiana troops. They would have looked quite similar to the Navy's overseas Compagnies franches version except for the anchor insignia on the cartridge box.67

Far left:
Soldier of the Louisiana troops, c.1716–1717. This plate shows the unusual arms and equipment of these troops at that time. The exact appearance of the musket is uncertain, but must have looked much like the contract 1716 Tulle shown. Instead of a cartridge box, the men had a powder horn and a bullet bag held by a narrow shoulder belt and a leather frog for a bayonet and a small hatchet (or tomahawk) hanging from another narrow shoulder belt. The uniform was a grey-white coat with blue cuffs, lining and blue breeches, red waistcoat (changed to blue shortly thereafter) and brass buttons. [Watercolor by Eugène Lelièpvre. Private collection] *Author's photo*

Left:
Soldier of the Louisiana Compagnies franches de la Marine, c.1754–1755. The musket would likely be at Tulle 1743 or a Model 1728 with bayonet. Note the "small hatchet" (or tomahawk) that replaced the sword in Louisiana from 1754. The uniform was grey-white with blue cuffs, lining, waistcoat and breeches, brass buttons and false gold hat lace. [Watercolor by Eugène Lelièpvre. Private collection] *Author's photo*

Louisiana did not have many hostile actions in its early years. They repulsed an "Alibamons" Indian attack in 1709 and took and retook Spanish Pensacola in 1719. Things were otherwise peaceful until disaster struck on November 28, 1729, when Fort Rosalie and its settlement (now Natchez) was overrun by a surprise attack of the Natchez Indians. The French eventually regained the initiative, but the colony was clearly too weak to withstand such events. The company of the Indies handed back its monopoly to a worried royal government. In 1731, the eight existing Louisiana companies became full-fledged royal Compagnies franches de la Marine and were reinforced by five more companies. The 4th Company of the Karrer Swiss Regiment

Right:

A soldier of the Canadian Compagnies franches de la Marine, c.1725. The Tulle musket he holds is based on the 1716 contract. It now has rings for a sling, added gradually to all military muskets at that time. He also has the socket bayonet that replaced plug bayonets in Canada from 1721 to 1725. The belt's frogs were now arranged parallel to accommodate both the sword and the bayonet's dark leather scabbards with brass mounts. The nine-hole belt-held cartridge box bore the anchor devise. The brass-mounted horn held a pound of powder. From about 1717–1718, the uniform of the regular infantrymen guarding the French domains in America, (but not including Louisiana) was a grey-white coat with blue cuffs, lining, waistcoat, breeches and stockings, brass buttons and "false gold" lace. [Reconstruction by Michel Pétard. Courtesy, National Historic Sites, Parks Canada]

was also posted in Mobile and New Orleans (see below). There were more campaigns against Indian nations in 1736, 1740 and 1752. In 1750, the garrison of Compagnies franches went from 13 to 37 companies, reduced to 36 in 1754 and 35 in 1759 when the Canonniers-Bombardiers artillery company was raised. Some of the troops posted in Illinois took part in the Ohio campaigns fighting the Anglo-Americans from Fort Duquesne during 1755–1759. The actual number of men in the troops had been greatly reduced by the time the Angoumois Regiment arrived in late April of 1762. Following the cession of Louisiana in 1763, French troops evacuated, except for six caretaker Compagnie franches that remained mostly in New Orleans until 1769 when a large contingent of Spanish troops arrived.

From 1731 to the 1760s, the Louisiana Compagnies franches were armed, equipped and uniformed exactly the same as those in Canada. The only difference came in the summer of 1754 when Governor Kerlérec ordered tomahawks to be carried by soldiers instead of bayonets (and surely swords also) when "on detachments," especially as "it is a good defensive arm" and "very useful to a soldier for cutting firewood or the pickets for his hut." The Illinois troops deployed in the Ohio were armed and dressed as Canadian troops and militiamen in a wilderness campaign.[68]

As in Canada, Louisiana Compagnies franches officers and men owned weapons suited for North American warfare. Captain de Lauze left "a musket and a pair of pistols garnished with yellow copper" in October of 1717. In 1724 at Fort de Chartres in Illinois, a soldier named Thomas purchased a "trade gun." In 1728, Lieutenant Franchomme sold at Fort de Chartres a pouch "of black deerskin decorated with porcupine quills" that would have been part of his frontier equipment. Lieutenant Jean-Baptiste de Saint-Laurent Montbrun, who passed away at Fort de Chartres in early 1748, had an old sword with a waist belt, a "Girard" musket, a "Thiolière" musket, a Tulle musket, a *ancre* (anchor) musket, an old musket and an assortment of knives. Captain D'Arradola (or Barrosola), who drowned in the Mississippi River near New Orleans in April of 1759, left amongst his possessions a sword with "silver moulding" (presumably its guard), a musket with its sheath and two powder horns, a bullet bag, a hunting knife decorated with silver, a middle (sized?) hunting knife, a waist belt trimmed with silver, and a "campaign" bag. The present city of St. Louis (Missouri) was settled as a result of many Illinois settlers having moved from the east to the west bank of the Mississippi rather than become British subjects. In 1767, an inventory of its government magazine listed 14 grenadier muskets, 30 tomahawks, two bayonets with scabbards and an old sergeant's sword. These and other items had been moved mostly from Fort de Chartres.[69]

ISLE ROYALE (LOUISBOURG)

Cape Breton Island, then called Isle Royale by the French, remained part of New France after 1713, and the garrison of Placentia was transferred there. In 1720, the town of Louisbourg was founded as the colony's capital, and work started on its substantial fortifications. Over the years, it became an important port, its harbor activity being the fourth in importance for North America by the early 1740s. It was besieged and taken in 1745, given back to France in 1748, and taken again ten years later. Its fortifications were destroyed in 1760 and the place abandoned during the later 1760s, by which time the island had been ceded to Great Britain.

Its garrison consisted of Compagnies franches with a detachment of the Karrer Swiss Regiment (until 1745, see page 118) and reinforced by metropolitan army battalions between 1755 and 1758. With regards to weapons issued to the troops Compagnies franches, they were the same models as in other colonies. Besides the weapons issued to the garrison, an order of July 10, 1723, specified that a further 100 "grenadier muskets with their socket bayonets" would be stored in the royal magazine. There were a few variations in the equipment, namely black pear-shaped powder flasks and black leather covering the nine-hole cartridge boxes in the 1740s and the 1757 adoption of metropolitan-type *giberne* (cartridge box) with shoulder belts.

Far left:

Private of the shipboard Compagnies franches de la Marine based in France, 1755. He carries the standard M.1728 musket or its Tulle derivative mounted in iron and is also armed with a straight-bladed, brass-hilted sword that may be of the half-shell model. Grey-white or white uniform with blue collar (the Compagnies franches in America having no collar), cuffs, lining (with small white anchors), waistcoat and breeches, grey gaiters, brass buttons, false gold hat lace, buff belts and slings. [Copy by Lucien Rousselot after the now vanished Tarascon Manuscript. Private collection] *Jean Boudriot photo*

Left:

Officer of Karrer's Swiss Regiment, c.1725. His silver-hilted sword is in the French Musketeer style with a white or silver ribbon attached to its guard. At the neck is a silver gorget. The uniform was red with blue cuffs, waistcoat (laced with silver), breeches, stockings and silver buttons. The hat had silver lace and white plumes edging the brim, the plumes being disallowed starting in 1729. [Detail from a print of a contemporary illustration. Private collection] *Author's photo*

Left:

Officer's gorget for a Swiss regiment of the French army, c.1730. Silver with gilded royal monogram and crown. [Print after J. Hilpbert. Private collection] *Author's photo*

Right:
Soldier of Hallwyl's Swiss Regiment, c.1763. He is armed with, possibly, a M.1728 army musket with iron ramrod, a bayonet and a sword or hanger. From 1752, Colonel Hallwyl kept the regiment's traditional red and blue uniform. It is uncertain if this was applied to its companies posted in Louisiana and the West Indies. [From a period watercolored manuscript. Anne S.K. Brown Military Collection, Brown University Library, Providence] *Author's photo*

Right, center:
Soldier of the Karrer Swiss Regiment, c.1725. From the 1720s, this regiment was in the Navy's establishment and provided detachments for garrisons in the West Indies and Fortress Louisbourg. It may have initially carried the army's Model 1717 musket. Its uniform was red with blue cuffs, lining, waistcoat, breeches and stockings, white metal buttons and white buttonhole lace at the waistcoat, "false silver" hat lace. [Reconstruction by Michel Pétard. Courtesy, National Historic Sites, Parks Canada]

Far right, above:
Soldier of Karrer's Swiss Regiment, c.1745–1750. He is armed with the army's M.1728 musket with its bayonet and a brass-hilted sword or straight-bladed saber. From 1732, its 4th company served in Louisiana at New Orleans and Mobile. [Watercolor by Michel Pétard. Private collection] *Author's photo*

Left:
Capt. Lt. Edmond-Antoine-François Sadouvilliers de Billaud (1705–1780) of Hallwyl's Swiss Regiment, c.1752–1763. He holds the muzzle of a musket. This is an interesting detail in an otherwise fairly formal portrait in that officers were not officially armed with muskets, but with swords and spontoons. Showing a cuirass was a portrait convention to denote an officer and only senior officers and heavy cavalry officers might actually have had them. The regiment's uniform was red with blue cuffs, silver buttons and hat lace. [Musée de l'Armée, Paris] *Author's photo*

WEST INDIES AND FRENCH GUYANA

The Compagnies franches posted in those territories were armed exactly the same as those posted in North America. The records of arms and equipment shipments to the West Indies and French Guyana are generally identical to those of North America. However, a note concerning a 1742 shipment of 1,500 muskets to Martinique stated that 500 of these to be further distributed to other Leeward islands were to have browned barrels, but they may have been meant to arm militiamen rather than regular soldiers. For equipment, there appears to have been no substantial exceptions. The white anchor on the gargoussier's flap was replaced by the royal arms in the later 1740s as in other colonies. The three companies of the Karrer (Halwyll) Swiss Regiment in the islands were also armed in a similar way to its detachments in North America and its HQ in Rochefort, France.[70]

Weapons

The period 1715–1763 saw an important evolution in the weapons carried by European troops. In the French armies, edged weapons continued their decline as battlefield arms for foot troops, halberds and spontoons were being eliminated in favor of muskets from 1758 for company sergeants and officers. Firearms (muskets in particular) were slowly and methodically improved during this period. The army Model 1717 infantry musket was the first real pattern musket that was to be followed in every detail by manufacturers supplying the French metropolitan army. The army Model 1728, with its barrel bands and other refinements, was something of a revolutionary musket in its day, and minor improvements were added to it in the following decades. The Tulle manufacture was the main supplier and often the sole supplier of portable military firearms to the navy from the end of the 17th century. As such, it provided the navy with firearms that generally followed the types of muskets and pistols used in the metropolitan army, except that various details were either somewhat different or were introduced some time later. The outstanding example

Left:

Officer of the Canadian Compagnies franches de la Marine, 1732. He is armed with a spontoon, a sword and wears a gorget. The 1732 probate inventory of Lt. Bailly de Messein specifies a brass-hilted sword with silver grip. The uniform, supplied to Canadian officers from 1732, was white with blue cuffs, lining, waistcoat, breeches and stockings, gold buttons and hat lace. The waistcoat was edged with gold lace. [Reconstruction from 1732 archives documents by Michel Pétard] *Courtesy, National Historic Sites, Parks Canada*

are the barrel bands introduced in 1743 for navy muskets, some 15 years later than in the army. The long-branched bayonets were laid aside during the early 1700s in the metropolitan army, but were still made in Tulle during the mid-1730s for naval and overseas troops.

From the middle of the 18th century, muskets from St. Etienne also occasionally provided muskets to the navy. The navy was now increasingly ordering muskets made at St. Etienne that were obviously of the army's Model 1728, and Tulle gradually lost its quasi-monopoly to furnish the navy's firearms. In 1740, some 1,500 St. Etienne muskets were sent to Haiti followed, in 1743, by 5,500 more for the "Islands of America" taken out of metropolitan army magazines, and some 1,200 were sent to Canada in 1745. They were immediately issued to the garrison. On February 3, 1750, arms makers Pierre Girard, Robert Carrier brothers and company at St. Etienne agreed to furnish 4,000 grenadier muskets to the navy that were accordingly delivered at the Rochefort naval base in 1751. This was followed by a large shipment of edged weapons and equipment for troops in America shipped in October of 1752, which consisted of:[71]

For Compagnies franches:
4,000 swords with brass guard and grip
   200 [sergeants] swords gilt guard and grip
4,000 cartridge boxes with nine holes
4,000 buff waistbelts
4,000 powder flasks garnished with brass
    90 drum slings with the king's livery
  100 waistbelts with the king's livery

For Canonniers-Bombardiers:
  10 [sergeants] sabers with gilt guard and grip
  80 sabers with brass guard and grip
  60 powder flasks of boiled leather
  80 *pulverin* of boiled leather

Below:
Officer of the shipboard Compagnies franches de la Marine, 1718. He is armed with a spontoon, a sword and wears a gilded gorget. The uniform was grey-white with blue cuffs, lining, waistcoat, breeches and stockings, gold buttons and lace. Gold lace on the coat was forbidden from 1729. [Copy of an original watercolor by Lucien Rousselot. Private collection]
Photo Jean Boudriot

Left:
Marine musket bayonet, c.1720s–1740. This example perfectly conforms to the Tulle contracts of 1729 and 1734. [Private collection]

Above:
Short-branched bayonet with a "hollow" blade, c.1716–1750. Specified in contracts as early as 1716, this blade type was to become standard on French infantry bayonets until the 1770s. This example was recovered in the 1960s from the French Lines at Fort Ticonderoga. [Private collection]

While the muskets now came from St. Etienne, the overseas Compagnies franches cartridge boxes (the old model with nine rounds carried on the waist belt), continued to be issued, although the Canonniers-Bombardiers, the metropolitan Compagnies franches, and the army regiments all had the large giberne cartridge box with its shoulder sling.

There were more St. Etienne orders during the 1750s. For instance, 1,000 muskets for Haiti in 1757, and in August of 1760, some 2,000 muskets from the royal manufacture of Charlesville loaded at Bordeaux destined for Canada. From this, it is clear that Tulle had lost its near-monopoly on supplying military weapons for the navy. That ministry was now in deep administrative turmoil, as was the Ministry of War and the government, as a result of repeated defeats during the Seven Years War. On December 21, 1761, a royal order prescribed that the royal arms manufactures of the metropolitan army would henceforth also supply the navy's ships and its marines and troops overseas. The government's overall objective was to make the organization, armament and equipment of all its troops on land, sea and overseas as seamless as possible. This included muskets, edged weapons and equipment now desired to be as identical as possible in all services. This would be gradually achieved from the late 1760s to the late 1780s.[72]

Left:
Compagnies tranches de la Marine cartridge box nine-hole wooden block and its black leather casing, first half of the 18th century. Found by archaeologists at Fortress Louisbourg. [Courtesy, National Historic Sites, Parks Canada]

Left:
Three nine-hole wooden blocks for cartridge boxes, c.1720. Traces of buff leather are still attached to the blocks. These accouterments carried by the troops of the Order of Malta were identical, apart from the flap with the white cross of St. John on black leather, to those carried by the Compagnies franches de la Marine in America. It is likely that these accoutrements were sent to Malta from France. [The Palace Armory, Valetta, Malta] *Author's photo*

Muskets

The Tulle contract of July 1716 called on the arms factory to furnish muskets for the soldiers of the Compagnies franches de la Marine. The two types issued were:[73]

- Ordinary musket (without a sling) — caliber 18; barrel: 3 feet, 6 in. long; four pins; cap not mentioned; rounded buttplate; flat lockplate, "S"-shaped counter-lockplate. No bayonet stud mentioned or bayonets issued with this musket.
- Grenadier musket (with a sling) — caliber 18; barrel: 3 feet, 6 in. long "with a stud to fix the bayonet," four pins; cap not mentioned; rounded buttplate; flat lockplate, "S"-shaped counter-lockplate; weight 4½ lbs.; "turning buckle" for the sling "to be slung over the shoulder"; walnut stock; socket bayonet with triangular blade (and most likely with a long branch).

Below:
Army musket lock, Model 1717. Stamped to St. Etienne and the gunsmith Pierre Girard (probably the elder active since the early 1700s). [Private collection] *Author's photo*

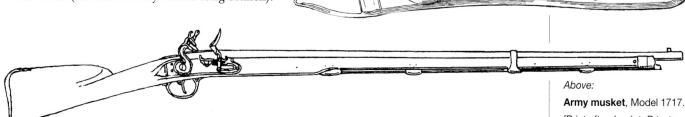

Above:
Army musket, Model 1717. [Print after Jandot. Private collection] *Author's photo*

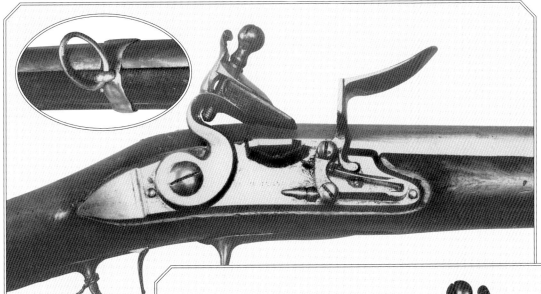

Left:
Army musket lock, Model 1717. Note the bridle at the spring. [Collection of the Royal Armouries, Leeds. Photo by Christian Ariès]

Left, inset:
Army musket, Model 1717. Barrel band with ring for the sling. [Collection of the Royal Armouries, Leeds]
Photo by Christian Ariès

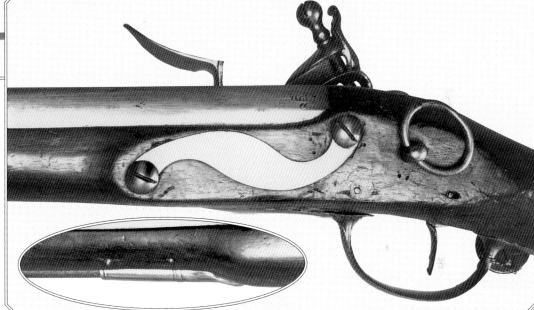

Right:
Army musket, Model 1717. Counter lockplate and ring for the sling. [Collection of the Royal Armouries, Leeds. Photo by Christian Ariès]

Right, inset:
Army musket, Model 1717. ramrod pipe. [Collection of the Royal Armouries, Leeds]
Photo by Christian Ariès

Right:
Army musket, Model 1717. Muzzle detail. [Collection of the Royal Armouries, Leeds]
Photo by Christian Ariès

Below:
Rampart Army musket, Model 1717. It is similar to the line infantry's, but has no bayonet nor bayonet stud, so its stock extends to near the barrel's muzzle. [Courtesy, Don Troiani]

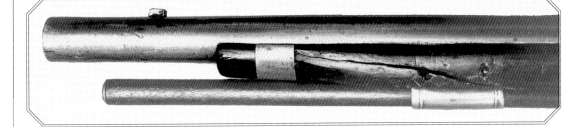

A new contract was agreed to on November 18, 1729. Tulle would furnish for the next five years grenadier muskets with bayonets for the Compagnies franches de la Marine. These were:[74]

- Grenadier musket — caliber 18; barrel 3 feet, 6 in. long, octagonal for 12 inches from the breech to the molding ring; four pins; a cap at the end of the stock, rounded buttplate; flat lockplate, "S"-shaped counter-lockplate; weight 4½ lbs.; bayonet with a 9-inch blade, 4-inch branch and 2.6-inch socket.

This was repeated with another five-year contract on September 13, 1734, for the same types of muskets for the Compagnies franches; indeed, both the 1729 and 1734 contracts have exactly the same specifications paragraphs. It is surprising to note that the molding ring was still retained on the barrel as well as the relatively archaic design of the bayonet with its long branch. These features appear to have disappeared by the early 1740s, the cannon barrels now being tapered and the bayonet blades much lengthened as was the practice in the metropolitan army as well as in most countries.[75]

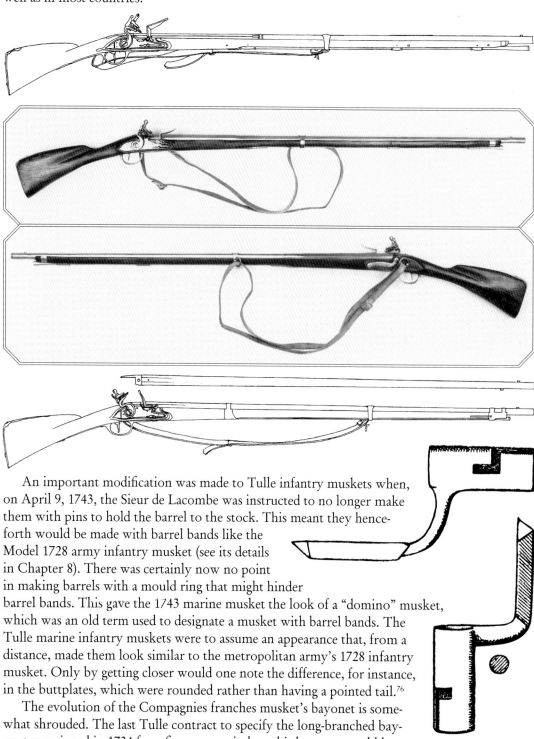

Left, top:
The Tulle marine musket reconstructed as per the 1729 and 1734 contracts between the Navy and the Tulle arms manufacture. No examples appear to have been definitely identified thus far. It was fastened with pins, and the lock was seemingly similar to that of the Model 1728 army musket. Its barrel was, however, octagonal with a mould ring. The bayonet specified in the contracts was the long-branched type. [Drawing by Michel Pétard. Private collection] *By kind courtesy of the artist*

Left, center:
Tulle military musket, 1729 and 1734 contract, right and left sides. Obverse side. [Reproductions by Kit Ravenshear. Courtesy, Fortress Louisbourg National Historic Site, Parks Canada]

Left:
Tulle military musket, 1743 modifications. Iron barrel bands were added, and the mould ring on the barrel had been eliminated so that the resulting musket was nearly similar to the army's Model 1728. [Drawing by Michel Pétard. Private collection] *By kind courtesy of the artist*

Left:
Bayonet sockets for army Model 1717 and 1754 muskets. [Print after Margerand] *Author's photo*

An important modification was made to Tulle infantry muskets when, on April 9, 1743, the Sieur de Lacombe was instructed to no longer make them with pins to hold the barrel to the stock. This meant they henceforth would be made with barrel bands like the Model 1728 army infantry musket (see its details in Chapter 8). There was certainly now no point in making barrels with a mould ring that might hinder barrel bands. This gave the 1743 marine musket the look of a "domino" musket, which was an old term used to designate a musket with barrel bands. The Tulle marine infantry muskets were to assume an appearance that, from a distance, made them look similar to the metropolitan army's 1728 infantry musket. Only by getting closer would one note the difference, for instance, in the buttplates, which were rounded rather than having a pointed tail.[76]

The evolution of the Compagnies franches musket's bayonet is somewhat shrouded. The last Tulle contract to specify the long-branched bayonet was signed in 1734 for a five-year period, so this bayonet would have been made until 1739. Thereafter, it is assumed that the army's 1728 model bayonet was adopted. Indeed, some muskets now came from St. Etienne that were certainly identical to the army's, as several surviving specimens and remnants show. The bayonet would have the usual "L"-shaped slot piercing its socket.

Right and below:
Officer's bayonet socket and elbow, 1750s. This remarkable artifact found at Fort de Chartres shows that some, perhaps nearly all, officers of the New France Compagnies franches had bayonets for their muskets.

However, there is slight evidence that a "Z"-shaped slot may have been used also. In the army, this first appeared with the bayonet of the Model 1754 musket, but this would be rather late in the period, and this weapon is very unlikely to have reached North America in numbers before the fall of Canada (as is discussed in Chapter 8). The most tantalizing objects are at least two such bayonets with Z slots

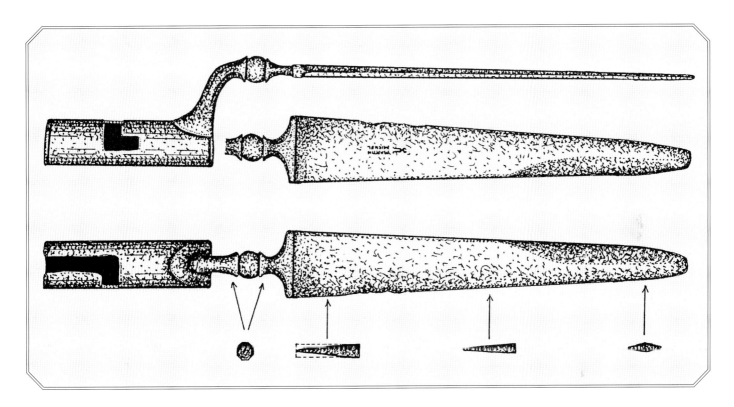

Above:
This type of design was associated with officer's bayonets. The line drawings show an intact example. [Drawings by Erik Goldstein]

found during archaeological research at Fort de Chartres that date from the 1750s. Louisiana was isolated during the Seven Years War, and very few supplies made it from France to the Gulf Coast, let alone to a fort that is about a thousand kilometers north of New Orleans that never had army troops in garrison, only Compagnies franches. This evidence points to bayonets of this design made before 1754, most probably for the Compagnies franches. The full story is presently unknown and perhaps will never be quite clear, except that some Compagnies franches soldiers posted in the center of North America in the middle of the 18th century had such bayonets.

Right:
Musket sling swivels, c.1740s–1750s. [Fort de Chartres State Historic Site, Illinois] *Author's photo*

Far right:
Musket sling swivel, c.1740s–1750s. Found in the remains of Fort Saint-Frédéric. [Crown Point State Historic Site, New York] *Author's photo*

Swords

Swords carried by the Compagnies franches remained in the Mousquetaire style with no substantial changes until the late 1740s. At that time, a new type of hilt with a *pontat simple* (half-shell) appeared for the enlisted infantrymen of the French army, and they made their way to America, although to what extent they replaced the Musketeer style is unknown. Compagnies franches Ensign Thomas Philippe Dagneaux, Sieur de la Sauzzaye, had "a sword with a silver grip" that may imply that only the wire grip was silvered or that the whole guard was silver. As late as 1760, there were many still in use that were of the older style, although wire-covered grips may have been more popular than previously. In any event, swords for infantry corporals and fusiliers were abolished definitively on March 20, 1764.[77]

Far left:
Soldier's sword, Compagnies franches de la Marine, c.1750–1763. This weapon had the *pontat simple* (half shell), which replaced the Mousquetaire type from about 1750. Drawing is taken from a specimen marked with an anchor on the pommel and inside the guard. [Drawing by Michel Pétard. Private collection] *By kind courtesy of the artist*

Left, center:
Brass pommel, pas-d'âne, knucklebow and knuckleguard of a Compagnies franche de la Marine soldier's sword. [Courtesy, Fortress Louisbourg National Historic Site, Parks] Canada

Near left and above left:
Soldier's sword brass knuckleguard and shell remnants, first half of the 18th century. [Fort de Chartres State Historic Site, Illinois] *Author's photo*

Left:
Soldier's sword brass scabbard tip, first half of the 18th century. The scabbard's leather could be either tucked in or covered the tip up to the end ball. [Fort de Chartres State Historic Site, Illinois] *Author's photo*

Left:
Soldier's sword with a brass half shell, c.1750s. This sword was carried by infantrymen from about the middle of the 18th century. This one was found in a well at Place Royale in Quebec City. It has a brass guard. [Centre d'interprétation de la Place Royale] *Author's photo*

Above and right:
Officer's sword and hilt, c.1700–1750. Gilded hilt. [Courtesy, National Historic Sites, Parks Canada]

Left:
Saber, first half of the 18th century. This saber with a brass guard belonged to François-Antoine Pécaudy de Contrecoeur (1676–1743) who was an officer in the Canadian Compagnies franches de la Marine. First a cadet, he became lieutenant in 1715, captain in 1727 and was knighted in the Order of St. Louis in 1738. His regulation weapon was the straight sword. However, on active duty in the wilderness, he preferred a sturdy grenadier's saber. The saber's blade has been mistakenly remounted reversed. [Musée du Château de Ramezay, Montreal] *Author's photo*

Below:
Hilt of Capt. Pécaudy de Contrecoeur's saber, first half of the 18th century. The brass guard appears to have traces of gilding and may originally have had two branches. The grip is of wood and seems a later replacement. The original grip was most likely of twisted brass wire. The blade has "VIVE LE ROY" (Long Live the King) inscribed along with etchings highlighted with gilt. [Musée du Château de Ramezay, Montreal] *Author's photo*

Right:
Spontoon versus sword fight, 1740. The illustration shows how to parry, with a sword, and strike with a spontoon or other types of polearms. Such action would have been more likely in the West Indies than in the Canadian wilderness. [Print after P.J.F. Girard's Traité des Armes, 1740. Courtesy, Stephen Wood collection]

Left:

Infantry drummer's sword and drum for a royal unit, c.1750. A fife case is laid on top of the drum and the drumsticks are below. The sword is the typical brass-hilted musketeer type and it has a red and white mixed sword knot with tassel. The buff waist belt is covered with the King's livery lace, a white chain on red or crimson ground. This was the type of arm, drums and accoutrements carried by drummers of the Compagnies franches in America. [Painting Nicolas Henri Jeaurat de Berty. Palace of Fontainebleau, France] *Author's photo*

Polearms

The 1758 order arming the officers and sergeants of the metropolitan army with muskets and bayonets instead of spontoons and halberds did not go unnoticed in the Ministry of the Navy, but no formal decision was made. In November of 1759, the minister commented that the officers of the Ile Royale Compagnies franches that were now in Rochefort, France, had asked to be armed like the *Troupes de Terre* officers. He felt it could be a good thing and that he was not "far from introducing" this practice in the "Troupes de la Marine," but for now, the officers were informed that it was not a pressing matter and it could wait for a while. There seems to have been no further steps taken in this matter before the Compagnies franches were disbanded. Officially, their officers continued to be required to appear at formal parades with swords and spontoons.[78]

Left:

Officer's iron pike head, first half of the 18th century. Found by archaeologists at Fortress Louisbourg. [Courtesy, National Historic Sites, Parks Canada]

Equipment

The cartridge box consisted of a slightly curved elm wood block into which were bored nine holes for cartridges. The block went into a buff leather container with two loops to slip it on the waist belt. In front of the cartridge box, but invisible because hidden by the flap, were two small pouches of soft buff leather, one for flints, the other for extra bullets.

The early decoration of the cartridge box leather flap is unknown. It may also have been plain. From c.1718, the flap was of reddish Russia leather that was embellished by a white leather anchor at the center and a white leather saw-tooth edging.

During the 1740s, the design of the wooden block remained similar at nine rounds, but some sent to Louisbourg in 1744 were now covered with black leather, a rather sombre model that seemed to have had few admirers. Shortly thereafter, the model with the white anchor was replaced in Canada and probably elsewhere by a new reddish brown flap bearing the king's coat

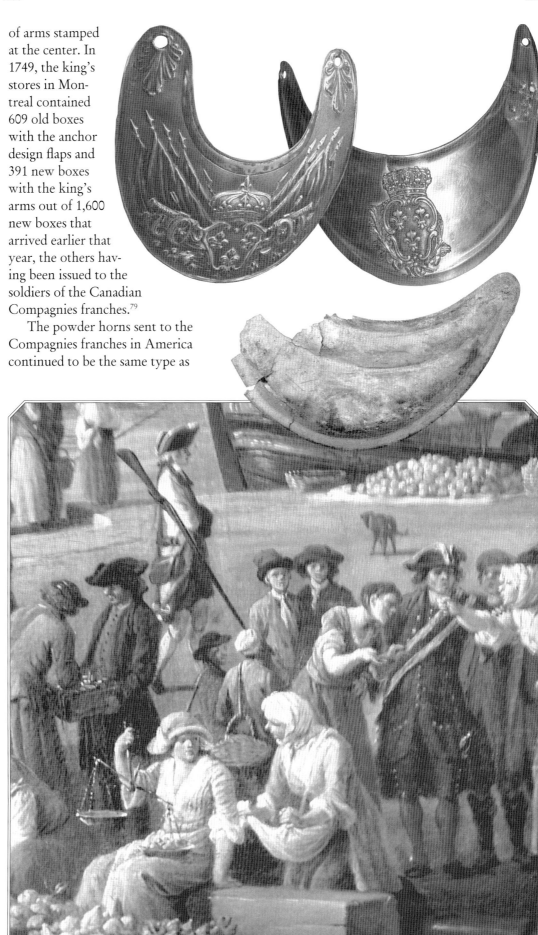

Near right:
Officer's gorget, c.1715–1725. Widely produced, this gilded copper gorget with stamped design features the royal arms and trophies. [Musée de l'Armée, Paris] *Author's photo*

Far right:
Officer's gorget, c.1750–1770. Gilded copper with a silver badge of the royal arms and trophies. This type was officially described in the 1767 dress regulations, but appears to have been in use from about the mid-18th century. This example has a Canadian provenance. [National Historic Sites, Parks Canada] *Author's photo*

Right:
Officer's gorget, first half of the 18th century. This was the popular double-bossed type. Canadian provenance. [Private collection] *Author's photo*

Right:
Port scene on Marseille's docks in 1754. The figure at the top is a marine of the metropolitan ship-borne Compagnies franches de la Marine with his musket slung over his shoulder and the giberne cartridge box with a shoulder sling. The figure on the right is a very rare depiction of an "Archer" peace officer. He wears an all-blue uniform with a blue bandolier and is armed with a white metal-hilted Musketeer-style sword. [Painting by Joseph Vernet. Musée de la Marine, Paris] *Author's photo*

of arms stamped at the center. In 1749, the king's stores in Montreal contained 609 old boxes with the anchor design flaps and 391 new boxes with the king's arms out of 1,600 new boxes that arrived earlier that year, the others having been issued to the soldiers of the Canadian Compagnies franches.[79]

The powder horns sent to the Compagnies franches in America continued to be the same type as in the late 1690s with brass bottom and top spout and an iron spring-actioned thumb piece. In 1736, however, Louisbourg officials asked "for 500 leather powder flasks and have mentioned that those made of horn garnished with brass rusted and broke easily, it was not desirable to [send them any more]." In 1744, some powder flasks, seemingly pear-shaped and covered with black leather, were sent to the Compagnies franches in Louisbourg. This appears to have been exceptional as later shipments mention *corne* (horn), including one of some 4,000 powder horns with their buff slings in 1752 for troops in America.[80]

This nine-hole belly cartridge box used by the colonial Compagnies franches was very different from what was used in the metropolitan land army since 1736 when it adopted the giberne that was a 19-hole cartridge box with its attached powder horn carried slung over the shoulder by a buff leather belt.

The metropolitan Compagnies franches serving as marines finally got the giberne at about the end of the 1740s, but not the Compagnies franches serving overseas. Some 4,000 nine-hole belly boxes, most likely stamped with the royal arms on the leather cover flap, were sent to Compagnies franches in the various territories in America during 1752.[81]

The arrival of metropolitan army battalions in New France from 1755 had an influence on the equipment of the Compagnies franches, at least in Louisbourg. There, during 1757, the Compagnies franches in garrison laid aside the belly boxes in favor of the extra 839 "red leather gibernes" that had been brought with two army battalions two years earlier. There may have been a similar effect

Left:

Soldier of the shipboard Compagnies franches de la Marine based in Brest, France, 1718. The musket is probably a 1716 contract iron-mounted soldier's firearm. A socket bayonet and a brass-hilted sword are also carried. The powder horn is slung on a narrow shoulder belt, and the ventral cartridge box had a reddish leather cover flap with a white anchor and toothsaw border. The uniform was grey-white with blue cuffs, lining, waistcoat, breeches and stockings, yellow metal buttons and hat lace. Below is a close-up of the soldier's 1718 watercolor showing the cartridge box open that reveals a wooden block bored with nine holes for the cartridge and the front leather pouches for flints and extra bullets. This conforms to many documents describing the equipment for the Compagnies franches posted in America. [Copy of an original watercolor by Lucien Rousselot. Private collection] *Photo by Jean Boudriot*

Far left:

Remains of a cartridge box cover, c.1750–1755. This item was found by archaeologist in a period refuse pit at Fort Beauséjour National Historic Site (Aulac, New Brunswick). The Russia leather of this cover seems to have been used by the fort's cobbler as a shoe sole. The royal arms stamped in the cover can be discerned at left. [Courtesy, National Historic Sites, Parks Canada]

Right:
Capitaine d'armes et sergent (Captain of arms and sergeant) of the metropolitan Compagnies franches de la Marine, c.1718. He is armed with his regulation halberd and sword. The waist belt, which has extra stitching, has a single frog for the sword scabbard. Captain of arms was a senior NCO in charge of portable weapons on board of a warship. This rank was not seen in the overseas Compagnies franches except for one posted in French Guyana during the 18th century. In 1718, their grey-white and blue uniform was similar that of a sergeant, but a gold lace edging the cuffs and pocket flaps was later added for a Captain of arms. [Copy of an original watercolor by Lucien Rousselot. Private collection]
Photo Jean Boudriot

in central Canada where seven army battalions were deployed between 1755 and 1757. Certainly, the wearing of shoulder cartridge boxes similar to those of army battalions by the Marine Battalion organized in 1757 from Canadian Compagnies franches is very likely. However, it is also obvious that many Compagnies franches soldiers, especially those not attached to the Marine Battalion serving with Montcalm's metropolitan battalions, continued to have the belly box gargoussier.

By February of 1760, the last year of the campaign in Canada, General Lévis' remaining troops in the Montreal area were desperate for equipment. According to his correspondence, he had run out of gibernes for his soldiers, be they metropolitan or Compagnies franches. Equipment was sought wherever it could be found, and a document of May 30th mentions that 263 gargoussiers, 371 powder flasks, as well as waist belts and musket slings, were amongst the supplies and

Right:
Grenadiers about to throw a grenade, 1740. The commands are to bite off the cap and light the fuse. Although there were no formal grenadier units in the regular colonial troops, grenades were occasionally used. The print shows grenadiers from the royal guard's infantry. They wore caps, as tricorn hats might get in the way when throwing grenades. [Print after P.J.F. Girard's Traité des Armes, 1740. Courtesy, Stephen Wood]

Left:

Military powder horn brass tops and bottoms, first half of the 18th century. [Fort de Chartres State Historic Site, Illinois] *Author's photo*

arms sent to Montreal from the government stores at Trois-Rivières. This would indicate that the French army under generals Montcalm and Lévis had a mixture of equipment up to the surrender of Montreal on September 8th. The army battalions had gibernes, as perhaps did some Compagnies franches soldiers also, but a lot of other men of the Compagnies franches still had their belly gargoussiers. Also, the small detachments of Compagnies franches scattered in forts and outposts west of Niagara surely never had new giberne equipment. There seems to have been no changes either for troops in Louisiana and the West Indies during the 1750s.[82]

Karrer (Halwyll's from 1752) Swiss Regiment

This regiment was raised on September 15, 1719, by François Adam Karrer and was initially part of the sizeable contingent of foreign troops in the metropolitan French army's Troupes de Terre Swiss units. These troops had a certain degree of administrative independence, because the Ministry of War hired them by a contract, termed a "capitulation," with a Swiss officer that recruited in Switzerland and managed the unit as its colonel. Swiss units had prerogatives, such as their own court martial system for discipline and legal redress. Unlike in the French units, which were recruited from natives of France that had to be Roman Catholic, Protestant soldiers could be enlisted and chaplains of that faith served with the unit. The Swiss regiments were known by their colonel's name. Their colonels were also solely responsible for the supply of weapons, equipment and uniforms, which were generally like those of the metropolitan infantry. The uniform coats for Swiss regiments, however, were red rather than grey-white, and they generally had blue facings with blue waistcoats and breeches.

Karrer's regiment had an unusual history for a Swiss unit, because in June of 1721, it was transferred from the Ministry of War to the Ministry of the Navy to provide detachments for overseas garrisons, with its 1st company acting as a strong depot stationed at the French naval base of Rochefort. In February of 1736, Colonel Karrer granted the regiment to his son Louis-Ignace Karrer, so that it kept its name until September 1, 1752, when Count Halwyll became its colonel. It was henceforth known as Halwyll's Regiment and continued to serve until ordered disbanded on June 1, 1763, a process only completed the following year. The Swiss regiment's overseas postings and main actions were:[83]
- 1st Company: 1723-1745, detachments at Louisbourg, Isle Royale (capture of Canso 1744, defense of Louisbourg 1745); 1746, detachment with Admiral D'Anville's expedition; in 1747-1749 a 30-man detachment at Quebec, Canada
- 2nd Company: 1723-1762: Martinique (defense of, 1762)
- 3rd Company: 1723-1763: Haiti
- 4th Company: 1731-1763: New Orleans and Mobile, Louisiana (Chikasaw campaign 1740)
- 5th Company: 1752-1763: Haiti

Above:

Military powder horn, c.1710s–1750s with brass ends and spout. A typical type carried in the French forces. In this version, the thumb-operated measure mechanism was at the base of the spout. [Private collection] *Simon Gilbert photo*

The regiment's first musket was almost certainly the army's Model 1717. Colonel Karrer bought some at St. Etienne. Surviving records show that, in early February 1729, he asked for a *passeport* (a shipping license) to ship 50 muskets with their bayonets from St. Etienne to Rochefort and from thence for the regiment's detachments in the West Indies. These were also very likely Model 1717 muskets, since the actual manufacture of the new army Model 1728 did not start until 1729. Later shipping passports to Colonel Karrer from St. Etienne would have been for Model 1728 muskets — for instance, a shipment of 200 muskets with their bayonets in 1732. This type of musket, with its subsequent improvements, appear to have been the regiment's standard weapon thereafter. Tulle muskets and their bayonets do not appear to have been purchased by colonels Karrer or Halwyll.[84]

The sword of Swiss troops had chances of being a sturdy saber rather than the somewhat decorative swords carried by French fusiliers. As elite troops, the Swiss could be armed like grenadiers. Records mention 52 sabers sent for Karrer's regiments in 1729 and 300 in 1732. Another 200 made by a cutler named Crochet are described as "sabers of the Swiss with iron grips and guards." These were delivered in November of 1737 "for service in the colonies" at 6 pound, 10 sols each. The guards of Swiss sabers could be *à la Wallonne* (Walloon style) with several branches, the blades slightly curved or straight. It could also be a straight-bladed, cavalry-style saber with the usual Musketeer guard.[85]

The soldier's equipment of Karrer/Halwyll's Regiment followed closely that of the metropolitan army. From the time it was raised and into the 1730s, it had the ventral gargoussier-type cartridge box slung on the buff waist belt. The reddish Russia leather flap was most likely stamped with the royal arms or left plain. With this came the powder flask (or horn) and its narrow buff shoulder belt. From the late 1730s or early 1740s, the regiment adopted, probably gradually over several years, the giberne cartridge box, probably with the same style of leather flap as before, with its own buff shoulder belt and the powder flask attached to the box.[86]

An officer in the 1750s could own a silver gorget, a powder flask garnished with silver, a musket furnished with iron with its bayonet, a knife garnished with silver with its gold and silver waist belt, two pistols, and a small silver-hilted sword. Sergeant Joseph Bock, who served with the half of the 4th Company of Halwyll's posted at Mobile, "drowned at sea" in early 1762. His inventory mentioned "one sword with a silver hilt" in his belongings.[87]

CHAPTER 6

Artillery
1500s to 1763

Gunners were present in America from the earliest expeditions of the 16th century. The ships and forts had cannons that would have been useless without the skills of men who knew how to operate them. Surprisingly, early gunners were considered as non-combatant experts in the alchemy of black powder and its propulsive powers when applied to pieces of artillery and their projectiles. Although they might become unwittingly involved in personal combat, this was not a gunner's first duty, and until the second half of the 17th century, troops were assigned to protect the gunners as well as their guns. A gunner, because of his knowledge, enjoyed higher pay and consideration.

Left:

Jacques Cartier having a small gun fired, 1535. This was done to frighten the Indians, and it was certainly a success. [Plate after H. Sandham in Picard's, *Les Français au Canada*, 1913] *Author's photo*

In French America, there is relatively little documentation regarding gunners until the last quarter of the 17th century and the advent of royal government. A royal order of May 12, 1678, creates a position of "King's Gunner" at Quebec City. Funds are also spend during the 1680s for such gunners in the West Indies and French Guyana, Martinique having three in 1691. These King's Gunners, also called "master gunners," were responsible for the care and maintenance of

Right:
Artilleryman and soldier, 1550s–1560s. The gunner holds a combination halberd and portfire rod and, although also armed with a dagger, he depends on the soldier nearby to defend him. In the French forces, the detachments of artillery guards tended to be Swiss soldiers. [Print after Marbot from contemporary prints. The cannon is from Tortorel's work on artillery. Canadian War Museum, Ottawa] *Author's photo*

Right:
Artillery battery, early 1600s. This print after contemporary artwork shows the various arms and equipments used by gunners at the time of Champlain's first settlements in North America. Note that the men serving the pieces are not armed and soldiers protect them. Print after Moltzheim. [Anne S.K. Brown Military Collection, Brown University Library, Providence] *Author's photo*

ordnance and training personnel in the maneuvers and firing of pieces of artillery. They were not considered part of the military establishment and were listed with civil officials such as legal staff. They were paid from civil rather than military funds, were not subject to the code of military justice and wore no uniforms. Larger colonies eventually had several gunners, the senior one known as the *Commissaire d'artillerie* (Artillery Commissioner).

The training was probably informal and given to various groups of soldiers and militiamen interested in artillery. In 1697, the king wished for a more structured organization in Canada and ordered Governor General Frontenac and Intendant Champigny to detach a soldier from each of the 28 Canadian Compagnies franches de la Marine to form an artillery school in Quebec City to drill "with cannons and mortars" under the direction of the King's Gunner. The training lasted six months, after which the men returned to various postings and were replaced by new trainees. Although this was not a new and official unit on the establishment, it was sometimes referred to as the "artillery company." In 1707, men were detached from the four companies in Acadia to form a squad of a dozen gunners. In 1735, two soldiers from each of the eight companies in Louisbourg formed a gunner's squad led by the master gunner. In February of 1744, an artillery school was formed in Mobile, Louisiana, by detaching a soldier from each of the 13 Louisiana Compagnies franches. In December of 1746, a training "company of Canonniers-Bombardiers" was formed in Martinique under the command of the colony's Commissioner of Artillery.[88]

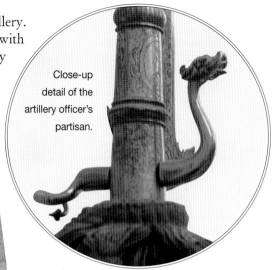

Close-up detail of the artillery officer's partisan.

Left:

Three partisans of various sizes and models, 17th century. The partisan at the center is arranged to hold the slow match cord used to fire cannons, revealing it as the weapon of an artillery officer. Its lower half is gilded. A gilt sun is on the upper half. The close-up above shows the gilded brass dragon that holds the match cord. The base of the weapon is gilded and etched, one of the etchings being of Louis XIV with a laurel crown. [Philadelphia Museum of Fine Art] *Author's photos*

Left:

Gunners serving a piece of artillery, 1640. Such a scene might well have been seen up on top of Québec City's Cape Diamond or in Martinique's Fort Royal. Gunners were not then organized into distinct units, but were considered as specialized artisans with professional skills. Note the partisan modified into a portfire rod. [Print after Moltzheim. Anne S.K. Brown Military Collection, Brown University Library, Providence] *Author's photo*

Bombardiers de la Marine

Due to their extensive knowledge of artillery, members of the sailing navy's marine artillery companies, the *Bombardiers de la Marine*, were occasionally detached, particularly from the Rochefort company, to various overseas territories to supervise ordnance and to provide artillery training in conjunction with the King's Gunners. In 1701 and 1702, of the Rochefort company of the Bombardier de la Marine, one was reported serving in Acadia and eight in Spanish America (for which see Chapter 10). Bombardier Candreau was given the rank of aide d'artillerie, which gave him officer status when he left for Placentia in 1710. Another was detached to Martinique and settled there while a sergeant of the Rochefort company and served at Isle Royale.

Right:
Gunner of the Brest Company of the Bombardiers de la Marine, 1703. He is armed with a grenadier (with sling) musket having iron furnishings and a brass-hilted sword. The accoutrements and cartridge boxes are of buff leather, except for the flap of the belly box that seems to have a pale fur-covered flap. The uniform is red with blue cuffs, lining, waistcoat, breeches and stockings, and brass buttons. The cap is covered with white fur speckled with black and has a blue crescent. The cuffs of a corporal and a sergeant, enhanced by yellow lace, are inset upper right. [Courtesy, Musée de la Marine, Paris, photo 11032]

Far Right:
Gunner of the Bombardiers de la Marine, c.1717. This bombardier private is armed with a brass-mounted grenadier musket, at least from the color of its buttplate, with its sling, bayonet and a brass-hilted saber. The buff accouterments hold a cartridge box with a dark red leather flap bearing a flaming bomb badge. The (invisible) powder horn was held by the narrow buff shoulder belt. The uniform was a red coat and breeches with blue cuffs, lining, waistcoat and stockings, white metal buttons and a tricorn laced with false silver lace. For dress parades, a grenadier-style cap was worn. [Original watercolor possibly by Vassé. Anne S.K. Brown Military Collection, Brown University Library, Providence] *Author's photo*

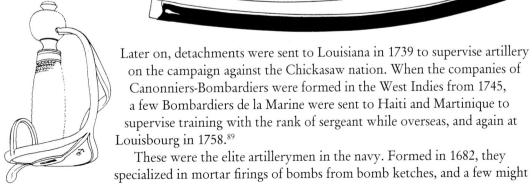

Saber of the Bombardiers de la Marine, c.1750–1763. Brass hilt. Note the small anchor mark. [Drawing by Michel Pétard. Private collection] *By kind courtesy of the artist*

Later on, detachments were sent to Louisiana in 1739 to supervise artillery on the campaign against the Chickasaw nation. When the companies of Canonniers-Bombardiers were formed in the West Indies from 1745, a few Bombardiers de la Marine were sent to Haiti and Martinique to supervise training with the rank of sergeant while overseas, and again at Louisbourg in 1758.[89]

These were the elite artillerymen in the navy. Formed in 1682, they specialized in mortar firings of bombs from bomb ketches, and a few might also be found detached on board large man-o-wars. They wore a red uniform trimmed with blue that included a unique cap and were armed with muskets and sabers. There was a 1713 royal order to establish a company of Bombardiers at Haiti that was to have the same uniform and armament, but it was never actually raised.[90]

Far left:

Gunner of the Bombardiers de la Marine, 1734. Member of the company at Rochefort. Armed with what would be a Tulle grenadier musket with iron furnishings, its sling, bayonet and a brass-hilted saber. Accouterments consisted of a buff waist belt and a cartridge box with dark red leather flap bearing a flaming bomb. The powder horn was held by a narrow buff shoulder belt. The uniform was a red coat with blue cuffs, lining, waistcoat, breeches and stockings, white metal buttons and an ornate grenadier-style cap. [Original watercolor. Private collection. Courtesy, Jean Boudriot]

Left:

Gunner of the Canonniers-Bombardiers, c.1743–1750. Armed with a musket mounted with brass and a brass-hilted double-branched saber. Accouterments consisted of a buff waist belt and a 30-round cartridge box with dark red leather flap held by a buff shoulder belt. The uniform was a blue coat with red cuffs, lining, waistcoat, breeches and stockings, white metal buttons and hat lace. [Watercolor by Michel Pétard. Courtesy, National Historic Sites, Parks Canada]

Canonniers-Bombardiers

All the training formations were not part of an official establishment of colonial artillery and did not have distinct arms or uniforms, although such units were finally raised in the various colonies by royal orders. They were:

- Canonniers-Bombardiers de l'Isle Royale — 1st Company ordered raised June 20, 1743; 2nd Company, raised February 1, 1758.
- Canonniers-Bombardiers de Saint-Domingue (Haiti) — 1st Company ordered raised December 19, 1745; 2nd Company, raised March 24, 1758.
- Canonniers-Bombardiers des Isles du Vent — 1st Company ordered raised April 30, 1747; 2nd Company, raised November 20, 1757.

Left:

Sabre probably belonging to a Canonnier-Bombardier, c.1744–1758. This item was found by archaeologists at Fortress Louisbourg. [Courtesy, Fortress Louisbourg National Historic Site, Parks Canada]

Below:
Brass hilt probably belonging to a Canonnier-Bombardier, c.1744–1758. The grip has a brass wire. This item was found by archaeologists at Fortress Louisbourg. [Courtesy, Fortress Louisbourg National Historic Site, Parks Canada]

- Canonniers-Bombardiers du Canada – 1st Company ordered raised April 10, 1750; 2nd Company, raised March 15, 1757.
- Canonniers-Bombardiers de la Louisiane – a single company ordered raised November 1, 1759.

The remarkable history of this relatively unknown artillery corps remains to be written in detail. Suffice it to say here that the Canonniers-Bombardiers were involved in nearly all major engagements between French and Anglo-American forces in North America and the West Indies between 1745 and 1762. This is because the companies were split into many detachments in most territories in which they served. The Canonniers-Bombardier company in the Windward Islands served from 1747 in Martinique, Guadeloupe and Grenada. Its second company, raised in 1757, had detachments in Marie-Galante and St. Lucia. Those in Canada from 1750 had detachments in Montreal and at forts as far as the Ohio. The Canonniers-Bombardiers in Haiti were mainly at Le Cap and Port au Prince. Those at Louisbourg were mainly posted in that seaport, but had a detachment at Fort Beauséjour between 1752 and 1755. The Louisiana company organized in 1760 was posted mainly in Mobile and New Orleans until transferred to Haiti in 1763 and disbanded.

The arms and equipment were inspired from those used by the Bombardiers de la Marine, but the uniform was dark blue with red trim and white metal buttons and lace. They wore tricorns laced with silver rather than grenadier caps.

The provisions regarding arms, equipment and uniforms in the June 20, 1743, royal order that created the first company of Canonniers-Bombardiers in Louisbourg was repeated in all subsequent orders authorizing such companies to be raised elsewhere in America. For arms and equipment, the order specified:[91] "The said company will be armed with a grenadier musket with its bayonet, leather cartridge box [giberne] with its leather shoulder belt, boiled leather priming powder flask [poulverin], a saber with its white and blue wool sword knot."

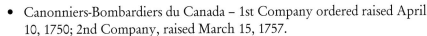

Above right:
Officer's sword, 1748. From its blade markings, "A", anchor and "1748", this quality sword likely armed an officer belonging to one the French navy's artillery units, since the letter "A" might stand for "Artillerie". [Detail of a plate by Maurice Bottet] *Author's photo*

Right:
Gun crew of the Canonniers-Bombardiers, c.1755– 1763. Two officers armed with swords. A corporal, a sergeant and a gunner each wearing a coat and a saber. [Watercolor by Eugène Lelièpvre. Courtesy, National Historic Sites, Parks Canada]

This is given in more detail in a 1744 bill for clothing, arms and equipment, which was also repeated for other companies later on:[92] "A grenadier musket with an iron ramrod and its bayonet. A Russia leather sling with its buckle."

The muskets made in Tulle during the 1740s for the Cannonniers-Bombardiers were not to have any special features other than brass furnishings. This was a long-standing distinction for French artillery troops. Thus, the only difference with the 1743 Tulle infantry musket was that it had a brass triggerguard, buttplate, sideplate and barrel bands.[93] "Saber with brass grip and double-branched guard, German blade, calf-hide scabbard tipped with brass. A blue, red and white wool sword knot" for corporals and gunners. For sergeants, the brass was gilded and the sword knot made of silk and silver thread.

The sergeants and corporals cartridge box was "of buff leather, double stitched with its [wood] block pieced with 19 holes, with a Russia leather cowhide [flap] cover embossed with a silver [washed badge of the] royal arms over two crossed anchors, the box having a raw linen [coutil] bag with two pockets." This box was worth eight pounds. The gunners cartridge box described as "like those of the corporals" was valued as seven and a half pounds, so it was not totally similar. The silver wash was possibly not added for the gunners.

There was the *poulverin* for priming and an additional powder pear (*poire à poudre* pear-shaped flask) of boiled leather. Thus, there were two powder flasks rather than one. All enlisted ranks had the same type of flasks.

Above:

Canonniers-Bombardiers gunners cartridge box, 1743–1766. No original example of this item is known, but this copy (made thanks to detailed records) gives a good idea of its appearance. The cover flap was of reddish brown Russia leather and was stamped with the corps' badge — the crowned royal arms over two crossed anchors. [Made by Jim Grahn, craftsman at Springfield, Ill. Lyle Cubberly collection] *Author's photo*

Corps Royal de l'Artillerie

During the reign of Louis XIV, the various types of metropolitan army gunners were gradually militarized. The advent of the *Fusiliers du Roi* regiment in 1671, originally a unit that was to guard artillery parks, but whose men evolved into being gunners, led to all army ordnance units being merged into the new *Corps Royal de l'Artillerie* of some 95 companies beginning in 1693. Often called *Royal Artillerie*, this corps was the metropolitan army's artillery unit. It included a few companies of miners and *ouvriers* (artisans). As seen above, the Ministry of the Navy had

Left:

Royal-Artillerie gun crew maneuvering a cannon at the port of Bordeaux, 1762. Gunners don't wear accouterments or coats, for ease of handling the gun. The officer wears his coat and sword at his left, beneath the coat. Royal-Artillerie's uniform was dark blue with red collar, cuffs, lining, waistcoat and breeches, yellow metal buttons and hat lace. Depictions of Royal-Artillerie are scarce, and this one has often been made into prints. The cannon appears to be a brass Vallières pattern piece mounted on a red carriage. [Detail from a painting by Joseph Vernet. Musée de la Marine, Paris] *Author's photo*

Right:
Gunner of the metropolitan Royal-Artillerie Regiment, 1757. This watercolor copied from an original rendering made in Germany during 1757 by one Christian Becker shows this gunner equipped for service in the field with his musket and a brass-hilted multi-branched saber with a straight blade. [Anne S.K. Brown Military Collection, Brown University Library, Providence] *Author's photo*

Right:
Sword of the Royal-Artillerie Regiment, c.1750s. Brass hilt. The blade is marked "Regiment Royale Artillerie". *Courtesy, Don Troiani*

its own ordnance units for its ships and territories in America. However, Royal Artillerie did send detachments to America.

The earliest detachments appear to have been ten miners that served in Martinique in 1721–1722, and another ten miners briefly at Louisbourg in 1722 for handling explosives related to building fortifications. Another half dozen miners went to New Orleans in 1739. Small detachments were sent to Canada beginning in 1755, but they only amounted to a few dozens officers and men that served under generals Montcalm and Lévis until 1760. That year, a sergeant and six gunners went to Louisiana to help form the Canonniers-Bombardier company there. In 1762, several officers and about 80 gunners of Royal-Artillerie arrived in Haiti. By a royal order of April 30, 1762, the two Haiti companies of Canonniers-Bombardiers were each expanded from 60 to 100 gunners and were led by the Royal-Artillerie officers. Traditionally, the colonial gunners served as garrison artillery, but this was now expanded to the use of field artillery as well. Three 12-pounders, six 8-pounders and sixteen 4-pounders with field carriages and ammunition were also sent to Haiti. These were brass field guns from the metropolitan artillery. Another 120 gunners with more officers arrived at the end of 1762. The two Haiti Canonniers-Bombadiers companies were ordered amalgamated into Royal-Artillerie on March 27, 1764, but this did not actually occur until late 1765 and 1766. In 1765, the metropolitan artillery detachment in French Guyana was replaced by new colonial artillery companies.[94]

Royal-Artillerie gunners being elite soldiers, they were armed with sabers or long, wide-bladed cavalry-style swords, as well as with muskets and bayonets. In effect, armament similar to grenadiers, the infantry's elite soldiers, and this became the hallmark for all artillery units as seen above with the Bombardiers de la Marine and the Canonniers-Bombardiers.

Royal-Artillerie muskets and bayonets were the same models as the army's, but the furnishings were of brass. Swords and sabers also, from the little evidence there appears to be, were similar to those carried by grenadiers and, like in the infantry, appear to have varied hilt models, some with a single branch and others multi-branched. The only way to know if they were a gunner's sword was if the name of the Royal-Artillerie was marked on the blade.

CHAPTER 7

Militiamen and Sailors c.1630 to 1763

All settlements since the 1500s had civilians assisting the few soldiers guarding the forts and early towns. Indeed, all appear to have been volunteers, if need be, and probably all had personal weapons. The organization of these volunteer militias was seemingly done locally or when a crisis occurred, everyone rallying around the settlement's leaders. In the 17th century, some militias in the West Indian islands became organized in a more permanent way. By the 1640s, Martinique, Guadeloupe and St. Kitts had militia companies. In Montreal, a volunteer unit was organized in 1663 and a permanent militia organization was formed from 1669, which eventually covered all of New France.[95]

(NORTH AMERICA) CANADA

The first corps of volunteer militia in Canada was formed in Montreal on January 27, 1663: "The Militia of the Holy Family of Jesus-Mary-Joseph." Its purpose was to assist the town's garrison (which amounted at that time to only 12 men), especially in mounting guard. Some 139 men enrolled, forming 20 squads of seven men each, including a corporal elected by his comrades. This unit, which mounted guards and patrolled the town's outskirts day and night, seems to have ceased its activities two years later, when regular royal troops arrived. But Montreal volunteers, nicknamed the "blue capots" because of their blue garments, are known to have taken part in expeditions with the Carignan-Salières Regiment against the Iroquois.[96]

The Canadian militia was organized from 1669; all men able to bear arms aged from 16 to 60 years of age were automatically part of it and could be mustered for various types of duties. All were enlisted in their locality's company, which was organized in each parish. Most were in villages along the St. Lawrence and Richelieu rivers, while some were in cities whose parishes might be larger so that two or three companies might be organized. Each militiaman was to have weapons and assemble for parades and training once a month. This was no paper organization, and royal officials were adamant that the militia would form a vital part of a community's social and military organization. Its officers were responsible for many aspects of civil administration that ranged from the pursuit of criminals and applying fire prevention regulations to taking censuses.

Left:
Militiaman armed with a matchlock musket and equipped with a bandoleer, c.1685–90. West Indian militiamen in towns would have had much the same appearance when armed and equipped as shown in this print after Anton Hoffmann, which illustrates the equipment remarkably well. [Private collection] *Author's photo*

Many of the officers and men in the early Canadian militia were former soldiers, while others were experienced woodsmen with activities in the fur trade. The militia thus contained a larger proportion of men who were familiar with the use of weapons than in other countries. Thanks to these abilities, a period of great explorations was launched in the 1660s that culminated with the discovery of the Great Western Plains and, in 1682, reaching the Gulf of Mexico by going down the Mississippi River. Naturally, these militiamen, especially those tempered by long experience in the wilderness, were past masters of the weapons they carried, that often were their only guarantee of survival, and they used them brilliantly in tactics largely borrowed from their First Nations companions and trading partners against common foes — usually the English and their native allies.

Right:
Officers or traders encounter First Nations warriors in Illinois, c.1690. Note the pistols slung at the waist belt. [Detail from Nicolas de Fer's map of North America published in 1698. Courtesy, Library and Archives Canada, NMC26825]

The *courreur des bois* and *voyageur militiamen* were, however, a minority — and a notorious one. They were those who took part in raiding expeditions into the largely unexplored center of the continent in the hopes of finding booty and glory. Most other Canadian militiamen were farmers, some of whom might have been voyageurs in their young days, and probably all quite familiar — as apparently were their wives and daughters — with firearms. The flintlock hunting musket was their favorite, and it is said that they were good target shots. A smoothbore in the hands of one who knows and loves his weapon can be lethal indeed to beast or man. Many would hunt in the fall, even in winter and early spring, then return to their fields in the summer. There were also fishing expeditions during which they learned how to handle canoes. One observer provided the following description of the Canadians of this era: "They are well proportioned, agile, vigorous, in perfect health, able to withstand all sorts of fatigue…and bellicose… born in a country with good air, nourished on good, abundant food…they are free from birth to engage in fishing and hunting and to go on canoe trips, during which there is much exercise." Another added that "Canadians are very brave" and more skilled at shooting muskets "than any others in the world."[97]

The variety of firearms that could be found in Canadian homes can be surprising. In December of 1669, the probate inventory of Toussaint Toupin, Sieur du Sault, of Quebec, revealed a small arsenal found at his residence, shop, warehouse, farm and a 20-ton small vessel. It included a flintlock musket "six feet long," another five feet long, one four feet, eight inches long, one of four and a half feet long, one "short" and another "longer" flintlock musket, two matchlock muskets, a carbine, a short *carabine* (rifled musket), several pistols, a small bullet mould for shot suitable for hunting "geese and ducks" and four swivel guns that must have been for the vessel. Toupin was a Quebec merchant as well as a land owner, which made him Seigneur of Belair, *sénéchal* (a civil legal official) of Lauzon and "master" of vessels. Some of the arms listed were surely meant to arm the crews of the small vessels. The rifled musket is an early mention of such a weapon in Canada.[98]

Keeping Canadians armed was a concern as, if they had flintlock muskets, some might trade them for fur with the First Nations. In 1673, Governor General Frontenac took steps to complete the organization of the militia and ordered that the companies of militia have frequent drills "every eight or 12 days at least" while noting that "most inhabitants have no weapons and no means to buy them." He had perceived the potential problem of having unarmed militiamen and, on February 12, 1674, strictly forbade inhabitants to barter their flintlock muskets, powder and shot. Those that defied his edict would be fined 50 pounds and the Indians participating in the trade would be shut in jail and be fined a moose's pelt. However, Frontenac had called for arms to be sent that "could be stored in an arms magazine in this country" as a "very important" measure. The king agreed, and in an April 1675 dispatch to Frontenac, he noted that the French people being "naturally brave" he never had difficulties arming them in France, but instead "often had to prevent them being armed." However, Canadians had to have access to arms to protect themselves from possible Indian attacks, and the king ordered weapons to be sent and stored in Canada. That year, 100 matchlock muskets and 12 partisans with four cannons and much ammunition were shipped to Canada. The matchlocks were not appreciated in a country used to flintlocks since the 1640s, and in 1677, some 500 flintlock muskets were sent to Quebec.[99]

The Canadian census of 1685 counted 1,810 firearms — undoubtedly nearly all flintlock muskets — in settlers' homes for 1,853 men. This was a considerable progress, since it showed that most men able to bear arms now had at least a flintlock musket. It was still not enough by 1687 because, on June 12th, Governor General Denonville ordered each man "capable of bearing arms, small or tall" to have and carry at all times a flintlock musket with enough powder and ball for 10 shots "so as to not be surprised or hurt by enemy savages." There were about 3,500 militiamen in 1710, and by 1750, the militia had grown to 11,687 men, divided into 165 companies commanded by 724 officers and 498 sergeants. All were supposed have at least a musket and a tomahawk.[100]

From the later 17th century right up to the September 1760 capitulation of Montreal, the question as to how well the Canadian militiamen were armed becomes somewhat murky. Obviously, Canadians did not wish to pay for muskets if they could get them for free during emergencies.

Supposedly, no firearms were handed out to militiamen, because they were expected to purchase their own. However, governors never ceased complaining that the Canadians lacked arms. In 1684, militiamen were loaned flintlock muskets, swords and canoes to fight the Iroquois; they had to be ordered to bring these flintlock muskets back, but the author of this study feels that few probably did if the authorities were resorting to ordering them to return weapons. The militiamen who "borrowed" the muskets likely viewed this as a bonus for their service and would have not declared them when censuses were taken. Obviously, many owned their own muskets, especially the

Below:

"Canadian on snowshoes going to war on the snow", c.1705. Although this print was engraved by one who was quite unfamiliar with what he was trying to illustrate, we can distinguish a very crudely rendered musket and a tomahawk at the waist belt; the bags at the waist are decorated with what might be beads on fringes. [Engraving in Claude Charles Le Roy Bacqueville de La Potherie's 1722 *Histoire de l'Amérique septentrionale...* Courtesy, Library and Archives Canada, C113193]

Right:
Militiaman armed with a matchlock musket, a sword and the equipment featuring a cartridge box, c.1700. Some West Indian militiamen used matchlock muskets as late as about 1715–1720. [Print after Anton Hoffmann. Private collection] *Author's photo*

more adventurous Canadians who volunteered to participate on raids. These had to be very hardy men, accomplished woodsmen and good fighters. A 1694 agreement by d'Iberville and Sérigny mentioned that Canadians joining them had to provide their own musket, powder horn and clothes in return for which they would receive half of the captured booty and half of the profits from seized merchandise. This explains how Canadian militiamen who volunteered to participate in raids were lured into these difficult and dangerous activities; the rewards could be great as long as they had weapons and knew how to use them expertly. To keep them armed, the Tulle arsenal agreed to furnish to Canada 600 hunting muskets a year for five years with a caliber of 28, a barrel of three feet, nine inches and a flat "half buccaneer" type lock.[101]

By 1729, the minister of the Navy approved the proposal made by Governor General de Beauharnois that muskets from the royal magazine could be issued to the militiamen who could not afford them. Some certainly could. Nevertheless, in 1745, little had changed in official statistics: about a third of militiamen reportedly had no muskets. A 1750 muster of the Côte St. Michel Militia Company near Montreal reported 38 muskets for it 55 militiamen. This perpetual shortage of muskets seems rather curious in view of the fact that Canadians had a reputation for being excellent shots according to several accounts. The Scandinavian scientist Pehr Kalm, visiting Canada in 1749, noted especially that "all the people born in Canada [were] the best marksmen in existence and rarely miss[ed]" their target, and that "there is not one of them who is unable to shoot remarkably well and does not possess a musket."[102]

Thus, it would seem every Canadian had his own musket and practiced target shooting. This apparent contradiction can be explained in two ways. First, militiamen in urban centers were less likely to own firearms than those living in the countryside, where about four in five Canadians lived. For example, by the 18th century, game had become rare in the Quebec City area so that about a quarter of the men eligible for the militia did not have firearms, simply because they had no use for them. Second, Canadians and the authorities were obviously playing a little game of hide and seek. Muskets were expensive and militiamen were not paid when on active service. In order to obtain a new musket without having to spend a lot of money, one could hide the good one he possessed and present himself unarmed for service or armed with a musket "so bad" that the authorities were obliged to provide another. The senior authorities must have had some complicity in this regard. Apart from the usual recriminations of government accountants, the governors were not unhappy to see this excellent militia armed with good muskets when the need arose. Up to the 1750s, it seems that 28 caliber hunting muskets were issued to militiamen who needed them. Thereafter, 18 caliber military muskets were issued in quantity to militiamen as well as bullets. Thus, as early as 1755, Chevalier Lemercier commented that three quarters of the Canadian militiamen on campaign were obliged to pare down the bullet's diameter "with their knives." In addition, militiamen in a wilderness campaign carried hatchets and often several knives, one sheathed at the waist, one at the leggings band, and a third suspended from the neck on a thong.[103]

While there was no prescribed uniform, Canadian militia officers followed, more or less, the traditional practice of wearing a gorget and a sword as insignias of officer status. As can be seen from the probate records below, these items had been owned by many officers since the 17th century and some also tended to have spontoons for parades. In more formal terms, Governor General Duquesne reminded militia officers in 1752 that he would not consider them as such unless they wore gorgets and swords. This was thereafter the rule, and it was applied. In 1759, General Bourlamaque did not recognize the authority of an officer of the Terrebonne Militia because he lacked a gorget.[104]

The probate inventory of militia captain Joseph Amiot, seigneur de Vincelot, at Cap St. Ignace on the south shore, who was also a fur trader and occasional corsair, gives an idea of the variety of weapons owned by a rural militia officer. In 1727, he was named commandant of the militia companies on the south shore of the Quebec area and was 70 years old when he passed away in 1735. He left "an old sword with its scabbard," two old buccaneer muskets with barrels four feet long, three others with a three-and-a-half-foot-long barrel, another "in the manner of a carabine [rifled musket]," a rifled carbine, a hunting knife mounted with brass with its belt and scabbard as well as a compass with its chain. Three years earlier, Captain Charles Dazée of the Ile Jésus (now Laval, north of Montreal) Militia listed only a flintlock musket amongst his belongings when his wife passed away.[105]

The area between Montreal and Quebec was the gouvernement of Trois-Rivières with many villages that are still visitor attractions today. Captain François Delpée of the Tennancourt Militia, who passed away in 1755, had a spontoon and a Tulle flintlock musket. His colleague at Bécancour, Captain François Bigot (not the intendant!), had a spontoon and a sword with a silver hilt when he died in 1756. François Rocheleau, who "when alive" was Captain of the Cap de la Madeleine Militia until 1759, owned "a regulation sword, a gorget, an officer's spontoon" and a "long flintlock musket with iron furnishings."[106]

Left:
Canadian militiamen, early 18th century. From left to right: a militiaman in winter dress, an officer and two militiamen wearing the short and medium length capot used in milder weather. All are armed with light caliber hunting (or trade) flintlock muskets, most of which were made in Tulle or in Saint-Étienne in France. Trade muskets had no bayonets, but militiamen always had a tomahawk and many carried three knives of various sizes: one at the chest hanging from the neck, a larger one slung in the waist sash and one fixed to the mitasse's garter. Militiamen in Canada did not have uniforms and used their own work clothing. Officers were distinguished by a gilded gorget and a sword. [Reconstruction after various period documents by Francis Back. Courtesy, National Historic Sites, Parks Canada]

Below:
Infantry officers, c.1730s. This French print shows well-dressed officers who would not have been out of place at a parade of urban militia in, for instance, Montreal or Quebec City in Canada or even Le Cap in Haiti or Fort Royal, Martinique. All are armed with a spontoon, a sword and both wear a gorget at the neck. [P.J.F. Girard's Traité des Armes (1740). Courtesy, Stephen Wood]

Ordinary militiamen would likely have at least a hunting musket, but their armament could also be quite varied. In 1701, the probate of François Breton living at Champlain in the Trois-Rivières district listed a "flintlock musket with a barrel four feet long" that could have been a long hunting musket. Joseph Chartrand at Rivière des Prairies (now Laval, north of Montreal) owned "a good long flintlock musket with a barrel of five feet with its furnishings" (which seems to be a buccaneer musket) and a "short" flintlock musket with a three and a half feet barrel when he died in 1732. François Guay of St. Denis on the shores of the Richelieu River had a buccaneer musket with a powder horn and ball bag, and "an old saber" when he passed away in 1750. Joseph Renault also had a buccaneer musket.[107]

There were also urban militia companies in Canada, and they were more like such units in European or West Indian towns. Probate records indicate that while some of them had the usual hunting muskets and knives, they also were armed with the more standard weapons and badges of rank, officers in particular.

One of the early captains of the Montreal Militia was the merchant Chabert Lemoyne, Sieur de Châteauguay, who passed away in 1685. In his house were found two "rather good" flintlock muskets with two more that were old, a short-rifled carbine, a pair of pistols and a sword with a silver hilt. In his storehouse were also two fine pocket pistols, 20 flintlock musket triggerguards with other furnishings, seven rifled carbines, six flintlock muskets of French manufacture and two from Holland, as well as a quantity of powder horns and powder flasks. His business was obviously a good place to purchase weapons.[108]

In 1694, Lieutenant Noël Langlois of the Beauport Militia, near Quebec City, also had "a brass gorget and a pike head" amongst his belongings as well as a "long" Tulle flintlock musket "having served for a long time," two other Tulle flintlock muskets of middle length and two old and short flintlock muskets, one of which was broken, a large English carbine (*un gros mousqueton anglais* — possibly a blunderbuss) and an old worthless pistol.[109] In Quebec City, Place Royale merchant François Rivière had a gorget, an old sword and a spontoon to perform his formal officer's duties in 1692, as well as an old flintlock musket and a pistol. Charles de

Monseigneur, an influential man and a member of the superior council, as well as naval commissioner, had a gorget, a silver-hilted sword "and another" with a brass hilt when he died in 1704. Claude Pauperet, Quebec merchant, had a "yellow brass gorget," an old rusty saber, two old pistols, a "bad" waist belt, an ammunition pouch and a "case to beat the drum" amongst his belongings when he died in 1707. Another Quebec merchant, Jean Crespin, member of the superior council, owned a pair of "pocket pistols" in 1734.[110]

Four years later, Trois-Rivières fur trader Jean Fafard, Sieur Laframboise, left three fine flintlock muskets with silver thumb-pieces and two marked with an anchor. Such muskets with silver thumb-pieces are also encountered in several other urban merchants' documents.[111]

Superior Council member Jean Eustache Lanouiller de Boiseles' probate revealed he owned two swords with silver wire grips, one soldier's sword, two old spontoons, two flintlock muskets and a saber with a horn grip when he passed away in 1750. In 1751, Joseph Durocher, Montreal merchant, had a gorget, a small sword with a brass guard and, for parades, "a spontoon mounted on its wooden" haft, possibly with a gilt spear. Another well-appointed Montreal militiaman, who also seems to have been an officer, was one François Baribeau, described as "voyageur merchant of the upper country," who died in 1754. His probate included "a sword with a silvered hilt with its buff belt embroidered with silver" and "a gilded brass and silver gorget" that may be a description of the silver badge fixed on the gilt gorget that was starting to be popular in the mid-18th century. However, it could also be the front of the copper gorget that was gilded and the back of it silvered, because one could argue that the badge did not appear in royal orders until 1767. Captain Charles Nolan Lamarque, bourgeois merchant in Montreal, also had a "regulation spontoon" and an old sword with its scabbard when he passed away in 1754. Captain Larchevêque in 1760 left a musket with a barrel of about three and a half feet long, two powder horns with their cords, and a small pocket pistol.[112]

In 1703, Charles Trépagny, a Quebec baker who certainly served in one of the city's companies, left "an old regulation flintlock musket" as well as an old Tulle musket. This shows that some city militiamen could have regulation flintlock muskets like soldiers. They were likely to have been carried by specialized units of urban militia. There was a squad of militia artillery in Quebec beginning in the early 18th century, and it was expanded into a company in 1752, the same year that an artillery company was formed in Montreal. Governor General La Galissonière proceeded to organize two elite "compagnies de reserve" for ceremonial occasions in both cities from amongst merchants and prosperous bourgeois that were commanded by nobles. He wished them to have uniforms, which was exceptional for Canadian Militia. The gunners had a so-far-unknown uniform that was most likely blue, while the bourgeois companies wore "scarlet with white waistcoat and cuffs," suggesting that these companies had standard military weapons and equipment like regular troops.[113]

West Indian freebooters were not the only corsairs roaming sea lanes; as early as 1708, the corsair ship *La Guyonne* out of Quebec flew France's white standard and long flame and had pistols, sabers, cartridge boxes, bullet bags, powder horns and a drum aboard.[114]

Below:

Pocket pistol, 18th century. A number of probate inventories mention these small pistols amongst the belongings of militiamen. This one has brass furnishings, barrel and lockplate. [Private collection. Courtesy, Rama/Wikimedia]

LOUISIANA

Settled from 1699, Louisiana was divided into two entities. These were the establishments on the coast of the Gulf of Mexico where Mobile and New Orleans, the capital of the colony, were situated. Much further north was the "Illinois Country" that was incorporated in 1717 into the colony of Louisiana. The majority of settlers in the "Illinois Country" were Canadians that had decided to move further west, and they brought with them the militia system they knew. They usually lived in family farms and small villages along the Mississippi River. Thus, the Canadian militia organization model by parish companies was prevalent in Upper Louisiana. Flintlock hunting muskets were seemingly the most common weapons in the Illinois. Jacques Bourdon, seemingly a trader at Kaskaskia who passed away in 1723, had some 14 muskets, a bullet mould and an old hunting horn. One Le Gras, who died in 1724 near Fort de Chartres, had three muskets, and in 1728, the deceased Gaussiaux left a pair of pistols, a flintlock musket, a hatchet and a powder horn. François Bastien who passed away at Prairie du Rocher in 1763 had two muskets. In effect, this was much the same as would have been possessed by a mildly prosperous rural militiaman in Canada. Clothing and other items listed in probate inventories suggest that the arms and appearance of Illinois militiamen, some of whom campaigned as far away as the Ohio and the Niagara area, were much the same as Canadian militiamen.[115]

In Lower Louisiana, on the Gulf Coast, the militia seems to have been organized beginning in the 1720s and appears to have been more akin to a West Indian planter's militia. In the mid-18th century, the Gulf Coast settlements of French Louisiana mainly consisted of the seaports of New Orleans and Mobile with plantations in the countryside. Both towns had militia units, and by the 1750s, New Orleans mustered about 400 militiamen divided into four companies of town bourgeois militia and a coast guard militia company. Mobile also had a few companies, including one of free Africans and one of artillery. Since 1730, the Louisiana Militia on the Gulf Coast had used the 1727 orders for the Windward Islands Militia as its basic regulations and general organization.[116]

By 1751, Militia officers in New Orleans were anxious to have uniforms. On May 25th, Governor Vaudreuil mentioned to the Minister of the Navy in Versailles that the town's militia "was learning the new [infantry] drill" and wished "to have regulation uniforms like those worn in the Windward Islands." Six days later, he reported that the New Orleans Militia had "made an arrangement" to have "the same uniform dress as that worn in the French islands." The infantry would have had white trimmed with red as in Martinique. The Captain Prevost of the Coast Guard Militia in the lower Mississippi area had a pair of pistols with silver furnishings and a spontoon. Weapons were sent from France to New Orleans. In 1732 for instance, apart from Indian trade muskets furnished with brass, 840 light hunting muskets and 720 "finer" light hunting muskets were sent from France. In 1748, 300 Tulle hunting muskets were shipped to Louisiana. Fourteen years later at Natchitoches, one Etienne Castambon owned a "demy Tule" (half Tulle) musket and a trade musket.[117]

ILE ROYALE

There seems to have been no formal militia organization at Ile Royale until the spring of 1741 when two companies of *Milice bourgeoise* — urban militia — were formed in the fortress town of Louisbourg and this had grown to four companies by the time of the 1745 siege. There may have been about 300 town militiamen during the 1758 siege, of whom 19 were killed and 29 injured. The garrison was predominant in this seaport fortress so that a strong militia organization was not as essential as in other colonies. There is little information on this militia, but the inhabitants of Louisbourg, many of whom were artisans and fishermen from France and sometimes in town for a temporary stay, were certainly far less familiar with weapons than Canadians. Louisbourg's civilian inhabitants did not own many weapons and this was not complained about by officials since they could easily be armed from the arms stored in the town's military magazine. They must have been issued weapons like the regular troops when besieged.[118]

THE WEST INDIES

In the 1660s, Louis XIV saw an opportunity to annex the western part of Hispaniola so it would become a French territory, seeing that most buccaneers were French and that some were trying to build plantations and other permanent settlements. French warships appeared to patrol the coast, and in a shrewd move, the king appointed Bertrand d'Ogeron, a noted buccaneer and planter, as his "governor of Tortuga" in June of 1665, bearing in mind that the island of Tortuga, which was a base for pirates that d'Oregon actually commissioned to attack the Spanish, was merely the capital for the whole of Haiti's coast. He then encouraged settlement, but the freebooters and buccaneers — often one and the same — disagreed and finally chased him out in 1674. The king now took a stronger grip on Haiti by appointing Jacques Neveu de Pouancey as governor, who arrived in 1676 backed with a naval force, and he proceeded to disarm the pirates, buccaneers and freebooters he encountered while encouraging sugar plantations that soon after thrived. The following year, he moved the capital from Tortuga to Port-de-Paix on the mainland. He also had fortifications built to protect the port of Le Cap (or Cap-Français, today Cap-Haitien) on the north coast that would become the colony's most important trade center.

On March 8, 1670, the king forbade commoners in the French West Indies from carrying swords, firearms and sticks with blades fixed, unless they were on government duty or chasing runaway slaves. By 1672, regular garrisons were no longer on the islands. The only sizeable force left to defend the islands were the inhabitants enrolled in the militia, and they had to be armed. Arms and ammunition were sent to arm the militiamen. A sampling of subsequent shipments reveals the types of weapons they used up to the early 18th century. The 1672 shipment to Martinique consisted of 200 matchlock muskets, 600 flintlock muskets, 100 carbines, 30 bullet moulds, 400 ammunition pouches, 600 powder flasks, 600 swords and 500 shoulder belts. In 1674, regular troops were again sent to the islands, but these soldiers would have already been armed. Additionally, in 1674, some 1,200 matchlock muskets, 400 carbines and 200 flintlock muskets were sent to the islands, but most or all of these were meant for the militia and sailors. To insure that enough firearms would be in the West Indies to arm its settlers organized into militia units, Louis XIV ordered on September 23, 1683, that merchant ship's captains bring a dozen flintlock muskets that would be sold to the inhabitants at 15 pounds each, an obligation that went on until 1774. In all probability, many of these weapons were "buccaneer" muskets.

Another shipment from September of 1683 gives an idea of the variety of arms sent. Some, notably matchlock muskets, may have been issued to soldiers, but most would have been to arm island militiamen and freebooter sailors:[119]

- Martinique: 100 match lock muskets, 50 flintlock muskets, 2,000 flints, 100 pikes, 50 spontoons (...) 24 halberds (...) 300 bandoleers garnished with their charges and cords, 200 cords and 200 charges to re-garnish the bandoleers in the stores (...).
- Guadeloupe: 20 flintlock muskets, 100 cutlasses, 100 iron pike heads.
- Sainte-Croix: 20 flintlock muskets, 1,000 flints (...).
- Marie-Galante: 20 flintlock muskets of five and a half feet long and of heavy caliber, 500 flints, a dozen cowhides to make charges and coverings for the weapons.
- Fort Royal at Grenada: 20 flintlock muskets of four feet long and of good caliber, 20 bayonets to put into said muskets, 24 belt pistols, 24 sabers, 200 bayonets, 500 flints for muskets and pistols (...)

Below:

Buccaneer on the island of Saint-Domingue (now Haiti) with his hunting dogs, mid-to-late 17th century. This somewhat crude print shows the very basic costume worn by early buccaneers, which consisted of little more than a rough and very dirty shirt, some sort of breeches (if any were worn), leggings and a small cap with a turned-down visor. The very long-barreled musket depicted here is possibly the earliest view of the Buccaneer musket *(fusil boucannier)* that was developed by the early buccaneers.
[Private collection]
Author's photo

MILITIAMEN AND SAILORS C.1630–1763

Right:
Buccaneer armed with a Buccaneer musket, late 17th century. The long barrel for this type of musket was initially developed to provide greater accuracy for shooting the wild pigs of Haiti. [Print after G. Ripart. Private collection] *Author's photo*

Below:
Militia cavalry trooper of the French West Indies, 1740s–1750s, armed with a Musketeer-hilted sword and a M1733 cavalry carbine. They were first uniformed in blue coats, but changed to scarlet with black cuffs in the early 1740s. [Watercolor by Michel Pétard. Anne S.K. Brown Military Collection, Brown University Library, Providence] *Author's photo*

There were no regular soldiers in Haiti when the following weapons were sent on September 20, 1686, "...for the coast of St. Domingue [Haiti] (...), 100 buccaneer arms [muskets], 50 pistols, 200 charged grenades, 48 pikes, 12 partisans, 1,000 lbs of slow match cord...," obviously for matchlock muskets already arming the militiamen. This was followed by the purchase of 200 buccaneer muskets for the inhabitants of the country [Martinique], 100 buccaneer muskets and 50 pistols to place in the forts of Haiti. In August of 1687, "the Sieur [Maximilien] Titon de la Roche has furnished and sent from Rochefort 400 fine flintlock muskets...to the islands of America...to be sold to the inhabitants..."[120]

A 1691 shipment of "ammunition" for the "islands of America" included 600 swords, 200 bayonets, 100 spontoons, 300 pouches, 500 ordinary flintlock muskets and 500 buccaneer flintlock muskets. A passport of August 18, 1700, mentioned 650 buccaneer flintlock muskets, 100 ordinary flintlock muskets, 100 grenadier flintlock muskets, 200 matchlock muskets and 200 pistols. During the years 1708 and 1709, 300 Tulle buccaneer muskets were sent to Martinique and another 300 "to St. Louis [Haiti]...for the inhabitants that don't have them..."[121]

All this was originally to arm only the inhabitants of European origin, but as early as the 1690s, there were also free African militiamen. Furthermore, arming some of the slaves for defense in an emergency was a definite option. On September 20, 1714, each inhabitant in Haiti was ordered to have in good working order a buccaneer musket, an ammunition pouch, a machete or a saber, and a bayonet for each ten African slaves in his plantation. He further had to have a pike ten feet long for each five African slaves. From August 10, 1739, militia dragoon troopers were each required to own "a regulation musket with its bayonet, a cartridge box, two pistols" and a sword with a long blade. Militia infantrymen were ordered to have "a regulation musket with its bayonet, a cartridge box, and a saber or a sword." Each inhabitant that owned four slaves or more was required to have, besides his regulation musket, "a buccaneer musket carried by an African." Companies of free Africans and free Mulattos would be armed with buccaneer muskets only, cartridge boxes, sabers and machetes and they were also permitted to have pistols.[122]

As seen above, and although some details may have varied after 1714 from what was done in Haiti, the militiamen in the other islands and in French Guyana were also under obligation to be armed. In French Guyana for instance, as early as 1678, some "200 buccaneer muskets for the inhabitants" were sent as well 100 matchlocks, 100 swords and 50 partisans. In the middle of the 18th century, the militia at Cayenne consisted of an infantry company and a dragoon company that were "exercised from time to time by their captains, and reviewed once in a year by the governor."[123]

A West Indian royal arms magazine would contain a variety of firearms. In 1718, the Martinique arms magazine had, amongst its weapons:[124] 256 Grenadier muskets, good and serviceable; 335 Buccaneer muskets with brass furnishings; 101 Buccaneer muskets for socket bayonets; 193 Matchlock muskets, good, both old and new. In bad condition and needing repairs: 171 Buccaneer muskets with iron furnishing; 104 Buccaneer muskets "with two fires"; 117 Buccaneer muskets, old, of different lengths.

Although weapons were often sent to the islands, there were never enough and this became a pressing problem during the Seven Years War. For instance, when Guadeloupe was attacked in 1759, a "quarter of the militia had no muskets, another quarter had small and bad hunting muskets and no bayonets." In 1762, when fears of a British attack were rampant in Haiti, an officer of the Léogane Militia wrote that "the militias are in general badly armed and some militiamen have no weapons." However, there were still about 200 muskets in the Léogane magazine, of which "part might be sold to arm those [militiamen] that have none." On May 4th of that year, militiamen in Haiti were reminded to have arms as ordered in 1739 by June 1st and those who did not have any would be issued muskets from the "King's magazines." There was no further mention of buccaneer muskets. Martinique in 1762 had over 10,000 "good grenadier muskets with bayonets," but nevertheless fell to overwhelming forces in February. There were limits to what militiamen could do, even well armed, in the face of regular enemy troops. The whole overseas defense policy would have to change (see Chapter 9).[125]

Above:

A gentleman cavalry officer, 1680s. He is armed with a broadsword with a fancy gilded guard and holds his "baton," which is symbolic of command in 17th-century France. Note the wide buff sword belt that was meant to provide some protection. Wealthy French West Indian gentlemen that served in militia cavalry troops likely assumed this appearance. [Contemporary print. Anne S.K. Brown Military Collection, Brown University Library, Providence] *Author's photo*

Weapons

Navy Weapons Regulations 1674 and 1689

By 1674, the King approved the definition made by the Ministry of the Navy as to the type of weapons that were to be found in naval arsenals. This was announced by a royal regulation of September 18th. By extension, these were also the weapons that would be used, in the future, in France's American territories. The printed regulation mentioned the weapons listed below, adding that the "usual practices were to be followed regarding their proportions," and these are mentioned in the draft manuscript of the regulation. We therefore combine the information given in both the draft and the printed version. They were:[126]

Shipboard sailor's matchlock musket — barrel: 3 ft., 8 in., held to the stock by four pins; octagonal at the breech and tapering for a third of its length; caliber: 8 lines (or 16 balls to the pound); serpentine 6-in. long, curved at 3.6 in.; barrel extends 2.6 in. beyond the walnut stock; forged iron ramrod pipes; wooden ramrod with iron tip; weight: 8 to 9 lbs. The ironwork on this type of musket was heavier and most likely cruder than on the marine's matchlock musket.

Musketoon — flintlock carbine; barrel: 3 ft. long; caliber 8 lines; weight: 5.5 lbs.

Pistol — flintlock; barrel: 1 ft. long; caliber 7 lines (20 balls); weight: 2 lbs.

Cutlass — "well sharpened" iron blade: 2.6 ft. long; 18 lines at widest part and 14 to 15 lines at narrowest

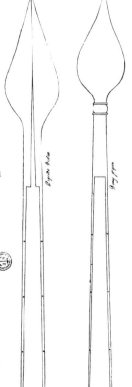

Left:

Naval boarding pike designs, c.1700. At left, a "hollow pike" and at right a half-pike. [Courtesy, Archives Nationales, Marine, G5, 202]

Right:
Cavalry troopers of later 1670s-early 1680s. The troopers have flintlock carbines whose butts rest upon pistol holsters. They also have a belt for a bullet bag and another for a sword. [Detail from a brass bas-relief by Martin Desjardins. Musée du Louvre, Paris] *Author's photo*

Below:
Armament of a French cavalryman, 1670s and 1680s. Weapons consist of a broadsword (C), a carbine (G) and pistols (E), buff leather jacket (A) with belts (E and B) and a pair of heavy cavalry boots (H) with spurs (K and I). Such mounted volunteer militia troops might be seen in the West Indies. [Print after Gaya's 1678 *Traité des Armes*. Private collection] *Author's photo*

Boarding axe – one side of the iron blade is to cut and the other has a hammer; the iron blade is 10 in. long, 3.6 in. wide, and the haft is 2 feet in length

Pike — iron pointed blade 5.6 in. long and 2.3 in. wide with "ears" up to 20 in.; ash wood haft 11.6 feet high

Half-pike — iron pointed blade 5.6 in. long and 2.3 in. wide with "ears" up to 20 in.; ash wood haft 7.6 feet high

Halberd — iron blade 9 to 10 in. long and 2 in. wide with ears 15 in. long with a hook

Partisan — iron blade 18 to 19 in. long by 2.9 in. wide; haft 6 feet long

The next general regulation "for the naval armies and the arsenals of the navy" was signed by the king on April 15, 1689. Although it went into great details of nearly every aspect of the navy, the part on weapons was remarkably short. As in 1674, the 1689 specifications for shipboard matchlock muskets were identical except that the barrel was now defined at 3 feet, 9 in.; otherwise, all other specifications were often repeated word for word and this regulation remained the theoretical one in force well into the second half of the 18th century.

This may have been a valid guide to the procurement of polearms and cutlasses during the 18th century, but, by the early 1700s, matchlock muskets had become redundant on board ships as well as on land. Furthermore, some weapons not covered by the 1674 or the 1689 regulations had appeared or were commonly in use. To be noted in particular is the appearance of the long-barreled buccaneer muskets that became a very popular weapon for sailors on board all types of ships, be they royal warships or pirates, as well as to arm West Indian militiamen.

While some sailors would be armed with firearms, it appears that many were expected to carry only edged weapons since they probably were not very familiar with the proper handling of muskets and pistols. For a visit by Louis XIV at the Brest naval base in 1679, the sailors were each armed with "a saber and a partisan or a spontoon" (meaning here a half-pike), and the marines were armed with the best and finest matchlock muskets for the royal review.[127]

Pistols

During the reign of Louis XIII (1610–1643), pistols assumed the technological features that typified them until the mid-19th century. Beginning in about the 1630s, the wheel-lock was replaced by the flintlock, which made it a less cumbersome weapon, ideal for cavalrymen as well as for sailors when boarding enemy ships. The pistol's barrels were initially fairly long. By the 1660, they had shortened to about 12 to 14 inches, although there were no set rules on such details. They were also handy for individuals concerned about personal security and, in a military context, were also likely to be carried discreetly by officers who were supposed to be armed only with swords and spontoons.

In a North American or West Indian context, pistols would be very handy for officers and militiamen when conducting raids, be they in the wilds of North America or in near-piratical operations in the Caribbean. From the 1660s, pistols also became handy for West Indian cavalry and dragoon units and remained an essential part of their armament thereafter. They were the only mounted units so armed until the 1770s when a few regular mounted companies served in the French islands. Thus, the West Indian cavalrymen were the only land-based troops to have pistols as a regulation weapon.

Left:
Cavalrymen, 1670s–1680s. The trooper at left is of the 1670s and early 1680s, because he wears the wide buff leather shoulder baldric to hold the carbine and buff shoulder sword belt (marked B and C), a buff leather sleeved jacket (A) and boots (D). The trooper at right dates from 1684. He wears a buff leather waist belt, which held a cartridge box containing "about 12 charges for pistols and carbines…packed in little rolls of paper" in the diameter of the caliber. The weapons consisted of a "saber or a sword" (E), pistols (F) and a carbine (G). [Manesson Mallet, *Les Travaux de Mars*, 1684 edition]
Author's photo

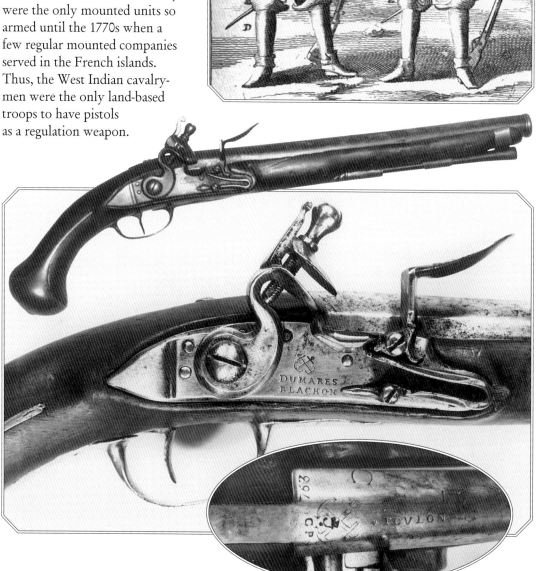

Left:
Navy pistol, c.1740s–1750s. The lockplate is marked "DUMARES BLANCHOND" with crossed anchors. Mounted with polished iron. [Private collection]
Author's photo

Left:
Lock of a Navy pistol, c.1740s–1750s. Marked "DUMARES BLANCHON", a gunsmith in Toulon, and with crossed anchors. [Private collection]
Author's photo

Left, inset:
Top view of a Navy pistol, c.1740s–1750s. Marked "TOULON", its place of manufacture, with crossed anchors and viewers' marks. [Private collection]
Author's photo

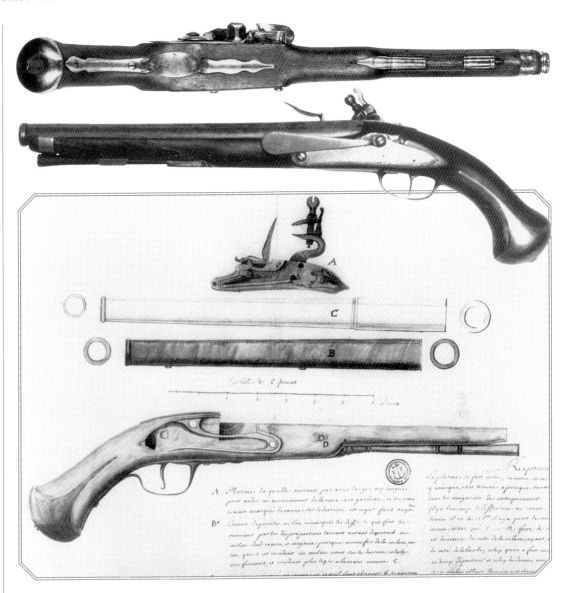

Right:
(top) **Underside of a Navy pistol** (below) The reverse lockplate side. Mounted with polished iron. c.1740s–1750s. [Private collection] *Author's photo*

Right:
Drawing of a navy pistol, 1693. This was the pattern drawing for the French navy's pistols introduced from November 10, 1693, and used into the 1760s. [Courtesy, Archives Nationales, Marine, G5, 202]

Navy Pistols

The other use was for sailors on board ships, so that royal arms magazines in all colonies always had a stock of pistols and they might be used for other purposes than naval operations. In North America, officers in particular appear to have always carried them in wilderness operations. From 1674 as seen above, a navy pistol was to have a 12-inch barrel and a caliber of 7 lines (20 ball caliber). This remained generally stable afterwards until the 1770s.

November 1697 Tulle contract: Navy pistols – 20 caliber; 12-inch barrel; round lockplate.

July 1716 Tulle contract: Navy pistols – 20 to 22 caliber; 12-inch barrel; iron furnishings unless brass is required; flat lockplate; weight: 1½ lbs.

November 1729 Tulle contract: Navy pistols – 20 caliber; 12-inch barrel; iron furnishings, brass is required for the Gardes du Pavillon and Gardes de la Marine (midshipmen); swivel buckle to carry slung over the shoulder instead of a hook as previously; flat lockplate; walnut stock; weight: 1½ lbs.

Army Pistols

West Indian militia cavalry troops might have used, on some occasions, the army's cavalry pistols rather than the naval models. Cavalry troops in the Caribbean tended to be made up of the wealthier men that were likely to privately purchase their arms and equipment as required by militia law. During the 18th century, they also provided their own mounts and uniforms. So far as arms are concerned, metropolitan cavalry pistols would have been high on the list. A royal order of May 16, 1675, specified that those pistols should have a 14-inch barrel, two inches longer than the navy's pistol, but otherwise, both types were generally similar in appearance. St. Rémy reported in 1697 that army pistols had a caliber of 18, a 13-inch-long barrel and an overall length of 20½ inches.

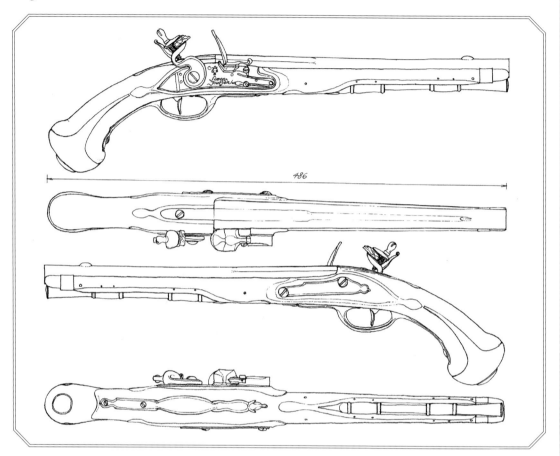

Left:
Model 1733 cavalry pistol. Some of these would likely have been used to arm French West Indian and Louisiana militia cavalry troops. [Plate by Jean Boudriot. Reproduced by his kind permission]

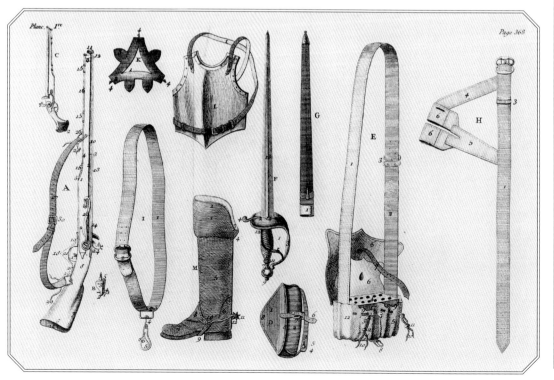

Left:
Cavalrymen's arms and equipment, 1750s. [Plate in La Porterie's 1754 *Institutions militaires pour la cavalerie et les dragons*. Private collection] *Author's photo*

Above, left:
Cavalry trooper of the 1730s is well armed, having a solid brass-hilted sword with a broad blade, a pistol in its holster and a carbine hooked to the broad buff shoulder belt. West Indian militia cavalrymen were unlikely to have heavy boots.

Above, right:
Rear view of the cavalry trooper of the 1730s shows how the solid brass-hilted-type sword with a broad blade is carried on the buff waist belt. The buff shoulder belt is wide to alleviate the weight of the carbine, whose butt is seen at right. [Watercolor by Parrocel. Courtesy, Anne S.K. Brown Military Collection, Brown University Library, Providence]

Between 1733 and 1734, the army's cavalry and dragoon pistol was more precisely defined with its barrel to be 11½ inches long with a 7-inch grip, a caliber of 18, as well as brass furnishings. This 1733 pistol was an elegant looking weapon whose appearance was very close to the navy's pistol. Although its barrel length had been shortened, some cavalrymen found them still too long and might shorten them to 10 inches. The Model 1733 pistol nevertheless remained the cavalry and dragoon's hand firearm until the advent of the 1766 pistol.

With regards to cavalry shoulder arms, these were also procured by some West Indian militia cavalry and dragoon units. By the May 16, 1675, order, the metropolitan army's cavalry and dragoons carbine was to be four feet long overall with the barrel three feet long. Its caliber was generally smaller, as it was meant to be a lightweight weapon with no bayonet. It remained thus fairly defined until the royal order of May 28, 1733, followed by the regulation of January 18, 1734, that introduced a new pattern of carbine. It was inspired by the 1/28 infantry musket, but was much shorter with a barrel 28 inches long. The caliber was 18, like the infantry musket. Shortly thereafter, the barrel was slightly lengthened to 29 inches and the butt also lengthened by half an inch from its original 13 inches. The furnishings were of brass except for the buttplate, which was of iron. The ramrod was of wood with an iron collar. The cavalry's version did not have barrel bands and its sling was fixed behind the triggerguard. The dragoon's version had barrel bands with the sling in front of the triggerguard. This was the army regulation carbine for mounted troops until 1766.

Rifled Carbines

In French, a rifle is called a *carabine*, hence a *carabinier* is a rifleman. Rifling the inside of a musket's barrel is said to have originated in 1498 when it was invented by Gaspard Zollner, a German gunsmith. By the mid-1550s, the practice had spread to other countries, and rifling (originally in straight lines) became spiral and had about five to nine groves, with cavalry carbines usually having seven. The ball had to be snug in the barrel, and a small mallet was needed to drive it down the bore. This gave this weapon markedly increased accuracy. The disadvantage was that rifled muskets took up to four times as long to reload and were expensive.

Rifled muskets, therefore, were used in very limited numbers by the French forces. Essentially, they were found in guard cavalry units, and from 1679, two troopers in each line cavalry company were to have rifled carbines. Some few might also be found in the navy and in overseas territories where they might be used by sailors, governor general's guards and militia cavalry. Manesson-Mallet mentioned in 1684 that "carabiniers were experienced troopers selected in (each) company. They must be...good shots. They have rifled carbines that shoot at 300 paces that are loaded with an iron ramrod."

The first regulation rifled carbine was defined by the 1734 regulations as "having the same proportions as the (cavalry) carbines, except that, at eight inches from the (barrel's) muzzle, the caliber will be reduced by a good half line to the breech, so there will be enough (thickness) for rifling." This was so the standard caliber carbine bullet could be driven down by only a ramrod without having to use a mallet. Much of the provisions of the 1734 regulation were repeated in 1766, only adding that the ramrod was of iron. Thus, the outside appearance of rifled carbines was similar to the standard cavalry carbine.

Insofar as French territories in America are concerned, guard units of the governors general of New France and the West Indies were armed with rifled carbines as seen in Chapter 3. Since riflemen were considered to be elite troops, a militia company of foot, or "Carabiniers," was organized at Le Cap (Haiti) during the 1730s, no doubt armed with rifled carbines to go with

Left:

Corps of Cavalry, Canada, 1759–1760. This 200-man regular unit raised amongst Canadians was the first cavalry unit in Canada and gave noted services during the 1759 siege of Quebec and the 1760 campaign. Its troopers appear to have been armed with sabers, pistols, carbines and muskets. The armament shown is according the royal order of 1750 for cavalry. The uniform was blue with red collar and cuffs and, seemingly, fur caps. The officers were detached from metropolitan army units and wore their own regimentals. [Plate by Eugène Lelièpvre. By kind permission of the artist and the Company Military Historians] their stylish scarlet coats faced with blue and trimmed with silver. The weapons and dress were privately purchased by the wealthy members of this and other such bourgeois volunteer militia units in the West Indies.[128]

In New France, rifled carbines were also occasionally present in government arsenals, not only in seaports, but in far-off forts. Fort Saint-Frédéric, for instance, had a few "rifled carbines." Some officers, be they of regulars or of militia, as well as some militiamen, privately owned such weapons also. Captain de Verchères had a small rifled carbine and a pair of fine pistols, an old Tulle musket as well as a spontoon when he died in 1752. Etienne Allaire at St. Ours, a village on the shore of the Richelieu River, owned an old rifled carbine when he passed away in 1752. They were certainly of French origin, although a few might be English, no doubt the result of booty after the capture of an Anglo-American fort. Such was probably the case in the 1750s for voyageur militiaman Antoine Sauvé whose 1760 probate mentioned a *carabine angloise* (English rifle) valued at 15 pounds as well as the more usual three Tulle muskets and two powder horns amongst his belongings. What rifles there were in Canada appear to have been used more for hunting than for warfare.[129]

Hunting and Trade Muskets

The hunting musket was the other widespread weapon that was especially prevalent in North America. As seen in Chapters 1 and 2, almost any weapon was found suitable for hunting in the early decades of the settlement of the French territories in America, with an early preference for flintlocks. By the second half of the 17th century, a distinct type of firearm evolved, which was lighter in weight, had a smaller caliber at 28 than military weapons, yet was sturdy, well balanced and easy to handle. It was the preferred arm of almost every French inhabitant and militiaman as well as with his allied warriors of the First Nations in North America. The hunting musket was also the trade musket. It was the same type of longarm that was traded with the Indians, although some of these were occasionally finely made with brass furnishings. These were more decorative and engraved, and were intended to be presented to chiefs.

As such, the hunting musket and the trade musket were not military weapons. There was a recommendation in 1755 by the Chevalier Lemercier that they should have bayonets, but this was seemingly never done. Thus, it is outside the scope of our study as far as details are concerned. There have been excellent studies published by Russel Bouchard, Kevin Gladysz, T.M. Hamilton, James A. Hanson and Dick Harmon, and the interested reader is referred to those works.[130]

While it may not have been made for warlike purposes, hunting muskets and their trade versions were soon seen on North American frontier battlefields being used by Canadian militiamen (who could also be called *coureurs des bois* and *voyageurs* if involved in the wilderness fur trade) and warriors of the First Nations. The smaller caliber of the hunting musket made it a lighter arm to carry than the military musket. This explains its popularity even in military expeditions when fur traders became serving militiamen, most of them obviously volunteers who might gain by seizing some booty.

Right:
Iron triggerguard, first half of the 18th century. This artifact appears to have been part of a hunting or a trade musket. [Fort de Chartres State Historic Site, Illinois] *Author's photo*

Below, top:
Tulle hunting musket, c.1720s–1750s. Mounted with iron fittings. Found in the Montreal area. [Courtesy, National Historic Sites, Parks Canada]

Below, bottom:
Tulle ordinary musket, 1716 contract. [Drawing by Michel Pétard. Private collection] *By kind courtesy of the artist*

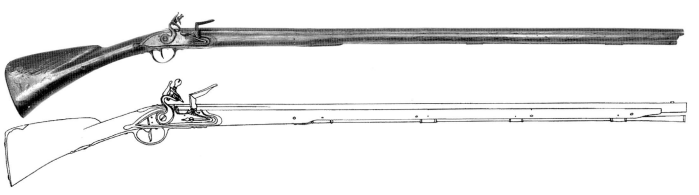

The men involved on arduous wilderness expeditions were likely to be soldiers and militiamen that were familiar with roaming in the wilderness and familiar with its First Nations inhabitants. Even the more agrarian Canadians in farms along the St. Lawrence River were reputed to be handy with weapons — invariably hunting muskets — and many were skilled in target shooting. Indeed, the local militia companies' assemblies in New France involved target shooting matches after church services rather than drill. Be they on farms or in a wilderness outpost, they knew a well-aimed shot from a light caliber hunting (or trade) musket could bring down a deer and, if circumstances commanded, a human foe.

Right:

Canadian militiamen, c.1700–1730. The exact significance of this ex-voto painting is lost, but it shows three Canadian men, two of whom appear to have perished, and a third giving thanks to Holy Mary (at the top of this large work, which has been cropped to fit). They are dressed in the typical Canadian costume of the time: a black neck cravat, a hooded capot, a waist sash, breeches and high winter mocassin-like boots. Of special interest are the two hunting muskets on the snowy ground — they are very dark and have scant details, but just enough to show they are the typical hunting muskets and were probably made in Tulle. The metal parts are not shiny and so appear to have been browned. This painting is somewhat unique in that it was surely painted in Canada and appears to be the only one showing the early costume and weapons of the French colonists. [Ex-voto painting of Notre-Dame de Liesse, Rivière-Ouelle (Quebec province). Courtesy, Centre de conservation du Québec]

March 1696 Tulle contract: Hunting musket – 600 per year for five years for Canada and Acadia – 28 caliber, 3 feet, 9 inches barrel, flat lockplate.
February 1716 Tulle contract: Hunting musket – "for Canada and other colonies if needed" – 28 caliber; 3 feet, 6 inches barrel, flat lockplate, walnut stock.
Royal regulation on muskets carried by merchant ships, November 15, 1728: "…the hunting muskets will have four feet long barrels and will be light."[131]
September 1734 Tulle contract: Hunting musket – 28 caliber; 3 feet, 6 inches barrel octagonal 12 inches from breech with mould ring, flat lockplate.

As early as 1709, there were proposals to add bayonets to the hunting muskets, but they were not considered strong enough to have them.[132]

Buccaneer Muskets

This weapon's evocative name was actually based on fact. Although nowhere to be seen in 20th and 21st-century pirate movies, the buccaneer musket was indeed a weapon originating with the somewhat lawless individuals that reamed the West Indies some three centuries ago and it was very popular until the middle of the 18th century.

Such men as buccaneers, freebooters and pirates needed weapons. Early on, they were supplied with knives and muskets made for them in western France, which they obtained by trading rawhide. A very sturdy and accurate firearm was needed from which evolved the long barrel for better accuracy and the sturdy club-like butt for solidity. Exquemelin stated in his 1678 *Buccaneers of America* that the better muskets were made by the gunsmiths Gélin in Nantes and Brachie in Dieppe during the 1650s to the 1670s. Later, other French ports shipped them out, not just to the buccaneers in Haiti, but also to other French islands. The early buccaneer muskets seemingly had matchlock locks, but it appears that flintlocks were favored early on. From the outset, the locks were made sturdy and large for rough use. The caliber was large for a hunting weapon, but it was meant to bring down deer or wild boar and, if need be, a Spanish soldier. So a military caliber was best, and it was usually 18 by the end of the 17th century.

With regard to its accuracy, some buccaneers claimed that their long-barreled muskets could shoot as far as cannons and that, according to Jean-François Bernard's 1689 *Nouvelle Manière de Fortifier les Places*, that they were certain "to kill at 300 paces and pierce a bull at 200." He felt royal armories should have stocks of these guns, observing that he preferred those with flintlocks because "…a good shooter could rarely miss a kill…" with a flintlock buccaneer musket and could aim "…at enemy officers or the bravest soldiers…". Consequently, Buccaneer muskets became much sought after by sailors, initially for privateers and pirate vessels, and later for French warships for long-range firing at enemy ships from the topsails.

French authorities saw the flintlock musket as the ideal weapon for its Caribbean settlers, and as early as 1683, merchant ships coming out of France to the islands were obliged by law to carry flintlock muskets to be sold to the settlers. The weapons shipped appear to have been exclusively buccaneer muskets. Over the years, further regulations directed merchant ships to carry buccaneer muskets to Canada as well, while Louisiana was excluded from this obligation. In a Tulle factory dispatch of September 19, 1693, a distinction is made between buccaneer muskets intended for West Indian merchants and ship owners, and those intended for the government. Caliber and proportions were the same for both, but for merchants and ship owners, they were made with good-looking furnishings — most likely of brass and engraved — while those intended for the government's services were to be plain. Presumably, the latter were also cheaper, but both types were equal as weapons.[133]

Above:
Gun furbishers in Nantes testing buccaneer muskets, c.1670. The length of the barrels and sturdy shape of the butts reveal the arms shown as buccaneer muskets. This seems to be one of the earliest images of this weapon. Note the cannon-like molding at the barrel's muzzle, a feature of early muskets. Nantes was an early center for making these arms. One of its gunsmiths, by the name of Gélin, was praised by Alexandre Exquemelin for the quality of his buccaneer muskets in his 1678 book about the "Sea Rovers" of America. [Print after Sébastien Leclerc. Courtesy, Bibliothèque Nationale, Paris]

Mid-17th century, as observed by Exquemelin: Buccaneer musket — 16 caliber; 4 feet, 6 inches long barrel; furnishings "different than those of ordinary hunting muskets in France." Bernard adds overall length at 5 feet, 8 inches. From the 1690s, the buccaneer musket usually had a barrel of 4 feet, 4 inches. There was also a shorter demi-boucanier (half-buccaneer) version whose barrel was four feet.

As seen below, a series of contracts for buccaneer muskets made at Tulle from the 1690 to the 1730s give various details that show a certain standardization of the basic features.

Tulle contract, November 1696: Buccaneer musket "300 for the islands of America including Canada" – 18 caliber; 4 feet, 4 inches long barrel; butt 14 inches long with a buttplate; walnut stock; weight: about 5 lbs.

Tulle contract, November 1697: Buccaneer musket — 18 caliber; weight: 5½ "like the ones delivered to the islands in May."

Buccaneer musket import regulation, Martinique, January 2, 1700: 18 caliber; 4 feet, 4 inches long barrel; brass furnishings.[134]

Request of August 9, 1712: "Mr. de Phelypeaux asks me from Martinique 300 buccaneer muskets made so as to be able to receive a socket bayonet of the caliber of 17 to 18 balls to the pound and with a barrel four feet long." The muskets were made, but it is not clear if they had bayonets, although they probably did, considering the shorter length of the barrel. If done, this addition of a bayonet was not widely followed thereafter. Subsequent documents specify a barrel of four feet, four inches without the mention of a bayonet.

Tulle contract, February 1716: Buccaneer musket – 18 caliber; 4 feet, 4 inches long barrel; flat lockplate; brass or iron furnishings; walnut stock; weight: 5½ lbs.

Royal regulation on muskets carried by merchant ships, November 15, 1728: "the buccaneer muskets will have four feet, four inches long barrels, 18 balls to the pound caliber…and will be light."[135]

Tulle contracts, November 1729 and September 1734: Buccaneer musket "for the inhabitants of the islands" – 18 caliber; 4 feet, 4 inches long barrel, held by five equidistant pins, octagonal for 13 inches from breech to molding ring; flat lockplate; brass or iron furnishings; walnut stock; buttplate 14½ inches long, 5½ wide and 2½ thick; weight: 5½ lbs.

Buccaneer muskets at Martinique, 1743: – 18 caliber; total length, 5 feet, 7 inches; barrel length, 4 feet, 4 inches; weight 7¾ lbs.[136]

Plug bayonets could be added to buccaneer muskets. With the advent of the socket bayonet, some were made with a lug on top of the barrel. However, this does not seem to have been widespread, possibly because of the extra expense of furnishing bayonets.[137]

Buccaneer muskets were now the primary firearm used by French West Indian militiamen and sailors, be they called *boucanniers* (buccaneers) or *flibustiers* (freebooters), from the mid-17th to the mid-18th centuries. A 1726 census of Martinique reported that 3,229 European men fit to bear arms had 4,750 buccaneer muskets, 2,442 pistols, 3,318 swords and bayonets and 2,417 cartridge boxes in their homes. This was quite an imposing arsenal, and there can be no doubt that they were well armed in case of an emergency.[138]

However, by 1740, Martinique's administrators did not feel that the armament was of suitable quality. The use of buccaneer muskets was questioned. Their supposed claims for accurate target shooting were increasingly in doubt, and their long barrels made them cumbersome. It was now felt that the standard military-style musket was best. That year, Martinique's governor general and intendant wrote to France for 2,000 grenadier muskets for issue to the militia. They even proposed a new musket model for this. Its caliber was to be of 24, the furnishings of brass, the barrel browned and the bayonet to have a flat blade and be one foot long, including its socket. It does not seem that this proposed model was made, but it does show a tendency to get away from buccaneer muskets. The metropolitan authorities agreed that new arms were needed, and at least 1,500 muskets had been received in Martinique with instructions to have the barrels browned locally and to distribute at least 500 in the Windward island. The note about the browning seems to indicate that these were standard infantry muskets that were browned once in the West Indies and not buccaneer muskets.[139]

Buccaneer muskets were also popular in North America during the first half of the 18th century, as shown in particular by Canadian probate records. However, by mid-century, authorities in France increasingly felt they were not as effective for target shooting as they were supposed

Above:

Members of the *Compagnie du Pacifique* in Patagonia, 1699. They are armed with Buccaneer muskets recognizable by their long barrels. [Print after an original Ms. Private collection] *Author's photo*

Below:

A shorter *demi-boucanier* (half-buccaneer) musket, c.1700s–1760s. Its barrel was 4 feet long (1,300mm) and overall length was 5 feet, 6.5 inches (1,692mm). Furnishings were generally of similar style and materials to the full-length buccaneer musket. [Plate by Jean Boudriot reproduced with his kind permission] *Author's photo*

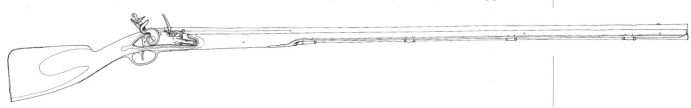

Right:
Buccaneer musket butt and lock, c.1740. This example was made in St. Etienne; the wood is oak and its furnishings are brass. [Musée de la Marine, Paris] *Author's photo*

Below, top illus.:
Typical outline of a buccaneer musket, c.1700s–1760s. This sturdy firearm had a very long barrel and its butt was large and solid. Its furnishings could be of brass or iron. This type had a barrel of 4', 4" long (1,408mm) and an overall length of 5', 6.5" (1,301 mm). The typical buttplate, triggerguard and sideplate designs are also shown.

to be and were cumbersome on board ships due to their very long barrel. They were, therefore, less in demand. In 1762, artillery inspector de Rostaing made tests in controlled conditions comparing the shooting accuracy of buccaneer muskets and standard army muskets of the same caliber. Even if the buccaneer musket had a longer barrel, it fared much worse than the army musket, while also being awkward to handle. Rostaing recommended its abolition to the minister of the navy, and it seems that no further orders for buccaneer muskets were made.

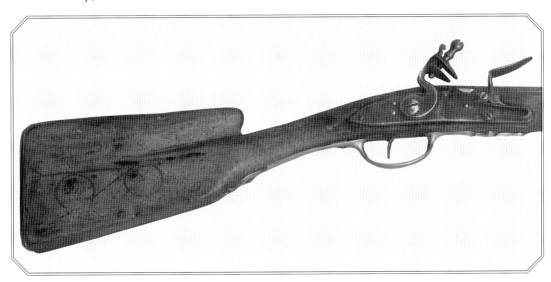

[Plate by Jean Boudriot reproduced with his kind permission] *Author's photo*

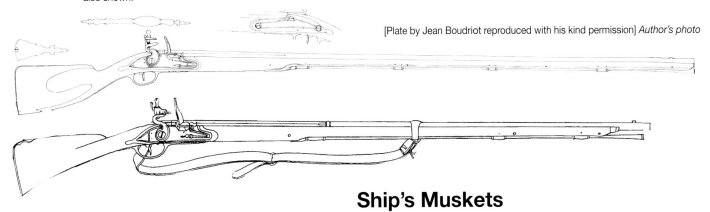

Ship's Muskets

Above, bottom illus.:
Tulle ordinary musket, 1729 and 1734 contracts. This musket had a barrel three inches shorter than the grenadier musket carried by soldiers of the Compagnies franches. It now also featured a sling, which would have been handy for sailors' landing parties. [Drawing by Michel Pétard. Private collection] *By kind courtesy of the artist*

By the late 1740s, buccaneer muskets were also increasingly frowned upon as a suitable arm for sailors on board warships and seem to have largely been discarded on board warships in favor of the ordinary muskets that were, from the late 1720s, made shorter than the soldiers' muskets.

As seen above, "ordinary" muskets had been made since the 17th century, and they basically denoted a weapon without a sling, whereas "grenadier" muskets had swivels screwed into their stocks to accommodate a sling. In 1729, Tulle started making ordinary muskets that henceforth defined them in a different way: they now had swivel rings for slings, but the barrels were made three inches shorter than the soldier's muskets. They had the same 18 caliber with a barrel length of three feet, three inches. This order was repeated in 1734 and probably again later on.

Also part of the Tulle contracts were mousquetons that had been used by ship's petty officers since the 17th century. These would have been the same models as those described above, yet some seem to have differences. The 1735 probate of Sieur Vincelot mentions several barrels at three and a half and four feet long that suggest a Quebec gunsmith may have shortened them and, in one case, rifled the bore.[140]

A few *Mousquetons à trompette* (trumpet carbines, meaning a blunderbuss whose barrel widened at the muzzle) were used mostly on ships, but they are occasionally noted in Canada and a dozen were found in store at Fort Saint-Frédéric between 1742 and 1757.[141]

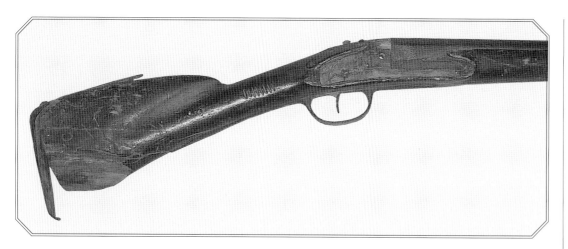

Right:

Part of a Model 1728 army musket that had a varied fate. It may have first armed a regular soldier and was then passed on to a Canadian militiaman, either as an issue or even as a purchase for hunting as well as for military activities. One notes eight notches behind the lock. The other side of the butt has the religious "I" cross and "S" logo marked with a knife that may also indicate a gift to an Indian warrior by missionaries or is simply a reassuring sign for its militia owner. In spite of various repairs and losing part of its stock, it has survived. It was found a few years ago by its present owner just south of Montreal and is recognized as a remarkable survivor of New France. [Courtesy, Kevin Gélinas Collection]

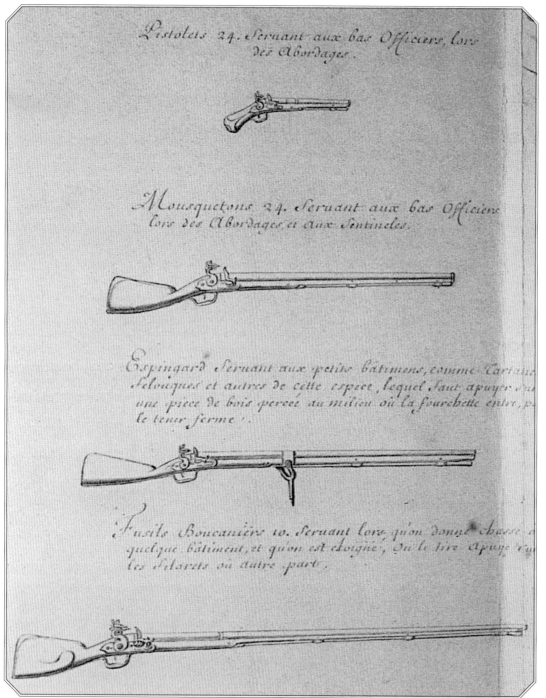

Right:

Firearms used on board a galley, c.1695–1715. These weapons were also found aboard the sailing navy ships. They were primarily used by sailors and petty officers when boarding or in close proximity to enemy ships. From top to bottom: a pistol, a carbine, an *espingole* and a buccaneer musket. [Undated document. Courtesy, Archives Nationales, Marine, G5, 203]

There were also some espingoles that were large, heavy muskets of high caliber fixed on swivels and used mainly on board ships and smaller watercraft. In 1722, the small ship *Le Chat Vernay* arriving at Quebec from St. Malo had four — three with iron barrels and one with brass.[142]

Edged Weapons

Swords and Sabers

In North America, militiamen all belonged to foot troops and preferred a tomahawk and knives as edged weapons instead of swords. Their officers were supposed to have swords and gorgets. Some of them still had to be reminded of this requirement as late as 1752. The type of swords would have been the same as for any officers and gentlemen — a Musketeer-style sword that was strictly a thrust weapon and useless for cuts.

In the West Indies, legislation prescribed swords for foot militiamen. The swords would presumably have been much the same as those carried by the regular soldiers, or else might be grenadier's sabers. They could vary a great deal in their details, often being privately purchased from merchants. The more prosperous planters, who were usually militia officers, would likely have quality weapons. For his part, the common militiaman might well bring a handy machete from the plantation if he did not wish to invest his money in a sword. Machetes appear to have been basically the same as modern ones, having a sturdy broad blade and a grip without a knucklebow or branches.

From the outset of France's settlements in America, there was no regular cavalry in the regular overseas troops of the Troupes de la Marine, nor were there any regular army cavalry corps sent during the 1750 and 1760s. The only exception could be the *Corps de Cavalerie* raised in Quebec in May of 1759 that served full time and was dissolved after the surrender of Montreal in September of 1760, although it was made up of Canadian militia volunteers led by French officers. There was no militia cavalry in New France before that.

The West Indian islands had militia cavalry troops from the second half of the 17th century. By the mid-18th century, large islands could boast groups of generally well-armed mounted militiamen. They were recruited from wealthier men who had to provide their mounts, arms, equipment and uniforms according to militia regulations. The richer men in the larger towns, especially in Haiti, further organized cavalry troops that were patterned after the royal guards and paraded in luxurious dress and accouterments armed with quality weapons. The weapons, equipment and dress of any West Indian militia cavalry unit was based on, or was the same as, those of the metropolitan cavalry and would have been imported from France.

Royal magazines housed edged weapons that could be issued to mounted units, although some arms, perhaps most, were privately bought by individual militia cavalrymen. In the mid-17th century, French cavalry swords were quite varied, and by the 1670s, everyone agreed that they were generally inadequate compared to those used by opposing troopers. They were often thrust weapons and so were at a disadvantage when opposed to cutting swords. This was corrected as of March 9, 1676, when the army's cavalry and dragoon trooper's sword blades were ordered to measure 33 inches in length (89.4 cm = 35.2 English inch) and be straight and pointed with both edges cutting. On February 22, 1679, the sword was termed a saber with its broad straight blade of the same length, which was maintained on January 16, 1734, except that sword blades could also have one cutting edge. This feature was applied to all cavalry sword blades (except hussars) from June 1, 1750, still at the same official length of 33 inches. This was not strictly followed, as some actual examples might have blades of 95 to 98 cm (37.4 to 38.5 English inches) and dragoons, who were supposed to have swords, had blades of 80 to 85 cm (31.4 to 33.4 English

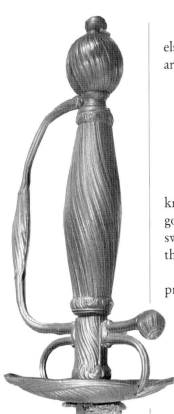

Above:
Gentleman's sword, c.1730–1760. Gilt brass hilt. This weapon was found in Place Royale, Quebec City's business hub in its Lower Town near the docks during the 18th century. It is associated with the Estèbe merchant family. An elegant weapon worn for a gentleman's everyday activities and for duty with the urban militia, in which he was likely an officer. [Centre d'interprétation de la Place Royale, Quebec City] *Author's photo*

Right:
Tomahawk, 1st half of the 18th century. The iron head was found during archaeological research on the fort's site. The handle is a modern reproduction. [Fort de Chartres State Historic Site, Illinois] *Author's photo*

inches). The terminology was confusing since, for some, a saber was an *épée forte* (strong sword) and usually denoted the heavy cavalry (and dragoon) sword with a broad straight blade. Eventually, the term of saber stuck to the curve-bladed weapon that armed light cavalrymen such as hussars.

Since the mid-17th century, the guard usually had one knucklebow, nearly always of brass, with a *pontat simple* (half shell) and a grip that could be either solid cast brass or a brass wire wrapped around a wooden cylinder. Another type of widely seen sword guard was the *à la Mousquetaire* style (Musketeer type) in brass that featured the *pas d'âne* with a wire-covered grip. Multi-branched types such as the Walloon, which was made of iron, could also be seen, and from 1729 to 1734, an experiment featuring a multi-branched iron hilt was considered for official adoption. Such swords were more difficult and expensive to make so that the type of hilt finally specified on January 16, 1734, was made of brass, a material that could easily be cast and shaped by almost any cutler, thus keeping costs down. The hand was not as well protected with the single knucklebow as on previous models, but the 1734 sword now had a full double shell.

Above:
Pipe tomahawk, mid-18th century. These luxury hatchets were especially prized by Indian warriors and chiefs, but Canadian militia and regular officers in the wilderness might also have them. [Canadian War Museum, Ottawa] *Author's photo*

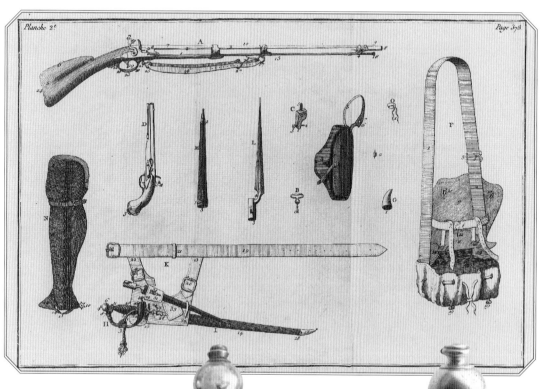

Some cavalrymen were not satisfied with this haphazard protection for the hand, and by about 1745, swords with double branches were increasingly seen. The order of June 1, 1750, specified that, henceforth, the guard would have two branches. The militia cavalry and dragoon troops in the West Indies certainly tried to have the same type of arms as in the regular army.

Left:
Dragoon's arms and equipment, 1750s. [Plate in La Porterie's 1754 *Institutions militaires pour la cavalerie et les dragons*. Private collection] *Author's photo*

Far left:
Brass hilt of a cavalry sword, c.1735–1750. This example has a half-shell guard and a wide and straight blade with one cutting edge according to the January 1734 order. [Private collection. Courtesy, Simon Gilbert]

Left:
Cavalry brass sword hilt, c.1750–1765. It has the two branches, made regulation on June 1, 1750. [St. Helens Island Museum, Montreal] *Author's photo*

Cutlasses

Although naval cutlasses were defined with measurements in 1674 and 1689, they were not an item that followed strict uniform rules before or after those dates. They were to be a solid hacking weapon for use at sea or on land, but not usually a luxury weapon. They were a favorite

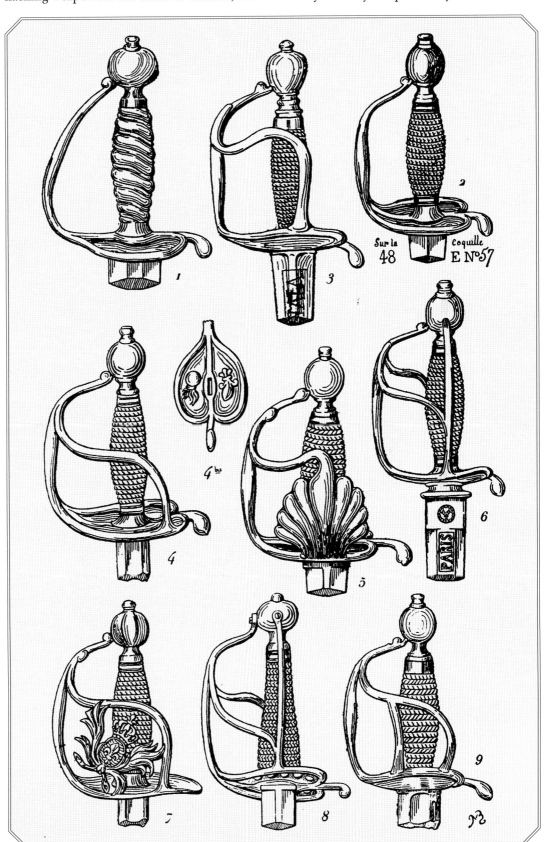

Right:
Brass sword hilts of cavalry and dragoons, 1700s–1760s:
1 – Early 18th century;
2 – (marked "48" and "E Nº57") c.1734;
3 – c.1750;
4 – c.1750;
4b – c.1750;
5 – c.1750 (branch ornamented by a shell, notably but not exclusive to the Royal Carabiniers Regiment);
6 – c.1750 (variant with extra branches);
7 – c.1750 (non-regulation more decorative branch obtained by some officers); **8** – Walloon style c.1730;
9 – multi-branched c.1760 (marked to the "Royal-Allemand Cavalry Regiment").
[Plate after Bottet]

weapon of 17th and 18th-century freebooters and sailors. Early engravings of corsairs and freebooters often show them armed with a variety of cutlasses, many having shell knuckleguards and/or thumb rings, others not, and always featuring broad blades of various lengths ranging from about 35 to 72 cm (14 to 28 English inches).

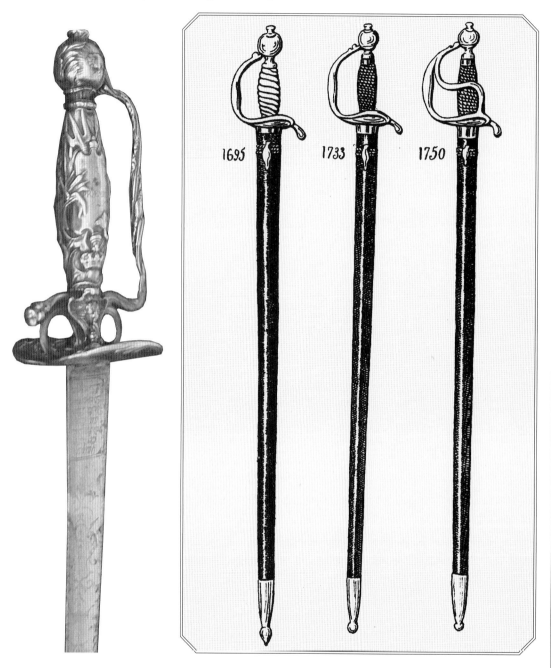

Left:
Épée d'honneur (sword of honor) awarded to Corsair Captain Pierre Anguier, 1746. This sword was given by the Minister of the Navy, Count Maurepas, upon instruction from King Louis XV, for Anguier's successful conveyance of troops and weapons to Scotland during the 1745–1746 uprising. This weapon has a silver hilt made by the Paris silversmith's guild mounted on a blade by Dunkirk furbisher Gaspard Certain. Such naval honor swords are extremely rare in France before 1789. Only three are known, and this is the only one in a public collection. They would be worn by the recipient at all official occasions on land or at sea. [Musée de la Marine, Paris] *Author's photo*

Far left:
Cavalry fortes épées (strong swords) or sabers, c.1695–1750s. This plate shows the main changes, especially notable at the hilts from the 17th century with the scabbards. [Plate after Bottet]

Cutlasses were not exclusively made for use at sea. Some were also shipped to be stored in overseas government arms magazines. At colonial seaports, some could be issued to warships and at forts defending the port, and its militiamen might also have some. In North America however, cutlasses might be found very far from the sea.

The navy did have a somewhat standard type of cutlass, usually termed a *sabre d'abordage* (boarding saber) or *sabre de bord* (shipboard saber) from the 1670s. Its style was called *à la Louvois* and its generally iron hilt looked much like the brass hilt of the sabers carried by grenadiers and cavalrymen of the land army. It may be that Louis XIV's minister of war, the Marquis de Louvois, successfully suggested its introduction in the navy. It was much criticized in its day, because it was made more cheaply since it was meant to be used by sailors only on occasions of close quarter combat such as boardings. Its guard was considered not solid enough and not offering

Above:

The fearsome buccaneer and pirate captain François L'Olonnois, active in the c.1660–1668 era. Born at Les Sables d'Olonne (France), hence his nickname, he came to the West Indies as an indentured servant and turned buccaneer in Saint-Domingue (now Haiti). His band of mostly French buccaneers from Haiti fought the Spaniards, first when France was at war with Spain and later as pirates. In this print from Alexandre Exquemelin's 1678 *De Americaensche zee-roovers*, he holds a cutlass with a shell guard. It appears to have been the favorite weapon with both the sailors and the early settlers of the French West Indies. [Courtesy, Lirbrary of Congress, Washington]

Above, right:

Captain Jean Bart, c.1695, France's most celebrated corsair during the reign of King Louis XIV, also served with distinction in the navy. This contemporary print shows him holding a cutlass with a knucklebow. A pistol is also hooked on his sash. From his neck hangs the grand knight's cross of the Order of St. Louis that Louis XIV personally awarded him in 1694. He has a slow match between his teeth as the sailor hands him small grenades. In his left hand, the sailor holds the grip of his cutlass, this one without a knucklebow. [Anne S.K. Brown Military Collection, Brown University Library, Providence] *Author's photo*

Right:

Two buccaneers of the 1670s. They wield a strong sword (or épée forte at left) and a cutlass (at right). Both of these weapons are shown without knuckleguards (shown close-up above) held by buccaneers above an unfortunate Indian and a Spaniard. Most of the freebooters appear to have been of French origin at that time. [After Alexandre Exquemelin's 1678 *De Americaensche zee-roovers*. Courtesy, Library of Congress, Washington]

enough protection to a sailor's hand. The blade was considered equally questionable being of indifferent quality and often not sturdy enough. It might not even be able to cut a thick rope. However, this first type of Louvois cutlass continued to be made the same until the middle of the 18th century.

In about 1756, an improved Louvois-type cutlass started to be made. It was generally the same as the original type except for its double shell guard, which was meant to give better protection to the sailor's hand. This type of cutlass continued to be made until 1779.

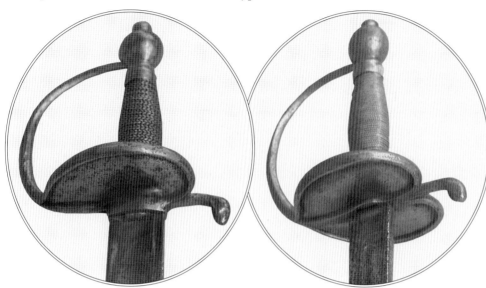

Starting around 1750, and perhaps before, another type of cutlass appeared that featured a brass guard having a single-shell counterguard bearing the bust of a ruler in Roman dress with ribbing on each side. This appears to have been a very cheaply made, but seemingly sturdy, all-purpose cutlass for the navy. The grip could be of bone or wood and the blade generally wide and long, but of no uniform model. A few examples have been found during archaeological research in North America, both at fort sites and in a wreck, as well as in private arms collections. It is hard to say if this type of sword was issued in great quantity.[143]

The buccaneers in Haiti also appear to have possibly developed and certainly popularized what is now known as a machete. They were said to originally have carried "a kind of short saber that they named 'machette' and several Flemish knives" during the 17th century. This handy short saber was probably used on warlike expeditions by land and sea, as well as being used as an essential tool of the sugar plantations all over the islands. The machette was the actual saber of many militiamen, especially those of African origin.[144]

Far left:

Boarding cutlass hilt of the Louvois style, c.1750. Sabers of this type started appearing as early as the 1670s as sailor's weapons. They usually had iron hilts with single-shell guards.

Centr left:

Hilt of boarding cutlass, improved Louvois type, c.1756–1779. Iron hilt.

Near left:

Boarding cutlass of the Louvois style, improved version, c.1756–1779. The guard was improved from about the mid-1750s when these saberswere made with double-shell guards in order to offer better protection to the sailor's hand. The hilt was of iron. [All above from Musée de la Marine, Paris] *Author's photos*

Below:

Boarding cutlass with a long curved blade, brass half-shell guard, ribbed and what appears to be the profile of a Roman emperor, bone grip. [Courtesy, Don Troiani]

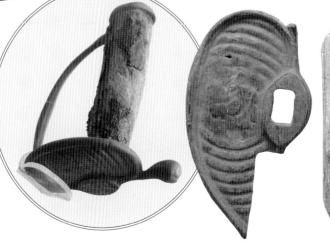

Right:

Boarding cutlass' guard, 1750s. This brass half-shell guard with a plain wooden grip was found by archaeologists at the site of Fort Saint-Frédéric. The guard's shell is ribbed and appears to bear the profile of a Roman emperor. [Crown Point State Historic Site, Crown Point, New York] *Author's photo*

Left:

Boarding cutlass' brass guard and bone grip remnants, 1750s. That these artifacts were found in Illinois and upper Louisiana shows that these crude types of sabers were distributed far and wide during the 1750s. [Fort de Chartres State Historic Site, Illinois] *Author's photo]*

Near right:
Boarding cutlass' guard and wide blade, 1750s. Brass half-shell guard, ribbed with appears to be the profile of a Roman emperor, and a plain wooden grip. This example has been mounted with a wide blade. [Courtesy, Don Troiani]

Far right, top:
Boarding cutlass' brass guard detail, 1750s. The crudely cast figure represents a ruler in Roman general's dress. From the wreck of the French frigate *Machault* sunk in July 1760. [Courtesy, National Historic Sites, Parks Canada]

Far right, bottom:
Boarding cutlass' brass guard, 1750s. This example comes from the wreck of the French frigate *Machault* sunk at the mouth of the Restigouche River (New Brunswick) in July of 1760. [Courtesy, National Historic Sites, Parks Canada]

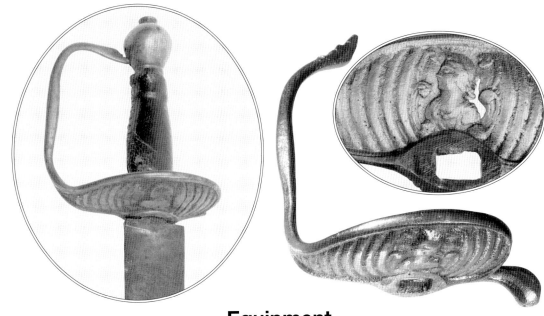

Equipment

The militiamen's equipment was generally his own personal property and could vary considerably. A Canadian militia volunteer woodsman such as a *coureur des bois* or a *voyageur* was likely to have had his own homemade pouch for bullets and his own powder horn that might also have been made locally hewn out of domestic farm animal horn or even a buffalo if out in the western territories. Regarding powder horns, the widespread Anglo-American cultural fashion of engraving them with elaborate, albeit naive, renderings of maps, figures and forts was not done in New France or, it seems, French colonies in general, even on personally owned horns. There seem to be no surviving, totally authentic horns that are unquestionably from that era in New France that have such decorations. This was obviously not a fashion in French domains. Otherwise, and especially for the more wealthy militia units found mainly in the West Indies, equipment that followed the equipment's patterns used by regular troops was sought after and used (see above and Chapter 9).

CHAPTER 8

Metropolitan Infantry 1746, 1755–1763

As seen in Chapter 3, metropolitan army units had been detached to the French West Indies and Canada during the 1660s. The policy from 1674 had been to garrison these territories with regular troops permanently there, the Compagnies franche de la Marine (see Chapters 4, 5 and 6). An adjustment to this defense policy occurred after the fall of the Fortress of Louisbourg in 1745. Admiral d'Anville's fleet of some 64 ships sailed from France in June of 1746 with the intent of recapturing the fortress. On board its ships were the regular metropolitan infantry regiment of Ponthieu and two embodied royal militia battalions, that of Saumur and that of Fontenay-le-Comte. There were also marine infantry and artillery contingents. The expedition was plagued by a series of misfortunes that included a catastrophic storm at sea, a deadly epidemic and Admiral d'Anville dying from a stroke. Some 44 ships managed to anchor in Chebucto Bay (now Halifax, Nova Scotia) in September and land some of these troops there to recuperate somewhat. All returned to France five weeks later, leaving the British in Louisbourg unscathed.

In 1754, the Jummonville Incident and the capture of Fort Necessity opened hostilities between France and Britain. In the summer of 1755, six battalions of the French regular army were sent to North America. They were the 2nd battalions of the regiments of La Reine, Landedoc, Béarn and Guyenne sent to reinforce Canada, along with Artois and Bourgogne who were intended to reinforce Louisbourg. In 1756, the 2nd battalions of La Sarre and Royal-Roussillon landed in Canada followed by the 2nd and 3rd battalions of Berry the following year. In 1758, Cambis and Volontaires-Étrangers arrived in Louisbourg, but were soon overwhelmed by greatly superior British land and sea forces. In Canada, Quebec fell in 1759, and the remaining French troops surrendered at Montreal on September 8, 1760.

The West Indies, which had not seen metropolitan troops since the 1660s, were sent a battalion of Royal Grenadiers, which was an elite unit of embodied royal militia that landed in Martinique during 1760. The French government realized it might lose its valuable Caribbean sugar islands and mustered a force of some 6,000 metropolitan army troops that landed in Haiti in early 1762, shortly after the fall of Martinique. By a royal order of April 30, 1762, the remnants of the existing 34 garrison companies of Compagnies franches de la Marine colonial infantry in Haiti were amalgamated into the regiments of Boulonnois, Foix and Quercy that were expanded to two battalions each. In addition, there was also the Royal-Barrois Regiment, the 300 metropolitan soldiers of the Piquets de Saint-Domingue and some 400 men to reinforce the Halwyll Swiss Regiment. Three NCOs of the Montcalm Cavalry Regiment were also to serve as lieutenants in

Above:

Grenadier of the Artois Regiment. From 1755 to 1758, Artois' 2nd battalion served at Louisbourg. The grenadiers were distinguished by their moustaches and by their large cartridge boxes. The uniform was grey-white with a red waistcoat and yellow metal buttons. [Formerly in the Library of the War Department, now at the Musée de l'Armée] *Author's photo*

Right:
Fusilier of the La Reine Regiment, 1757. From 1755 to 1760, La Reine's 2nd battalion served in Canada. He holds a Model 1728 infantry musket. The uniform was grey-white with red cuffs and collar, blue waistcoat and white metal buttons. [Formerly in the Library of the War Department, now at the Musée de l'Armée] *Author's photo*

Below:
Fusilier of the La Sarre Regiment, 1757. From 1756 to 1760, La Reine's 2nd battalion served in Canada. This is a rare rear view of a soldier wielding his sword, which seems to be the *pontat simple* (half-shell) guard type. The blade shown is rendered somewhat short by the unknown artist. The uniform was grey-white with blue cuffs and collar, red waistcoat and yellow metal buttons. [Formerly in the Library of the War Department, now at the Musée de l'Armée] *Author's photo*

Below, right:
Fusilier of the Angoumois Regiment, 1759. Ten companies of this regiment garrisoned in New Orleans, Louisiana, in 1762–1763. They most likely were armed with the Model 1728 infantry musket. The uniform was grey-white with blue collar, cuffs and waistcoat, and white metal buttons. This illustration by Taccoli shows that only the bayonet is carried. No sword is visible. [Courtesy of the Royal Library, Madrid]

Haiti and train the local militia cavalry. Furthermore, about 600 Grenadiers-Royaux that had been exchanged following the capitulation of Martinique.

The lesser colonies in the area were not omitted. For French Guyana, a detachment of 80 to 100 men from the Bigorre Regiment arrived at Cayenne in July of 1762. To reinforce Louisiana, ten companies of the Angoumois Regiment were posted in New Orleans and its surrounding area from April 1762 to October 1763 when transferred to Haiti. About 6,400 officers and men from the French regular metropolitan army were sent from France to Haiti, Louisiana and French Guyana in 1762 alone. It is not without interest to note that this was nearly double the number of metropolitan regulars that had been in Canada in late 1759 and early 1760.[145]

Weapons

The six battalions that arrived in North America during the summer of 1755 landed at Quebec and Louisbourg with an impressive amount of arms, artillery, ammunition, clothing and supplies of all sorts, many intended as a reserve. For the troops in Canada, this included:

1,000 rampart muskets
1,400 infantry muskets with iron ramrods
4,000 Tulle hunting muskets
200 pairs of pistols
30 officers sword hilts
30 sergeant's sword hilts
100 grenadier saber's hilts
600 leather belts for sergeants
1,000 priming powder horns
4,000 beef horns each containing 1 lb. of powder
40 drums
3,520 tomahawks (*cassetêtes*)
100 rifled carbines

2,000 iron ramrods
200 hunting muskets for officers
200 officer's sword blades with scabbards
100 sergeant's sword blades
400 grenadier saber's blades
200 leather belts with buckles for officers
4,000 cartridge boxes (*demi gibernes*) of 30 rounds with their belts
400 spontoons
1,500 musket slings
80 drum heads
600 axes

Below:

Fusiliers in formation, armed with the Model 1728 infantry musket with its bayonet and Musketeer-type swords. The accoutrements are the shoulder cartridge box giberne and the sword belt. The figures wear the blue-faced red uniform of the Gardes-Françaises Regiment, but the arms, equipment and general appearance of these soldiers was much the same as the line infantry. [Print after Eisen. Anne S.K. Brown Military Collection, Brown University Library, Providence] *Author's photo*

Below, left:

Cartridge box of a line infantry fusilier, c.1736–1767. The block had holes for 30 cartridges. Some 4,000 were sent to Canada with the metropolitan infantry battalions in 1755. [Reconstruction by Michel Pétard]

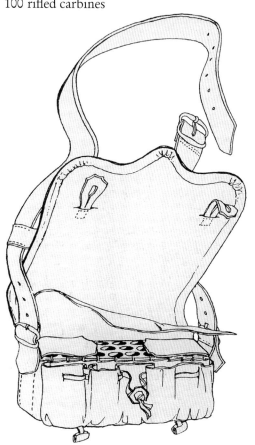

METROPOLITAN INFANTRY 1746, 1755–1763

Right:
Bayonet for the Model 1754 infantry musket. [Private collection] *Photos courtesy of Erik Goldstein*

Below:
Open original cartridge box of a line infantry fusilier of a metropolitan regiment, c.1736–1767. Brown leather. [Musée de l'Armée, Paris] *Author's photo*

The same types of supplies were delivered at Louisbourg, but in lesser quantities.[146] Of the above items, the most surprising were the 1,000 rampart muskets. The only one known to have been produced in quantity was the Model 1717 army rampart musket, so this, although old, was probably what was sent to Canada and stored at Quebec and possibly Montreal. These were not issued to troops on campaign due to their extra weight. Curiously, none are listed in the stores in October 1755, so it is uncertain if they actually arrived in Canada. Perhaps they were on the ships intercepted by Admiral Boscawen. The 100 rifled carbines are somewhat a mystery as to who they were intended for. There were 33 in store at Quebec on October 8, 1755, but none listed elsewhere, nor were any requested. Only a dozen would be necessary for the guard of the governor general, and there were no militia cavalry units in Canada, so they were likely used on board navy ships. Items such as the 4,000 Tulle hunting muskets and the 3,520 tomahawks were certainly intended for the Canadian militiamen and the allied warriors.[147]

The metropolitan troops arrived fully equipped. The soldiers of the Guyenne Regiment's 2nd battalion received new muskets in early April when they boarded the ships. These were likely Model 1728 muskets, since the men were instructed to detach the slings from their old muskets to put it on the new one, the sling arrangement on the Model 1754 musket being different. Once arrived, the cartridge boxes and uniforms were issued to all the soldiers in early July. For the upcoming campaign, the swords of private fusiliers were withdrawn and kept in stores; only the grenadiers kept wearing their sabers. Furthermore, all fusilier sergeants were also armed with a musket with its bayonet and a 30-hole giberne instead of the halberd. By February of 1760, the army that General Lévis reorganized in Montreal was lacking many items, including cartridge boxes for the soldiers of the battalions. For a replacement to those who needed them, they were instead given a powder horn and a bullet bag.[148]

Muskets

The standard infantry weapon in the metropolitan army was the Model 1728 musket. It was probably the most modern musket of its day, because its barrel was fixed to the stock with metallic barrel bands rather than by pins. This made it easier to take the musket apart for cleaning and minor repairs as well as minimizing damages associated with removing pins. It was also a well-balanced weapon, not too heavy and generally quite reliable and sturdy. The battalions that came to North America from 1755 were probably already armed with the 1728 or its spinoffs of 1741 (iron ramrod, nail-head shape) and the so-called 1746 model's very minor changes (octagonal barrel, bridle removed between the pan and the steel on the lock, which actually weakened the lock's action). It was named the 1746 model, largely amongst later collectors, although it was very similar to the 1728. On the whole, soldiers

Below:
Model 1728 infantry musket, 1750s. [Courtesy, Craig Nannos]

liked the 1728, as it proved to be a reliable and not too heavy a weapon. It came with its bayonet that made it a small pike over six feet high, and its sling was usually of the reddish-brown Russia leather.

Left:
Lock of a 1728 infantry musket, 1750s. It is marked faintly with the small crowned "S E", above that denotes St. Etienne. [Courtesy, Craig Nannos]

Below:
Muzzle detail of a 1728 infantry musket, 1750s. [Courtesy, Craig Nannos]

Left:
Markings on army firearms. [Print after Jandot. Private collection]
Author's photo

Above:
Model 1728 infantry musket, c.1750. [Courtesy, Don Troiani]

Left:
Lock of a 1728 infantry musket, 1750s. Marked faintly to St. Etienne by its crown and "S E" stamp. [Courtesy, Don Troiani]

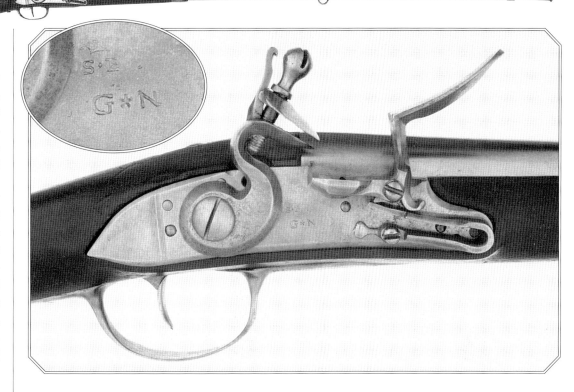

Above:
Model 1728 army musket. This example was made in St. Etienne. [Courtesy, National Historic Sites, Parks Canada]

Right:
Lockplate of the Model 1728 army musket. The mark "G ∗ N" is to Grange Neuve, a St. Etienne gunsmith. The small crowned "S • E" above identifies St. Etienne. [Courtesy, National Historic Sites, Parks Canada]

Some changes to the basic 1728/1746 model musket were made in 1754, and this resulted in those muskets being called Model 1754. The lock was made stronger by reinstating the bridle removed in 1746, but the most visible feature was the musket sling that was henceforth fixed under the musket from the triggerguard's front to the second band. Was this Model 1754 used in North America? It seems extremely unlikely. Although its specifications were defined by late September 1754, the contract for making it was not signed until December 20th. It must have been several weeks or months before work on the first examples of the new muskets actually started, and when finished, they still had to be viewed, proofed, accepted, packed, shipped and stored in a royal arms magazine.

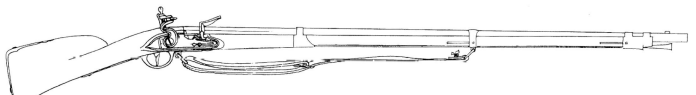

Above;
Model 1754 infantry musket. [Drawing by Michel Pétard]
Author's photo

Meanwhile, troops were gathering at Brest and sailed for Canada in early April of 1755. Some or all soldiers received new muskets that would have already been made and in store at royal arms magazines. The same is likely true for contingents sent to Canada and Louisbourg in the following years. So far, there seems to exist no verifiable evidence from protected archaeological sites in North America regarding pieces that unquestionably belong to this type of musket.

If any such muskets made it to the shores of America, they would have been carried by the troops sent to the West Indies during the early 1760s, especially by some of the 6,200 men that landed in Haiti and lower Louisiana during 1762. But there are no definitive clues as to which model of army musket armed these regiments.

Since the late 17th century, grenadier company officers in the metropolitan infantry were armed with muskets and, usually, sabers instead of spontoons and swords. These muskets and sabers could be of various types, and in the first half of the 18th century, it was not uncommon to see grenadier officers carrying light hunting muskets with short bayonets, these often having a wide flat blade. There was no regulation regarding their arms until the royal order of May 1, 1754.

Their musket was specified to be of 18 caliber, constructed like the soldier's, but with a barrel of four feet, six inches, two inches shorter than the Model 1728 musket for enlisted men. The furnishings were to be of polished iron and the weapon made finer so that its weight would be about seven pounds. Its bayonet had a blade of 8½ inches instead of the soldier's 14-inch blade.

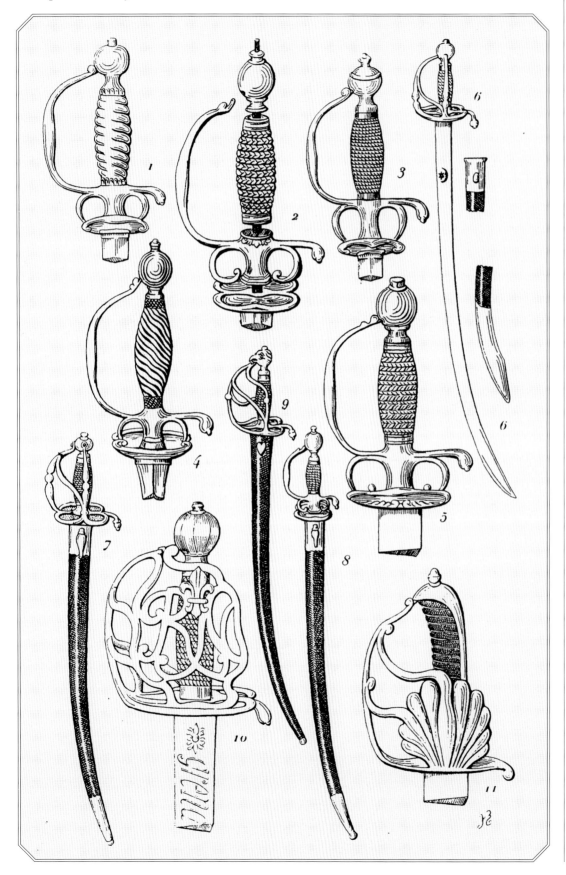

Left:
Infantry soldier's swords and sabers, 1700s–1760s.
1 – Infantry soldier's sword with brass hilt, early 18th century;
2 – Infantry soldier's sword with brass hilt, c.1730;
3 – Infantry soldier's sword with iron hilt, early 18th century;
4 – Infantry sergeant's sword with iron hilt and ebony grip, regulation model, 1750s;
5 – Sword-hilt type commonly used by infantry and cavalry during the first half of the 18th century grenadier's sabers, c.1700–1766;
6 – Grenadier's saber with brass hilt and brass scabbard mountings;
7 – Grenadier's Walloon-type saber with iron hilt, which were popular with Swiss and German regiments in the French army;
8 – Saber with a brass sword hilt;
9 – Saber with an iron Walloon-type hilt;
10 – Grenadier's saber of the Royal-Nassau Regiment, c.1750s;
11 – Saber hilt of the Corsican Legion, c.1765. These last two examples show the remarkable variations that could be seen in certain units, usually at the officer's expense, from about 1760. The shell addition appears to have been a popular style from the early 1760s and is seen in a later print of the Hainault Regiment.
[Plate by Maurice Bottet]
Author's photo

Swords

Metropolitan officers in fusilier companies and battalion staff were armed with straight-bladed swords, nearly always of the musketeer style, while grenadier officers had sabres. Generally, these were private purchase, so the variety in details of decoration was obviously great and suited to the officer purchasing the sword or saber. The usual rule of thumb was that the guard's metal should match the gold or silver of the regimental button, but this appears to occasionally have been overlooked by some officers. A sergeant's model sword was introduced in 1750 for metropolitan infantry regiments. It had an iron guard with a white metal grip. This could vary, as proven by the surviving sword of Sergeant Raby of the Guyenne battalion in Canada. It had a white metal grip with gilt decorations. (See illustrations on page 167.)

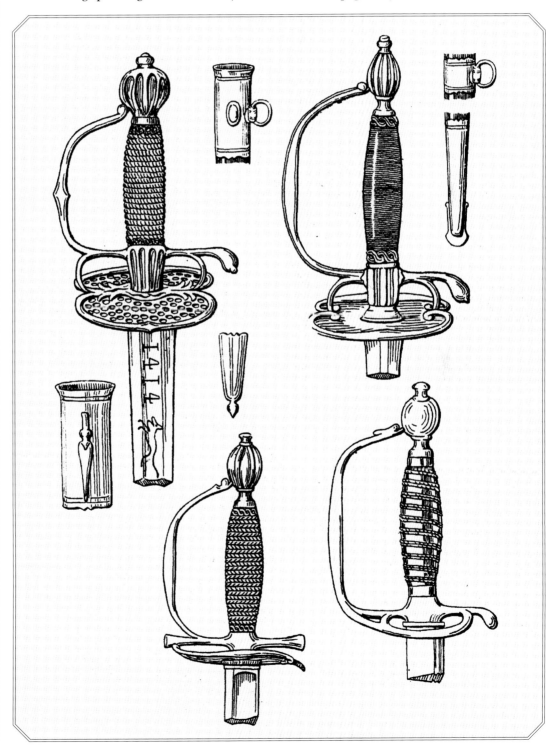

Right:
Officer's sword hilts, c.1745–1760s. Many types were seen, usually based on the Musketeer hilt. [Plate by Maurice Bottet]
Author's photo

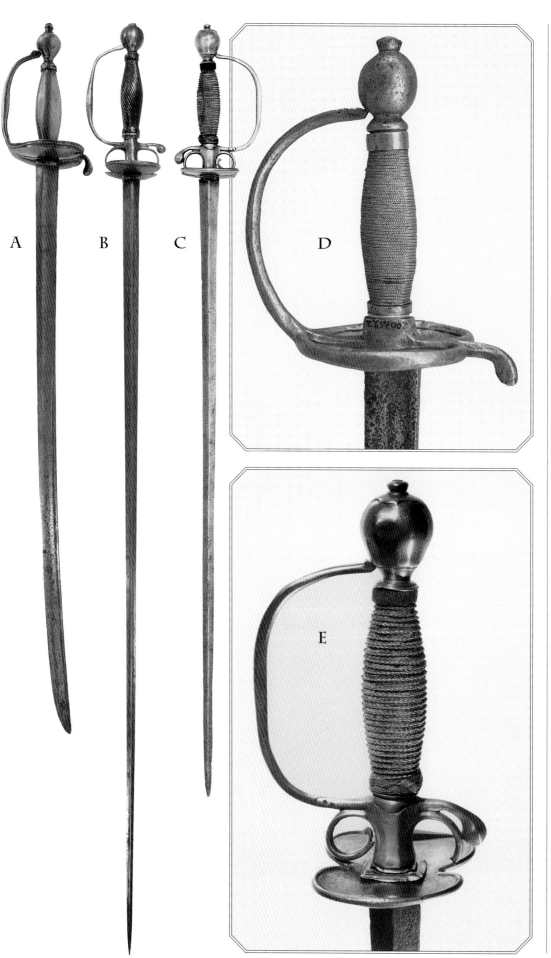

A:
Grenadier's saber, 1750s. Brass guard.
[Courtesy, Don Troiani]

B:
Sergeant's sword, 1750s. Iron hilt and ebony grip.
[Courtesy, Don Troiani]

C:
Sergeant's sword, 1750s. Iron hilt and white metal wire grip.
[Courtesy, National Historic Sites, Parks Canada]

D:
Grenadier saber hilt, 1750s. [Musée de la Marine, Paris. Courtesy, Rama/ Wikimedia]

E:
Sergeant's sword hilt, 1750s. [Courtesy, National Historic Sites, Parks Canada]

A:
Sergeant Pierre Raby's sword, 1750s. Kept by Sergeant Raby after his discharge from the Guyenne Regiment at Montreal on September 15, 1760, this sword remained in the family with his discharge certificate signed by General Lévis. White metal hilt with the small etching of a cavalryman below the grip highlighted in gold. The guard is 16 cm high, the blade 72 cm long and 2.5 cm wide below the guard. [Private collection] *Author's photo*

B:
Hilt detail of Sergeant Raby's sword of the Guyenne Regiment, 1750s. Born in 1723, Raby joined the Guyenne Regiment in August of 1754 and was promoted to sergeant in 1755 when he came to Canada. There, he wed Gabrielle-Françoise Brouillet on November 23, 1756. After many campaigns, he chose to stay in Canada after the surrender of Montreal on September 8, 1760, and passed away in 1775 at the nearby village of Terrebonne. [Private collection] *Author's photo*

C:
Maker's mark on the blade of the sword of Sergeant Pierre Raby of the Guyenne Regiment, 1750s. The shop named Le Tête Noire (the black head) located on the *Pont St. Michel* (St. Michael's bridge) in Paris was where it was sold and possibly made or assembled. [Sketch by Francis Back]

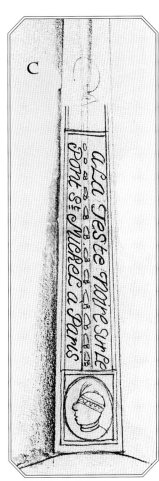
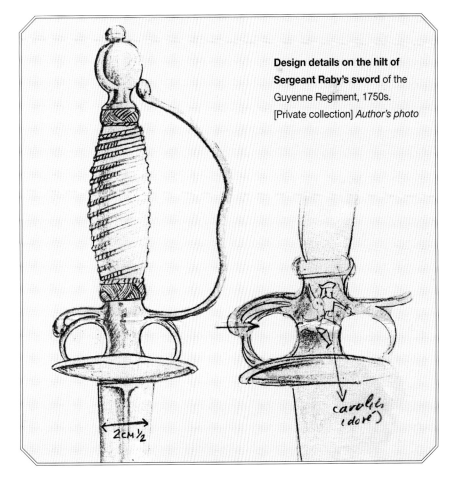

Design details on the hilt of Sergeant Raby's sword of the Guyenne Regiment, 1750s. [Private collection] *Author's photo*

Polearms Replaced by Muskets

Before the later months of 1758, the regulation weapons for metropolitan infantry officers and sergeants of fusilier companies were spontoons and halberds with swords. On October 31, 1758, a royal regulation was issued, but it was corrected, printed and distributed on December 9th. This definitive version concerned "the armament of the officers and sergeants of fusiliers," who were now introduced to firearms. Henceforth, they were to be armed and equipped as follows:

Fusilier company officers — a musket of 18 caliber, barrel four and a half feet long, "of the same construction as that of the soldier's of the latest model with the difference that it will be better finished and lighter (in weight), with the furnishings in polished iron..." The bayonet had an 8½-inch blade "three quarters hollowed, and cutting at its tip." The musket was to weigh "seven pounds at most." Fusilier sergeants would receive the same type of muskets as their men.

This December 1758 regulation applied to the Ministry of War's French and foreign infantry, as well as to the royal militia in France. It did not apply to troops administered by the Ministry of the Navy nor those administered by the *Compagnie des Indes* (East India Company), but it was the usual practice to adopt such measures brought out by the Ministry of War sooner or later. This order would have been known in America by the summer of 1759.

In Canada, Quebec was then being besieged, and arms and ammunition were scarce. In any event, this was nothing new. Since the arrival of the battalions in 1755, firearms were commonly used on campaign by officers and sergeants. One can doubt that the finer points about specially made officer's light muskets, peculiar cartridge boxes and shoulder epaulets were ever seen in Canada. General Levis' army, in 1760, had some of its men using knives for bayonets, and large arms supplies from France could not get through. It was different in Haiti, especially from 1762, when thousands of French metropolitan army regulars landed there to considerably reinforce its garrison. By then, the officers and NCOs of these troops would have been rearmed and reequipped according to the new regulation.

Battalion and regimental field officers (majors, lieutenant-colonels, and colonels) continued to be armed with spontoons until 1766. By the May 1, 1754, regulations, spontoons were to be seven feet long, the spear's blade to be eight inches with four inches of socket, including two narrow extensions on the sides that were six lines wide and 18 inches long each having six small holes in which to screw the spear into the wood. It was to have five feet, nine inches of wood (which had an inch diameter) and three inches of heel, the whole weight being three pounds.

Equipment

Beginning in 1736, metropolitan army infantrymen below the rank of sergeant wore a cartridge box held by a buff shoulder belt. This *demi-giberne* (half cartridge box) originally had 19 holes, but this was raised up to 20 by the order of January 19, 1747, and later up to 30. Its wooden box was in a Russia or black leather container that had small linen pouches for flints and a Russia or black leather cover flap. The flap was sometimes stamped with the royal arms. It was held by a buff leather shoulder belt "without nails or holes" for corporals and privates and also with cords to hold a wooden powder flask and a priming powder flask that hung behind and below the cartridge box. This equipment replaced the waist cartridge box that had been worn since the early 1700s. The enlisted men also had buff waist belts with frogs with which to hold the sword and bayonet scabbards.

Metropolitan infantry grenadiers were said to have somewhat larger cartridge box containers, supposedly to hold a few grenades, although this may not have been a universal practice. Grenadier sergeants were armed with muskets rather than halberds and also wore the cartridge box with its shoulder belt. The 1747 order mentioned that their cartridge pouches had small cowhide leather pouches rather than linen and that they were to be "well stitched, without nails, without holes."[149]

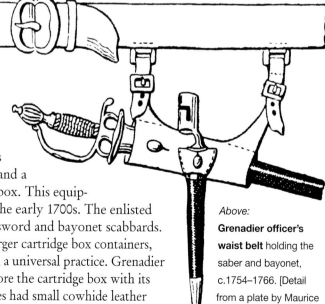

Above:
Grenadier officer's waist belt holding the saber and bayonet, c.1754–1766. [Detail from a plate by Maurice Bottet] *Author's photo*

A:
Fusilier officer's cartridge box, c.1760. The badge on the reddish leather flap has the arms of Navarre, which associates this artifact with the Navarre infantry regiment. Buff shoulder belt. [Musée de l'Armée, Salon de Provence. Courtesy, Raoul Brunon]

B:
Grenadier officer's cartridge box, 1758 Pattern. View with cover flap closed. Red Russia leather, silver thread crowned grenade and border. This item is marked "1762". [Musée du Royal 22e Regiment, La Citadelle, Quebec City. Courtesy, David Ledoyen]

C:
Grenadier officer's cartridge box, 1758 Pattern. View with cover flap open. Note the mark "MDLXII" (1762). [Musée du Royal 22e Regiment, La Citadelle, Quebec City. Courtesy, David Ledoyen]

D:
Grenadier officer's cartridge box, 1758 Pattern. View of cartridge holder with eight holes. [Musée du Royal 22e Regiment, La Citadelle, Quebec City. Courtesy, David Ledoyen]

The fusilier officer's cartridge box ordered in December of 1758 was called a *demi-giberne* (or half-cartridge box) having eight holes for the cartridges with a red morocco or black leather flap ornamented by a fleur-de-lis at its center, embroidered in gold or silver depending on the uniform of the unit, lined and edged with white leather. Officers were further distinguished by a "cloth epaulette, covered by a lace of silver or gold, placed on the shoulder" to accommodate the cartridge box's shoulder belt. The belt was of stitched white leather, one and a half inches wide, with a buckle. The sergeant's cartridge box had twelve holes, its flap having a fleur-de-lis stamped and washed in gold or silver and the belt of stitched yellow buff leather. The sergeant's cloth epaulet was plain without lace. Grenadier company officers already had similar light muskets, but from December 1758, their cartridge box

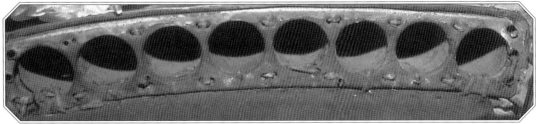

flaps were ordered to be similar to the fusilier officers' with the difference that a grenade badge embroidered in gold or silver was to be at the flap's center. Grenadier sergeant's flaps were to have a stamped grenade washed in gold or silver.

As seen above, the army in Canada had run out of cartridge boxes in the spring of 1760, having even issued the old nine-shot gargoussiers left in the stores, and resorted to issuing bullet bags and powder horns as a last-gap measure.

CHAPTER 9

Era of the American War of Independence 1760s–1780s

After the Seven Years War, the French navy went through a period of reorganization and expansion. This included a major overall of the weapons systems used on board all vessels as well as those that armed marines and colonial troops. This was a gradual process that occurred from 1763 and went on for at least two decades. However, the main transformation of the navy's weapons systems, for its crews, marines and overseas troops, occurred mainly between 1763 and 1773.

In terms of metropolitan harbor and overseas territorial administration, there was an initial concept that surfaced towards the end of the Seven Years War. This concept was that the army should take over duties related with all aspects of land defenses both at home and abroad. This culminated in the royal order of December 10, 1762, that assigned 23 metropolitan infantry regiments to serve as marines on board ships and in some overseas territories. Artillery and engineering services in harbors, ships and most colonies would also be rendered by the metropolitan corps. The Ministry of the Navy argued that "real" marines and "real" colonial troops were still necessary, while major naval bases, both at home and abroad, should be under the authority of senior naval officials. All these discussions had an impact on weapons systems of both the navy and the army.

Left:
Grenadier company of the Angoumois Infantry Regiment, c.1763–1767. Note that the grenadier officer has a saber as his men and the field officer wears a sword. From 1763, the French army went through radical changes to modernize and make it one of the most lethal forces in Europe. Its arms, equipment and uniforms were totally changed. Regiments now had the new Model 1763/1766 musket, new white leather accouterments and new white uniforms with, for Angoumois, green facings and yellow buttons, the elite grenadiers now having bearskin caps. This regiment was posted in Louisiana in 1762–1763 and then Haiti until 1766. [Print after Jacques Onfroy de Bréville. Private collection]
Author's photo

The matter of having well-adapted personnel to perform duties also surfaced. The 100 marine companies of the metropolitan-based Compagnies franches de la Marine had officially been disbanded in March of 1762, and well over 150 companies of the various overseas colonial Compagnies franches had also been gradually disbanded from 1760 to 1763, the lone survivors being the six companies marooned in Louisiana until a substantial Spanish garrison finally relieved them in 1769.

In Versailles, meanwhile, naval officials successfully argued that the military capacity of the navy had to be maintained both at home and overseas. The argument that the navy's expertise would be maintained simply by incorporating its infantrymen and gunners into the army also waned as time passed. For one thing, many left the service after the war, leaving few real veterans, and the new recruits could not fill the knowledge gap. Army officers were also horrified to find their battalions depleted by tropical fevers in the West Indies, and even worse, the soldiers seemed to perish at a higher proportion than ever before. This was due to the frequent rotation of regiments. The immune proportion of men would go back to Europe to be replaced by new soldiers that were subject to tropical diseases. No one then understood the medical causes of the

A:
Gunner of the Royal-Artillerie Regiment, c.1767. Detachments of this metropolitan artillery corps garrisoned various West Indian islands until the early 1770s. They were generally armed like infantrymen, but their muskets had brass furnishings, and they all had hangers. [Print after Lattré. Anne S.K. Brown Military Collection, Brown Univ. Library, Providence] *Author's photo*

B.
Grenadier of the Port-au-Prince Regiment, 1773. Grenadiers were armed with a saber, here shown as the Model 1767 *briquet* type. The musket appears to be the Model 1763–1766. The regiment's uniform was a dark blue coat with red collar and cuffs, and white metal buttons. [Print after Lattré. Private collection] *Author's photo*

C.
Fusilier private of the Troupes Nationales de Cayenne in French Guyana, c.1776, had exactly the same weapons, accouterments and uniform as his comrade in the colonial Ile-de-France Regiment (shown) posted at Mauritius in the Indian Ocean. He was armed with what appears to be the 1763–1766 musket with its bayonet. The uniform was white with dark blue facings and white metal buttons. [Anne S.K. Brown Military Collection, Brown University Library, Providence] *Author's photo*

D.
Fusilier of the Martinique Regiment, c.1776. He is seemingly armed with the standard 1763–1766 musket with its bayonet and its scabbard hung on the waist belt. The coat was dark blue with buff collar and cuffs, white piping and turnbacks, and white metal buttons. [Anne S.K. Brown Military Collection, Brown University Library, Providence] *Author's photo*

fevers, but as far as the French authorities were concerned, its effects might be lessened if, as in the past, units were posted permanently in overseas territories. It might also be substantially less expensive, since battalions would not have to be moved back and forth from Europe. This approach was agreed to, and a compromise was reached in 1765–1766. French Guyana, Haiti, Senegal, Mauritius and La Réunion (in the Indian Ocean) would be henceforth garrisoned by specific overseas units that came under the authority of the Ministry of the Navy. The new regular colonial units raised were: *Troupes Nationales de Cayenne* (French Guyana); *Légion de Saint-Domingue* (Haiti); *Légion de l'Ile de France* (Mauritius and La Réunion); *Volontaires d'Afrique* (West Africa).

From 1769, three companies of dragoons were added to the Légion de Saint-Domingue, which already had a strength of 30 companies of foot troops. To this could be added the *Compagnie franche de Saint-Pierre et Miquelon* (posted on the islands of Saint-Pierre and Miquelon off Newfoundland's southern coast), which had existed since 1763 as a provision in the Treaty of Paris.

Martinique, Guadeloupe and a few smaller Windward Islands continued to be garrisoned by metropolitan regiments. As years passed, officials and leading residents in those islands reported back to Versailles that having troops who were permanently linked to the colony was much more preferable, since their officers and men often integrated into local society, which made them ever more familiar with West Indian ways.

Left:

Gendarme of the royal guard, c.1776. Posh mounted militia units in the West Indies (notably at Le Cap in Haiti and in Martinique) were dressed, armed and equipped like the *Gendarmerie de la Garde* in Versailles. They had sabers, pistols and carbines and wore scarlet coats having a black collar, lapels, cuffs, turnbacks, waistcoat, breeches, saddle cloth and pistol holster covers, gold buttons and lace. [Anne S.K. Brown Military Collection, Brown University Library, Providence] *Author's photo*

Left:

Gunner and miner of the Royal Artillerie Regiment, 1776. The gunner is armed with musket, bayonet and the unseen artillery short sword that was held by the shoulder belt with a buckle. The 1776–1779 uniform was a blue coat and breeches, red cuffs, piping and turnbacks, yellow metal buttons, white waistcoat and stockings. The miner is shown in undress wearing a white waistcoat with red cuffs and blue cap with red band, piping and lily. [From an original unsigned manuscript. Anne S.K. Brown Military Collection, Brown University Library, Providence] *Author's photo*

By 1772, the whole notion of transporting metropolitan regiments to provide regular overseas garrisons was abandoned. Henceforth, metropolitan battalions would be sent only as reinforcements to an area that might be more threatened, or in case of war. The existing colonial units were merged into a new organization that greatly expanded the overseas permanent force. On December 30, 1772, seven new regiments were created, three in the East Indies and the following in the West Indies: Du Cap (Haiti); Port-au-Prince (Haiti); Martinique and Guadeloupe. The troops in French Guyana and Saint-Pierre and Miquelon were maintained.

Artillery services performed by the metropolitan *Corps royal de l'artillerie* were also gradually replaced by new colonial regular Canonniers-Bombardiers companies from 1764 in French Guyana, Haiti (1768), Martinique and the Leeward Islands (1774). Of the ten metropolitan engineers sent to Haiti, four had died and three had gone back to France by 1766. Colonial engineers, therefore, reappeared in Haiti, and the navy also resumed control of higher command of overseas territories.

Meanwhile, the once moribund French navy had undergone a massive reorganization and construction program that, by the mid-1770s, made it the world's second strongest naval force. The third strongest navy was that of France's Spanish ally, so for the first time since the early 18th century, Great Britain's realm over the seas could seriously be challenged.

From March 1, 1762, the shipboard marines also went through a number of reorganizations. The remnants of the Compagnies franches and the artillery bombardiers were amalgamated into three new brigades of the Corps royal de l'artillerie to provide gunnery services in naval bases, vessels and colonies while, starting on December 10, 1762, some 23 metropolitan line regiments were assigned infantry duties on ships, naval bases and overseas. Soldiers unused to naval ways and shipboard conditions did not always make ideal marines, and from September 24, 1769, the three artillery brigades were reorganized and expanded to each have a bombardier company, four gunner companies and three fusilier companies. Officers were henceforth solely from the navy.

In 1772, the navy again assumed complete authority over its marines, and on February 18th, eight new regiments of marines were organized, each having a company of bombardiers, one of gunners and seven of fusiliers. The regiments were named after French seaports: Brest, Toulon, Marseille, Rochefort, Bayonne, Saint-Malo, Bordeaux and Le Havre. This complex organization was abolished on December 26, 1774, in favor of an expanded infantry *Corps royal de l'infanterie de la Marine* of 100 fusilier companies with three companies of bombardiers as distinct units. The organization had reverted back to what it had been from the 1690s to the early 1760s. It was that flexible organization that provided marines and bombardiers on French warships during the American War of Independence, sometimes

Above:
Gunner of the Royal Artillerie Regiment, 1786. Except for a fourth button on the sleeve (reduced to three in 1786), this plate shows the uniform, arms and accouterments of the metropolitan artillery gunners from 1779, many of whom served in America. The musket had brass furnishings. The uniform was dark blue with red cuffs, turnbacks, piping and brass buttons. [Print after Hoffman. Anne S.K. Brown Military Collection, Brown University Library, Providence] *Author's photo*

Right:
Trooper of a hussar company of the 2nd Legion, *Volontaires Étrangers de la Marine,* c.1778–1780. [Period print. Musée de l'Armée, Salon de Provence. Courtesy, Raoul Brunon]

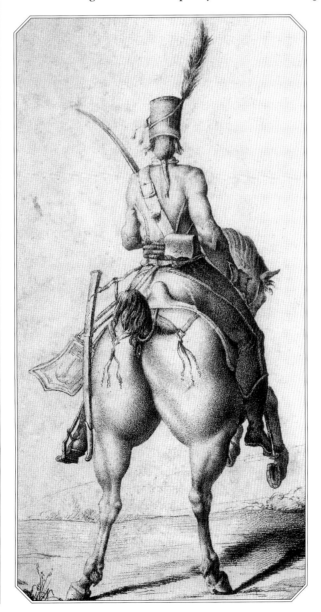

serving on land such as at the 1781 siege of Yorktown.[150]

When hostilities broke out in 1778, the Ministry of the Navy sponsored the organization of the *Volontaires Etrangers de la Marine* recruited amongst French and German volunteers. This legionary corps was intended for overseas service. It had three legions of mixed infantry, artillery and hussar units. Its 1st Legion was sent to the West Indies and its 3rd Legion to the East Indies. The 2nd Legion remained as a depot in France until reorganized as the *Volontaires Etrangers de Lauzun* — Lauzun's Legion — after the name of its commander, the Duke of Lauzun, and sent to the United States with Gen. Rochambeau's army in 1780.

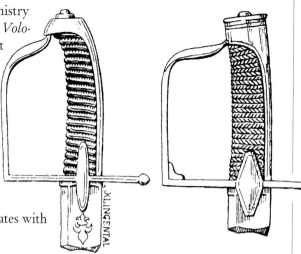

Left:
Hussar sabers, 1770s. Far left, the Model 1779 saber with its hilt at center. A variant is at left. The metal hilt and scabbard fittings could be yellow or white depending on the unit's button color. It would have been yellow/gilt for Lauzun's Legion's hussars in the United States.
[Detail from a plate by Maurice Bottet]
Author's photo

Left:
Hussar trooper of Lauzun's Legion, c.1780. He is armed with a carbine (carried at right), a saber and pistols. This rare print of this unit has some stains but shows the arms clearly. Lauzun's hussars in the United States had a sky-blue dolman and pelisse, red collar, cuffs and breeches, yellow cord, lace and buttons, black *mirleton* cap with yellow lace. [Anne S.K. Brown Military Collection, Brown University Library, Providence]
Author's photo

Metropolitan Army Units Detached Overseas

In 1775, the "shot heard 'round the world" at Concord, Massachusetts, had immediate repercussions in the corridors of power at Versailles, and six metropolitan army battalions were ordered to reinforce the French West Indies in November of that year. Following the American victory at Saratoga, five more battalions went to the Caribbean followed by two more in April of 1778. War between France and Britain broke out in July. Adding to the eight colonial battalions, there were now 21 infantry battalions in the French West Indies, and many were deployed in operations against the British colonies. Some 22 additional metropolitan infantry battalions were sent to America from 1779 and all remained until 1783.

Left: Bayonet and scabbard for the 1763 and 1766 model infantry muskets.

Photos courtesy of Erik Goldstein

Right: **Grenadier of the Saintonge Regiment,** 1779. Certain period prints can sometimes be more misleading than a careful modern reconstruction. This print, published at Stratsbourg by M.P.F. d'Isnard in 1779, has the correct uniform colors for the February 19, 1779, dress regulations (except that the lapels should be edged with green piping), but the musket had four barrel bands, and the grenadier's Model 1767 short saber should be carried by a shoulder belt. On other examples of this series, the musket sometimes has no barrel bands. [Private collection] Author's photo

The Metropolitan Army Infantry Battalions Deployed in America between 1778 and 1783 were:

Regiment	Location	# of Batts.	Length of Service
Auxerrois	Martinique	1	Nov. 1775–July 1783
Viennois	Martinique	1	Nov. 1775–July 1783
Armagnac	Guadeloupe	1	Nov. 1775–July 1783
Agenois	Haiti	1	Nov. 1775–July 1783
Cambrésis	Haiti	1	Nov. 1775–July 1783
Gâtinois	Martinique	1	Nov. 1775–July 1783
Gâtinois	Haiti	1	Oct. 1777–July 1783
Agenois	Haiti	1	Oct. 1777–July 1783
Viennois	Martinique	1	Oct. 1777–July 1783
Auxerrois	Guadeloupe	1	Oct. 1777–July 1783
Armagnac	Guadeloupe	1	Oct. 1777–July 1783
Walsh	Martinique	1	April 1778–March 1784
Hainault	Martinique	1	April 1778–1783
Champagne	Martinique	1	Jan. 1779–July 1783
Dillon	Martinique	1	March 1779–Sept. 1783
Foix	Martinique	1	July 1779–1783
Enghien	Martinique	2	Feb. 1780–July 1783
Touraine	Martinique	2	Feb. 1780–July 1783
Royal-Comtois	Martinique	1	Feb. 1780–Feb. 1784
Soissonois	United States	2	May 1780–July 1783
Bourbonnois	United States	2	May 1780–June 1783
Saintonge	United States	2	May 1780–June 1783
Royal-Deux-Ponts	United States	2	May 1780–June 1783
Rl-Hesse-Darmstadt	West Indies	1	Dec. 1781–April 1783
Auvergne	Martinique	2	Sept. 1782–July 1783
Berwick	Martinique	1	Sept. 1782–1783
Rouergue	West Indies	2	Nov. 1782–April 1783

Metropolitan Artillery Units:

Regiment	Location	# of Batts.	Length of Service
Metz	West Indies	1 Bn.	Oct. 1777–1783
Metz	United States	2 Cos.	May 1780–June 1783
Auxonne	United States	1 Bn.	May 1780–June 1783
Metz	United States	4 Cos	1781–1783
Grenoble	Martinique	1 Co.	1781–1783
La Fère	West Indies	4 Cos.	1782–1783

It should be noted that Agenois, Gatinois and Touraine were detached from the West Indies to join General Rochambeau's army in the United States during September and October of 1781. From March 1781 to September 1782, nearly 11,000 men — the equivalent of about 17 battalions — were sent to reinforce units in the West Indies. Thousands were also detached to serve as marines on board warships.

Very few metropolitan cavalrymen were sent to America. In October of 1777, a company of dragoons from each regiment of Condé and Belzunce were sent to Haiti and briefly served at Savannah in September and October of 1779. They returned to France in 1783.

Left:
Saintonge Regiment, c.1776–1783. This plate shows the typical armament and equipment of French metropolitan infantrymen at the time of the American War of Independence. Saintonge served in the United States from 1780 to late 1782. A fusilier (left) was armed with a Model 1777 army musket and his bayonet, which was carried in a scabbard attached to the cartridge box belt. Officers (left, center) were armed with swords. Drummers (center, right) were armed with a short saber. Grenadiers (right) were each armed with a musket (shown as a Model 1777), a bayonet and a short Model 1767 saber. The figures in the foreground wear the 1779 uniform of white trimmed with green and with yellow metal buttons. The grenadier and fusilier in the background wear the 1776 uniform of white with orange facings, light blue collar and white metal buttons, the fusilier having the short-lived frock. [Plate by Eugène Lelièpvre. Private collection] *Author's photo*

WEAPONS
Navy and Overseas Troops

Following the end of the Seven Years War, it became a departmental priority to have a sufficient number of weapons to arm the regular troops who were posted overseas and were under the responsibility of the Ministry of the Navy. It was decided to obtain 18,500 muskets and 750 pairs of pistols. Of these, 10,400 muskets were to go to America with 500 pistols going to Haiti and 250 for Martinique. Some of these weapons were kept in store as reserve weapons. By 1770, only 2,000 muskets and 469 pairs of pistols remained to be delivered.[151]

While weapons for all these troops tended to be similar to those used in the army beginning in the 1760s, there were some alterations favored by naval officials, especially on muskets, that became peculiar to naval and overseas troops as well as for shipboard muskets and pistols. The most visible difference was the use of brass furnishings, instead of iron. Artillery troops, on land and sea, traditionally had brass furnishings, and this became a standard feature for marines and overseas infantry from the 1760s. This feature was introduced between 1762 and 1769 when the shipboard marines and bombardiers were amalgamated into the metropolitan artillery. Brass was certainly a better option than iron in a saltwater environment, and by 1770, it seems to have been a common practice. In the case of metropolitan marines, all musket furnishings were of brass. Proposals were made in 1772–1773 concerned the "bronzage" (browning) of musket barrels, claiming this would afford an even better protection against the elements, but this does not seem to have been done during manufacturing in France, although it could be done locally overseas. Brass-furnished weapons already cost about 10 percent more than iron-mounted ones.[152]

For regular colonial troops in the overseas territories, there was a small but important difference — the sling band fixed in the middle of the barrel was of white metal. This appears to have appeared fairly early as shown by a musket in Craig Nannos' collection (see illustration on page 180), which generally has the features of a 1763 infantry musket, but made with brass furnishings and the iron barrel band for the sling. In 1779, this officially became a feature of the colonial troops musket model introduced that year.

However, until the late 1770s and early 1780s, it is uncertain if overseas colonial infantry consistently had muskets with brass or with iron furnishings. Few details are given in shipping documents. For instance, the 50 muskets sent in 1771 to the Compagnie franche de Saint-Pierre et Miquelon are simply noted as being with bayonets, slings and iron ramrods. We suspect that muskets, some with iron furnishings and others with brass, were delivered to the overseas territories. They largely received metropolitan army muskets in the 1760s and it is unlikely that all would have had their iron furnishings changed to brass, especially if intended as reserve weapons for local militia and volunteers. In 1766, some 6,800 muskets intended for the East and West Indies were ordered by the Ministry of the Navy at Maubeuge and St. Etienne. They were most likely the light 1763 (1766) model. Most of the later replacement weapons appear to have been made at St. Etienne, and many were shipped to various overseas territories in the early 1770s.

They were the subject of a scathing March 1775 report sent from Pondichery, India.

Below:
Bombardier de la Marine private and other ranks of the *Corps Royal de l'Infanterie de la Matine*, 1774–1782. The gunners, NCOs and corporals amongst these naval troops were armed with brass-mounted muskets, bayonets and brass-hilted short sabers. The models of weapons could vary, especially sabers. Accoutrements were somewhat different for naval troops than for the land army forces. They continued to have the waist belt after 1779 that supported the bayonet and the saber scabbards and did not have a separate shoulder belt for the latter weapon. [Drawing by Eugène Lelièpvre. Private collection] *Author's photo*

The musket received there appeared to be, at first sight, "of the best quality," but when taken apart to be browned — a local practice — the barrels were found to have been old and made-up from several pieces previously cut up, some barrels having up to eight different marks on them and several being cracked. The authorities proceeded to proof 100 muskets of which 17 burst. This was done in the presence of Governor Bellecombe, who was so upset that 25 of the barrels, along with a formal report, were sent back to the minister of the navy in Versailles complaining that it was more than likely that "all the colonies had most probably been generally infected by these dangerous weapons" and demanded new arms. The arms manufacture at Tulle was still producing weapons for the navy, and between 1766 and 1770, some 18,000 muskets were shipped to Haiti to arm its militia.[153]

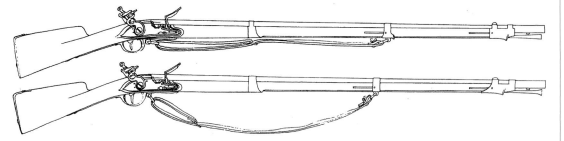

Left:

Metropolitan army infantry muskets 1763 and 1766 models. From the top: Model 1763, Model 1766 (or the "light 1766" also sometimes designated the 1763–1766) at bottom. [Drawing by Michel Pétard. By kind courtesy of the artist] *Author's photo*

Left:

Lock of the French colonial infantry musket, c.1770. This item is surcharged "US", indicating it was transferred by French ordnance into American service. [Courtesy, Craig Nannos]

Left:

Sideplate of the French colonial infantry musket, c.1770. [Courtesy, Craig Nannos]

ERA OF THE AMERICAN WAR OF INDEPENDENCE 1760s–1780s

Above:
Infantry NCO and corporal, c.1766. Both are armed with muskets, bayonets and short sabers. The muskets are not rendered with total exactness, but appear to be the army's infantry Model 1763. The uniform and equipment are in the new "Prussian" style introduced from 1763. These two figures may belong to the Swiss Guards. [Anne S.K. Brown Military Collection, Brown University Library, Providence] *Author's photo*

Right, top:
M.1763 dragoon musket.
[Print after Jandot. From Hick's 1938 *Notes on French Ordnance*] *Author's photo*

Right, center:
Metropolitan army dragoon Model 1770 musket.

Right, bottom:
Metropolitan army infantry Model 1774 infantry musket.
[Both courtesy, Don Troiani]

The main weapons used in the navy and its overseas troops generally were:

Muskets of c.1763–1777 — Metropolitan infantry muskets were usually made at Saint-Etienne with various minute modifications (see above and in illustrations). When the metropolitan army introduced its new infantry musket in 1777, the navy was quite satisfied to use its same technical specifications, but with the provision that, for marine and overseas service, the furnishings would be of brass rather than of iron. This was a minor adjustment that manufacturers easily dealt with, and it was made as the Marine musket Model 1777 and the Marine musket Model 1779 following minor adjustments.

Marine musket Model 1777 — All brass furnishings, made in Maubeuge and St. Etienne.

Marine musket Model 1779 — The same as above except for the swivels for the sling and the grip behind the trigger, which were henceforth made of iron.

In July of 1778, some 3,500 Model 1777 marine muskets were ordered at Maubeuge. Saint-Etienne also received a substantial order, but production went slowly at first — 1778 saw 627 marine muskets; in 1779, 241 marine muskets; in 1780, 5,523 marine muskets; in 1781, 1,342 marine muskets and in 1782, 640 marine muskets.

With some 8,373 from St. Etienne plus 3,500 from Maubeuge at war's end, the need for marine muskets was fulfilled. It must be observed that Charlesville did not make any Model 1777/1779 marine muskets. Surprisingly, neither did Tulle until an order for 6,000 was made in 1791. Thus, examples bearing the Tulle markings date from the French Revolution and not the American War of Independence. The main specifications for the Model 1777/1779 marine musket are: overall length, 59.8 inches; barrel length, 44.7 inches; caliber, 0.69 English inches; weight, 9.5 lbs.; bayonet, Model 1770–1771.

Overseas troops also needed to be rearmed, and in 1779, the navy introduced a musket for its regular colonial troops. The Model 1779 colonial troops musket had the same specifications as the Model 1777/1779 marine musket except for one detail — the barrel band of the musket sling was made of iron.

It is very difficult to ascertain which unit was issued what sort of the new marine or colonial muskets at a given time. It would seem that the three legions of the Volontaires Etrangers de la Marine raised from 1778 had them. According to a January 1780 inspection of the 1st Legion at Martinique, they had new weapons and equipment. This would most likely indicate the Model 1777 marine musket.[154]

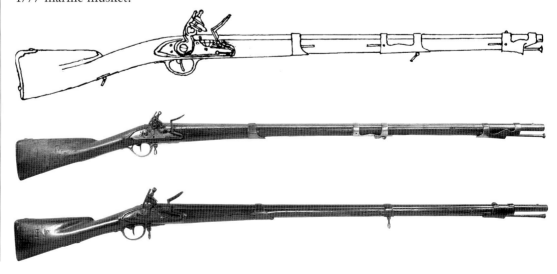

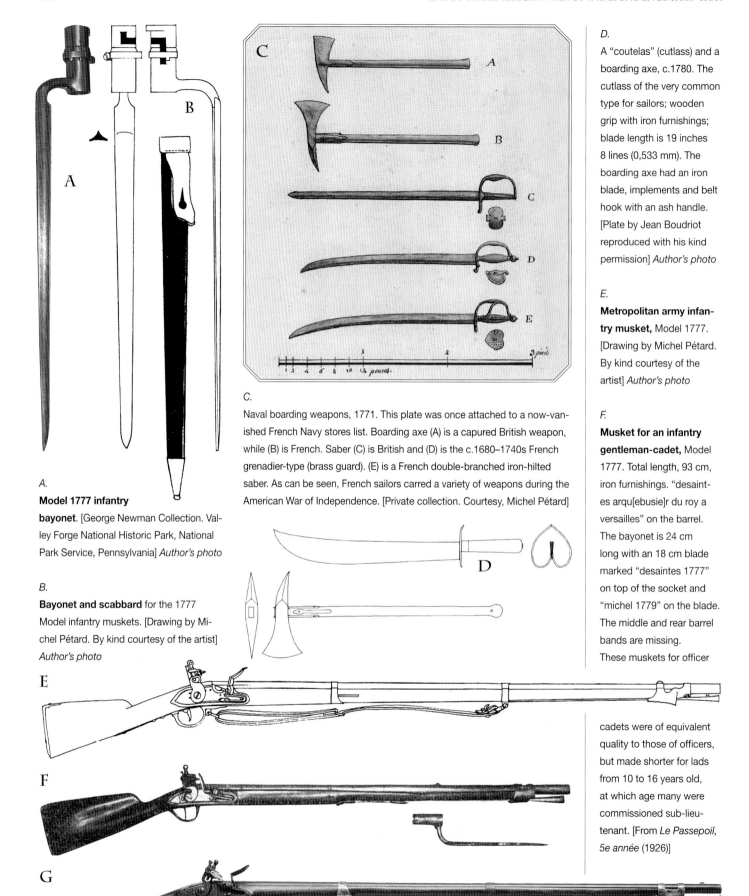

A.
Model 1777 infantry bayonet. [George Newman Collection. Valley Forge National Historic Park, National Park Service, Pennsylvania] *Author's photo*

B.
Bayonet and scabbard for the 1777 Model infantry muskets. [Drawing by Michel Pétard. By kind courtesy of the artist] *Author's photo*

C.
Naval boarding weapons, 1771. This plate was once attached to a now-vanished French Navy stores list. Boarding axe (A) is a capured British weapon, while (B) is French. Saber (C) is British and (D) is the c.1680–1740s French grenadier-type (brass guard). (E) is a French double-branched iron-hilted saber. As can be seen, French sailors carred a variety of weapons during the American War of Independence. [Private collection. Courtesy, Michel Pétard]

D.
A "coutelas" (cutlass) and a boarding axe, c.1780. The cutlass of the very common type for sailors; wooden grip with iron furnishings; blade length is 19 inches 8 lines (0,533 mm). The boarding axe had an iron blade, implements and belt hook with an ash handle. [Plate by Jean Boudriot reproduced with his kind permission] *Author's photo*

E.
Metropolitan army infantry musket, Model 1777. [Drawing by Michel Pétard. By kind courtesy of the artist] *Author's photo*

F.
Musket for an infantry gentleman-cadet, Model 1777. Total length, 93 cm, iron furnishings. "desaintes arqu[ebusie]r du roy a versailles" on the barrel. The bayonet is 24 cm long with an 18 cm blade marked "desaintes 1777" on top of the socket and "michel 1779" on the blade. The middle and rear barrel bands are missing. These muskets for officer cadets were of equivalent quality to those of officers, but made shorter for lads from 10 to 16 years old, at which age many were commissioned sub-lieutenant. [From *Le Passepoil, 5e année* (1926)]

G.
Colonial infantry musket, c.1770. Brass furnishings except for the iron middle band. [Courtesy of Craig Nannos]

ERA OF THE AMERICAN WAR OF INDEPENDENCE 1760s–1780s

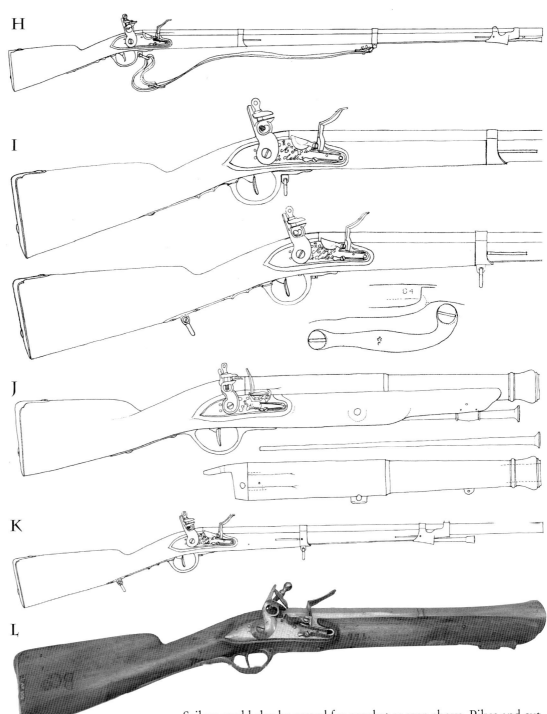

H. Model 1777 marine and Model 1779 colonial infantry musket. The outline of both muskets was similar. The difference was in the details. The 1777 marine musket had all brass furnishings. The 1779 colonial infantry muskets did also, except for the iron band at the middle of the stock for the sling. [Drawing by Michel Pétard. By kind courtesy of the artist] *Author's photo*

I: Lock and butt detail of the Model 1777–1779 marine and colonial muskets (top) and the Model 1777 ship's musket (bottom). Note the sling swivel placement differences. The sideplate is common to all models. [Plate by Jean Boudriot reproduced with his kind permission] *Author's photo*

J. Espingole (swivel gun) used generally on ships and longboats, c.1780. Its barrel was of brass and measured 21 inches (0,569 mm) long and had a 32 mm caliber. Overall length came to 3 ft., 9 ins. (0,996 mm). Its furnishings were of brass. [Plate by Jean Boudriot reproduced with his kind permission] *Author's photo*

K. Ship's mousqueton (carbine or short musket), M1779. This 16-caliber weapon had brass furnishings, a barrel length of 2 ft., 4 ins. (.758 mm); overall length of 3 ft., 7 ins. (1,165 mm). [Plate by Jean Boudriot reproduced with his kind permission] *Author's photo*

L. Shipboard blunderbuss musket, Model 1779. This weapon, called a *tromblon* or *mousqueton à trompette*, armed certain senior sailors when in close-proximity combat. Brass barrel and furnishings, small wooden ramrod. [Musée de la Marine, Paris] *Author's photo*

Sailors could also be armed for combat as seen above. Pikes and cutlasses remained relatively varied after 1760, but firearms underwent a gradual change with the demise of the Buccaneer muskets and also that of the navy pistol, which had remained basically the same since the late 17th century. From 1777, radically different ship's muskets and pistols were introduced. While the calibers remained the same, the weapons themselves were much smaller and less heavy and cumbersome.

Ship's mousqueton (carbine) Model 1779 had brass furnishings and was made only in Tulle. This weapon was nearly identical to the Model 1777 cavalry carbine, but before 1786, its lock was inspired by the 1770 lock that was slightly higher. There were other minor modifications after 1784, and this weapon was made until 1806. The main specifications for the Model 1779 ship's musketoon are — Overall length, 46.1 in.; Barrel length, 29.8 in.; Caliber, 16; Weight, 7 lbs.

Ship's pistol Model 1779, 1st type. The navy found no merits to the army's Model 1777 box pistol and, instead, introduced its own pistol. With the outbreak of war with Great Britain, the navy needed all the new pistols it could get, and they were all made at Tulle. Production of the 1st type started in 1779 and ended in about 1782. A carbine lock was rushed into production to meet the demand, so it was somewhat large for the pistol's proportions. It should be noted that, before the Republican Year 13 (1803), Tulle pistols were stamped with marks only at the top of the rear of the barrel. The main specifications for the Model 1779 ship's pistol Model 1779, 1st type are — Overall length, 13.3 in.; Barrel length, 7.5 in.; Caliber, 16; Weight, 2.4 lbs.

Ship's pistol Model 1779, 2nd type was made from 1783 to 1787 and generally resembled its predecessor, except that its lock was smaller and suited to this pistol's proportions. It also made the pistol slightly lighter. The main specifications for the ship's pistol Model 1779, 2nd type are — Overall length, 13.3 in.; Barrel length, 7.5 in; Caliber, 16; Weight, 2.2 lbs.

We should note that some gunsmiths in Tulle also made pistols and muskets for naval officers. These were not official weapons, but were very handy for officers engaged in battles. The pistols generally followed the navy's Model 1777, but were more ornate with some engraving, the butt end having an animal's head and the furnishings being generally of iron rather than brass.

Overseas colonial troops officers were issued firearms, except for senior field officers who only had swords. A January 1783 issue to 39 officers of the Troupes Nationales de Cayenne battalion specified the following:[155] three regulation swords with their shoulder belts for senior officers, 36 regulation swords with their shoulder belts for other officers, 36 regulation muskets with bayonets. Edged weapons for marine and overseas troops usually conformed to the army's models described on page 186.

Below, left:

Model 1779 Navy pistol, 1st type.

Below, right:

Model 1779 Navy pistol, 2nd type. [Both plates by Jean Boudriot reproduced with his kind permission]

Author's photo

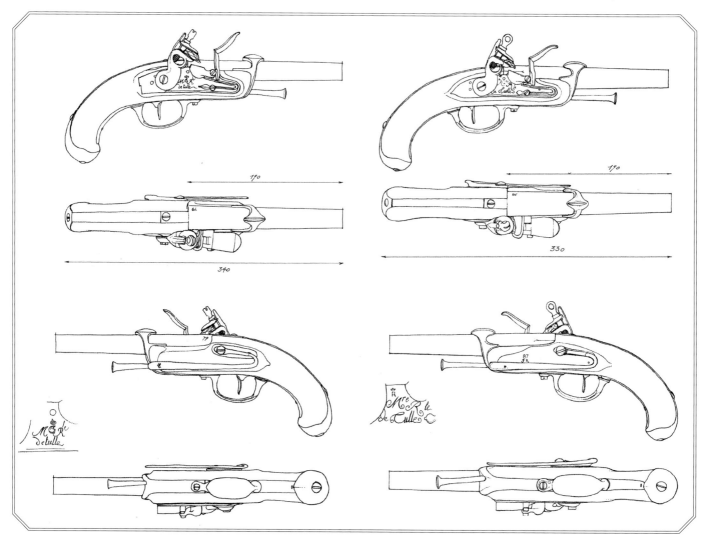

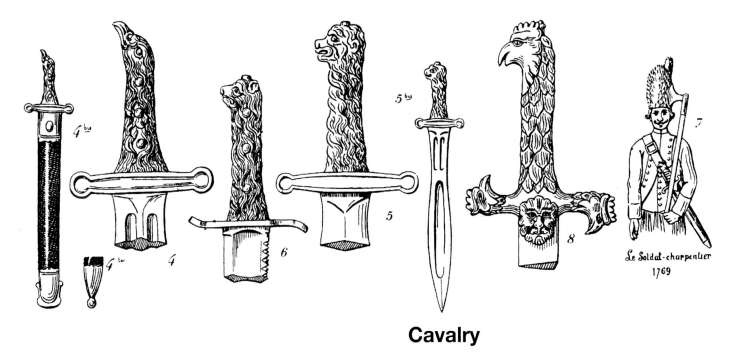

Above:
Royal-Artillerie and infantry sapper's hangers, 1760s–1780s, inspired by the Roman and hunting swords of Antiquity with grips bearing animal heads:
4, 4b and 4c – Gunner's brass-hilted saber of Royal-Artillerie, c.1770
5 and 5b – Marine artillery's brass-hilted saber, c.1770
6 – Carpenter-soldier's (later called sapper) brass-hilted saber, c.1769
7 – Blade etching of a carpenter-soldier, c.1769; 8: Sapper's brass-hilted saber, c.1784.
[Detail from a plate by Maurice Bottet]
Author's photo

Right:
Sergeant's sword of the Dauphin Dragoon Regiment, 1779–1786. Gilt Musketeer style guard.
[Courtesy of Czerny's International Auction House, Sarzana, Italy]

Cavalry

The notion of having regular cavalry companies amongst the post-1763 troops under the Ministry of the Navy may seem strange, but there are two instances for overseas units. Three companies of dragoons attached to the Legion de Saint-Domingue for service in Haiti existed from November 1769 to their 1773 amalgamation into the new colonial infantry regiments. In 1770–1771, they were issued with "300 sabers including 15 for NCOs" and "150 pairs of pistols whose bronzed [browned] barrel must be eight inches and six line long" and made at Saint-Etienne. These weapons were most likely the same as for metropolitan dragoon regiments.[156]

The detachments of Condé and Belzunce dragoons in Haiti from 1777 to 1783 (and the siege of Savannah in 1779) had the same armament and equipment as in France. From 1767, dragoon trooper's swords had an iron hilt that looked somewhat crude, but very solid with good protection for the hand. In 1779, officers adopted a more genteel-looking gilt hilt that featured a fleur-de-lis on the lower part of the side branch. There are no particular provisions for dragoon NCOs in the regulations, but a 1779–1783 naïve portrait of a Dauphin Dragoon Regiment's sergeant shows him holding a gilded Musketeer sword guard that may have been a traditional distinction associated with that rank.[157]

An especially interesting item was the brass helmet that had been worn by French dragoons since 1763. But for a few exceptions, such protective armor for troopers had not been seen since the mid-17th century, and these helmets constituted a timid comeback of armor onto the battlefield. The style of the helmets was in a vaguely neoclassical fashion inspired by the discoveries of Greek and Roman vestiges during the 18th century. Some such helmets were sent to the American army (see Chapter 10).

The hussar companies of the Volontaires Etrangers de la Marine that were raised starting in 1778, were to be uniformed, armed and equipped like other hussar units. Their saber was described as "in the Hungarian style, with a brass hilt, the blade wide and curved" with a leather knot and a carbine. As noted above, its 2nd Legion was reorganized as Lauzun's Legion in May of 1780, and 600 of its men, including 300 hussars, were sent to the United States at part of Gen. Rochambeau's army. At that time, half of the hussars were further armed with lances, quite an unusual

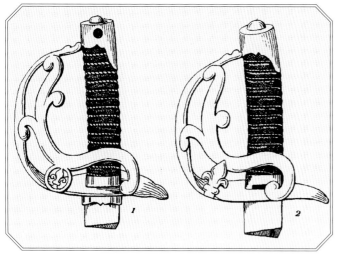

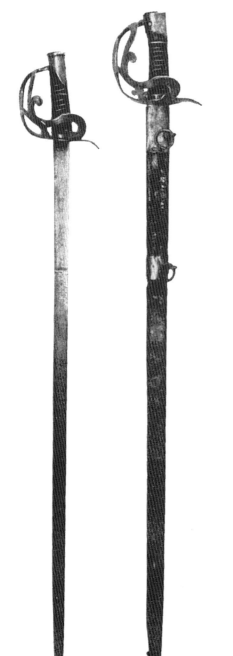
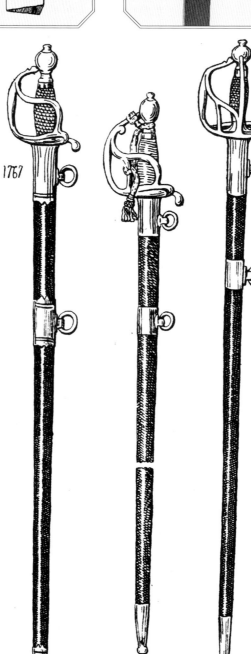

Above, left:

Cavalry and dragoon's troopers saber hilts, 1779–1783. These hilts were of polished iron. [Detail from a plate by Maurice Bottet] *Author's photo*

Above, right:

Cavalry and dragoon saber hilts, 1779. Left: officer. Right: private trooper. [From *Le Passepoil*, 28e année (1947)]

Far left:

Cavalry and dragoon sabers, 1779. Officer's on left. Private trooper's on the right. The blade was 90cm long. [From *Le Passepoil*, 28e année (1947)]

Near left:

Cavalry *fortes épées* (strong swords) or sabers, c.1767–1779. The first sword at left is the regulation type with its scabbard. The swords at the center and right have multi-branched hilts that are variants of the Model 1767 seen in some units, in this case the Royal-Allemand and Royal-Champagne cavalry regiments. [Plate after Bottet]

Right:
Trooper of the Belzunce Dragoon Regiment, c.1776–1779. A company from this regiment served in Haiti from 1777 to 1783. They were armed with the dragoon saber, pistols and the dragoon musket shown in this print, hooked to the shoulder belt. By the 1776 regulations, dragoons wore dark green coats upon which Belzunce had white lapels and cuffs, red collar and white metal buttons. Artois had buff lapels and cuffs, white collar and white metal buttons. From 1779, Belzunce had *aurore* (an orange-red shade) cuffs and lapels and Condé buff lapels and dark green cuffs, both having a dark green collar and white metal buttons. [Anne S.K. Brown Military Collection, Brown University Library, Providence] *Author's photo*

From left to right:
Model 1767 infantry short saber "Briquet" or hanger for grenadiers and NCOs. Its hilt was of cast and polished brass. [Fort Ticonderoga Museum. Author's photo]

Corps Royal de la Marine brass "Briquet" saber hilt, 1772–1774. This weapon armed NCOs, gunners and grenadiers of the marine regiments.

Corps Royal de la Marine brass "Briquet" saber hilt, 1772-1774. This saber very likely armed many NCOs of the 100 company "Corps Royal d'infanterie de la Marine of 1774–1782. [Both swords from Musée de la Marine, Paris. Courtesy of Rama/Wikimedia]

weapon for cavalry at that time. Their already fine and unusual appearance was noted. Von Closen mentioned that "Lauzun's Legion and its lancers, especially, made an extremely favorable impression" at a review near Newport, Rhode Island, in July of 1781. By September 18, 1781, they were joined by the hussars of the 1st Legion that were brought up from the West Indies and participated at the siege of Yorktown. Their weapons were well handled in a fight with the British Legion's cavalry, its Col. Banastre Tarleton losing a few fingers to a French hussar's saber before being runoff with his troopers at Gloucester Point on October 3rd.[158]

Infantry Edged Weapons

The armament of NCOs went through a short and confusing period following a regulation of March 20, 1764, that brought back the halberd for sergeants. These new halberds, along with a new sergeant's sword, were to be of a new model that would be later communicated. However, no new model appeared and instead came the order of January 1, 1766, that definitely confirmed the 1758 orders in that all sergeants and corporals were to be armed with muskets and equipped with cartridge boxes. This specified that they would be armed with sabers. Drum-Majors, at last in the colonial legion of Saint-Domingue (Haiti) and Ile de France (Mauritius), were armed with a sword having a "silver grip and a knuckle bow of silvered brass with a blue silk and silver sword knot." They also were issued with a "cane with a silver pommel engraved with the king's [coat of] arms."[159]

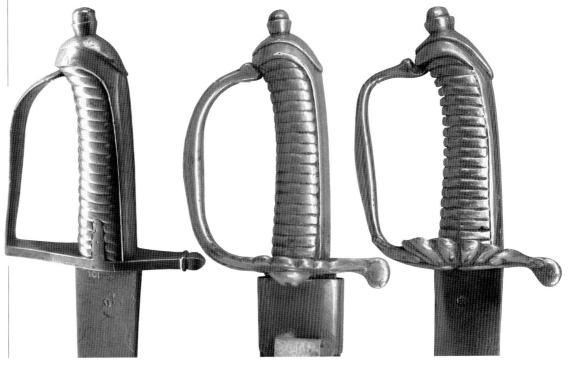

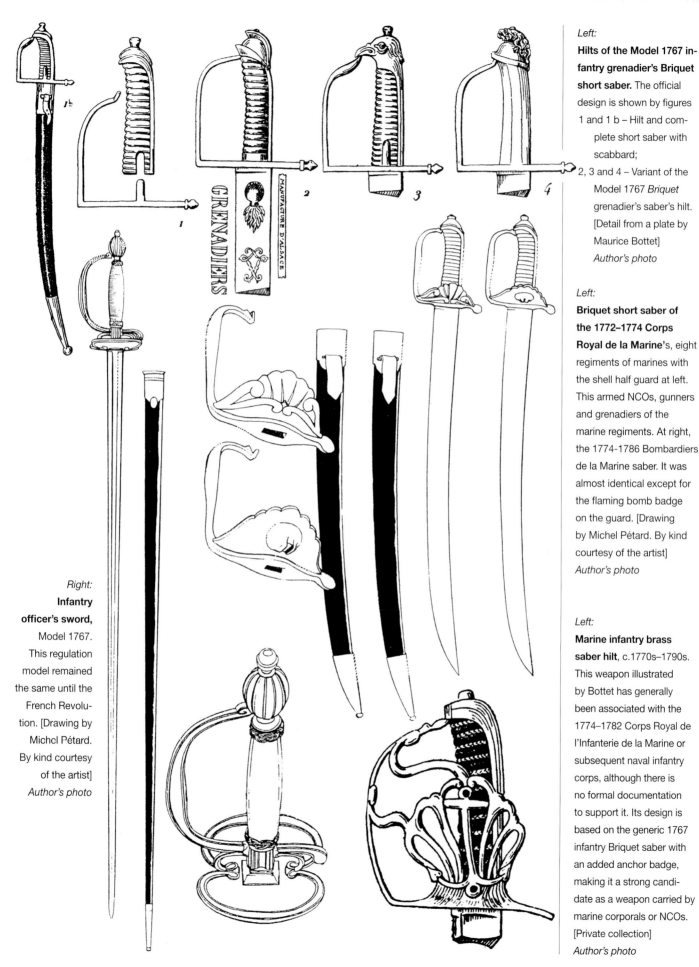

Left:
Hilts of the Model 1767 infantry grenadier's Briquet short saber. The official design is shown by figures 1 and 1 b – Hilt and complete short saber with scabbard; 2, 3 and 4 – Variant of the Model 1767 *Briquet* grenadier's saber's hilt. [Detail from a plate by Maurice Bottet] *Author's photo*

Right:
Infantry officer's sword, Model 1767. This regulation model remained the same until the French Revolution. [Drawing by Michel Pétard. By kind courtesy of the artist] *Author's photo*

Left:
Briquet short saber of the 1772–1774 Corps Royal de la Marine's, eight regiments of marines with the shell half guard at left. This armed NCOs, gunners and grenadiers of the marine regiments. At right, the 1774-1786 Bombardiers de la Marine saber. It was almost identical except for the flaming bomb badge on the guard. [Drawing by Michel Pétard. By kind courtesy of the artist] *Author's photo*

Left:
Marine infantry brass saber hilt, c.1770s–1790s. This weapon illustrated by Bottet has generally been associated with the 1774–1782 Corps Royal de l'Infanterie de la Marine or subsequent naval infantry corps, although there is no formal documentation to support it. Its design is based on the generic 1767 infantry Briquet saber with an added anchor badge, making it a strong candidate as a weapon carried by marine corporals or NCOs. [Private collection] *Author's photo*

ERA OF THE AMERICAN WAR OF INDEPENDENCE 1760s–1780s

From 1767, a standard infantry saber — the *sabre-briquet* — for grenadiers, chasseurs, NCOs and corporals was introduced in all the French land forces. It had a D-shaped brass guard that included the ribbed grip. It was widely issued to both the metropolitan and the colonial infantry regiments and was in use for decades to come. There were some exceptions, as there is evidence that some units appear to have used their own models instead. As an example, a period print of "bravery rewarded" at the capture of Grenada on July 4, 1779, shows a grenadier wearing a distinct saber that features three branches and a shell (see illustration below). The Navy's gunners and bombardiers also had slightly different models starting in 1772. Marine and overseas infantry corporals and NCO's sabers were also based on the generic 1767 infantry briquet saber and might also have a more elaborate guard with an added anchor badge.

The swords of infantry officers could be quite varied in details. Field and fusilier company officers retained the basic Musketeer style while grenadier officers had sabers. The regulation of April 25, 1767, tried to impose a more uniform style of sword for all infantry officers. It called for a Musketeer-style sword with a gilt hilt, except for the grip, which was silver and with a long blade of 26 inches (703 mm). The staff officer's sword had an even longer blade at 28 to 29 inches (760 to 780 mm). Grenadier officers were supposed to exchange their sabers for this new sword, but there is no evidence they ever did. Fusilier officers that already had their silver-hilted swords

Below:
Hainaut Regiment Grenadier Sergeant Horadou's ornate saber guard is shown in this detail of a contemporary print of the July 3, 1779, capture of Grenada by the French. During the assault, Lieutenant de Vence was set upon by several British gunners who were then beaten back by Horadou. Count d'Estaing saw the incident and promoted Horadou on the spot to the rank of officer. [Courtesy, Anne S.K. Brown Military Collection, Brown University Library, Providence]

Right:
Grenadier of the Soissonnais Regiment, c.1780. He is armed with the standard musket with its bayonet and, as a grenadier, with a Model 1767 saber that was carried by its own shoulder belt. Soissonnais served in the United States from 1780 to late 1782. [Plate after Hoffman. Anne S.K. Brown Military Collection, Brown University Library, Providence] *Author's photo*

were also adamant, as previously, that they would wear them to the death. To calm down irate officers, a regulation of March 1, 1768, specified that officers could have the sword of their choice that they "ordinarily wore" on duty laid over their coffins. As years went by, new officers were required to have the Model 1767 sword. Portraits seem to show that they sometimes opted for a gilt grip instead of the regulation silver.

Equipment

The overseas units had the same type of equipment as metropolitan troops. This included the regimentally marked brass plates on the cartridge box flap. From 1779, the brass plates were no longer issued for the boxes, but they continued to be seen until old accouterments were replaced. This could take several years for troops stationed overseas.[160]

After the end of the Seven Years War, the militias in the various islands were gradually re-raised and, from 1768, were subjected to a series of royal regulations aimed at streamlining their organization. Militiamen in Haiti were each required to have when mustered, for infantry, a military musket with its bayonet, and for dragoons and cavalry, a saber, a pair of pistols, a musket with its bayonet and a horse with its saddlery. Martinique had similar regulations. By 1769, the militia's strength stood as follows:[161]

Saint-Domingue (Haiti) • 211 dragoon companies; 608 infantry and artillery companies; 3 Grenadier à cheval cavalry companies; 25 hussar companies; 6 Carabiniers cavalry companies; 5 Gendarmes companies; 3 heavy cavalry companies — total of 857 companies totaling 14,200 men of which 4,940 were free mulattos or blacks.

Martinique • 7 dragoon companies; 48 white infantry companies; 13 free mulatto and black companies; 1 Gendarmes company; 8 artillery companies; 1 German fusilier company — total of 73 companies totaling 3,900 men.

St. Lucia • 2 dragoon companies; 10 white infantry companies; 5 free mulatto and black companies — total: 17 companies totaling 850 men.

Guadeloupe • 11 dragoon companies; 35 white infantry companies; 13 free mulatto and black companies; 12 artillery companies; 1 German fusilier company — total: 72 companies totaling 3,600 men.

Marie Galante and dependencies • 1 dragoon company; 6 white infantry companies; 1 artillery company; 2 companies at the Saints; 1 company at Désirade — total: 11 companies totaling 550 men.

Cayenne • No reports, but about 1,500 men.

Grand total of militiamen in the West Indies and Guyana: 24,600.

To arm all of these militia formations, some 22,000 muskets "of the same caliber as dragoon," 454 hussar carbines, 853 cavalry carbines and 4,881 pairs of pistols were ordered on May 28, 1769, to be sent to the West Indies. In all, some 33,000 firearms (including 9,762 pistols) were ordered. By 1770, some 7,500 infantry muskets had been received at Martinique and Guadeloupe. Thus, this massive rearmament program was well under way and was most likely completed by the time the American Revolution broke out. Government storehouses in the post-1763 French West Indies could contain other types of arms apart from weapons made in France. In 1771, some 545 British muskets were sent to Martinique along with 723 others "of various calibers" and 20 carbines needing repairs so as to have a surplus of weapons available. This was seen as being "very useful in case of war" to arm ships and estates, "and even corsairs" who might need them. Guadeloupe also received 401 muskets of irregular calibers for the same purposes. On the whole, it was felt that 7,666 warlike firearms of various sorts should be stored in Martinique and 3,277 in Guadeloupe. To encourage good shooting, starting in 1768 a militiaman that proved proficient

Above:

Infantry grenadier, 1780s. This rear view shows the Model 1767 saber with its red saber knot wrapped around the guard and the pommel. Note also the small strap that ties to a waist button to keep the cartridge box from flapping. [Detail from a painting in the Musée d'Alsace, Stratsbourg. Courtesy, Francis Back]

Below:
Field officer of the La Reine Infantry Regiment, c.1770. This portrait shows the officer on duty wearing the regulation gilt gorget with its silver coat-of-arms badge and armed with the gilded sword hilt with its regimental silver sword knot. This was the regulation appearance that was common to all infantry field officers. La Reine's uniform from 1767 was white with red collar, cuffs and lapels, silver buttons and epaulets for officers. [Private collection]

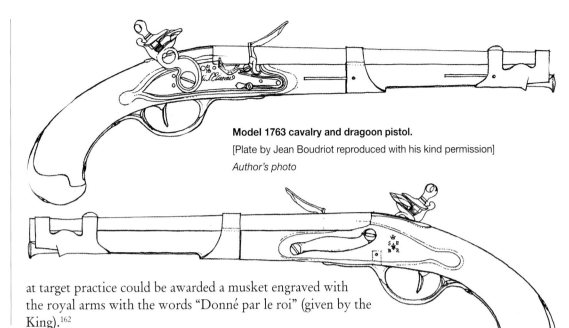

Model 1763 cavalry and dragoon pistol.
[Plate by Jean Boudriot reproduced with his kind permission]
Author's photo

Right:
Officer's gorget, c.1770–1790. Gilt with silver royal coat-of-arms badge. Yellow and gold silk cord. This was the 1767 regulation gorget. The narrow crescent was the fashion for French gorgets at the time of the American War of Independence. [Private collection]

at target practice could be awarded a musket engraved with the royal arms with the words "Donné par le roi" (given by the King).[162]

The second half of the 18th century was a period of unprecedented wealth in the French West Indies. Some even reckoned that one fifth of Europe's overseas trade passed through the ports of Haiti, especially Le Cap, which was then arguably one of the world's most prosperous towns. This spawned militia units that were armed, equipped and uniformed with previously unseen luxury. Their service mainly consisted of being reviewed by the governor four times a year, which became occasions for celebrations and competition as to which units had the finest arms and uniforms. By the 1770s, the dress of some corps was "as brilliant as those of (the guard units) of the King's Household." Amongst the many lavishly uniformed units in Le Cap and Martinique were the mounted *Gendarmes* in the same dress and arms as those of the royal guard at Versailles, those in Martinique being armed with a saber, two pistols and a lightweight carbine. The 1778 company of *Mousquetaires* in Guadeloupe was armed with a saber, a pistol and a dragoon musket.[163]

Advertisements in *Affiches Américaines*, a periodical published at Le Cap in Haiti, gives an idea of the type of arms owned by the inhabitants, all of whom were militiamen. These advertisements show that the descendants of the buccaneers had become rich planters or merchants and their arms and equipment were possibly amongst the finest that could be found anywhere in the Americas. The Chevalier de Puilboreau lost a "pistol garnished with silver, with a ramrod" near Le Cap (December 3, 1774). Sold at the Duquesne plantation were muskets, pistols and swords "garnished with silver" (September 21, 1779). One Dupin living near Limonade in Haiti reported having a quality dragoon saddle lined with crimson velvet with its green saddle cloth stitched with white lace and pistol holsters. This must have been for a militia dragoon company (March 2, 1780). The Grandjean household at Grande-Rivière had a silver-hilt-

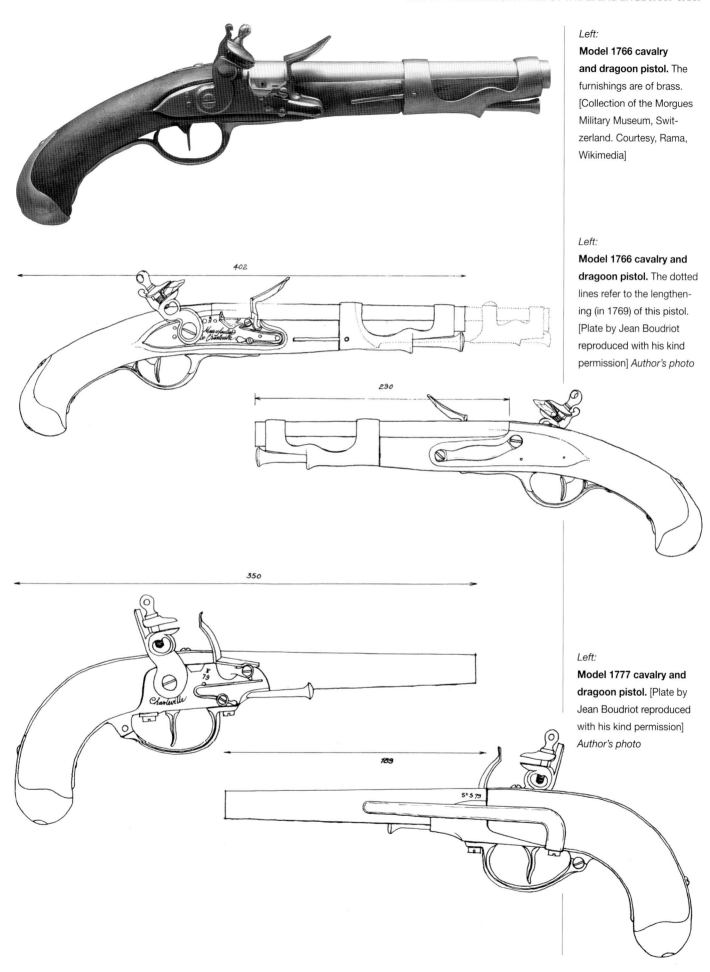

Left:
Model 1766 cavalry and dragoon pistol. The furnishings are of brass. [Collection of the Morgues Military Museum, Switzerland. Courtesy, Rama, Wikimedia]

Left:
Model 1766 cavalry and dragoon pistol. The dotted lines refer to the lengthening (in 1769) of this pistol. [Plate by Jean Boudriot reproduced with his kind permission] *Author's photo*

Left:
Model 1777 cavalry and dragoon pistol. [Plate by Jean Boudriot reproduced with his kind permission] *Author's photo*

ed sword, a blue silk sword belt and carbine belts with silver buckles and hooks; obviously for a militia cavalry unit (March 18, 1780). Yet another individual lost near Montrouis a "hunting knife with an ivory grip showing a wolf's head, whose jaw is slightly broken, the scabbard quite worn as well as its belt of green silk mixed with gold" (April 25, 1780).

During the American War of Independence, a number of specialized and volunteer units were formed. There were two types of corps. New volunteer companies such as Guadeloupe's mounted Mousquetaires would muster for active service for the length of time of a campaign, such as participating in an attack on a British island. For instance, Martinique's *Cadets de Saint-Pierre* took part in the 1778 capture of Dominica. Some units were raised specifically for

full-time duty amongst local inhabitants, who preferably volunteered, but who could also be drafted.

The first such corps, raised in Martinique in July of 1778, was the company-strong *Volontaires de Bouillé* named after Governor General the Marquis de Bouillé and armed with musket and bayonet, saber and a belly cartridge box held by a waist belt. In Haiti, the *Grenadiers-Volontaire de Saint-Domingue* were organized in March of 1779 amongst white creole volunteers with the *Chasseurs-Volontaires de Saint-Domingue* whose enlisted men were mulattos and Africans led by European officers. Both gained fame at the siege of Savannah (U.S.A.) in September of 1779. Detachments of the Chasseurs-Volontaires de Saint-Domingue also served with distinction as marines on board French navy warships in several West Indian naval battles and part of the unit garrisoned at Grenada until 1783. There was also the *Chasseurs-Royaux de Saint-Domingue*, recruited

Far right:
Lieutenant of the Angoumois Infantry Regiment, c.1767–1770. From 1763, fusilier company officers such as the one shown wore white leather waist belts with belt plates and Musketeer-hilted swords. This lieutenant, off duty since he dos not wear his gorget, sports a Nivernois-style hat with an elaborate powdered hair arrangement. [Print after Jacques Onfroy de Bréville from a period portrait. Private collection] *Author's photo*

Right:
Private of the Chasseurs-Volontaires de Saint-Domingue, 1779–1783. This battalion, recruited amongst free Africans in Haiti, served with distinction at Savannah and in several naval battles, as well as providing part of the garrison of Grenada. It was armed like metropolitan infantry chasseurs, including the short saber. The musket could be of several types produced during the 1770s for the navy or the army. Its uniform was dark blue, including lapels that were probably edged with yellow piping, yellow collar, green cuffs, hunting horn badges on the turnbacks and epaulets, the hat having a white plume tipped yellow. [Watercolor by Michel Pétard. Anne S.K. Brown Military Collection, Brown University Library, Providence] *Author's photo*

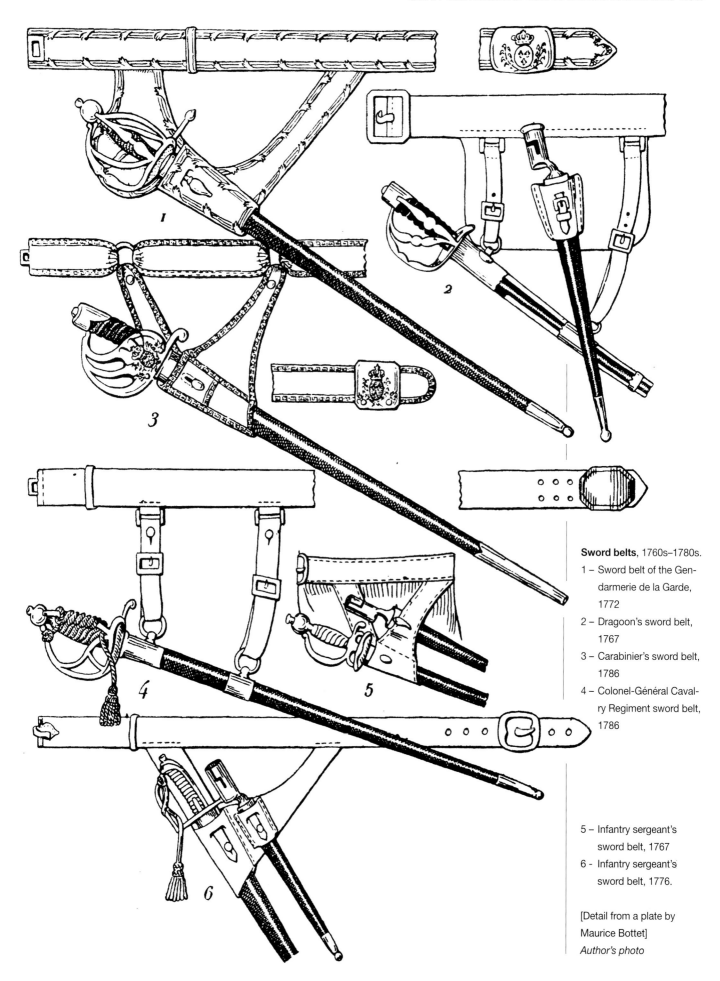

Sword belts, 1760s–1780s.
1 – Sword belt of the Gendarmerie de la Garde, 1772
2 – Dragoon's sword belt, 1767
3 – Carabinier's sword belt, 1786
4 – Colonel-Général Cavalry Regiment sword belt, 1786
5 – Infantry sergeant's sword belt, 1767
6 – Infantry sergeant's sword belt, 1776.

[Detail from a plate by Maurice Bottet]
Author's photo

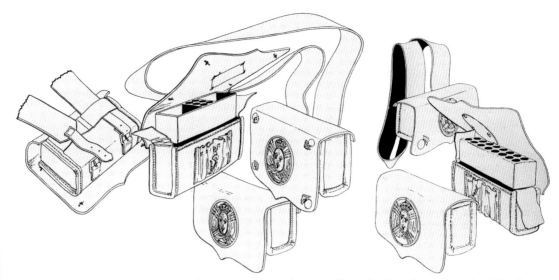

Right:
Infantry cartridge boxes, Model 1767. The boxes were of blackened leather with white belts. Until 1779, they were issued with brass badges on the flap, plain thereafter. The one with small grenade badges at the flap's corners is for grenadiers. The wooden box for sergeants and enlisted men had three compartments, the central one holding six cartridges in holes, the two others containing a dozen each. At right is the smaller model for officers that held 16 rounds. The flap for grenadier officers had two small grenades. [Drawing by Michel Pétard. By kind courtesy of the artist] *Author's photo*

amongst Haiti's mulattos and Africans in 1780, who contributed a detachment to the 1781 Spanish-led siege of Pensacola. Similar types of units called *Volontaires Libres* were raised starting in late 1782 at Martinique and other French smaller islands.

The 1779 *Grenadiers-Volontaires* and Chasseurs-Volontaires de Saint-Domingue had "weapons furnished from the king's magazine" in Haiti. This consisted of a musket with its bayonet and a Briquet saber. So did the 1780 Chasseurs-Royaux de Saint-Domingue except that, for enlisted men, the saber was replaced by a "strong machete, in the country's style."[164]

Exactly what type of weapons these various units carried will probably never be known in detail. The wealthy members of the more "posh" units, such as mounted Gendarmes and Mousquetaires, may well have had privately purchased arms emulating those of the royal guard. The volunteer units serving as regulars, those serving part-time and the militiamen could have had quite a variety of weapons. We have seen that some 33,000 firearms were ordered in 1769, and all were probably delivered by the mid-1770s. These were in addition to older serviceable arms already in store, as well as others that were sent from the mid-1770s. Needless to say, probably every model of weapon described in this chapter may well have armed volunteer and militia corps at the time of the American War of Independence.

Below, far right:
Waist belt to carry the Model 1767 saber for NCOs and grenadiers and the fusilier's bayonet. White leather with brass metal parts. Note the small leather cap to cover the top of the bayonet. [Drawing by Michel Pétard. By kind courtesy of the artist] *Author's photo*

Right:
Infantry fusilier's accoutrements, 1779. From 1779, privates and corporals had the bayonet scabbard attached to the cartridge box belt. Drummers had a belt with a single frog for the short saber. Grenadiers and chasseurs had an additional frog for the bayonet. [Drawing by Michel Pétard. By kind courtesy of the artist] *Author's photo*

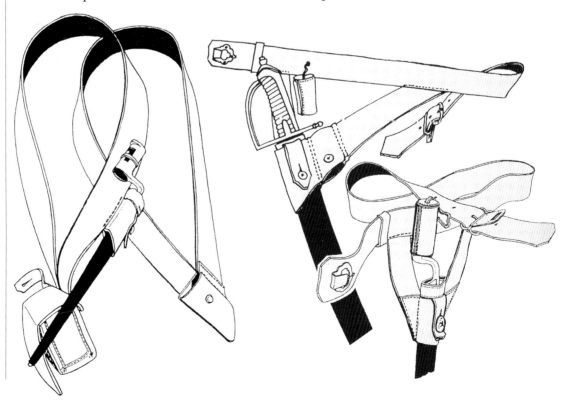

CHAPTER 10

Weapons Furnished to Allied Powers

Arms to Spanish America

French weapons were used by individuals in the Spanish, Dutch and British colonies beginning in the 16th century, either as the result of private purchases or as booty. The accession in 1700 of Louis XIV's grandson, Philippe Duke of Anjou, as King Felipe V of Spain "and the Indies," made France its ally at a time when the Spanish armies and their armament were moribund, if they existed at all, especially in "the Indies," as its overseas territories were termed. With war about to be declared over this Spanish royal succession, the French government became involved in furnishing weapons and other military supplies to the Spanish forces of Felipe V.

In February of 1701, arrangements were made to have shipped "without delay" French arms and ammunition for the Spanish colonies in America. Louis XIV felt that they would be "employed most usefully" at Cartagena de Indias (Columbia), Portobello (Panama), Vera Cruz (Mexico) and Havana (Cuba). The arms shipment consisted of: 50 cannons of 36 and 24 lbs. caliber; 8 mortars; 2,000 flint or matchlock muskets and carbines; 2,000 swords or sabers.

With this came ammunition and also a few artillery officers and Bombardiers de la Marine to serve the artillery and train gunners in case there were not enough qualified Spanish artillerymen. Supplies were again sent the following year with several more French officers to serve in the main Spanish bases as advisors. The officers and bombardiers came back to France in 1703.[165]

In February of 1707, arrangements were made in Rochefort to ship 500 flintlock muskets to Havana, Cuba, in answer to a request from the King of Spain. Two months later, the warship *Atlas* was preparing to sail for Buenos Aires laden with arms and ammunition, as well as a detachment of a sergeant and 20 men from Rochefort. The following year, a report from Santiago de Cuba mentioned that its garrison had only 40 flintlock muskets, so there were still important needs. Meanwhile, King Felipe V made enquiries as to having more flintlock muskets made in France for the Spanish garrisons in America. By 1709, it was Cartagena de Indias (in present-day Columbia) that needed weapons, and in August, the King of Spain retained the Tulle arsenal to furnish ordinary and grenadier muskets as well as pistols before the end of the year. However, payment problems delayed delivery until January of 1710 when Spanish doubloons came into the coffers of Tulle.[166]

Arms to the United States

The outbreak of the American Revolution in 1775 drew much interest in France. That Britain's American colonies were in open revolt against their government signaled France that the time to avenge the humiliations of the Seven Years War might be approaching. For the Americans, who then had no weapons industry, it was vital to obtain arms shipments from Europe, and the obvious nation that had a large production capacity was France. The American Congress sent Silas Deane as an envoy to France, where he arrived in early June of 1776 hoping to obtain military arms as well as monetary credit.

On 1August 16, 1776, Silas Deane wrote from Paris that he "had learned that in the late reform of the French Army, they had shifted their arms for those of a lighter kind, the heavy ones, most of which were the same as new, to the amount of seventy or eighty thousand, lay useless in magazines, with other military stores, in some such proportion, I apprehended it no way impossible to come at a supply from hence, through the agency of some merchant, without the Ministry being concerned in the matter. In such case the merchant would be accountable to the Ministry, and the Colonies to the merchant, by which means a greater time of payment might be given, and more allowance in case of our being disappointed." At that time, the firm of Roderique Hortalez & Co. was promising to ship French arms, ammunition and other military supplies to the Americans "notwithstanding the open opposition which the King of France, his ministers, and the agents of administration show, and ought to show, to everything that carries the least appearance of violating foreign treaties and the internal ordinances of the kingdom." This royal government's "open opposition" to any gun-running was, of course, only for official diplomatic purposes. Senior ministers, with the blessing of King Louis XVI, had in fact organized a massive covert operation to provide military supplies to the Americans.

Right:
Playright and covert diplomat Pierre Caron de Beaumarchais, c.1777. He secretly managed the French government's gun-running operations between 1776 and 1778. [Print after portrait. Private collection] *Author's photo*

Right:
Beaumarchais' "hotel" in Paris, c.1780s. It was a large building, from which much business was conducted by the famous playright and secret arms smuggler. It was situated close to the old castle of "La Bastille" (at right), which had become a prison for state prisoners. [Painting by J.B. Génillion. Musée Carnavalet, Paris] *Author's photo*

This firm of Hortales & Co. was fictitious, as was its merchant owner. Lodged in the fine Hotel de Hollande, it was the creation of the playwright and covert diplomat Pierre Caron de Beaumarchais, who had been recommended to Deane by Count Vergennes, the Minister of Foreign Affairs at the French court. Hortales & Co. was secretly supported by the French government to supply the Americans with weapons. On June 10, 1776, a million French pounds had secretly been transferred by Vergennes to Beaumarchais to fund the purchases. The average price for a musket was 25 French pounds (or livres), which came to five U.S. dollars, a great saving since American-made muskets cost an average of $12.30 each. These secret transactions appear to have been partly or wholly made at Beaumarchais' mansion near the present Place de la Bastille in Paris. In April of 1777, Benjamin Franklin, the American ambassador at the French court in Versailles, reported that 80,000 muskets had been purchased for 220,000 pounds that "were the King's arms and second-hand, but so many of them are unused and exceptionally good that we esteem it a great bargain if only half of them should arrive."[167]

Left:

Lock of a French infantry Model 1763 musket supplied to the United States. It was made at the St. Etienne royal arsenal. The rear of the lockplate has the letters "US", indicating that it was in American military service. [Springfield Armory Museum, National Park Service, Springfield, Massachusetts] *Author's photo*

Left:

View of the lower barrel breech of a French infantry Model 1763 musket supplied to the United States. Note the "M1763" marking. [Springfield Armory Museum, National Park Service, Springfield, Massachusetts] *Author's photo*

In December of 1776, Deane was hoping for "thirty thousand fusils (muskets), two hundred pieces of brass cannon, thirty mortars, four thousand tents, and clothing for thirty thousand men" from French officials who were somewhat unsure about supplying arms to the Americans. He confided to John Jay that "Mr. Beaumarchais has been my minister in effect, as this court is extremely cautious." The French playwright had indeed been very active. On February 28, 1777, Beaumarchais informed Congress that he had "the honor to fit out for the service of Congress, by the way of Hispaniola, the ship *Amelia*, loaded with field and ordnance pieces, powder and leaden pigs. As the season is too far advanced that the ship might go straightway to your ports, I have charged M. Carabane, my correspondent at Cape François (Haiti), to reverse the whole cargo on Bermudian or even on American ships, if he finds any at her arrival in that port, and to transmit to you as soon as possible. This is the fourth ship I have addressed to you since December last, the other three have steered their course towards your eastern ports. The first is the *Amphitrite* of 480 tons, Captain Sautrel, loaded with cannons, muskets, tents, entrenching tools, tin, powder, clothing, etc. Left Havre de Grace on the 14th of December, 1776. The second is the *Seine*, from the same port, Captain Morin, of 350 tons, loaded with muskets, tents, mortars, powder, tin, cannons, musket balls, etc. The third is the *Mercure*, of 317 tons, Captain Herand, from Nantes, loaded with one hundred thousands of powder, 12,000 muskets, the remainder in cloth, linen, caps, shoes, stockings, blankets, and other necessary articles for the clothing of the troops." In all, some 30,000 muskets, 200 pieces of artillery, gunpowder, clothing

Above and right:
Model 1763/66 French infantry musket supplied to the United States with a Model 1766 flat lock marked "Charleville". The lock may have been added or replaced before it was shipped from France. [Courtesy of National Historic Sites, Parks Canada]

Right, below:
American Continental infantrymen, c.1780. They are armed with French muskets, as most Americans fighting the British army in the United States carried firearms supplied from France. [Painting by H.C. McBarron. Anne S.K. Brown Military Collection, Brown University Library, Providence] *Author's photo*

Far right, top:
Dragoon officer's helmet, c.1780. From 1763, protective armor made a comeback in the form of the dragoon's brass helmet. Hundreds were sent to the American army. Brass with a black mane and an imitation leopard skin fur turban. [Musée Lambinet, Versailles] *Author's photo*

Far right, bottom:
Colonel Benjamin Talmadge, 2nd Continental Light Dragoon, 1780s and General Washington's chief intelligence officer. He wears a French dragoon helmet. [Print published in his 1858 memoirs]
Author's photo

and camp equipage for 25,000 men. The *Seine* was intercepted by a British ship off Martinique, but the *Amphitrite* arrived at Portsmouth, New Hampshire, and the *Mercure* at Philadelphia in March of 1777 bringing 21,000 muskets and 100,000 pounds of powder. It was the first time in American history that such a large quantity of military supplies arrived from Europe.[168]

The types of arms sent to the U.S. were varied. As alluded to above, some were obviously the "heavy" Model 1763 infantry musket that had been stored when the "light" 1763 was introduced in 1766. Others could be of various later models, more or less used, but some were new. All were to be in working order, so that some were repaired and might have parts from different models. Those delivered at Nantes came from a maker named La Tuilerie, a fictitious name that veiled the real source of these muskets, which were the royal arms manufactures who shipped muskets specifically for the Americans at the behest of Beaumarchais. More of the arms were delivered in two other ships later in 1777.

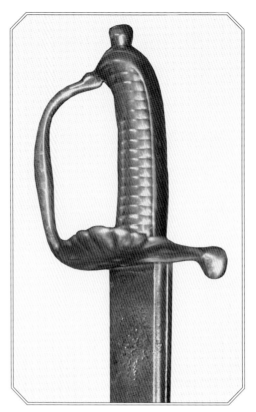

Left:

Briquet saber marked by its French makers "Grenadiers de Virginie" (Virginia Grenadiers), 1780s. It follows the French Navy's Model 1772 briquet saber for gunners, grenadiers and NCOs of the *Corps Royal de la Marine* regiments of marines with a half shell added to the guard of the Model 1767 army briquet saber. The blade has the "Grenadiers de Virginie", mark although there were no grenadiers in the American army. [Fort Ticonderoga Museum, Ticonderoga, N.Y.] *Author's photo*

The account books of Carcier de Monlieu, one of Beaumarchais' suppliers at St. Etienne, reveal some details regarding part of this later shipment. It included 16,080 soldier's muskets with their bayonets; 2,700 officer's muskets, possibly the officer's infantry Model 1754, and 4,943 dragoon muskets, probably the Model 1754.[169]

By 1778, France and Britain were drifting towards hostilities, and war broke out between the two nations in June. By then, about 80,000 muskets had been received in the United States. There was no further need for fictitious gun-running companies, and French supplies now flowed into the United States. It is estimated that, during the war, at least 102,000 and possibly over 115,000 muskets were sent. Most were metropolitan army models, especially the 1763 and 1766 (or light 1763) patterns, but also included were about 15,500 marine muskets that had been

Left:

Sword of General Lafayette, c.1775–1783. Gilt hilt including wire-wrapped grip. The pommel has a neoclassical figure sitting. This weapon is said to have been the weapon he usually wore when serving with the American army. [Musée de l'Armée, Paris] *Author's photo*

Right:
Hilt of the small sword belonging to Col. Marinus Willett of New York, c.1785. One of ten elegant swords ordered in 1777 by the U.S. Congress and awarded to various officers for meritorious action. The hilt was silver, richly ornamented with gold. The oval on the grip has the American eagle. The base of the blade is blued and gilded. The maker was C. Liger of Paris. [Courtesy, The Metropolitan Museum of Art, New York. Bequest of George Willett Van Nest, 1916]

Below:
Design for the hilt of a small sword c.1780. Note the neoclassical attributes that were then very popular. [Courtesy, The Metropolitan Museum of Art. Gift of John Blair, in memory of his father, Claude Blair, 2011]

made at Tulle, St. Etienne and Maubeuge between 1778 and 1783.

Apart from firearms and bayonets, a document of 1781 mentions a shipment of 1,500 dragoon's brass helmets for the American army. Since 1763, French dragoons wore such helmets, and the American troopers were now to wear this latest item of French armor. The likenesses of at least two American officers show them wearing these French brass dragoon's helmets.[170]

Swords and sabers were far less common than firearms amongst the supplies that came from France. American regiments did not have grenadiers, and their corporals were not armed with hangers. Furthermore, Americans could produce good edged weapons, notably cavalry sabers, so there was no urgency to obtain such weapons overseas. There are surviving "Grenadiers de Virginie" short sabers in American collections that may have been a possibly private shipment. On the other hand, fine officer's swords were made in France and exported to many countries. American officers who could afford it were soon ordering dress small swords from Paris and would continue to do so for many decades to come.

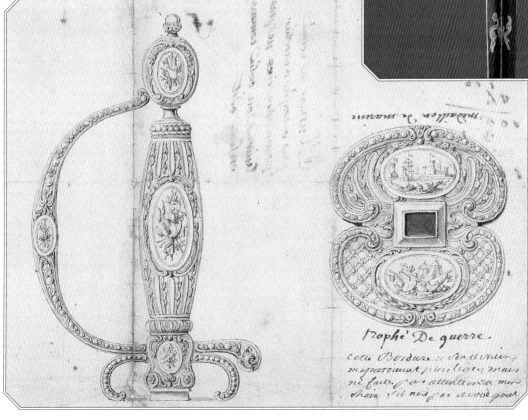

CHRONOLOGY

1504 — First recorded appearance of armed Frenchmen in America.
1540–1580s — Armor and crossbows mentioned, as well as firearms and edged weapons.
1600–1630s — Armor initially worn in Canada, later discarded.
1640s–1650s — Flintlock muskets widely adopted in Canada; same in Haiti as long-barreled buccaneer flintlock muskets.
1660s–1670s — Swords with Musketeer hilts become prevalent in foot and mounted troops.
1683 — September 23 – Merchant ships ordered to transport 12 flintlock muskets for sale to West India islands inhabitants.
1690 — Tulle arms works begin production for the Navy.
1703 — Matchlock muskets abolished in metropolitan infantry.
1717 — Introduction of Army Model 1717 infantry musket.
1728 — Introduction of Army Model 1728 infantry musket. Features barrel bands.
1729 — Tulle military muskets henceforth all have slings.
1741 — Iron ramrod on Army Model 1728 infantry musket. Tulle follows suit for the Navy.
1743 — Barrel bands added to Tulle military muskets.
1750 — Cavalry swords to henceforth have hilts with two branches.
1754 — Introduction of Army Model 1754 infantry musket.
1761 — Henceforth, the arsenals making army weapons (Charleville, St. Etienne, Maubeuge) are officially allowed to supply the navy. Arms supplied to marines and colonial troops henceforth essentially similar to the army's models. In practice, brass furnishings often appear to replace the army's iron furnishings.
1763 — Introduction of Army Model 1763 infantry musket.
1766 — Introduction of Army Model "Light 1763" also termed Model 1766 infantry musket.
1767 — Infantry short sword named "briquet" introduced for NCOs, grenadiers and chasseurs.
1770, 1773, 1774 — Several so-called models with minute changes.
1774 — September 10 – Obligation to transport muskets for sale to West India islands inhabitants canceled.
1777 — Introduction of Army Model 1777 infantry musket.
1777 — Introduction of Navy Model 1777 marine infantry musket.
1779 — Introduction of Navy Model 1779 colonial infantry musket.

APPENDIX I
METROPOLITAN ARMY INFANTRY MUSKETS MAIN FEATURES 1717 TO 1777

We use Jean Boudriot's allocation of models. Measures given in 18th-century French feet and inches (please see conversion tables at beginning of this book). The data is mainly compiled from Boudriot and Bonnefoy.

Model 1717
Total length: 4 feet, 11 inches
Barrel length: 3 feet, 8 inches
Round barrel with a flat on the top
Bayonet stud on top barrel
Barrel fixed to stock by four pins
Lock: flat
Ramrod: wood
Ramrod held by ramrod pipes
Furnishings: iron, sling buckles on left side
Weight: 8 ½ lbs.
Bayonet: triangular full blade, total length 17 inches, two slots in L-shape in socket
Production: 58,000
(The Model 1717 rampart musket is nearly similar, but has no bayonet nor bayonet stud so its stock extends to near the barrel's muzzle)

• • •

Model 1728
Total length: 4 feet, 11 inches
Barrel length: 3 feet, 8 inches
Round barrel with a flat on the top
Bayonet stud on top barrel
Barrel fixed to stock by bands
Barrel band spring at muzzle band
Lock: flat
Ramrod: wood with an iron tip; all iron from 1741
Furnishings: iron, sling buckles fixed on left side
Weight: 8 ½ lbs.
Bayonet: triangular hollowed blade, total length 17 inches, two slots in L-shape in socket

• • •

Model 1741
The so-called "Model 1741" is similar to the 1728 except that the ramrod tip is of iron with a nail head shape from that date, changed to pear shape from 1750.

• • •

Model 1746
The so-called "Model 1746" is similar to the 1728 with the 1741 iron ramrod except that the barrel is now octagonal and the bridle linking the pan and steel on the lock is removed.

• • •

Model 1754
Total length: 4 feet, 11 inches
Barrel length: 3 feet, 8 inches
Barrel: octagonal
Bayonet stud on top barrel
Barrel fixed to stock by bands
Barrel band spring at muzzle band and middle bands
Lock: flat
Ramrod: iron with inverted triangular tip
Furnishings: iron, sling buckles fixed under stock
Weight: 9 ¾ lbs.
Bayonet: triangular hollowed blade, total length 17 inches, three slots in Z-shape in socket

Model 1763
Total length: 4 feet, 8 inches
Barrel length: 3 feet, 6 inches
Barrel: round with two small flats, one on each side
Bayonet stud under the barrel
Barrel fixed to stock by bands
Barrel band spring at muzzle band and middle bands
Lock: flat
Ramrod: iron with pear shape tip
Furnishings: iron, sling buckles fixed under stock
Weight: 10 lbs.
Bayonet: triangular hollowed blade, total length 17 inches, three slots in Z-shape in socket

• • •

Model 1766 (or Light 1763)
Total length: 4 feet, 8 inches
Barrel length: 3 feet, 6 inches
Barrel: round with two small flats, one on each side
Bayonet stud under the barrel
Barrel fixed to stock by bands
Barrel band spring at muzzle and middle bands
Lock: flat
Ramrod: iron with nail head tip
Furnishings: iron, sling buckles fixed under stock
Weight: 8 ¾ lbs
Bayonet: triangular hollowed blade, total length 17 inches, three slots in Z-shape in socket

• • •

Model 1770
Total length: 4 feet, 8 inches
Barrel length: 3 feet, 6 inches
Barrel: round with two small flats, one on each side
Bayonet stud over the barrel
Barrel fixed to stock by bands
Barrel band spring at muzzle and middle bands
Lock: semi-rounded
Ramrod: iron with nail head tip
Furnishings: iron, sling buckles fixed under stock
Weight: 9 lbs
Bayonet: triangular hollowed blade, total length 16 ¼ inches, one slot with ring on socket

• • •

Model 1771
Same as above, but the bayonet stud is under the barrel

Model 1773
Total length: 4 feet, 8 inches
Barrel length: 3 feet, 6 inches
Barrel: round with two small flats, one on each side
Bayonet stud over the barrel
Barrel fixed to stock by bands
Barrel band spring at muzzle, middle and rear bands
Lock: rounded
Ramrod: iron with nail head tip
Furnishings: iron, sling buckles fixed under stock
Weight: 9 lbs.
Bayonet: triangular hollowed blade, total length 17 inches, three slots in Z-shape in socket (same as 1763–1766)

• • •

Model 1774
Total length: 4 feet, 8 inches
Barrel length: 3 feet, 6 inches
Barrel: round with two small flats, one on each side
Bayonet stud over the barrel
Barrel fixed to stock by bands
Barrel band spring at muzzle, middle and rear bands
Lock: semi-rounded
Ramrod: iron with pear shape tip
Furnishings: iron, sling buckles fixed under stock
Weight: 9 ¼ lbs
Bayonet: triangular hollowed blade, total length 16 ¼ inches, three slots with spring on socket

• • •

Model 1777
Total length: 4 feet, 8 inches
Barrel length: 3 feet, 6 inches
Barrel: round with two small flats, one on each side
Bayonet stud under the barrel
Barrel fixed to stock by bands
Barrel band spring at rear
Lock: semi-rounded with brass pan
Ramrod: iron with pear shape tip
Furnishings: iron, sling buckles fixed under stock
Weight: 9 ½ lbs
Bayonet: triangular hollowed blade, total length 17 ¼ inches, three slots with ring on socket

APPENDIX II
ARMS PRODUCTION

Infantry musket for the metropolitan army:
Model 1717: 58,000 (and about 80,000 rampart muskets)
Model 1728: 770,000
Model 1754: 270,000
Model 1763: 130,000
Model 1766 (or light 1763): 300,000 (includes Model 1770 and 1771)
Model 1773: 29,000
Model 1774: 66,000
Model 1777: 300,000

In all, over two million metropolitan infantry muskets were made at St. Etienne, Charleville and Maubeuge from 1717 to 1789. There are no consistent statistics for firearms other than infantry muskets made at St. Etienne, Charleville and Maubeuge between 1717 and 1777. The statistics from 1777 give an idea of the production output.

Firearms (other than infantry muskets) made from 1777 to 1789:
Dragoon muskets: 40,294
Officer's and gentlemen cadet muskets: 2,450
Muskets for the navy: 6,106
Artillery muskets: 10,368
Rifles: 1,300
Cavalry carbines: 25,293
Hussar carbines: 9,235
Pistol pairs: 29,812
Muskets directly delivered to regiments: 13,010
Pistol pairs delivered to regiments: 596
Carbines delivered to regiments: 1,012
Total: 139,476

Production at Tulle from 1777 was about 7,000 firearms a year and possibly up to 9,000 from 1783. This included marine and colonial infantry muskets and ship's muskets. It would have thus made some 35,000 firearms by 1783 and another 54,000 by 1789 for a total of about 89,000.

APPENDIX III
TROUPES DE LA MARINE

In 1695
Based in France:
Compagnies franches de la Marine . 100 companies
Bombardiers de la Marine . . . . 3 companies
Gardes de la Marine . . . . 3 companies
Compagnies franches des Galères . . 15 companies
Gardes du Pavillon Royal des Galères . 1 company
Pertuisaniers des Galères

Based in America:
Compagnies franches de la Marine:
    of Canada . . . . .28 companies
    of Acadia . . . . .2 companies
    of Placentia . . . . .2 companies
    of the Islands (Including Haiti) . .14 companies
    of French Guyana . . . . .4 companies

In 1735
Based in France:
Compagnies franches de la Marine . 50 companies
Bombardiers de la Marine . . . . 3 companies
Gardes de la Marine . . . . 3 companies
Gardes du Pavillon Amiral . . . . 1 company
Karrer's Swiss Regiment . . . . . . 1 company depot
Cadets de Rochefort . . . . 1 company
Compagnies franches des Galères . . 15 companies
Gardes du Pavillon Royal des Galères . 1 company
Pertuisaniers des Galères

Based in America:
Compagnies franches de la Marine:
    of Canada . . . . .28 companies
    of Haiti .16 companies
    of the Islands . . . . .10 companies
    of Isle Royale . . . . .8 companies
    of Louisiana . . . . .13 companies
    of French Guyana . . . . .6 companies
Karrer's Swiss Regiment Haiti . . . . . . 1 company
Karrer's Swiss Regiment Martinique . 1 company
Karrer's Swiss Regiment Louisiana . . . 1 company
Karrer's Swiss Regiment Louisbourg. . ½ company

In 1755
Based in France
Compagnies franches de la Marine . 100 companies
Bombardiers de la Marine . . . . 3 companies
Gardes de la Marine . . . . 3 companies
Gardes du Pavillon Amiral . . . . 1 company
Halwyll's Swiss Regiment . . . . . 1 company depot
Cadets de Rochefort. . . . . 1 company
Dépôt des colonies (Isle de Ré)
Pertuisaniers in several ports

Based in America:
Compagnies franches de la Marine:
    of Canada . . . . .30 companies
    of Haiti .34 companies
    of the Islands . . . . .20 companies
    of Louisiana . . . . .36 companies
    of French Guyana . . . . .10 companies
    of Isle Royale . . . . .24 companies
Canonniers-Bombardiers Isle Royale. . 1 company
Canonniers-Bombardiers Haiti . . . . . . 1 company
Canonniers-Bombardiers Islands . . . . . 1 company
Canonniers-Bombardiers Canada . . . . 1 company
Halwyll's Swiss Regiment Haiti . . . . 2 companies
Halwyll's Swiss Regiment Martinique. 1 company
Halwyll's Swiss Regiment Louisiana. . 1 company

In 1780
Based in France:
Corps royal de l'infanterie de la Marine
. . . . 100 companies
Bombardiers de la Marine . . . . 3 companies
Gardes de la Marine . . . . 3 companies
Gardes du Pavillon Amiral . . . . 1 company
Cadets-gentilhommes des colonies. . . . 1 company
Dépôt des recrues des colonies
Pertuisaniers in several ports

In America:
Régiment du Cap Haiti . . . . 2 battalions
Régiment du Port au Prince Haiti. . . . 2 battalions
Régiment de la Martinique Martinique . . . .
. . . . 2 battalions
Régiment de la Guadeloupe Guadeloupe
. . . . 2 battalions
Bataillon de la Guyane French Guyana
. . . . 8 companies
Canonniers-Bombardiers Haiti . . . . . 3 companies
Canonniers-Bombardiers Islands . . . 3 companies
Volontaires Etrangers de la Marine West Indies
. . . . 1 legion
Lauzun's Legion United States
. . . . 300 infantry and 300 Hussars

Note: There were also police paramilitary *Archers de la Marine* units in several naval bases in France. Overseas, the intendants and commissaires-ordonateurs each also had, from the 1660s, at least one *Archer de la Marine* at their service and were their guards in formal occasions. They were armed with swords and carbines. Canada had, from 1677 to 1760, a small *Maréchaussée* police unit armed the same way. Haiti also did in the 18th century, which grew to a sizeable corps that featured uniformed mounted troops armed like cavalry with sabers, pistols and carbines. After the French East India Company went out of business in 1770, the company's troops were disbanded and the Ministry of the Navy assumed responsibility for the garrisons of territories in Africa, the Indian Ocean and India. In 1780, the units posted in Africa and east of the Cape of Good Hope consisted of the Volontaires d'Afrique battalion, the Isle de France and Pondichery regiments, the Compagnie franches de Madagascar, a legion of the Volontaires Etrangers de la Marine, Canonniers-Bombardiers companies and Sepoy units. All were armed as the overseas troops in America by weapons shipments from France.

GLOSSARY

Ancre musket — Anchor musket. Could also be a pistol. Basically a firearm marked with an anchor (ancre in French), sometimes two anchors crossed, usually on the lock.

Arquebuse — Arquebus. This longarm appeared in Spain in the mid-15th century as a lighter version of the hand cannon. It was a matchlock weapon whose caliber might be as light as 48 balls to the pound in the 16th century. It was gradually replaced by the matchlock musket (see Mousquet) in the later 16th and early 17th centuries. Its lightness seems to have been appreciated by the early inhabitants of New France (see also Haquebut).

Blunderbuss — see Mousquetons à trompette.

Boucanier musket — Buccaneer musket. Long-barreled musket originating from the buccaneers and freebooters. Became a naval weapon and even prescribed for West Indian Compagnies franches in 1695 (see Chapters 4 and 7).

Carabine — rifled musket. In a military context often confused in translation with an English carbine, which was usually a cavalry weapon (called mousqueton in French) carried by elite troopers. It was, in effect, a rifled cavalry carbine that was more expensive due to the rifling, and especially in guard units, that could have luxury furnishings and finishing. The "carabine" could also be found on French naval ships in small quantities. Its occasional presence in overseas territorial arms magazines was likely due to supplying ships and possibly the guardsmen that attended the governor generals (see chapter 3). For the non-military uses, see Gladysz, *The French Trade Gun in North America 1662-1759*, bearing in mind that some privately purchased rifled musket belonged to Compagnie franches officers and could have been used in wilderness campaigns.

Domino musket — Musket with barrel bands, introduced in 1728 for army muskets and 1743 for navy muskets.

Espingole — type of swivel gun. Heavy musket with large caliber barrel held by a fork planted in a wood railing or post; mostly used on board ships, bateaux and other small crafts. Their barrels were substantial and made of either brass or iron. The firing mechanism was a flintlock.

Esponton — Spontoon. Also called a demi-pique (half-pike) since it was shorter by half at about seven feet high and intended for infantry officers beginning in the 16th century with the sword. It was the officer's official weapon until 1764 in the French army. Found in many probate inventories in America.

Fusee — or Fuzee. An anglicized version of the French word fusil that denotes a flintlock musket. In the 17th century, it also meant a lighter musket than the matchlock, and in Britain, the term fusee came to mean a light musket for hunting or for officers by the 18th century. This term was not used in France.

Fusil à deux coups — Double-barrel musket. An expensive civilian hunting musket. Uncommon but known to have been owned by at least two Canadian Compagnies franches officers as an unofficial weapon. Also, a musket of five shots (thus five barrels) was owned by Canadian Captain Duplessis-Fabert at the beginning of the 18th century.

Fusil Canadien — Canadian musket. This denomination appears for 79 muskets stored at Fort Carillon (Ticonderoga) in 1756, but not for other years. Stores listed at other places never use this denomination. No details are provided to give an idea of their general appearance and caliber. What these muskets were is left to conjecture. We feel they were possibly muskets made from various gun parts by Canadian gunsmiths, most likely for use by Canadian militiamen, and might have been more akin to hunting muskets.

Fusil à Domino — see Domino musket.

Fusil Grenadier — Grenadier musket. Appears in the army towards the last quarter of the 17th century to denote a musket fitted with a sling (called a grenadière), so it could be slung over the shoulder by infantry grenadiers while they hurled grenades. In the French army, four grenadiers per infantry company appeared in 1668 and grenadier companies in 1670. Other armies followed suit. There were no grenadiers in the Troupes de la Marine until the 1770s and then only in isolated circumstances, but soldiers of the Compagnies franches and Bombardiers received muskets with grenadières from the early 18th century. This handy feature was gradually added to muskets for all soldiers.

Fusil ordinaire — see Ordinaire musket.

Galères musket — Galley musket. Muskets that were used in the French Mediterranean galley fleet based in Marseille. The Troupes de la Marine also had 15 Compagnies franches des Galères that served as marines on board the row galleys. Their arms were generally similar to those of the metropolitan and overseas Compagnies franches de la Marine, as were their uniforms, except that they had red as the facing color instead of blue. The galley fleet was abolished in 1748 and its personnel and troops incorporated into the sailing navy in the Mediterranean fleet. As for the row convicts, they were kept in the "Bagne [prison] de Marseille" making cloth for uniforms. See Boudriot and Pétard's *Marine Royale* and Gladysz, *The French Trade Gun in North America 1662-1759* for illustrations and data on Galley fleet muskets.

Gargoussier cartridge box — This primitive use of the word gargousse stems from the name given to artillery charges. Consequently, the new containers were named gargoussiers, but these were actually infantry cartridge boxes slung on the waistbelt.

Gorget — hausse-col in French. Originally a piece of armor that protected the neck, it evolved into a badge identifying officer status in Western Europe (and also non-commissioned-officers in Germany) during the 17th century. It then assumed a crescent shape and was worn below the neck. It was usually made of copper that could be gilded. German troops in French service had polished iron gorgets, and Swiss troops had them silvered. As illustrated in this book, the decoration of the gorget in the first half of the 18th century varied, most seemingly being plain or with a double boss, the smaller at the top, while rarer examples are fully embossed with trophies, the royal arms and other devices. For French units, the somewhat universal model consisting of a gilt crescent with a silver badge bearing the crowned royal arms with palm leaves at the sides was formally adopted by royal orders in 1767. The question remains as to whether it was the result of previous practices or a totally new concept. Gorgets were worn by unit officers, but not by generals, staff officers or engineers. It remained part of full dress in the French forces until 1882.

Grenadier musket — see Fusil Grenadier.

Haquebut — several spellings. Circa 1475-1550 firearm that could be somewhat different than the Arquebuse (see above) being defined by Peterson's *Encyclopedia* as a heavy weapon requiring support, as a powerful arm with a sling and as a portable weapon. Vanished by the mid-16th century.

Hallebarde — Halberd. This was a polearm handled by hallebardiers in the 15th and 16th centuries. They were considered elite soldiers, and this weapon became the badge of elite soldiers of ceremonial guard units and infantry sergeants. The halberd itself had a head that combined a spear and an axe blade, which was sometimes artfully etched. It armed sergeants until 1758 in the metropolitan army and until the early 1760s in the Troupes de la Marine infantry.

Hausse-col — see Gorget.

Mousqueton — **Carbine.** In a military context, a mousqueton was basically a short musket mostly used by cavalry. Some were also used by the navy as ship's armament.

Mousquetons à trompette — Trumpet carbines, meaning a blunderbuss whose barrel widened at the muzzle. Also called a tromblon. Used mainly on ships, but a few might have been found in the larger forts.

Mousquet — **matchlock musket.** This was the most common denominator from the 17th century, but it could also have a snaphance or wheel-lock mechanism (mostly in the 16th century). Abolished officially in the French infantry in 1699.

Ordinaire musket — **ordinary or common musket.** Denotes a musket without a sling, as opposed to the Grenadier musket (q.v.). This term appeared in the last third of the 17th century.

Pertuisane — **Partisan.** A polearm related to the halberd (q.v.) that appeared in the 15th century, suited for close quarter combat in the 16th and 17th centuries on land and sea while becoming also a polearm of choice for some officers with the esponton (q.v.) and also carried by elite guard units, for instance the Gardes de la Manche of the royal bodyguard. Its head featured a wide and flat blade with two pointed extensions at its bottom. Officer's and guardsmen's partisans could be intricately etched and gilded and/or silvered. From 1670, army officers were not to carry partisans. However, they continued to be used in the navy for colonial West Indian militias and by constabulary units. Until 1748, the galley fleet based in Marseille had a corps of Petruisaniers des Galères that detached nine soldiers on each of the 15 galleys with more in port. A small unit of Pertuisianiers was associated with the guard of convicts in Martinique starting in 1764.

Pique — **pike.** Pikes, which were about 14 feet high, were common in European infantry units and gradually went out of use during the 17th century and were abolished in 1703 in France. While infantry pikes were sent to French America in the early 17th century, they were little used if at all. Pikes were also used by navy sailors when boarding in hand-to-hand combat, and the pikes found in government arms depots from the later 17th century were most likely of this type and for this purpose (see Chapter 7).

Rampart musket. Basically a somewhat heavier version of the regulation metropolitan infantry musket for use in fortified places, seemingly first defined in 1717. It had the same dimensions as the standard weapon, except that it had a heavier caliber at 16 and a heavier barrel. It had no bayonet. About 70,000 to 80,000 of the army 1717 rampart model were made, but only a few thousand of the Model 1728 and none thereafter. It was a metropolitan army musket, but some may have been obtained by the navy for its ships or the overseas territories it administered. In 1747, the Marquis de la Galissonière, Governor General of New France, asked for some to be sent to Canada and, on January 13, 1748, the Minister of the Navy answered that he had asked if the magazine at Rochefort could supply them (AC, B, 87).

Spontoon — see Esponton.

Tromblon — **a blunderbuss musket.** See Mousqueton à trompette.

ABBREVIATIONS

In general, the abbreviation is followed by the series identity letters and numbers and the volume or box number. Dates and names are given rather than folio or page numbers, some ledgers bearing up to three different numbers on a folio or page by eager clerks or archivist. In the case of Archives Nationales du Québec documents, they have the name of the notary and the document's description.

AB	Archives Raoul et Jean Brunon, Musée de l'Armée, château de l'Empéri, Salon-de-Provence, France.
AC	Archives des Colonies (Archives Nationales, Outremer, Aix-en-Provence, France)
AG	Archives de la Guerre (Service Historique des Armées, Vincennes, France)
AM	Archives de la Marine (Archives Nationales, Paris, France)
AN	Archives Nationales, Paris, France.
ANQM	Archives Nationales du Québec à Montréal.
ANQQ	Archives Nationales du Québec à Québec.
ANQTR	Archives Nationales du Québec à Trois-Rivières.
AR	Archives de la Marine de Rochefort (Rochefort, France).
CO	Colonial Office (at The National Archives, Kew, UK).
KM	Kaskaskia Manuscripts (at Randolph County Courthouse, Chester, Illinois).
LAC	Library and Archives Canada, Ottawa.
MC&H	Military Collector & Historian, Journal of the Company of Military Historians.
RAPQ	Rapport de l'Archiviste de la Province de Québec.
TNA	The National Archives, Kew, UK.
WO	War Office (at the The National Archives, Kew, UK).

SELECT BIBLIOGRAPHY

Ariès, Christian, *Armes Blanches Militaires Françaises* (Nantes, 1966–1983). An excellent series of installments illustrated by Michel Pétard on various types of swords and polearms.

Bonnefoy, François, "Les Armes de guerre portatives en France, du début du règne de Louis XIV à la veille de la Révolution, (1660–1789) de l'indépendance à la primauté" (Paris: Librairie de l'Inde, 1991), 2 volumes. Doctoral thesis at the Sorbonne (University of Paris), certainly the most essential, exhaustive and finest study on the topic.

Brooker, Robert E., *Armes de Poing Militaires Françaises du XVIe au XIXe Siècle et Leurs Incfluences à l'étranger* (La Tour-du-Pin: Portail, 2006). The best and most complete study on pistols.

Bottet, Maurice, *L'Arme Blanche de Guerre Française au XVIIIe Siècle* (Paris, 1910). The pioneering, well-illustrated and still quite useful work on swords and polearms.

Bouchard, Russel, *The Fusil de Tulle in New France 1691–1741* (Bloomfield, Ontario, 1998). The classic study on this topic.

Bouchard, Russel, *Les armes à feu en Nouvelle-France* (Québec: Septentrion, 1999). Survey of the use, regulations and trade of firearms followed by descriptions of the main types. Well illustrated with photos and line drawings.

Boudriot, Jean, *Armes à feu françaises: modèles d'ordonnance* (Paris, 1961–1971). The various cahiers (folders) with their clear drawings (by the author) and excellent texts are still the best source on regulation portable firearms in the 18th century.

Boudriot, Jean, *Le Vaisseau de 74 Canons* (Paris, 1973–1977), 4 volumes. When it first appeared, this massive study of a 1770s-1780s 74-gun ship-of-the-line from its keel to its masts tops with everything it contained as well as the men who sailed in her, revolutionized and set a new standard for such naval studies. Volume 2 deals partly with arms and ordnance, but other aspects of these topics are also found in Volume 4. While thousands of illustrations are by the author, Michel Pétard also illustrated the parts of the 4th volume that were devoted to the officers and men of the crew and the marines.

Boudriot, Jean and Michel Pétard, *Marine Royale XVIIe–XVIIIe Siècles: Uniformes, Équiments, Armement* (Paris, 2003). Outstanding and important study beautifully illustrated with a wealth of color illustrations reproducing period documents with excellent plates showing arms, uniforms and equipment as well as line drawings of officers and marines of the French Navy from the 1660s to 1789. It should be noted that this does not cover the overseas troops, but remains an essential source to consult for any study regarding the material culture of garrisons posted in America.

Encyclopedia of Firearms, edited by Harold L. Peterson (New York, 1964). Still an outstanding work.

Gladysz, Kevin, *The French Trade Gun in North America 1662–1759* (Mowbray, Woonsocket, R.I., 2011). This work, in fact, covers a great deal more than trade guns. It is extremely well documented on all types of muskets more or less related to trade guns and includes many military muskets. These are illustrated by over 800 images showing all aspects of furnishings on several types of muskets since their styles are often seen in several models that range from military to hunting weapons. Much recommended for any arms library.

Goldstein, Erik, *The Bayonet in New France, 1665–1760* (Museum Restoration Service, Ontario, Canada, 1997).

Hicks, James E., *Notes on French Ordnance 1717–1936* (Mount Vernon, N.Y., 1938) reprinted as *French Military Weapons 1717–1938* (Norman Flayderman & Co., New Milford, Conn., 1964).

Margerand, G., *Armement et Équipement de l'armée Française du XVIème au XXème Siècle* (Paris, 1945). Very useful study, somewhat indifferently illustrated, but reproduces many key archival documents. The information on 1760s–1770s bayonets is interpreted erroneously and has since been corrected by Boudriot.

Neumann, George, *The History of Weapons of the American Revolution (New York, 1967)*. Profusely illustrated and covers in fact from the 16th century to 1783.

Lenk, Torsten, *The Flintlock* (London, 1965). The classic work on this topic from the original 1939 Swedish publication, excellently translated by J.A. Urquart. Much recommended for any arms library.

Pétard, Michel, *Équipments militaires de 1600 à 1870*, volumes 1 and 2 (Saint-Julien-de-Concelles, [France] 1984 and 1985). The finest study on the equipment of soldiers in 17th and 18th-century France, beautifully illustrated. The text also contains many archival extracts. The complete series, which goes on to 1870, has ten volumes and is the definitive source regarding all aspects of French army and navy accoutrements, illustrated by thousands of line drawings and plates.

Pétard, Michel, *Des Sabres et des Épées* (Nantes: Éditions du Canonnier, 1999–2005), three volumes. The first volume (1999) deals with the pre-1804 period. An admirable and most complete survey of sabers and swords used in the French army from the 17th century to 1870, illustrated by hundreds of color plates.

Pétard, Michel, *Le Sabre d'abordage* (Nantes: Éditions du Canonnier, 2006) — text and captions both in French and English. The definitive work of naval boarding sabers, illustrated with many color plates.

Pétard, Michel, *Les Sabres des Hussards* (Nantes: Éditions du Canonnier, 2010). A complete detailed study of Hussar sabers from the 17th century to the early 21st century, illustrated by a wealth of color plates and photos.

Peterson, Harold L., *Arms and Armor in Colonial America 1526–1783* (New York, 1956). The pioneering and still pertinent study, well illustrated.

Pitous, J.P., *Les baïonnettes réglementaires françaises* (Paris, 1973).

ENDNOTES

1. Xabi Otero et al, *Euskaldunen Labrador* (Nafarroa, 1990), p. 25; AC, Dépôt des Fortifications des Colonies, mémoires, Canada, No. 327; René Chartrand, "Les Vikings au Groenland et dans l'arctique canadien," *Prétorien*, No. 16 [Paris], (octobre-décembre 2010).

2. Two pieces of artillery of copper and brass; two half pieces of the same materials; six "berches" (a small brass gun) and iron petteraros; the said artillery mounted on its carriages and supplied with instruments...; 1,600 pounds of balls of different calibers for the artillery, plus 300 balls with sticks and chains (to damage enemy ships); 500 pounds of grapeshot for the artillery. From Gonneville's account in: *Les Français en Amérique pendant la première moitié du XVIe siècle*, edited by C.A. Julien (Paris, 1946), pp. 27–28, 41.

3. From Verrazano's account in: *Les Français en Amérique...*, pp. 54, 70.

4. Jacques Cartier, *Les voyages de Jacques Cartier*, J. Dumont, ed. (Montreal, 1969), pp. 103, 130, 139, 174.

5. *A Collection of Documents Relating to Jacques Cartier and the Sieur de Roberval*, H.P. Biggar, ed., (Ottawa, 1930), pp. 275–278; Cartier, pp. 248–250, 258–259.

6. Jean de Lery, *Histoire d'un voyage fait en la terre du Brésil, autrement dite Amérique* (La Rochelle, 1578), preface, pp. 64, 117; Arthur Heulard, *Villegagnon* (Paris, 1897) puts the number of settlers at 290, but others such as de Lery mention 600.

7. Charles de La Roncière, *La Floride Française* (Paris, 1928), pp. 70, 87–89; Solis de Mera, Gonzalo, *Pedro Menendez de Aviles*, translated by Jeanette Thurber Connor (Florida State Historical Society: Deland, 1923), pp. 114, 121.

8. *New American World: A Documetary History of North America to 1612*, David B. Quinn, ed., (Arno and Hector Bye: New York, 1979), IV: 45–46. Jones and the pilot Edward Spicer were humanely taken back to France and eventually reached England where they made their claim totalling £3,961.

9. Pierre de Bourdelle, abbé de Brantôme, *Discours sur les colonels de l'infanterie de France* [written c.1580–1600] and edited by Étienne Vaucheret (Paris and Montreal, 1973), pp. 120, 144, 162–165, 210.

10. Marc Lescarbot, *Histoire de la Nouvelle-France* (Paris, 1617), books 4 and 5, and *Relation dernière de ce qui s'est passé au voyage...en la Nouvelle France depuis 10 mois...* (Paris, 1612), n.p. It is interesting to note that the Indian woman called a sword 'Ech'pada' which is obviously "Espada" the Portuguese and Spanish word for sword. In French, it is "épée."

11. Clarence-Joseph d'Entremont, *Histoire du Cap-Sable*, (Ermice, LA, 1981): II: 476.

12. Alaric Faulkner, "Gentility on the Frontiers of Acadia 1635–1674: An Archaeological Perspective," *New England/New France 1600–1850*, The Dublin Seminar for New England Folkife Annual Proceedings (Boston University, 1989), pp. 82–100.

13. Joan Dawson, "The Governor's Goods: The Inventories of Personal Property of Isaac de Razilly," *Nova Scotia Historical Review*, 1985: 99–112; Francis Back, "Gouverneur de l'Acadie 1635", *Cap-aux-Diamants*, No. 48 (1995): 48.

14. *Mémoires des commissaires de Sa Majesté très chrétienne...*, (Amsterdam, 1755) II: 407–408.

15. Gabriel Sagard, *Le grand voyage au pays des Hurons* (1632 Paris edition revised and annotated by Jean Dumont in the 1969 Montréal edition), pp. 134–136, 209.

16. Samuel de Champlain, *Voyages du sieur de Champlain* (1613–1632 editions revised and annotated by C.-H. Laverdière in the 1870 Québec edition as *Oeuvres de Champlain*), I : 342–344, 362, 397; René Beaudry and Jean Le Blant, *Nouveaux documents sur Champain et son époque* (Ottawa, 1967), pp. 204, 285, 351.

17. *Oeuvres de Champlain*, III: 994, 1229–1130; *Mercure françois*, XIX (1633), p. 816; Archives de La Rochelle (France), B, 5654, No. 156, Inventaire...dans le navire Saint-Pierre, 28 August 1618; early arms and armor is illustrated in Wallhausen, F.J., *L'art de la guerre* (Paris, 1615).

18. M. Faillon, *Histoire de la colonie française en Canada* (Montréal, 1865), Volumes I and II.

19. For instance, flintlock muskets are mentioned by period chronicler Dollier de Canson from 1651 in his *Histoire du Montréal* (Montréal, 1868). See also the *Relations des Jésuites* (published yearly; we have used the 1858 reprint).

20. "Inventaire en état des lieux du fort St. Louis", *Canadian Antiquarian and Numismatic Journal*, April 1890, pp. 153–156; Archives du Séminaire de Québec. Verreau 11, No. 16, Colbert de Feronne to de Seuil, Brouage, 27 May 1662.

21. Yves d'Evreux, *Suitte de l'histoire des choses plus memorables advenues en Maragnan es années 1613 et 1614* (Paris, 1615), pp. 27, 133; *Histoire véritable de ce qui s'est passé de nouveau entre les François et les Portugais en l'Isle de Maragnan des Toupinsambous* (Paris, 1615), pp. 7–11.

22. Jean-Baptise Du Tertre, *Histoire générale des isles de S. Christophe, de la Guadeloupe, de la Martinique et autres dans l'Amérique* (Paris, 1654), pp. 24, 335.

23. "Le commandeur de Poincy à Saint-Christophe," *Revue d'histoire des colonies françaises*, 1915: 294.

24. *L'histoire de l'Isle de Grenade en Amérique*, anonymous 1659 account edited by Jacques Petitjean-Roger (Université de Montréal, 1975), pp. 52–53, 122, 134, 225.

25. Sébastien Deher, quoted in Richard Brzezinski, *The Army of Gustavus Adolphus, 1 Infantry* (London: Osprey Military, 1991), p. 17; "Mémoires de Messire Robert Arnauld D'Andilly," *Collection des mémoires relatifs à l'histoire de France*, M. Petitot, ed., (Paris, 1824), XXXIII: pp. 333–334; illustrations of soldiers by Abraham Bosse, *Figures au naturel tant des vestements que des postures des Gardes-Françaises du Roy très chrétien* (Paris, 1643).

26. The most hilarious and outlandish example of a prank causing a black powder accident, found by this author, was on 3 April 1677, at the British fort in Bombay, India. The storekeeper decided to send up some gunpowder to dry on the North East bastion. Meanwhile, at the guard house, a certain Corporal Staunton had a sense of humor and took: "an old bandileer [bandolier] and filled it with wild fire [priming powder], intending to tie it to the tail of a dog, then in the guard [house], and [Corporal Staunton] running to the gate, the dog not being [found] in the way, he took the bandileer, there being a [lighted slow match] string tied to it and flung it towards the Old Judge's House, but the wind being very strong, it blew it upon the bastion and fired all the powder which was 35 barrels all English. There were 8 Coolies tending it and 1 Centry who were all burnt to death, whereof 6 blown into the ditch and the parade, and some limbs blown over the fort. All the doors in the Fort were blown open, and made most part of the Town shake." Corporal Staunton was not hurt, but was kicked out of the garrison after being made to run the gauntlet three times for his little prank. One is amazed he was not executed! Found in: Arthur E. Mainwaring, *Crown and Company* (London, 1911), p. 60, quoting a 1677 report.

27. Except for pikemen in Swiss regiments in French pay who kept their steel helmets.

28. BN, Fonds Français, 10,251, Ordonnance pour l'entretenement de gardes, 11 December 1663; César de Rochefort, *Histoire naturelle et morale des Antilles* (Paris, 1650, p. 54; AM, B3, 6, Supplément de la dépense, 9 July 1667; probate of Governor General Vaudreuil, 19 June 1726 in: *Inventaire des testaments, donations et inventaires du regime français*, P.-G. Roy, ed., (Quebec, 1943), III: 213.

29. Jean-Baptise Du Tertre, *Histoire générale des Antilles habitées par les Français* (Paris, 1671), III: 268, 302; *Colonising Expeditions to the West Indies and Guiana*, V.T. Harlow, ed. (London: Halkuyt Society, 1925), p. 237; Moreau de Saint-Méry, *Loix et Constitutions des colonies françaises de l'Amérique sous le vent* (Paris, 1784-1787) I: pp. 151, 156, 166; AG, A1, 183, 202 and 213.

30. AM, B3, 6, Sommes destinées...de Baas...ses gardes, 9 July 1667.

31. AC, C11A, 2, Etat general..., 1666; On this regiment, see: Régis Roy and Gérard Malchelosse, *Le Régiment de Carignan* (Montreal: G. Ducharme, 1925); Jack Verney, *The Good Regiment: The Carignan-Salières Regiment in Canada 1665–1668* (Montreal and Kingston: McGill-Queen's, 1991).

32. *Inventaire des testaments, donations et inventaires du regime français*, P.-G. Roy, ed., (Quebec, 1941), III: pp. 272–278; ANQQ, Paul Vachon, Inventaire de François Pollet, Sieur de la Combe Pocatière, 14 April 1672; ANQM, A. Adhémar, Inventaire de Pierre Dupras, Sieur du Bray, 10–15 October 1678.

33. ANQM, Antoine Adhémar, No. 5419, Inventaire de Dominique La Motte, 27 November 1700. He was appointed captain of the King's Domain Guards, a customs unit, the year before he passed away. On the Fort Frontenac garrison see: AC, C13C, 3, *Mémoire sur les dépenses du Sieur de La Salle au Fort Frontenac* (1675–1684).

34. AC, B, 4, Ordonnance...Gardes du Sr Comte de Frontenac, 15 April 1672; ANQQ, Pierre Duquet, Inventaire des biens de feu Thomas de la Mouguère, 3 June 1678; ANQM, C. Mauge, Inventaire de feu Philippe de Carrion, Sieur Dufresnoy, 21 December 1683.

35. AC, C11A, 113, Autre dépense à cause de l'habitation de Plaisance, 1663.

36. Monsieur de Lamont, *Les fonctions de tous les officiers de l'infanterie...* (Paris, 1669), p. 17. The morality of a sergeant was to be spotless and not, to quote, " toujours attaché au cul d'une putain [always attached to the ass of a prostitute]..."

37. AC, B, 9, Cannons, affust..., 5 June 1680; AC, F1A, 2, Note, 6 December 1680; AM, B2, 60, Note, 6 June 1687; AC, B, 13, Estat..., January 1689.

38. AC, B, 14, Estat..., Versailles, 10 September 1692; B, 18, Minister to Sr. Bégon, Versailles, 13 July 1695, 5 and 26 September 1696.

39. AC, B, 18, Ordonnance du roi, 12 October 1695; AR, IE, 599, H. Jules to Delacombe, 7 November 1697; AC, B, 21, Passeport, 18 August 1700; B, 31, Minister to Bégon, Versailles, 21 March 1708.

40. AC, B, 7, Ordonnance de fonds...Sr. de Baas...sa compagnie de gardes, 10 April 1676.

41. AC, F1A, 1, Etat des armes...Cayenne, 21 April 1677 and June 1679; AC, B, 13, Etat des Munitions...Cayenne, 1687.

42. AC, C11A, 6, Mémoire de La Barre, 13 November 1684; C11A, 7, to Denonville, February 1685; Denonville to Minister, Paris 3 April 1685; AC, F1A, 2, Canada...17 April 1685; F1A, 7, Canada...24 November 1692.

43. ANQQ, Louis Chamballon, Inventaire des biens de feu François Marie Renaud d'Avesne des Méloizes, 16 May 1699; ANQTR, Daniel Normandin, Inventaire de Marie Anne Babie veuve de Sieur de Lusignan, 19 June 1699.

44 ANQQ, Louis Chamballon, Inventaire de feu Jacques de Joibert, Seigneur de Soulanges, 2 May 1703; ANQM, Antoine Adhémar, No. 6398, Inventaire des bien de Mr. Le Gay, 22 February 1703 gives also the belongings of an officer whose name is unclear; ANQM, Michel Lepailleur, Inventaire du feu Daniel de Grelon, Sieur Duluth, 22 February 1710; ANQQ, NF 25, 452, Inventory of Nicolas Rousselot, Sieur de la Prairie, 14 July 1711; ANQM, Antoine Adhémar, No. 9470, Inventaire Jacques Lepicard Dumesny de Noré, 24 February 1714; ANQM, M. Lepailleur, No. 1718, Inventaire de Louis Mallerais, Sieur de la Moillerie, 20 December 1714; ANQM, Michel Lapailleur, No. 603, Testament de l'honorable Pierre Goudot, 30 May 1708.

45 ANQM, Michel Lepailleur, No. 1254, Inventaire de feu François Lefebvre, Sieur Duplessis Fabert, 24 November 1712.

46 ANQQ, Louis Chamballon, Inventaire de Thomas Farabezolles, 21 July 1711.

47 AC, C11A, 8, Etat des vivres et munitions..., March 1686; *Journal de l'expédition du Chevalier de Troyes à la Baie d'Hudson en 1686* (Beauceville, 1918), pp. 7–8. The raiders departed Montreal on March 29. Their arduous inland route, planned to take the English posts by surprise, took them along the Ottawa River, Lake Temiscamingue, Lake Abitibi and the Abitibi River, finally arriving at Moose Factory on June 20. The next day, they easily captured the fort from astounded British traders. Fort Charles and Albany, fell almost as easily. De Troyes arrived back in Montreal in October with his soldiers. The Canadian volunteers, were left behind in the various trading posts.

48 Archives de La Rochelle, B, 5682, No. 374, Estat du chargement de l'*Aimable* [bound for Acadia], 3 July 1684. Ammunition and civilian clothing was also sent on this and two other ships.

49 AC, C11D, 2, Meneval to Seignelay, 7 September 1689; B, 16, Estat des munitions, 14 January 1693; C11D, 2, Mémoire à Monseigneur...fort...de la rivière Saint-Jean, 1695; F1A, 10, Mémoire pour le fort Royal, 1701; AR, 1E, 51, Pontchartrain to Bégon, Versailles, 19 March 1704; AC, C11A, 29, note by Bégon, Rochefort, 10 March 1708.

50 AC, F1A, 3, Rolle des soldats destinez pour Plaisance, La Rochelle, 15 April 1687; F1A, 7, État des munitions, 20 January 1691; B, 17, Mémoire de ce qui est nécessaire... Placentia, January 1694; AR, 5E2, 7, Plaisance, 1701; AC, C11C, 3, Durant de L Garenne to minister, Placntia, 10 October 1702; AM, B2, 166, État des munitions, 14 February 1703; AR, 1E, 65, Pontchartrain to Bégon, Fontainebleau, 15 August 1708.

51 *Lettres de Cavelier de La Salle*, Pierre Margry, ed. (Paris, 1879), II: pp. 378–380.

52 AC, F1A, 10, Mississippi 1701, Extrait des certificates des fournitures...; AC, F1A, 11, Estat des dépenses du Mississippi, 1703 and 1704.

53 Chenevrières, M. de, *Détails militaires* (Paris, 1750), I: pp. 1–2.

54 Antoine Boudet, *Histoire générale de la Marine* (Paris, 1757), III: pp. 55–56.

55 Yves Cayre, *Histoire de la Manufactures d'armes de Tulle 1690-1970*, n.p., (1970), pp. 18–19.

56 François Bonnefoy, *Les Armes de guerre portatives en France...*, II: pp. 597–599.

57 René Chartrand, "Du manche à la douille", *Journal des Armes*, I: 1215.

58 ANQM, Michel Lepailleur, No. 603, Testament de Pierre Goudot, 30 May 1708.

59 AC, B, 12, Etat des canons, armes..., 20 September 1686.

60 Alain Manesson Mallet, *Les Travaux de Mars*, (Paris, 1684), III: 18. Some "gibicieres" with "poires à poudre" are mentioned in New France as per AC, B, 16, Estat des munitions, 14 January 1693. The small "pulverin" priming flask was often mixed up with the powder flask holding a pound of powder.

61 AR, 1E, Vol. 38, Minister of the Navy to Rochefort Intendant Bégon, 29 Feb. 1696. This primitive use of the the word "gargousse" from the name given to artillery charges so that the new containers were named "gargoussiers," but these were actually infantry cartridge boxes.

62 AC, F3, 13, Ordonnance du roi, Versailles, 1 May 1743.

63 ANQQ, Boissseau, No. 1546, Inventaire de Catherine Trefflé et Nicolas Bailly, Sieur de Messein, enseigne des troupes, 6 March 1739; ANQQ, Boisseau, No. 321, Inventaire de Madeleine Levasseur et Henri Albert, Sieur de Saint-Vincent, officier des troupes, 23 June 1742; AC, B, 110, minister of the Navy to Mr. De Ruis, Versailles, 23 November 1759. ANQM, Panet, No. 1243, Inventaire de feu Sieur de la Morandière, 28 January 1761. He was a colonial King's Engineer and in his belongings were two scarlet uniforms, which was these engineer's regulation dress, De la Morandière also owned a violon.

64 ANQM, Chevremont, No. 258, Inventaire de Joseph Dejourdy de Cabagnac, 27 March 1737; ANQM, Danré de Blanzy, No. 5099, Inventaire...J.-B. Jarret de Verchères, 8 August 1752; ANQM, Henri Bouron, Inventaire du défunt Sieur de Bouat, 12-15 September 1753; ANQM, Pierre Panet, No. 788, Inventaire...Sieur de Saint-Michel, 12 April 1758; ANQM, P. Panet, No. 1,113, Inventaire de François de Marillac, 19 October 1759; ANQM, Danré de Blanzy, No. 8254, Inventaire de Joseph Langy, 26 April 1760; ANQM, P. Panet, Inventaire du...Sieur Chevalier de la Corne, 19 April 1762.

65 ANQM, Gervais Hodiesme, No. 42, Dépot d'argent pour André Duplessis dit Lajoye, 17 April 1753; ANQM, Danré de Blanzy, No. 6573, Inventaire... Pierre François de Sarrobert, sergent d'infanterie, 8 January 1756; ANQM, F. Simonnet, No. 253, Inventaire de feu Jean Megret dit St. Jean, 24 August 1758.

66 ANQM, Documents judiciaries, 06-MT1, 1/161, Procès de François Bertrand, Henri Davout, Pierre Beauvais, Joseph Gorel, Jean-Marie Ballet, soldats déserteurs du fort Sandosket, Trial at Montreal on 22 January 1752.

67 AR, 1E, 569, Minister to Montholon, 23 October 1714, also mentions 200 Tulle hunting muskets with brass furnishings to be sent; AC, C11A, 4, Armement des quatres companies de la Louisiane, June 1716; AC, B, 42, Mémoire sur l'habillement et armement, c. 1718; AG, A1, 2592, Troupes, Postes, Forts, Biloxi, 22 January 1721; AC, B, 43, Habillement general des 10 Compagnies, 1724 and Etat général des dépenses, 1728.

68 AC, C13A, 38, Kerlérec to Minister, 15 September 1754; René Chartrand, "The Troops of French Louisiana 1699-1769", MC&H, XXV, No. 2 (Summer 1973): pp. 57–65.

69 Louisiana State Museum, Archives and Manuscripts, Inventory of Sieur de Lauze, 26 October 1717. He was seemingly posted at Dauphine Island and acting as major when he died. He also had a used white uniform coat with blue cuffs and brass buttons. *The Village of Chartres in Colonial Illinois 1720-1765*, documents translated and edited by Margaret Kimball Brown and Lawrie Cenas Dean (New Orleans, Polyanthos, 1977), p. 820; KM, 48/1/20/1, Inventory of Jean-Baptiste de Saint-Laurent Montbrun, 20 January 1748; LAC, MG1-E, 9, Inventaire d'Arradola, 19 April 1755. He served on the staff as "Aide-Major" at the time of is death. A lot of clothing was also listed, including several regulation uniforms and various items suited to social and outdoor activities. Frederic L. Billon, *Annals of St. Louis in its Early Days* (St. Louis, 1886), pp. 47–49.

70 AC, B, 74, Minister to Mssrs. De Clieu & Marin, 28 March 1742.

71 AC, C11A, 91, Etat des pièces d'artillerie et des munitions de guerre...Québec, Montréal, les Trois-Rivières, dans les forts Saint-Frédéric, Niagara et Frontenac, 1 September 1747, reported only 503 St. Etienne muskets left in the Montreal royal arms magazine; AC, F1A, 38, Colonies 1751, Minister to Srs. Pierre Girard, Robert Carrier, Marly, 12 May 1752. Each musket came to 17 livres 10 sols.; AC, B, 96, Passeport..., Fontainebleau 1 November 1752.

72 AC, F1A, 45, Full payment to Le Jay, 1 August 1760; AC, F1A, 46, Payment to royal manufacture of Charlesville, 1 August 1760; Bonnefoy, *Les Armes...*, I: 73 and II: 599-600.

73 AM, B1, 5, Traité entre le roi et M. de La Combe, Dunkirk, July 1716.

74 AN, K, 909, No. 44, Notice sur la manufacture de Tulle, 19 November 1729.

75 AN, K, 909, No. 45, Notice sur la manufacture de Tulle, 13 September 1729.

76 Note kindly shared with the author by Jean Boudriot.

77 G. Margerand, *Armement et équipement*, p. 52; ANQM, Danré de Blazy, No. 8236, Inventaire de Thomas Philippe Dagneaux, Sieur de la Sauzaye, 11 April 1760. He also left a regulation white cloth coat lined with blue serge and blue velvet cuffs, white cloth breeches; an old white coat lined blue and brass buttons, a blue waistcoat trimmed with gold lace and buttons.

78 AC, B, 110, Minister to Ruis, 23 November 1759.

79 AC, C11A, 96, Inventory of the king's stores, Montreal, 20 September 1749.

80 AM, B2, 247, Envoyé à Rochefort à destination des colonies; AC, B, 54, Matériel pour les îles et colonies, 1730; AR, 1E, 125, Minister to M. de Beauharnois, Versailles, 14 September 1736; AR, 1E, 125, À envoyer dans les colonies pour 1737; AC, F1A, 35, "100 fournimens de cuir noir en poire avec leur banderole en peau de buffle", Louisbourg, 1744; AC, B, 92, Matériel pour colonies, marine et galères, 1750; AC, B, 96, Passeport..., Fontainebleau, 1 November 1752.

81 AC, B, 96, Passeport..., Fontainebleau, 1 November 1752.

82 AG, A1, 3417, No. 307, Dans les magasins de Louisbourg, 15 December 1756; AC, C11B, 37, Pour les troupes, 1758; *Lettres du chevalier de Lévis concernant la guerre du Canada*, H.R. Casgrain, ed. (Montreal, 1889), pp. 274–277; ANQQ, M173/634, Jean-Claude Panet, Factures des marchandises et munitions, Trois-Rivières, 30 May 1760.

83 Zur-Lauben, Baron de, *Histoire militaire des Suisses au service de la France* (Paris, 1751), III: pp. 320–321, 502-505; May de Romainmotier, *Histoire militaire de la Suisse et celle des Suisses dans différends services de l'Europe* (Lauzanne, 1787), V: 473–476, VI: 280, 294; Lemau de la Jaisse, *Sixième abrégé de la carte générale du militaire de France* (Paris, 1740), p. 114-115; AR, 1A, 7, L.A. de Bourbon to Marquis de Ste Maure, 20 June 1721; AC, F1A, 23, Régiment Suisse de Karrer, Extrait du Fond, April 1724; AG, Xg, 87, Ordonnance du roi pour le licenciement du régiment suisse de Hallwyl, 1 June 1763; monthly musters in: AG, Yb, 685 and AG, Xi, 31 and 32.

84 AC, B, 53, Note to Karrer, 15 February 1729; AC, B, 56, Passeport au Sr Karrer, 1 January 1732.

85 AR, 1E, 113, Régiment Suisse de Karrer, Estat..., 25 May 1729; AC, B, 56, Passeport au Sr Karrer, 1 January 1732; AC, F1A, 34, Marine 1737 note dated 27 January 1738.

86 A few shipment records of "gibernes" survived: AC, B, 92, Passport to Karrer, 1 October 1748 includes 45 "gibernes"; AC, B, 94, Passport to Karrer, 1 October 1749 lists 30; AC, B, 96, Passport to Karrer, 27 March 1752 lists 20.

87 "Records of Superior Council of Louisiana," *Louisiana Historical Quarterly*, XXIII, 1940: 918; LAC, MG1-E, 389, Inventory of Captain Jean-Grégoire Volant, Halwyll's Regiment, 27 September 1761; TNA, High Court of the Admiralty, 32/195, correspondence pertaining to Hallwy's 3rd Company captured on board *La Biche*.

88 For a survey of the colonial artillery before 1789, see: René Chartrand, "L'artillerie coloniale française 1534–1791," *Carnet de la Sabretache*, nouvelle série, No. 109-E, 4e trimestre (1991): pp. 109–117.

89 The Bombardiers de la Marine had three companies, one based at Brest, one at Rochefort and one at Toulon. AC, F1A, 10, A Rochefort pour la solde..., 2 May 1702; AR, 1E, 70, Pontchartrain to Bégon, Versailles, 18 June 1710; AM, B1, 6, Note by Mr. Beauharnais, Rochefort, 20 April 1716; Jean Peters, *Les artilleurs de la marine sous Louis XIV* (Paris, 1995), pp. 57–67; AC, B, 85, Minister to Caylus, 30 April 1747, mentions 8 or 10 bombardiers sent to Martinique; AC, B, 105, Minister to Drucour, 24 December 1757, mentions 10 Rochefort bombardiers to form the new company at Louisbourg.

90 AM, B1, 8, Règlement du roi au sujet d'une Compagnie de 60 Ouvriers sous le nom de Compagnie d'Artillerie...dans l'Isle de la Tortue et la coste de Saint-Domingue, 20 April 1713. The order was repeated on 18 February 1726 (AC, B, 49) and 28 September 1736 (AC, B, 64), but the colony's budgets in AC, F1A, show no financial provisions for such a unit nor was it mentioned in any musters or correspondence of troops in Haiti.

91 AC, C11G, 12, Ordonnance concernant l'établissement d'une Compagnie de Canonniers à l'Isle Royale, 20 June 1743.

92 AC, F1A, 34, Habillement pour une nouvelle compagnie de canonniers, 5 November 1743; AC, B, 82, Passeport...compagnie de Canonniers-Bombardiers nouvellement établie à St. Domingue, 17 December 1745.

93 AR, 1E, 144, Minister to Givry, 26 July 1747.

94 For details on Royal-Artillerie's organisation, see Louis Susane, *Histoire de l'Artillerie française* (Paris, 1874), pp. 182–195; AC, F2C, 3, Beauharnois to Council, 23 and 28 April, 4 May and 9 June 1722; AC, C11B, 6, Verville to Council, 3 December 1722; AR, 1E, 126, Minister to Beauharnois, 5 and 12 March 1737; Moreau de Saint-Méry, *Loix et constitutions des colonies françoises sous le vent* (Paris, 1784-1790), 4: 720; AC, F1A, 50, Circulaire aux intendants des colonies, 15 February 1763.

95 Jean-Baptiste Du Tertre, *Histoire générale des isles...*, p. 469.

96 ANQM, Ordonnances, box 1663–1670, Montreal, January 27, 1663. Ordinance of the Governor founding the militia of the Sainte-Famille de Jésus-Marie-Joseph with a roll of its soldiers.

97 Ruette d'Auteuil, "Mémoire sur l'état présent du Canada", 12 December 1715, RAPQ, p. 59; *Relations par lettres de l'Amérique septentrionale (années 1709 et 1710)*, edited by Camille de Rochemonteix (Paris, 1904), p. 6.

98 ANQQ, Gilles Rageot, Inventaire de Toussaint Toupin et de feu Marguerite Boucher, 24 December 1669. This included a cassock and an old tabard that might indicate that Toupin had been a governor's guardsman.

99 *Ordonnances, commissions, etc., des gouverneurs et des intendants de la Nouvelle-France 1639–1706*, P.-G. Roy, ed., (Beauceville, 1924), 2 volumes, I: pp. 164–165; RAPQ, 1926–1927, pp. 47, 80; AC, B, 6, Mémoire des armes, 1675 and B, 7, Mémoire des armes, 1677.

100 The 1685 census is in: *La correspondance de Vauban relative au Canada*, Louise Dechênes, ed., (Ministère des Affaires culturelles: Québec, 1968), pp. 48–49; Ordonnances, commissions..., II: pp. 163–164; AC, C11A, 95, Recapitulation des Milices, 1750.

101 ANQM, Ordonnances 1684–1689, Ordonnance de l'intendant de Meules, 10 October 1684; AC, C11A, 13, Convention que MM. d'Iberville et Sérigny, 8 August 1694; AR, 1E, 599, De par devant le conseiller...Sieur de La Combe (Tulle), 25 March 1696. The contract also called for five chief's muskets; on 25 May 1694, another agreement mentioned 110 light muskets with fine furnishings for the "Gardes de la Marine" (midshipmen) at Rochefort, 300 grenadier muskets for Compagnies franches, 200 muskets of a small caliber for Canada and five muskets for Indian chiefs.

102 P.-G. Roy, *Inventaire des Papiers de Léry* (Quebec, 1939), I: 215; AC, C11A, 83, Beauharnois to Minister, 4 November 1745; AC, C11A, 95, Rolle de la compagnie de Côte St. Michel, 1750; Kalm, Pehr. Voyage de Pehr Kalm au Canada en 1749. Translated and annotated by Jacques Rousseau and Guy Béthune. (Montreal: Cercle du Livre de France, 1977), pp. 413–414, 552.

103 AC, C11A, 100, Lemercier to Minister, 20 October 1755; AC, C11A, 103, Milice du Canada, 1758; Steve Delisle, *The Equipment of the New France Militia 1740-1760* (Bel Air, MD, 1999), p. 32.

104 *Bulletin des recherches historiques*, VIII (1902): pp. 156–157; Sieur de Courcelle, "Mémoire sur le Canada," RAPQ, 1924–1925, p. 103.

105 ANQQ, Nicolas Boisseau, No. 119, Inventaire de Marie-Gabrielle, widow of Charles Joseph Amiot, Sieur de Vincelot, 24 May 1735; ANQM, Raimbault fils, No. 793, Inventaire de Charles Dazée, 30 Janvier 1732.

106 ANQTR, Jean Le Proust, Inventaire de François Delpée, 12 August 1755; ANQTR, Jean Le Proust, Inventaire de François Bigot, 4 May 1756; ANQTR, Jean Le Proust, Inventaire de François Rocheleau, 22 January 1759.

107 ANQTR, Daniel Normandin, Inventaire de François Breton, 16 December 1701; ANQM, Chaumont, Inventaire de Joseph Chartrand, 28 Janvier 1732; ANQM, A. Foucher, No. 268, Inventaire de François Guay, 22 April 1750 and No. 287, Inventaire de Joseph Renault, 22 June 1750.

108 ANQM, B. Basset, No. 1617, Inventaire des biens de...Chabert Lemoyne, vivant Sieur de Châteauguay, premier Capitaine de la Milice de l'Isle de Montréal, 27 March 1685.

109 ANQM, F. Genaple, No. 1057, Inventaire de Noël Langlois vivant Lieutenant de la Milice de Beauport, 8–9 January 1694.

110 ANQQ, NF25, Inventaire de François Rivière, 23 January 1692; ANQQ, F. Genaple, No. 1843, Inventaire de Charles de Monseignat, 8 January and 14 February 1704; ANQQ, Louis Chamballon, Inventaire de Charles Pauperet, 7 April 1707; ANQQ, Nicolas Boisseau, No. 93, Inventaire de feu Jean Crespin, 13 January 1734.

111 ANQTR, Poulin, No. 260, Inventaire de Françoise Marchant, widow of Jean Fafard, Sieur Laframboise, 27 July 1739; ANMQ, Porlier, No. 944, Inventaire de Louis d'Ailleboust, Sieur de Coulonges et de feu Marguerite Lefournier Duviers, 15 January 1743; some 200 fine muskets made at St. Etienne had a barrel four feet long with a silver thumb-piece and back sight as per LAC, Gradis documents, micro F1600, 15 June 1757.

112 ANQQ, NF 20-28, Inventaire de feu Jean Eustache Lanouiller de Boiseles, 5 December 1750; ANQM, Danré de Blanzy, No. 4447, Inventaire de Joseph Durocher, 18 March 1751; Danré de Blanzy, No. 5994, Inventaire de François Baribeaux, 10 July 1754; ANQM, Panet, Inventaire des biens de feu Sieur Larche, 17 November 1760.

113 ANQQ, F. Génaple, No. 1805, Inventaire de Charles Trépagny, 2-5 July 1703; Sieur de Courcelle, "Mémoire sur le Canada", RAPQ, 1924–1925, p. 103.

114 ANQQ, NF25, 422, Papiers relatifs à...La Guonne, 1708.

115 On the Illinois Militia, see the fine study by: Winstanley Briggs, "The Forgotten Colony: Le Pays des Illinois," PhD thesis, University of Chicago, December 1985; Natalia Mare Belting, *Kaskaskia Under the French Regime* (New Orleans, 1975), pp. 43, 45–46; *The Village of Chartes in Colonial Illinois*, Mary Kimball Brown and Lawrie Cena Dean, ed., pp. 342, 808, 820, 934-935.

116 LAC, MG 18, H24, Ordonnance concernant les Milices des Isles du Vent, 1 October 1727, copy registered on 18 February 1730 by the Louisiana Superior Council at New Orleans; Louis Narcisse Baudry des Lozières, *Voyage a la Louisiane* (Paris, 1802), p. 63 – in 1769, Milhet and Caresse, both New Orleans Militia officers, wore their uniforms when executed by a Spanish firing squad; Huntingdon Library (San Marino, Calif.), LO 9, Vaudreuil to Loubœy, 17 October 1746; LO 284, Vaudreuil to Minister, 25 May 1751; LO 9, same to same, 31 May 1751; probate of Sieur Prevost, Coast-Guard Militia captain, 14 July 1769, *Louisiana Historical Quarterly*, Vol. 9 (July 1926), p. 457; in Illinois, some officers may have had uniforms. The 1771 probate of Lt. Louis Lambert, St. Louis Militia, mentions a uniform as per: Gregory M. Franzwa, *The Story of Old St. Genevieve* (Patrice Press: St. Louis, 1967), pp. 42–43 ; AC, C8A, 51, Governor General Champigny to Minister, 12 July 1740 and AC, C8A, 53, same to same, 14 December 1741; AC, F1A, 30, Etat des merchandises propres à la Louisiane [June 1732]; AC, B, 86, Minister to Givry, 17 November 1747.

117 Inventaire des biens du Sieur Provost, 14 July 1769 in *The Louisiana Historical Quarterly*, Vol. 9, No. 3, (July 1926), p. 457; Natchitoches County Courthouse (Notchitoches, La.), Conveyance [Archives], Vol. 1, No. 305, Etat des effets de différentes espèces..., 20 September 1762.

118 AC, C11B, 72, Duquesnel to Minister, 17 May 1741; John R. Dunn, *The Militia in Isle Royale* (National Historic Sites Service Manuscript Report Number 31, Fortress of Louisbourg, September 1971), passim; Hugh Boscawen, *The Capture of Louisbourg 1758* (University of Oklahoma: Norman, 2012), p. 350; John Johnston, *Endgame 1758* (University of Nebraska: Lincoln, 2007), p. 274. In 1756, one notes a request for 50 Tulle trade guns probably intended for allied Indians as per AC, C11B, 37, Prévost to Minister, 29 November 1756.

119 Moreau de Saint-Méry, *Loix et constitutions...*, I: 192; AC, B, 4, Armes et munitions, 21 January 1672; AC, B, 6, Armes et munitions, 23 March 1674; AC, A, 14, Ordonnance du roi, 10 September 1774; Moreau de Saint-Méry, *Loix et constitutions...*, II: 574. AC, B, 10, Etat des merchandises qui seront envoyées de Rochefort aux Isles de l'Amérique, Fontainebleau, 24 September 1743.

120 AC, B, 12, Estat...que le Roy veut estre envoyé à la coste de St. Domingue, 20 September 1686; AC F1A, 3, Comparaison des dépenses des Isles...,1686 to 1687; AC, F1A, 3, Minister to de Lubort, Versailles, 1 August 1687. From 1665 to 1716 Maximilien Titon and his grandson Maximilien-Louis had the exclusive right to supply weapons to the French army.

121 AC, B, 14, Munitions, 4 September 1691; AC, B, 21, Passeport, 17 August 1700. Ordnance was also sent: 30 cannons in 1672 and 2 mortars in 1691; ,AC, B, 32, Minister to Sr. Barthome [?],27 April 1709.

122 AC, A, 24, Ordonnance du roi, 23 September 1683; The 1714 order was only applicable from the end of 1717 when it was officially registered at the superior councils. There was a militia company of free Africans at Le Cap as per Moreau de Saint-Méry, *Loix et constitutions...*, III: p. 86 (a regulation regarding this unit in 1724) and III: p. 571.

123 AC, B, 7, Etat des armes, 8 June 1678; Thomas Jefferys, *The Natural and Civil*

124 *History of the French Dominions in North and South America*, (London, 1761), II: p. 220.

125 AC, C8A, 24, Armes de guerre, 15 January 1718. The rather mysterious buccaneer muskets "à deux feux" (with two fires) might mean two barrels and two locks, but this would make such a weapon unbearably heavy.

126 Musée de l'Armée à l'Empéri (Aix-en-Provence), Archives Brunon, dossier W9, Les Milices..., Léogane, 19 mars 1762. The Léogane Militia had ten companies including one of artillery, one of cavalry, one of "carabiniers" possibly armed with rifled carbines and three of free mulattos and Africans; Moreau de Saint-Méry, *Loix et constitutions*..., IV: 456. LAC, MG18, M (Monkton Papers), 52, Contraste des operations... de la Guadeloupe et de la Martinique, 1762.

127 Antoine Boudet, *Histoire générale de la Marine* (Paris, 1757), III: 55-56. The draft of the 1674 regulation (kindly noted and shared by Jean Boudriot) also mentioned a flintlock musket with rounded lock plate – barrel: 4 feet long; caliber 8 lines; weight: 8 lbs., but this was not retained in the final version.

128 *Lettres, instructions et mémoires de Colbert*, Pierre Clément, ed. (Paris, 1864), III: letters Nos. 525, 529.

129 Moreau de Saint-Méry, *Description topographique, physique, civile, politique et historique de la partie française de l'île de Saint-Domingue* (Philadelphia, 1797) I: 496.

130 ANQN, Danré de Blanzy, No. 5099, Inventaire des biens de feu J.B. Jarret, Sieur de Verchères, 8 August 1752; AC, C11A, 82, Etat des munitions...Saint Frédéric, 1743 and C11A, 98, Etat des munitions...Saint Frédéric, 1752 both list the same (?) four "carabines rayées;" AC, C11A, 89, Etats des fonds..., 1747 lists a shipment of "6 Carabines rayées" by the French merchant Gradis; ANMQ, Soastre, No. 463, Inventaire des biens de feu Etienne Allaire, 11 February 1752; ANQM, Thomas Vautier, No. 438, Inventaire des biens de feu Antoine Sauvé, 23 May 1760.

131 AC, C11A, 100, Lemercier to Minister, 20 October 1755; Russel Bouchard, *Les Fusils de traite en Nouvelle-France* (Chicoutimi, QC, 1976); Kevin Gladysz, *The French Trade Gun in North America 1662–1759* (Mowbray: Woonsocket, RI, 2011); T.M. Hamilton, *Colonial Frontier Guns* (Chadron, Neb., 1980) and *Indian Trade Guns* (Union City, Tenn., 1982); James A. Hanson and Dick Harmon, *Firearms of the Fur Trade* (Museum of the Fur Trade: Chadron, Neb., 2011).

132 AR, 1E, 599, Tulle contracts, 25 March 1696 and 7 November 1697; AM, B1, 5, Tulle contract 1716; Archives de La Rochelle, B, 111, Lettres patentes du roy et règlement..., 15 November 1728; AN, K, 909, No. 43 Notice sur...Tulle, 18 November 1729 and No. 44 13 September 1734.

133 AR, 1E, 402, Intendant of Rochefort to minister, 18 January 1710.

134 AC, A, 24, Ordonnance du roi, 23 September 1683; AC, 22, severals ordinances excluding Louisiana from 1718; AC, A, 14, Arrêt, 10 September 1774; Yves Cayre, *Histoire de la Manufactures d'armes de Tulle 1690–1970*, pp. 25-26 quoting 1693 dispatch; Jean Boudriot, "Le fusil boucanier français," *Gazette des armes*, No. 40 (1976).

134 Moreau de Saint-Méry, I: 628.

135 Archives de La Rochelle, B, 111, Lettres patentes du roy et règlement..., 15 November 1728.

136 AC, C8A, 55, Etat des proportions, 2 August 1743.

137 AC, C8A, 24, Armes de guerre, 15 January 1718.

138 AC, C8A, 37, Recencement, 16 February 1727. The various small batteries spread along the coast had 85 cannons. There were also 530 white servants, 284 aged and infirm men, 241 free mulatto and black men, 13,696 black and mulatto slaves in the prime of life.

139 AC, C8A, 51, Governor General Champigny and Intendant La Croix to Minister, 21 June 1740; AC, B, 74, Minister to De Clieu and Marin, Versailles, 28 March 1742.

140 ANQQ, Nicolas Boisseau, No. 119, Inventaire de Marie-Gabrielle, widow of Charles Joseph Amiot, Sieur de Vincelot, 24 May 1735.

141 AC, C11A, 82, Etat des munitions...Saint-Frédéric, 1742; AC, C11A, 102, Etat des pieces...Saint-Frédéric, 2 October 1757.

142 ANQQ, NF25, 609, Trial concerning the wreck of *Le Chat Vernay* at Quebec, 8 October 1722. Six old sabers and ten pistols were also reported on board.

143 Examples were found at Quebec City, Fort Beauséjour, Fort Saint-Frédéric (Crown Point, N.Y.), Fort De Chartres and in the *Machault* sunk in 1760.

144 *Almanach de Saint-Domingue, Historique, Curieux et Utile pour l'année bissextile 1775* (Nantes, 1775), p. 25.

145 The number of metropolitan regular soldiers in Canada in April 1760 was reported to be 199 officers and 2,712 NCOs and privates according to the *Journal des campagnes du chevalier de Lévis en Canada de 1756 à 1760* (Montréal, Beauchemin, 1889), p. 257.

146 AC, C11A, 100, Etat general des approvisionnement (for Canada, 1755); C11B, 36, Etat des effets (for Isle Royale, 31 December 1755).

147 AC, C11A, 100, Etat des différentes armes...à Québec, 8 October 1755; État des ustencilles...à Montréal, 20 October 1755.

148 "Campagne de 1755, livre d'ordres," *Mémoires de la Société historique de Montréal*, cinquième livraison (1900), pp. 2, 6, 24; RAPQ, 1934–1935, p. 68; Lettres du chevalier de Lévis concernant la guerre du Canada, H.R. Casgrain, ed. (Montreal, 1889), pp. 274–277.

149 M. de Héricourt, *Élémens de l'art militare* (Paris, 1756), I: pp. 237–238.

150 Victor Nicolas, *Le livre d'or de l'infanterie de la Marine* (Paris, 1891), pp. 13–26.

151 AC, C8B, 13, Colonies (note), 25 July 1770. Another 1,600 were to arm outgoing recruits to America at the depot in Isle de Ré (near La Rochelle, France).

152 AR, 3A, 1 and 13, Reports and memos on browning, 1772–1773; AB, 32 Arm., Observations sur la difference des prix entre la Manufacture de Tulle et celle de Charleville, undated but c.1780–1785. A Tulle brass-mounted musket with bayonet cost 21 livres, 19 sols and 6 deniers (inclusive of 2 livres, 4 sols and 4 deniers for the bayonet) while a Charleville musket without bayonet was 18 livres and 3 sols.

153 AC, C12, 22, Saint-Pierre et Miquelon, armement des troupes, 1771. A 1776 document in the same volume mentions that the magazine contained 173 muskets with bayonets, 172 cartridge boxes with slings, 88 swords and 106 waistbelts. LAC, MG18, K3, 1 (Lotbinière papers) printed report from Pondichery, 22 March 1775; figures from Bonnefoy, I: 359.

154 AC, D2C, 15, Revue...Volontaires étrangers de la Marine, Martinique, 26 January 1780.

155 AC, C14, 56, Troupes Nationales, 1 January 1783.

156 AC, B, 137, to Régisseur de l'habillement, Versailles, 30 November 1770 and to Mr. Boiroyer, Versailles, 24 December 1770.

157 *Manuel du Dragon*, by an officer of dragoons, (Paris, 1777), pp. 194–195; AG, XC, 57, Inspection at Charleville of Belzunce Dragoons by the Duke of Brissac, 29 July 1782.

158 *The Revolutionary Journal of Baron Ludwig Von Closen 1780–1783*, translated and edited by Evelyn M. Acomb, (Chapel Hill: University of North Carolina, 1958), pp. 91, 142.

159 AC, B, 125, À Messieurs les régisseurs de l'habillement, 13 September 1766.

160 AC, B, 143, Minister to de Boisroger, 31 December 1772; AC, C9, 147, Inspection, Du Cap Regiment 24 September 1779, the regiment had 1,436 cartridge box plates, 1,466 waistbelts and 36 drum slings.

161 AC, C8A, C8B, 13, Colonies [armament report], 25 July 1770. The document contains detailed breakdowns of each type of unit by district; Moreau de Saint-Méry, *Loix et constitutions*..., V: 166; AG, Xi, 1, Ordonnance du roi concernant les milices de la Martinique et de Sainte-Lucie, 1 September 1768.

162 AC, C8A, 70, Observations...25 and 26 September 1771; *Les Annales du Conseil souverain de la Martinique* (Bergerac, 1786) II: p. 263.

163 *Essai sur l'histoire naturelle de l'isle de Saint Domingue* (Paris, 1776), p. 12; Moreau de Saint-Méry, *Description*..., I: p. 497; *Les Annales du Conseil souverain de la Martinique*, II: p. 266; Boyer-Peyreleau, *Les Antilles françaises, particulièrement la Guadeloupe* (Paris, 1823) II: p. 144.

164 AC, F3, 262, Ordonnance pour la levee...Volontaires de Bouillé, 1 July 1778; Moreau de Saint-Méry, *Loix et constitutions*..., V: pp. 861–862, VI: 28; AM, A1, 131, No. 53, Ordonnance du roi, 30 August 1782; AC, F3, 262, Ordonnance pour la creation...Volontaires Libres de la Martinique, 27 October 1782.

165 AM, B2, 153, Ponchartrain to the Duke of Harcourt, Versailles, 17 February 1701; AC, B, 24, Pontchartrain to the Count of Marsin, Versailles, 29 March 1702; *Mercure Galant*, March 1704, p. 75.

166 AR, 1E, 59, Pontchartrain to Bégon, 16 February and 27 April 1707; AC, B, 31, Ponchartrain to Rouzol, Versailles, 24 October 1708; B, 31, Pontchartrain to Amclos, Versailles, 5 December 1708, Jean Peter, *Les manufactures de la Marine sous Louis XIV* (Paris, 1997), pp. 90–91. The number of weapons furnished in 1709 is not given.

167 *American archives*, Peter Force, ed., 5th series (Washington, 1843), p. 1114; *The Revolutionary Diplomatic Correspondence of the U.S.*, Francis Wharton, ed., (Washington, 1889) II: pp. 131, 210, 276; Arcadi Gluckman, *United States Muskets, Rifles and Carbines* (Buffalo, 1948), pp. 60–61.

168 Louis de Loménie, *Beaumarchais et son temps* (Paris, 1856), II: pp. 132–140; Neil L. York, "Clandestine Aid and The American Revolutionary War Effort: A Re-Examination," *Military Affairs*, XLIII (February 1979): pp. 26–30.

169 Thomas Balch, *Les Français en Amérique pendant la guerre de l'indépendance des États-Unis* (Paris, 1872), pp. 69–70; Dominique Venner, *Les armes américaines* (Paris, 1978), pp. 49–51.

170 Arcadi Gluckman, *United States Muskets, Rifles and Carbines*, pp. 59–61; Robert M. Reilly, *United States Martial Flintlocks* (Lincoln, R.I.: Mowbray, 1986), pp. 24–25; Library of Congress, Continental Congress, Laurens Papers, 1, Fournitures pour le mois de mai 1781; likenesses of Lt. Col. Benjamin Talmadge in his *Memoirs* (New York, 1858) and of Lt. Col. Thomas Seymour by John Trumbull at Yale University.

INDEX

A

Abenakis (Indians), 83
Acadia, xiii, xiv, 45, 82–84, 122, 123
Affiches Américaines, 189
Agenois Infantry Regiment, 175
Alibamon (Indians), 102
Allaire, Etienne, 145
Amelia, 196
Amiot, Joseph, Seigneur de Vincelot, 132
Amphitrite, 196, 198
Angoumois Infantry Regiment, 103, 160
Anjou, Philippe, Duke d', 194
Antartic America, 30
Argall, Capt. Samuel, 45
Argenteuil, Lt. D', 81
Arnaud, Col., 60, 62
Artois Infantry Regiment, 158
Atlas, 194
Aulnay, Charles Menou d', 46–48
Austrian Succession, War of, 98
Aviles, Don Pedro Menendez de, 38

B

Baas, Jean-Charles de, 68
Baribeau, François, 134
Basques, 19, 41
Bastien, François, 135
Bastille, Place de la, 195
Bayonne (France), 41
Bayonne Marine Regiment, 173
Béarn Infantry Regiment, 158
Beauharnois (or Beauharnais), Charles, marquis de, 131
Beaumarchais, Pierre Caron de, 195, 196, 198
Bellecombe, Guillaume de, 178
Belzunce Dragoon Regiment, 175, 183
Berry Infantry Regiment, 158
Bicheur, Louis Le, Sieur de La Roche, 56
Bigorre Infantry Regiment, 160
Bigot, Capt. François, 132
Biteaux, L., 56
Brachie, 147
Brazil, xiii, 19–21, 45, 57, 59
Bray, Pierre du Pras, Sieur du, 68
Bréda, Treaty of, 82
Brest (France), 87, 89, 163
Brest Marine Regiment, 173
Breton, François, 133
Boiseles, Jean-Eustache Lanouiller de, 134
Bois-le-Comte, 34
Bock, Sgt. Joseph, 119
Bombardiers de la Marine (Bombardiers of the Navy), 123, 194
Bonnavista (Newfoundland), 84
Bordeaux, 108
Bordeaux Marine Regiment, 173
Boscawen, Adm. Edward, 161
Bouat, Ens. de, 100
Bouillé, François Claude Amour, marquis de, 191
Boulonnois Infantry Regiment, 158
Bourdon, Jacques, 135
Bourgogne Infantry Regiment, 158
Bourlamaque, 132
Buccaneers, xv, 58, 87, 136, 147, 156
Buenos Aires, 194

C

Caen (France), 57
Cabagnac, Lt. Joseph Dejourdy de, 99
Cambis Infantry Regiment, 158
Canada, xiii, xiv, 22, 50, 68, 74, 78, 98, 99, 108, 114, 117, 125–128, 131, 147–149, 158, 160, 161, 163, 168
Canonniers-Bombardiers, 103, 107, 108, 122–125, 127, 173
Candreau, Bombardier, 123
Canso, 118
Canson, Dollier de, 56
Cap de la Madeleine, 132
Cap Rouge, 30
Cap St. Ignace, 132
Cape Breton Island, xiii, 104
Cape François (see: Le Cap, Haiti), 196
Carabane, Mr., 196
Carib (Amerindians), 59
Carignan-Salières Infantry Regiment, 68
Carrier, Robert, 107
Cartagena de Indias (Columbia), 194
Cartier, Capt. Jacques, 22, 23
Casco Bay (Maine), 21
Castambon, Etienne, 135
Cayenne (French Guyana), xv, 65, 78, 91, 137
Céronne River (France), 88
Chalours, Comm. Duperron, 70
Chambelle Regiment, 65, 68
Champagne Regiment, 60
Champigny, Jean Bochard de, 122
Champlain (Canada), 133
Champlain, Samuel de, 50, 52, 54, 55
Charlesfort, 37
Charlesville (France), 108, 179
Chartier, Louis, 46
Chartrand, Joseph, 133
Chasseurs-Royaux de Saint-Domingue, 191, 193
Chasseurs-volontaires de Saint-Domingue, 191, 193

Château Saint-Louis, 57
Chazy, Sieur de, 68
Chebucto Bay, 158
Chickasaw (Indians), 123
China, 21
Christopher Columbus, 19
Closse, Lambert, 57
Colbert de Terron, Charles-Jean, 57
Coligny, Gaspard de, 30, 37
Compagnie des Indes (Company of the Indies or East India Company), 101, 102, 168
Compagnie d'Occident (Western Company), 101
Compagnies franches de la Marine, 74, 75, 78, 81–84, 86, 87, 89, 93, 95, 96, 98, 99, 101–103, 106–112, 114–118, 122, 158, 171
Compagnie franche de Saint-Pierre et Miquelon, 172, 177
Commissaire d'artillerie (Artillery Commissioner), 122
Concord (Massachusetts), 175
Condé Dragoon Regiment, 175, 183
Corne, Capt. de la, 101
Corps de Cavalerie (Canada), 151
Corps Royal de l'Artillerie, 126, 173
Corps royal de l'infanterie de la Marine, 173
Côte Saint-Michel Militia Company (near Montréal), 131
Coupar, 57
Courreur des bois, 129, 145, 157
Crespin, Jean, 134
Crown Point (N.Y.), 101
Crozat, Alexandre, 85, 101, 102

D

D'Anville, Jean-Baptiste de La Rochefoucauld de Roye, duc, 118, 158
D'Arradola, Lt., 103
Dauphin Dragoon Regiment, 183
Dauphine, 21
Dazé, Capt. Charles, 132
Deane, Silas, 194, 196
Delpé, Capt. Charles, 132
Denonville, Jacques-René, marquis de Brisay de, 80, 130, 132
Desormeaux, Dollard, 56
De Troyes, Chevalier Pierre, 82
Dieppe (France), 19, 21, 147
Dominican Republic, xv
Donacona (Indian chief), 22
Doussin, René, 56
Du Cap Colonial Infantry Regiment, 173
Ducasse, Adm. Jean-Baptiste, 76
Dufresnoy, Lt. Philippe de Carrion, Sieur, 70
Duluth, Capt. Daniel de Grelon, Sieur de, 81
Dupéret, Jean, 21

Dupin, 189
Duplessis, Sgt. André, 101
Duplessis-Besançon, Mr., 62
Duquesne, Michel Ange, marquis de Menneville, 132
Duquesne (plantation, Haiti), 189
Durocher, Joseph, 134
Dutch forts, 55

E

East Indies, 173, 177
Essomericq, 20
Espoir, 19
Estrées, Victor Marie d'Estrées, duc d', 78

F

Fabert, Capt. Duplessis, 81
Fafard, Jean, Sieur Laframboise, 134
Falmouth (U.K.), 41
Farabezolles, Sergeant Thomas, 81
Felipe V (King of Spain), 194
Flintlock (introduced), 62
Florida, xiii, 37
Franchomme, Lt., 103
Francis I (King of France), 21, 23
Franklin, Benjamin, 195
French style (à la Française) lock, 62
French West Indies, defined, xv
Frères de la côte (Brethrens of the Coast), 58
Frontenac, Louis de Buade, comte de, 70, 83, 84, 122, 130
Fort Beauséjour, 125
Fort Biloxi, 86
Fort Caroline, 37, 38
Fort de Chartres, xiv, 101, 103, 111, 135
Fort Coligny, 30
Fort Conti, 70
Fort Duquesne, 103
Fort Necessity, 158
Fort Pentagouet, 46
Fort Rosalie, 102
Fort Sandusky, 101
Fort Saint-Frédéric, 101, 145, 149
Fort Saint-Joseph, 83
Fort Saint-Louis, 57, 58, 83 (Acadia), 85 (Texas)
Fort Sainte-Marie, 45, 47
Fort Sainte-Marie-amongst-the-Hurons, 63
Fort San Mateo, 38, 40
Fusiliers du Roi Infantry Regiment, 126

G

Gardes-Françaises Infantry Regiment, 60
Gardes de la Marine, 141
Gardes du Pavillon, 141
Gargot, Nicolas, 70
Garrison soldiers, 68-69
Gassiaux, 135
Gaspé (Canada), 22
Gatinois Infantry Regiment, 175
Gélin, 147
Girard, Pierre, 103, 107
Gloucester Point (Virginia), 185
Godé, Nicolas, 56
Gonneville, Capt., 19, 20
Goudot, Surgeon-Major Pierre, 81, 92
Grande-Rivière (Haiti), 189
Grandjean (household, Haiti), 189
Great Britain, xiii, 182
Great Western Plains, 129
Greenland, 19
Grenada, xv, 59, 75, 125, 136, 187, 191
Grenadiers de Virginie, 199, 200
Grenadiers-volontaires de Saint-Domingue, 191, 193
Guadeloupe, xv, 59, 75, 98, 125, 128, 136, 138, 172, 188, 189
Guadeloupe Colonial Infantry Regiment, 173
Guadeloupe Mousquetaires, 189, 191, 193
Guards, Governor General's, 65, 68, 70, 73, 78, 144
Guay, François, 133
Gustav Adolf I (King of Sweden), 59
Guyana (French), xiii, xv, 59, 65, 67, 68, 78, 91, 98, 106, 121, 160, 172, 173
Guyenne Infantry Regiment, 158, 161, 165

H

Haiti, xv, 58, 75–77, 93, 108, 118, 123–125, 127, 156, 160, 163, 168, 172, 175, 177, 178, 183, 189, 191, 193, 196
Halifax (Nova Scotia), 158
Halwyll's Swiss Infantry Regiment, 118, 158
Havana (Cuba), 194
Havre de Grace (France), 196
Heny II (King of France), 30, 44
Henryville, 30
Herand, Capt. 196
Hispanolia, xv, 58, 196
Hochelaga, 22
Hollande, Hotel de, 195
Honfleur (France), 20
Hudson's Bay, 82
Hurons (Amerindians) 63, 101

I

Iberville, Pierre Le Moyne d', 131
Ile Jésus, 132
Ile Royale, xiii, xiv, 104, 114, 118, 123, 124, 135
Ile Saint-Jean (Prince Edward Island), xiv
Iles du Vent (Windward Islands), 124
Illinois, xiv, 103
Illinois, pays des (Illinois Country), 101, 135
Indian Ocean, 172
Iroquois (Indian Confederacy of the Five Nations), 50, 55, 68, 70

J

Jackonsville (Florida), 37
Jacquet, 41
Jemsec, 82
Jones, Capt. Hugh, 41
Jummonville Incident, 158

K

Kalm, Pehr, 131
Karrer Swiss Infantry Regiment, 102, 104, 118, 119
Kaskaskia, 135
Kerlérec, Louis de, 103
King's Gunner, 121, 122, 123

L

La Barre, Joseph-Antoine Le Febvre de, 79, 80
La Belle, 85
Labrador, 19, 41
Lacombe, Matrial Fénis de, 88, 110
La Guyonne (Canadian corsair ship), 134
Le Havre Marine Regiment, 173
La Hève (Acadia), 46
Lallier Infantry Regiment, 65, 68
Langlois, Lt. Noël, 133
Langy, Capt. Joseph, 101
Languedoc Infantry Regiment, 158,
Larchevêque, Capt., 134
La Reine Infantry Regiment, 158
La Réunion, 172
La Sarre Infantry Regiment, 158
La Prairie, Capt. Nicolas Rousselot, Sieur de, 81
La Salle, Robert Cavelier de, 69, 84, 85
La Tuilerie, 198
Laudonnière, René Goulaine, 37
Lauze, Capt. de, 103
Lauzun, Armand Louis de Gontaut, duc de, 174
Lauzun's Legion, 174
Laval, 133
Le Cap, xv, 125, 136, 144, 189
Le Cap Gendarmes, 189
Le Chat Vernay, 151

Leeward Islands, French, xv, 173
Légion de l'Ile de France, 172, 185
Légion de Saint-Domingue, 172, 183, 185
Le Gras, 135
Lemercier, Chevalier François-Marc-Antoine, 132, 145
Lemoyne, Capt. Chabert, Sieur de Châteauguay, 133
Léogane (Haiti), 138
Léry, Jean de, 30
Lescarbot, Marc, 45
Lévis, Francis de Gaston, Chevalier de, 117, 118, 127, 161, 168
L'Homme, Jacques, 20
Louis XIII (King of France), 139
Louis XIV (King of France), 65, 74, 84, 87, 126, 136, 139, 154, 194
Louis XVI (King of France), 195
Louisbourg, xiv, 98, 104, 114, 116, 118, 123, 125, 127, 135, 158, 160, 163
Louisiana, xii, xiv, 84, 85, 98, 101, 102, 111, 118, 123, 125, 135, 160, 163, 171
Louvois, Michel Le Tellier, marquis de, 154, 156
Lucière, Dominique de La Motte, 69, 70
Lusignan, Capt. de, 81

M

Machault, 101
Maranhao (or "Maragnan", Brazil), 57
Marie-Galante, 75, 125, 136
Marillac, François de, 100
Marseille (France), 87, 89
Marseille Marine Regiment, 173
Martinique, xvi, 59, 63, 67, 74, 75, 98, 106, 118, 121, 123, 125, 128, 136-138, 147, 148, 158, 160, 172, 173, 177, 179, 188, 189, 191
Martinique Cadets de Saint-Pierre, 191
Martinique Gendarmes, 189, 193
Martinique Colonial Infantry Regiment, 173
Martinique Volontaires de Bouillé, 191
Matagorda Bay (Texas), 85
Matchlock, introduction, 43
Maubeuge (France), 177, 179, 199
Mauritius, 172
Measurements, described, xvii
Megret, Sgt. Jean, 101
Méloizes, Ens. des, 80
Mem de Sa, 34
Mercure, 196, 198
Mésy, Augustin de Saffray de, 57
Messein, Ens., 99
Metropolitan army artillery units in America (1777-1783), 175
Metropolitan army infantry battalions in America (1778-1783), 175
Mexico, Gulf of, xiv, 84, 85, 101
Michigan, Lake, 101
Ministère de la Marine (Ministry of the Navy), vii, xiii
Milan (Italy), 43
Militia (Canada), 128-134, 145, 146. 157
Militia artillery companies (Canada), 134
Militia reserve companies (Canada), 134
Militia, of Beauport (Canada), 133
Militia, of Bécancour (Canada), 132
Militia, of Cap de la Madeleine (Canada), 132
Militia of the Holy Family of Jesus-Mary-Joseph (in Montreal), 128
Militia, of Montréal, 133
Militia, of Québec City, 133, 134
Militia, of Tennancourt (Canada), 132
Militia, of Terrebonne (Canada), 132
Militia (Ile Royale), 135
Militia (French Guyana), 137, 188
Militia (Louisiana), 135
Militia artillery company (Louisiana), 135
Militia (of Free Africans in Louisiana), 135
Militia Bourgeois (Louisiana), 135
Militia Coast Guard (Louisiana), 135
Militia (West Indies), 135-137, 157, 188
Militia cavalry (West Indies), 140, 141, 143, 144, 152
Militia, of Guadeloupe, 188
Militia, of Haiti, 137, 138, 188
Militia, of Marie-Galante, 188
Militia, of Martinique, 138, 188
Militia, of Léogane, 138
Militia, of St. Lucia, 188
Miquelet (lock), 62
Mississippi River, xiv, 84, 85, 101, 103, 129, 135
Mobile, 85, 103, 119, 122, 125, 135
Moillerie, Ens. Louis Mallerais, Sieur de la, 81
Monein, Capt., 44
Monlieu, Carcier de, 198
Mont, Sieur de, 45
Montbrun, Lt. Jean-Baptiste de Saint-Laurent, 103
Montcalm Cavalry Regiment, 158
Montcalm, Louis-Joseph de, marquis de, 118, 127
Montréal, 56, 74, 115, 118, 125, 128, 130, 132, 158, 161
Montseigneur, Charles de, 133-134
Morandière, Capt. de la, 99
Morin, Capt., 196
Mouguère, Capt. Thomas, de la, 70
Moyne, Jacques Le, 40

N

Nantes (France), 147, 196, 198
Natchez, 102
Natchez (Indians), 102
Natichitoches, 135
Navarre Infantry Regiment, 67
Negroli family (of Milan), 44
New Amsterdam (New York), 55
New France, defined, xiii
New Orleans, xiv, 85, 103, 111, 125, 127, 135, 160
Newfoundland, 41, 172
Newport (R.I.), 185
Niagara River, 70, 135
Noré, Capt. Jacques Lepicard, Dumeny de, 81
Normandie Infantry Regiment, 67

O

Ogéron, Bertrand d', 136
Ohio, 103, 125, 135
Orange (Albany, N.Y.), 55
Orléans Infantry Regiment, 65, 68

P

Paris, Treaty of, 172
Parquet, Governor du, 59
Parris Island (S.C.), 37
Pauperet, Claude, 134
Pauphile, Michel, 88
Penobscot (Maine), 46
Pensacola, 102
Pertuisaniers, 93
Pentagouet, 82, 83
Piedmont (Italy), 43
Piquets de Saint-Domingue, 158
Placentia, xiii, xiv, 41, 70, 84, 89, 104, 123
Philadelphia, 198
Platine à chenapan (snaphance lock), introduction of, 43
Pocatière, Capt. François Pollet, Sieur de la Combe, 68
Poitou Infantry Regiment, 65, 67, 68
Pondichery (India), 177
Ponthieu Infantry Regiment, 158
Port-de-Paix, 136
Port au Prince, xv, 125
Port-au-Prince Colonial Infantry Regiment, 173
Port Daniel (Québec), 22
Port Royal (Acadia), 45, 46, 83, 84
Portobello (Panama), 194
Porto Seguro (Brazil), 20
Portsmouth (N.H.), 198
Portuguese, 34
Pouancey, Jacques Neveu de, 136
Prairie du Rocher, 135
Prevost, Capt. 135
Protestants, 30, 34
Poutraincourt, Sieur de, 45
Puiloreau, Chevalier de, 189

Q

Quebec City, 23, 74, 78, 80, 98, 101, 118, 121, 122, 129, 131–134, 151, 158, 161, 168
Queen Anne's War, 98
Quercy Infantry Regiment, 158

R

Raby, Sgt. Pierre, 165
Raverdière, Daniel de la Touche del La, 57
Razilly, Isaac de, 45
Recife (Brazil), 21
Red Bay (Labrador), 41
Redon, Pierre (of Paris), 44
Ribault, Capt. Jean, 37, 38
Richelieu, Cardinal de, 46
Richelieu River, 128, 133
Rio de Janeiro (Brazil), 30, 34
Rivière, François, 133
Rivière des Prairies, 133
Roberval, Jean-François de La Rocque de, 23
Rochambeau, Jean-Baptiste Donatien de Vimeur, comte de, 174, 175, 183
Rochefort (France), 79, 87, 89, 106, 107, 114, 123, 136, 194
Rochefort Marine Regiment, 173
Rocheleau, Capt. François, 132
Roderique Hortalez & Co., 195
Rostaing, Phillipe Joseph, comte de, 149
Roy, Simon Le, 57
Royal Artillerie, 126, 127
Royal-Barrois Infantry Regiment, 158
Royal Grenadiers, 158, 160
Royal Militia Battalion of Fontenay-le-Comte, 158
Royal Militia Battalion of Saumur, 158
Royal-Roussillon Infantry Regiment, 158
Royan (France), 40
Ruyter, Adm. Michiel de, 74

S

Sagard, Father Gabriel, 52
Sarrobert, Sgt. François de, 101
Sainte-Croix Island (Maine), 45
Sainte-Croix (West Indies), 75, 136
St. Denis (Canada), 133
Saint-Domingue (Haiti), xv, 58, 75, 76, 124, 136
Saint-Ètienne (France), 80, 87, 89, 98, 107, 119, 177, 179, 183, 198, 199
Saint-Jean-de-Luz (France), 41
St. John River (New Brunswick), 45, 83
St. John's (Newfoundland), 84
St. Kitts (or Saint-Christophe), 59, 67, 75, 128
Saint-Malo (France), 23, 151
Saint-Malo Marine Regiment, 173
Saint-Michel, Lt. de, 100
St. Lawrence River, 22, 128
St. Louis (Haiti), xv, 137
St. Louis (Missouri), 103
St. Lucia, 59, 125
St. Ours (Canada), 145
Saint-Père, Jean de, 56
Saint-Pierre et Miquelon, 172, 173
Santiago de Cuba, 194

Salvador de Bahia (Brazil), 30
Saratoga, 175
Sault, Toussaint Toupin, Sieur du, 129, 130
Sautrel, Capt., 196
Sauzzaye, Ens. Thomas Philippe Agneaux, Sieur de la, 112
Savannah (Georgia), 175, 183, 191
Scottish soldiers, 30, 34
Seine, 196, 198
Senegal, 172
Sérigny, Joseph Le Moyne de, 131
Seven Years War, 98, 170, 177, 188
Soulanges, Capt. Jacques de Joibert, Seigneur de, 81
Soullard, 70
Spanish America, 123, 194
Spanish spy, 23
Spanish Succession, War of, 89, 98
Swiss company (of soldiers), 102

T

Tarleton, Col. Banastre, 185
Thomas, soldier, 103
Titon, Maximilien, 80, 87, 136
Tortuga, 58, 136
Tour, Françoise-Marie de La, 47, 48
Tour, Charles de La, 45, 47, 48
Touraine Infantry Regiment, 175
Toulon (France), 87, 89
Toulon Marine Regiment, 173
Tracy, Alexandre de Prouville, marquis de, 65, 68, 73
Traversy, Ens. François, 68
Trépagny, Charles, 134
Trois-Rivières, 56, 74, 118, 132–134
Troupes de la Marine, vii, 74, 86, 92, 98, 114
Troupes de Terre, vii, 86, 114, 118
Troupes Nationales de Cayenne, 182
Tulle (France), 76, 77, 80, 88, 89, 98, 100, 101, 103, 106–110, 126, 131–136, 145–149, 161, 178, 179, 182, 194, 199
Twelve Apostles, 64, 79, 93

U

United States, xiii, 195
Utrecht, Treaty of, 83, 84

V

Vallets, Jean, 56
Verchères, Capt. J.-B. Jarret de, 100, 145
Vasseur, Capt. Le, 58
Vauban, Sébastien Le Prestre, Seigneur de, 89
Venezuela, 59
Vera Cruz (Mexico), 194
Vergennes, Charles Gravier, comte de, 195
Versailles (France), 98, 135, 172, 189, 195
Verrazano, Giovani da, 21
Vikings, 19
Vincelot, Sieur de, 149
Villegagnon, Nicolas Durand de, 30, 34
Volontaires d'Afrique, 172
Volontaires de Bouillé (Martinique), 191
Volontaires Étrangers de la Marine, 174, 179, 183, 185
Volontaires-Étrangers Infantry Regiment, 158
Volontaires Libres, 193
Voyageurs, 129, 145, 157

W

West Africa, 172
West indies, xiii, 58, 74, 106, 121, 136, 151, 171, 173, 175, 177, 189
Windward Islands, xv, 125, 148, 172
Wheel-lock, (invention of), 43

Y

Yorktown (Virginia), 185

Z

Zollner, Gapard, 143

More Flintlock Musket Titles Available from this Publisher

(SEE ORDERING INFORMATION BELOW)

French Military Small Arms
VOLUME I: FLINTLOCK LONGARMS

First of two volumes by Didier Bianchi. *(Translated from the French by Eric A. Bye, M.A., C.T.)* The most extensive guide to French flintlock military longarms ever to be published in English. Concentrates on identification and service use, covering everything from Infantry Muskets, Rampart Guns, Dragoon Muskets, Cavalry Musketoons, Constabulary Musketoons, Naval Muskets, Hussar Musketoons, Foot and Mounted Grenadier Muskets, Arms of the Mamelouks, Lancers' Musketoons, Royal Muskets, Muskets of the Bodyguards and much more. More than 550 outstanding color photographs.
SOFTCOVER • 136 pgs. • 11"x8.5"

British Military Flintlock Rifles 1740-1840

by De Witt Bailey. Until now, there has been little information available about these rifles and which units carried them into battle. Starting with the Seven Years War, the whole story is told right through the American Revolution, the Napoleonic Age and to the end of the flintlock era. Each rifle is illustrated in 320 exceptional photographs. The types of rifles include such famous weapons as the Baker, the Ferguson, the Pattern 1776 and the rifles used by German mercenaries and royalists in the American Revolution. **HARDCOVER • 336 pgs. 8.5"x11"**

$47.95 + $4.50 p/h

The Brown Bess
Identification Guide and Illustrated Study of Britain's Most Famous Musket

by Eric Goldstein and Stuart Mowbray. A pattern-by-pattern full-color guide, this book covers them all, including the India Patterns! 1,000 color photos.
SOFTCOVER • 160 pgs. • 11"x8.5"

Small Arms of the British Forces in America 1664-1815

De Witt Bailey's long-awaited book on British firearms used in American wars is finally here. If it was used in the Revolutionary War, the War of 1812 or the French and Indian Wars, it's in here! The Brown Bess information alone is staggering! Over 400 photos covering muskets, pistols, rifles, etc. 376 pages includes specific regimental issue data from official Ordnance records. **HARDCOVER • 376 pgs. • 8.5"x11"**

MUSKETS of the REVOLUTION

by Bill Ahearn. The exciting, true story of the guns that fought the American Revolution. Not just a technical study of old firearms, this is a tribute to the bravery of the men who fought on both sides of that epic conflict and a celebration of the weapons that have become so much a part of our national character. Includes many never-before-published photos! Nearly 500 photos and illustrations.
HARDCOVER • 248 pgs. • 8.5"x11"

$39.99 + $4.50 p/h

$39.99 + $4.50 p/h

$59.99 + $4.50 p/h

$49.99 + $4.50 p/h

MOWBRAY PUBLISHING • 54 E. School St. • Woonsocket, RI 02895
800-999-4697 • Outside U.S. 401-597-5055 • email: orders@manatarmsbooks.com
www.gunandswordcollector.com Personal Check, Money Order, VISA, M/C and Amex Accepted